East Asian Pop Culture

Hong Kong University Press thanks Xu Bing for writing the Press's name in his Square Word Calligraphy for the covers of its books. For further information, see p. iv.

TransAsia: Screen Cultures

What is Asia? What does it mean to be Asian? Who thinks they are Asian? How is "Asianness" produced? None of these questions can be answered without talking about the screen-based media. Asia today is becoming a transnational public space in which all kinds of cross-border connections proliferate, from corporate activities to citizen-to-citizen linkages. All of this mediated and shaped by media — from Japanese and Korean television series, Hong Kong action films, video piracy, J-Pop and K-Pop, to a variety of subcultures facilitated by internet sites and other computer-based cultures. And outside Asia, films are packaged and marketed at film festivals and by DVD distribution companies as "Asian," and the descendents of migrants are not only identified by others as "Asian" but also increasingly identify themselves as "Asian," and then turn to "Asian" screen cultures to find themselves and their roots.

The continued reliance on national frameworks in politics, economics and other social sciences, media studies, film studies, and other disciplines and fields is becoming obsolete. This series on trans-border screen-based culture in Asia aims to not only spotlight new research but also promote more groundbreaking research in this area.

Series Editors: Koichi IWABUCHI and Chris BERRY

Series International Advisory Board

Ackbar ABBAS (University of Hong Kong)

Ien ANG (University of Western Sydney)

Yomi BRAESTER (Washington University)

Stephen CHAN (Lingnan University)

CHUA Beng-Huat (National University of Singapore)

Ian CONDRY (Massachusetts Institute of Technology)

DAI Jinhua (Peking University)

John Nguyet ERNI (Lingnan University)

Annette HAMILTON (University of New South Wales)

Rachel HARRISON (School of Oriental and African Studies, University of London)

Gaik Cheng KHOO (Australian National University)

KIM Kyung-Hyun (University of California, Irvine)

KIM Soyoung (Korean National University of Arts)

Helen Hok-Sze LEUNG (Simon Fraser University)

Akira Mizuta LIPPIT (University of Southern California)

Feii LÜ (National Chengchi University)

LÜ Xinyu (Fudan University)

Eric MA (Chinese University of Hong Kong)

Fran MARTIN (Melbourne University)

MOURI Yoshitaka (Tokyo National University of Fine Arts and Music)

Meaghan MORRIS (Lingnan University)

NAM Inyoung (Dongseo University)

PANG Laikwan (Chinese University of Hong Kong)

Michael RAINE (University of Chicago)

Bérénice REYNAUD (California Institute of the Arts)

Lisa ROFEL (University of California, Santa Cruz)

Krishna SEN (Curtin University of Technology)

Ubonrat SIRIYUVASAK (Chulalongkorn University, Bangkok)

Eva TSAI (National Taiwan Normal University)

Paola VOCI (University of Otago)

YOSHIMI Shunya (Tokyo University)

ZHANG Zhen (New York University)

East Asian Pop Culture
Analysing the Korean Wave

Edited by

Chua Beng Huat and Koichi Iwabuchi

香港大學出版社
HONG KONG UNIVERSITY PRESS

Hong Kong University Press
14/F Hing Wai Centre
7 Tin Wan Praya Road
Aberdeen
Hong Kong

ISBN 978-962-209-893-0

British Library Cataloguing-in-Publication Data
A catalogue record for this book is available from the British Library.

Secure On-line Ordering
http://www.hkupress.org

Printed and bound by Pre-Press Limited, Hong Kong, China.

Hong Kong University Press is honoured that Xu Bing, whose
art explores the complex themes of language across cultures, has
written the Press's name in his Square Word Calligraphy. This
signals our commitment to cross-cultural thinking and the distinctive
nature of our English-language books published in China.

"At first glance, Square Word Calligraphy appears to be nothing
more unusual than Chinese characters, but in fact it is a new way
of rendering English words in the format of a square so they
resemble Chinese characters. Chinese viewers expect to be able to
read Square Word Calligraphy but cannot. Western viewers, however
are surprised to find they can read it. Delight erupts when meaning
is unexpectedly revealed."

— Britta Erickson, *The Art of Xu Bing*

Contents

Acknowledgements

This collection of essays is the result of a workshop organized by the Cultural Studies in Asia Research Cluster at the Asia Research Institute, National University of Singapore. The aim of the Cluster is to promote collaborative research in contemporary cultural practices which are influenced by intensifying transnational exchanges across historical, linguistic and cultural boundaries in Asia. ARI serves as a site for bringing researchers together in collaborative endeavours of research, conferences and publications. Its funding of this workshop is gratefully acknowledged. We would also like to thank the members of the 'events team' at ARI, especially Ms Alyson Rozells, for their skills and efficiency in organizing the logistics of the workshop. Professor Chen Kuan-Hsing, who was then Visiting Fellow at ARI, provided insightful comments throughout the two-day workshop. As the research assistant to the Cultural Studies Cluster, Ms Laavanya Kathiravelu was the first to read through and carry out initial editing of the manuscript, for which we are indebted.

Chapter 8 was previously published under the title of "Transnational Media Consumption and Cultural Identity: Young Korean Women's Cultural Appropriation of Japanese TV Dramas", in *The Asian Journal of Women's Studies* 12(2), 2006. Permission of the editors for republication in this volume is gratefully acknowledged.

Contributors

CHUA Beng Huat is in charge of the Cultural Studies Research Cluster at the Asia Research Institute and Professor of Sociology, National University of Singapore. In the past few years, he has been actively engaged in collaborative work in the field of East Asian pop culture. He is founding co-executive editor of *Inter-Asia Cultural Studies*. His most recent book, as editor, is *Election as Popular Culture in Asia* (2007).

Yukie HIRATA is a PhD candidate in the Department of Sociology, Yonsei University, and teaches in the Department of Interdisciplinary Studies, Dokkyo University, Seoul.

Koichi IWABUCHI teaches media and cultural studies at the School of International Liberal Studies, Waseda University, Tokyo. His English publications include: *Recentering Globalization: Popular culture and Japanese transnationalism* (Duke University Press, 2002); *Feeling Asian Modernities: Transnational consumption of Japanese TV dramas* (ed. Hong Kong University Press, 2004); and *Rogue Flows: Trans-Asian cultural traffic* (co-ed. with S. Mueke and M. Thomas, Hong Kong University Press, 2004).

Dong-Hoo LEE is an associate professor in the Department of Mass Communication at University of Incheon, Korea. She has published articles on transnational program adaptation and digital mobile culture in Korea.

Her research interests include media flow in the age of globalization, the cultural consequences of new communication technology, and medium theory.

Keehyeung LEE teaches in the School of Journalism and Communication at Kyung Hee University, Seoul, South Korea. He specializes in media and cultural studies. His work includes 'Beyond the fragments: Reflecting on communicational cultural studies in South Korea'(2005); 'Speak memory! *Morae Sigye* and the politics of social melodrama in contemporary South Korea', *Cultural Studies Critical Methodologies* (2004).

Lisa Y. M. LEUNG is an assistant professor in the Department of Cultural Studies at Lingnan University, Hong Kong. She has published journal articles on the localization of international women's magazines, the globalisation of Chinese satellite TV, and gender and cross-cultural analysis of flows of media and cultural products across Asia, including several book chapters that examine transnational reception of Korean dramas.

Tania LIM received her PhD in Media and Communications from Queensland University of Technology, Brisbane, Australia. She now works on media policy issues at the Media Development Authority of Singapore. Her research areas are the development of Asian film and television industries, new media and globalisation, youth media and consumerism.

Angel LIN is an associate professor in the Department of English and Communication, City University of Hong Kong. She works in the areas of critical discourse analysis, urban ethnography, critical pedagogy, feminist media studies and youth cultural studies.

Yoshitaka MŌRI is an associate professor of sociology and cultural studies at Tokyo National University of Fine Arts and Music. His research interests are postmodern culture, media, art, the city and transnationalism. His recent publications include *Karutyuraru Stadeizu Nyumon* (The introduction to cultural studies, with Toshiya Ueno) 2000 and 'Culture = politics: The emergence of new cultural forms of protest in the age of *Freeter*', *Inter-Asia Cultural Studies* (2005).

Doobo SHIM is associate professor in the School of Culture and Communications at the Sungshin Women's University, Seoul, Korea. His research interests include: the impact of globalization on Korean media industry, dynamics of Asian media industries, and international communication theories. He has published in *Media Culture and Society, Journal of Communication Inquiry*, and *Prometheus*.

Avin Hei Man TONG is a research associate in the Faculty of Education, The Chinese University of Hong Kong. She received her MA in Communication from the Chinese University of Hong Kong. She has been researching topics in youth cultures, media audience studies and feminist cultural studies.

Eva TSAI is an assistant professor in the Graduate Institute of Mass Communication, National Taiwan Normal University. Her work has appeared in the anthology *Feeling Asian Modernities* (Hong Kong University Press, 2004), and journals such as *Modern Chinese Literature and Culture, Inter-Asia Cultural Studies*, and *Japan Forum*. She is writing a book about the production of love by the East Asian cultural industries.

Fang-chih Irene YANG is associate professor at the Department of English in National Dong Hwa University, Taiwan. She has published articles on the localization of international women's magazines in Taiwan, the production and reception of popular music, sexual politics in variety shows, politics of translating post-feminism from the West to Taiwan, and reception of Korean dramas in Taiwan.

Introduction
East Asian TV Dramas:
Identifications, Sentiments and Effects

Chua Beng Huat and Koichi Iwabuchi

In an anthology published in 1995 with the title, 'to be continued ... Soap Operas around the world' (Allen 1995), the only Asian country that rated an entry (Rofel 1995) was an analysis of the People Republic of China (PRC) TV's drama, 'Yearning' (渴望, fifty episodes, 1990), a melodrama credited as marking 'the maturity of soap opera as a full-blown Chinese genre' (Lu 2001:215).[1] The date of the production and screening of this melodrama shows us that the PRC is a very new entrant in this genre of media entertainment. Thus, the absence of analysis of this genre in other East Asia locations in a collection that claims to cover 'soap operas around the world' is at its most generous attributable to the 'space limitation' in a book and at worst, the lack of knowledge of the editor of soap operas in East Asia. The fact is TV soap operas or melodramas have been part of the staples of popular entertainment in East Asia since, at least, the early 1970s.

Take Singapore, for example, which did not have television until 1961. The now famous Hong Kong/Hollywood star, Chow Yun Fat, was introduced to the Singapore audience in the mid-1970s as the main character in the popular TV drama series, *Man in the Net* (网中人), imported from Hong Kong. At the scheduled hour of every week night, in all the neighbourhoods in the public housing estates, in which more than 85% of Singaporeans reside, the sounds from the television sets, turned in unison to the one and only Chinese language channel, would echo through the outdoor spaces that were devoid of people because all the residents were at home glued to the television sets, which were then often 'shared' with neighbours, watching the latest instalment of *Man in the Net*. In the days of nascent industrialization, Singapore was both too poor in national economy and too small in domestic population and market to support a vibrant media industry; indeed, even today, the small domestic market remains an obstacle even though the wealth issue has been long solved.

Since then, Singapore has been receiving waves after waves of TV dramas from different parts of East Asia: Chinese period-costumed melodramas of long suffering but eventually triumphal daughters-in-law in wealthy, large and complicated extended families, came from Taiwan throughout the 1980s, followed in the 1990s by Japanese urban 'trendy' dramas of romances among young professionals dressed from head to toe in international designer togs, living in well appointed apartments and dining in upscale, especially Western, restaurants in the most trendy locations in the city of Tokyo. Each of the 'trendy' dramas series was a visual metaphor for capitalist-consumerist modernity. It is this consumerist modernity that is part of the fascination and captivates the audience of Japanese trendy dramas in the rest of East and Southeast Asia, especially those in the developing nations who aspire to improvements in their material life.[2] Just as the popularity of the Japanese dramas waned, came the Korean TV dramas in the late 1990s and early 2000s. The flood of Korean pop culture — films, pop music and especially TV dramas — into the rest of East Asia came to be known very quickly as the 'Korean Wave' (韓流) by the PRC audience in 1997. By mid-2005, as one drama series was followed hot on the heels by another on TV broadcast, Korean TV dramas became part of the daily programming of many free-to-air and satellite television stations in East Asia and, thus part of the routine viewing habits of their respective audiences.

Singapore, as a media consumption location, thus suggests that there are potentially three sources of East Asian TV dramas in any East Asian locations: a historical stream of Chinese language(s) dramas in all the predominantly ethnic Chinese locations, including the PRC, Hong Kong, Taiwan and Singapore, an island-nation with 75% ethnic Chinese population, and in the past decade and a half, Japanese and Korean TV dramas. Indeed, it is the arrival of the latter two in the rest of the region that provides the material basis for a discursive conceptualization of an 'East Asian pop culture' sphere with an integrated cultural economy.[3]

Uneven Flows and Exchanges

The flows and exchanges within this East Asian pop culture sphere have been governed firstly by the disproportionate massive ethnic Chinese consumer market relative to those of Japan and Korea. Texts of imported media programme are regularly dubbed and subtitled in Chinese script in Hong Kong and Taiwan for local broadcast but subsequently re-exported to other ethnic communities in the global Chinese diaspora and more recently to the PRC. It is this massive global ethnic Chinese consumer market that makes dubbing, translating and subtitling a potentially profitable investment. Consequently, the flows and exchanges of TV dramas have been very unequal within the region. Drama serials tend to flow from Japan and Korea into ethnic-Chinese locations, while only a trickle of the dramas from the latter locations enter the Korean or Japanese market; indeed, no Hong Kong TV drama has ever been screened on Japanese television to date.

Secondly, differences in domestic economic capacity and the history of the media industry have determining effects on the exporting and importing of TV dramas in a particular location. For example, as the wealthiest country in Asia, domestic consumers alone are able to support the Japanese TV drama industry, in spite of the high cost of production. This had lead to an initial reluctance to seek overseas markets. The popularity of Japanese TV dramas was initiated by illegal broadcasting through private satellite stations in places like Taiwan and underground private consumption in Korea. The popularity of Japanese TV dramas in the rest of East Asia came as a surprise to the producers and the additional profits serendipitous. It motivated the Japanese producers to produce dramas that consciously attempt to capture this overseas market. However, the drama series *Romance 2000*, also titled *Love 2000*, which was telecast simultaneously in Tokyo, Taiwan, Hong Kong and Singapore, was such an obvious failure that it might have put a stop to such experiments. With the additional difficulties of policing intellectual property copyrights, Japanese drama producers may be said to be returning to cultivating the domestic market, with the exception of some joint productions with Korea television stations since the late 1990s.

Thirdly, memories of colonization and wars have influenced the flows and exchanges of pop cultures within East Asia. With the PRC as the nation's antagonist constantly on the political radar screen, Taiwanese youth have been favourably disposed to Japanese pop culture, and are colloquially known as 'ha-ri-zu' (哈日族) — 'keen consumer of Japanese media and Japanese-style goods' (Lee 2004: 144) — often to the chagrin of their parents and other elders who have bitter memories of the history of Japanese colonization of Taiwan. The same bitter history of Japanese colonization led South Korea to impose an official total ban on the import of all Japanese cultural products in 1945. This was not lifted until 1998 with the signing of the Joint Declaration of the New 21st Century Korea-Japan Partnership, when media products flowed freely between the two nations. However, the official ban did not make Korea impermeable to Japanese pop culture; even the government-owned Korean Broadcasting Station was guilty of the illegal importation of Japanese pop culture. With a constant stream of underground importation, Japanese pop culture had been 'copied', 'partially integrated', 'plagiarized' and 'reproduced' into Korean products; so much so that Kim Hyun-mee suggests that 'Japanese [pop] culture in Korea had already set its roots deep into the emotional structure of Koreans' (2002:4) by the time of the Joint Declaration.

The aggregate result of the multiple determining factors on East Asian pop culture development, especially of TV dramas, is one of uneven and unequal flows and exchanges across national and cultural boundaries. First, there has been a historical stream of exchanges and flows within predominantly ethnic-Chinese areas, truncated by the 40 years of communist economic regime in the PRC, reconnected again after its economic marketization in 1978 and gaining vitality by the early 1990s when the film and television industry in the PRC were liberalized. Second, there has been the flow of Japanese TV dramas into the rest of the region without corresponding import of TV dramas from elsewhere until 2004 when the Korean TV drama series, *Winter Sonata*, was broadcast by NHK. And finally, since the late 1990s, the strong export and flow of Korean TV dramas into the rest of East Asia as part of the Korean Wave, which has the backing of the government as cultural export industry. We are concerned at this juncture with the latest of these developments, namely, the arrival of and respective local receptions of Korean TV dramas, as part of the larger 'Korean Wave' phenomenon, in the rest of East Asia.

Korean TV Dramas

The penetration of Korean TV dramas into East Asian markets in the late 1990s is the consequence of felicitous timing. The post-1997 Asian Financial Crisis that savaged the Korean national economy contributed to the stepping-up of the exporting of Korean pop culture as part of the national export industry. The same crisis had led television industries in the other affected East Asian economies to look for cheaper programmes than the relatively expensive Japanese dramas. The confluence of these two separate industry strategies led to the rapid importation and screening of Korean TV dramas in the rest of East Asia, except Japan, creating the so-called 'Korean Wave' in the region.

Take Singapore again as an example. In 1999, the tightly government controlled media sector, which has very severe restrictions on local and foreign ownership, opened a gap for a new free-to-air television station. This new station was owned by the local monopoly newspaper publisher, the Singapore Press Holdings (SPH). In 2001, it started operating with two channels, an English language Channel I and a Mandarin Channel U (尤 for 'excellence'). This was an uphill venture because the government-owned television station, with three free-to-air channels had already be in existence for more than thirty years and had well consolidated audience base. This was very quickly apparent, as the locally produced English language programmes on Channel I failed abjectly to establish an audience and was shut down within two years of its establishment, reducing the channel to broadcasting news and imported programmes from the US. It eventually shut down completely in 2004.

The Mandarin Channel U, on the other hand, was able to carve out and take away a significant segment of the local audience from its established rival through a strategy of half locally produced programmes and half imported programmes from Japan, Hong Kong (with TVB) and Korea. Parenthetically, it should be noted that this was a repeat of how STAR TV used Japanese trendy dramas as a means of establishing its audience base in Hong Kong, where the two existing local stations had already captured 90% of the audience on the island. The locally produced programmes were largely variety shows, which copied the format well established by Japan and Taiwan stations — high energy, rapid-fire commentaries from a team of programme hosts whose sole objective is to make fun of and embarrass the guests in the show. From the point of preparing to launch the new channel, the station had already bought a store of Korean TV dramas because the latter had by then proved popular in Hong Kong and Taiwan.[4] The popularity of the Korean dramas in Singapore pushed the state-owned Channel 8 and the new Channel U into a bidding war for similar drama series, culminating in the highest price being paid of the serial, *All In* (2003), rumoured to be up to forty thousand Singapore dollars per episode. Such fierce competition for imported programmes, not restricted to Korean TV dramas, was cannibalizing the stations and led eventually to the merger of the state-owned and SPH-owned stations into a joint-stock monopoly in 2004. In 2005, Channel U reconfigured itself as the station that showcases 'pan-East Asian' pop culture, reflecting the stabilization of flows of East Asian pop culture throughout the region.

Perhaps the drama series that has the greatest impact on all the predominantly ethnic-Chinese locations in East Asia is Korea's *Dae Jang Geum*

(大长今) —*Jewel in the Palace* (2003), which chronicles the rise and tribulations of the first female imperial physician in 16th-century Chosun Dynasty. The serial was first exported to Taiwan and was very well received. It was subsequently screened on TVB in Hong Kong to record breaking audience ratings. The Taiwan mandarin version was then bought by a provincial satellite station, Hunan Satellite Television, and broadcast at the national level in the PRC. In early 2006, it was broadcast on subscription-only cable television in Singapore. It was so popular that it was immediately rebroadcast after the completion of its first run and finally, a third broadcast was done on the above-mentioned free-to-air Channel U.

As a rule the Japanese and Korean TV dramas that cross national boundaries to the ethnic-Chinese predominant locations are of the contemporary urban romance genre. Historical period costumed dramas, of which many are produced in Japan and Korea, are not exported as the audiences in the latter locations may not have the prerequisite historical and cultural knowledge to sustain their interest in the usually longer series of historical dramas. *Jewel in the Palace* is thus an exception. In this case, the 'close' cultural affinity between the Chosun Dynasty and Chinese history was an important bridge to its success; for example, the written texts in the drama, from imperial edicts to recipes for food and medicine, were written in Chinese script. This facilitated 'indigenization' through dubbing and subtitling. Riding on this affinity, the Hong Kong television station took additional effort to 'indigenize' the series by, for example, providing brief explanations of the narrative before the broadcasting of each episode and, often giving the Chinese equivalent of the ingredients in the on-screen menu or medical prescriptions. Such local television station investments are central to the popular success of the series.

In Japan, undoubtedly the singular Korean TV drama that has had an immense impact on audiences is *Winter Sonata*, starring Bae Yong Jun in the male lead character. The series was first shown on NHK-owned cable television late at night in 2003 to boost its sagging ratings. Popular requests caused it to be shown again in early 2004. Then, on 3 April 2004, Bae Yong Jun arrived in Tokyo and was mobbed by 5,000 mostly middle-age fans who turned up to welcome him, instantly creating a media spectacle. Following which, NHK rebroadcast the series on a terrestrial station, again with record viewer ratings. The series propelled Bae into stardom in Japan, earning him the title 'Yon-sama' and 'Lord (/Prince) Yong'. NHK earned a phenomenal sum of money through tie-up products such as DVD sets and a novelized book. Beyond the television screen, *Winter Sonata* also spawned behavioural changes among its Japanese middle-aged female audiences including, among other things, turning them into enthusiastic tourists to Korea, earning the latter a substantial amount of tourist dollars.

Themes and Essays

The success of Korean TV dramas in the rest of East Asia is evidenced by the fact that they are now part of the daily programming of many local television stations in both afternoon and evening schedules. Nevertheless, academically this pan-East Asian transnational pop culture phenomenon has yet to be submitted to a more systematic comparative analysis, both in terms of its reception and consumption in different locations, and in terms of a comparison with similar genre entertainment from other parts of East Asia. This is the background that motivates the analyses in this collection of essays from different locations in the region.

Section I examines the political economy and current state of play in the television industry in East Asia. Regional media production is promoted by national policy and South Korea is the best exemplar of this. Shim Doobo explores the rise of the 'Korean Wave' in the new millennium in terms of governmental and corporate support. He empirically examines government support, investments of chaebols (Korean conglomerates), and processes of capital accumulation in the media sector. The development is no linear evolution and the continuous efforts of the producers to improve their own production techniques should not be ignored, but the governmental promotional policy is undoubtedly a most prominent factor in the rapid growth of the Korean media industry, a development strategy that has now been taken up by other Asian states. The intensification and dynamic circulation of media cultures in East Asian markets is not restricted to expanding the export of cultural products from one location to the rest of the region, as exemplified by the Korean Wave. Coining the term, 'renting strategies', Tania Lim shows how media producers in East Asia mutually appropriate celebrities, icons, contents and program formats of East Asian pop culture for their own productions and co-productions in their bid to garner stronger positions in their respective TV territories and the regional TV marketplace. Transnational Asian popular media texts have been used by provincial/local media operators as a resource to compete successfully with the dominant national players. Leung charts how Hunan Satellite TV, a regional station in the PRC, succeeds in using Korean media — through its successful bid for one of the most popular Korean TV programs, *Dae Jang Geum* — as a vehicle to establish its footprint in the competitive national

TV media space. The station had to juggle with a multitude of forces — state, ideological, ethnic, and economic — at the national level, in order to assume a leading role among the various national, terrestrial and cable/satellite, broadcasters. The case of Hunan Satellite TV throws light on the dynamics that mediate the local with the national via the transnational, in an increasingly intensified 'globality' where the development of communication technologies and the rise of East Asian media flows enable 'local' or 'regional' players to escape subordination to the national center.

Thematically, the essays in Section II are concerned with transnational-crosscultural receptions of TV dramas in different locations across East Asia. The crisscrossing of national and cultural boundaries logically raises the question of how an audience watches/reads imported TV dramas within East Asia. Chua aims to answer this question by developing a comprehensive, relatively formal, conceptual framework for the analysis of pan-Asian, trans-national pop culture consumption. At one level he examines the circulation and reception of media products in locations where an ethnic-Chinese population predominates, namely the PRC, Hong Kong, Taiwan and Singapore. Within this 'Pop Culture China', Japanese and Korean films and TV programs are usually dubbed as a means of 'domesticating' the foreign. However, the 'reduced' foreignness is preserved in the visual elements as part of the desired viewing pleasure. Next, drawing on existing TV drama audience studies throughout East Asia, it can be demonstrated that audiences in the different locations read imported products along a linear temporality defined by capitalist-consumer modernity, specifically in terms of nostalgia for a 'less-capitalist' past where life was more vigorous or desire for a more consumerist future. Finally, the possible emergence of a pan-East Asian 'community of consumers' and its implication is examined.

Lin and Tong's comparative analysis of the meaning-making activities of Hong Kong and Singaporean female audiences of Korean TV dramas found that these audiences are adept in using Korean dramas to construct and confirm their own multiple, at times conflicting, subjectivities, which seem to be rooted concurrently in 'tradition' and 'modernity', to negotiate everyday life tensions and dilemmas experienced in contemporary urban living, and to construct what they see as their distinctive 'Asian' modern femininities. These modes of consumption contrast with those of Japanese female audiences, whose responses are explored in the next two contributions in this section.

Here, it needs to be stressed that the impact of Korean TV dramas on Japan merits special attention, not least because of the lingering importance of colonial/postcolonial relations between the two countries. The very significant impacts of the Korean Wave in Japan are undoubtedly results of the entangled history of the two countries, Korea being colonized by Japan for close to four decades (1910–1945). The essays by Mori and Hirata analyze the impact of the Korean TV serial drama, *Winter Sonata*, in Japan. Each shows that the effects of Korean TV dramas on Japanese audiences are such that new cultural-political phenomena have emerged, which have a potential impact on the people-to-people relations between the two countries, beneath the continuing difficult international relations of the two nations.

Through interviews with middle-aged female fans of the drama and Yon-sama (Bae Yong Jun), which constitutes the predominant fan base in Japan, Mōri shows how the fans are actively involved in a various post-text cultural practices such as organizing fan meetings, learning Korean culture and language, and participating in *Winter Sonata* fan tours in Korea. Some of the audiences have even started to reconstruct postcolonial memories of the war between Japan and Korea. Although male-dominated social discourse in Japan easily dismisses the *Winter Sonata* and Yon-sama phenomena as a 'trivial fad of unhappy women', Mōri argues that the emergence of new cultural subjectivities of middle-aged housewives and their political possibilities should be taken seriously in their own right, in spite of having been marginalized or even ignored in a traditional political sense. This is precisely what Hirata has done in her empirical study of the Japanese women fans turned tourists who traveled to the shooting locations for *Winter Sonata*. The number of Japanese who traveled to Korea in 2004 grew by 35.5 percent compared with the previous year due to these women fans of Korean TV dramas. Based on fieldwork and interviews, Hirata elucidates the changes in the Japanese tourist's view of Korea, which also testifies to the change in gender dynamics of Japanese tourists to Asia. Obviously, consumption of *Winter Sonata* has provided the Japanese women fans an opportune moment for the self-reflexive review of not just the state of their own lives and interpersonal relationships but also of Japan's historical relationship with Korea.

While the rest of East Asia is watching Korean dramas, whose reception is discussed below, a significant segment of the domestic Korean audience at home is watching imported Japanese TV dramas. Lee Dong-Hoo studies ethnographically how young Korean women, from their late teens to early thirties, watched and related Japanese TV dramas to their daily lives. Constrained by conventional gender systems, these women react negatively to home-grown dramas and embrace the Japanese media products in building cultural capital for their own subjectivity formation. Lee examines, firstly, the ways in which the fans create or experience transnational consumption space, within which they negotiate their cultural or gender identities in an age of globalization. Secondly, how their reception experiences have been hybridized as their self-reflexive reading becomes more inter-textual and inter-cultural, with an increasing propensity to select, compare and appropriate cultural products from various countries.

Section III covers the nationalistic reactions and negative 'backlash', which are at once political and ideological, that might be generated by massive cultural cross-border regional flows, of the Korean Wave. At home, critics point to the economic motivations and unbecoming nationalism behind the gleeful celebration of the 'acceptance' of Korean 'culture' by other Asians. Lee Keehyeung critically analyzes three competing positions on the Korean Wave in South Korea developed by the South Korean government, cultural producers and critical intellectuals; namely, neoliberalism, state-centric nationalism, culturalism cum post-colonialism. Reflecting on previous studies on the historical formations and trans-border flows of South Korean and Japanese popular cultures in Asia, Lee seeks to provide alternative, non-nationalist ways of envisioning the flow of South Korean popular culture across Asia so as to further inter-regional cultural understanding and dialogues. Elsewhere, the prominent presence of Korean pop culture begins to attract xenophobic reactions against a Korean 'cultural imperialism'. For example, in Taiwan, the popularity of Korean dramas has been described by the mass media as an 'invasion of Korean Wave', a discursive construction that is embedded in economic and cultural nationalism, which are both predicated on the masculine conception of a nation. In contrast, there is another discourse that takes on a feminine form, addressing the question of how women consume Korean drama affectively, particularly that of the male body. This feminine discourse circulates in newspaper entertainment pages and fan websites that have women as its implicit reader/consumer. Yang critically interrogates these three public discourses on the Korean Wave from a feminist perspective. She suggests that the fan/women discourse functions as a 'mode of containment' that marginalizes women's speech to 'female complaint'. However, she argues that 'complaint' itself is both resistant and containment, self-expressive and self-confining and concludes with an attempt to re-read the fan discourse through Heidegger's notion of 'technology' in the hope of transforming the existing public sphere which leaves women no place to speak. Picking up the thread of the politics of the national, Tsai explores the inter-Asia cultural space where different strands of nationalisms meet and compete to define, shape, and discipline the legitimacy of border-crossing pop stars. While many successful transnational celebrities in inter-Asia embody cosmopolitan mobility, limits to their fluid identity are exposed when unresolved historical tensions and new conditions of intra- and inter-national cultural politics flare up. The stalled career of Aboriginal-Taiwanese diva A-mei is generally perceived as a casualty of the clash between Taiwanese and PRC nationalism. BoA, a young South Korean pop singer based in Japan, was recently compelled to pledge her patriotism during a territorial dispute between Korea and Japan. Tsai's analysis highlights an emergent issue of how inter-Asia celebrities can become implicated in national identity battles, in an era where the intensification of transnational cultural flows seems bound to engender the nationalization of sentiments and politics.

However, how the *Winter Sonata* phenomenon has influenced, constructively or otherwise, the social positioning and recognition of resident Koreans in Japan, most of whom are the descendants of expatriates under Japanese colonial rule, remains a question and an issue. This issue is conceptualized and examined by Iwabuchi through the complexities of how transnational media flows of the Korean Wave intersect with postcolonial and multicultural issues in the Japanese local. He suggests that as the Korean Wave has significantly bettered the image of Korea, social recognition of resident Koreans has also improved. Nevertheless, in spite of this improved perception, a lack of understanding of the historically embedded experiences of resident Koreans remains, as the resident Koreans in Japan are often unproblematically associated with the culture and people of South Korea in such a way that postcolonial and multicultural issues are subsumed under the inter-national framework.

Conclusion

Using Korean TV dramas as an analytic vehicle, the essays in this volume collectively provide a multi-layered analysis of the emerging East Asian pop culture space in terms of intensifying production, marketing, circulation and consumption. By closely examining the political economy of the TV industry, audiences of the regional media flows in terms of gender subjectivity constructions, perceptions of colonial-postcolonial relationships and, nationalist responses to trans-national media culture exchanges, the essays highlight the multiple connectivities and socio-political implications of popular cultural flows and exchanges in East Asia. This series of contextually grounded analyses of the actual pop cultural circulation across national, cultural and geopolitical boundaries demonstrates the effects pop culture has on the imagination, meaning-making and meaning-changing and negotiation of difference — audience and their imagined regional counterparts, transnational fans and their 'idols' and even, postcolonial relations between the colonizer and colonized — on their consumers. This volume, along with already published works of its contributors, demonstrates the presence of an East Asian pop culture that co-exists side by side with US domination in the global media industry. We hope that it offers to readers further empirical and conceptual insights into cultural globalization, which cannot be ascertained in existing US-centric analyses.

I

Television Industry in East Asia

1

The Growth of Korean Cultural Industries and the Korean Wave

Doobo Shim

Introduction

Since the 1980s, Korea had been under daunting bilateral (largely from the United States) and multilateral pressures to open its markets, in the name of globalization, in various sectors including the cinema and television. These global economic dynamics influenced Korea Inc.'s industrial formations. While taking on the defensive, the Korean economy began to promote production and commodification of media and cultural content, including film, television programming, animation, etc., against the backdrop of the worldwide diffusion of "information society" discourses. The media liberalization measures, also pushed for by citizens who were fed up with long years of state control of the media, led to a considerably competitive domestic media environment that eventually cultivated commercially sensitive productions. Ironically, the global media market openings in the 1990s facilitated the export of Korean popular culture.

By early 2006 Korean cultural productions, including television drama, film, pop music, etc., have become widely consumed by audiences in Asia. Starting with *What Is Love All About* and *Stars in My Heart* in the late 1990s, and *Winter Sonata* and *Dae Jang Geum* in recent years, Korean television drama, and its stars including Bae Yong Jun, Ahn Jae Wook, Lee Byung Heon, and Kim Hee Seon, have enchanted Asian audiences. The popular consumption of Korean television dramas has coincided with that of cinema. Starting with *Shiri*, *Joint Security Area* and *My Sassy Girl*, Korean films have become regular fixtures in theatres across Asia. At the same time, Korean pop music, or K-pop, has also produced such international celebrities as H.O.T., BoA, and Rain ("Bi"). The regional media call this new popular cultural phenomenon in Asia the *Korean Wave* (or, *Hallyu*).

The everydayness of Korean pop culture in Asia is evidenced by the fact that it has become material for a song 〈我不是 宋承宪〉("I am not ... Song Seung Heon") in Malaysia. Two male singers express the feelings of a man who has a girlfriend infatuated with the Korean actor Song Seung Heon. Its words, "You want me to say *Salanghe* ("사랑해") / You complain that our romance is not like that in the Korean soap opera ... . You order me to have only a pack of Korean instant noodles a day ...",[1] show how much Korean popular culture is embedded in people's lives in Asia.

In order to account for the growth of Korean popular culture into an export industry and its international appeal, this chapter examines the trajectory of Korean popular culture industries linking them to global and local political economic relations and the domestic cultural environment. Because of time and space constraints, this chapter focuses on cinema and television dramas for its analysis of the development of Korean popular culture. For a start, we shall discuss the government policies and domestic conglomerates' business moves that helped transform the Korean cinema industry, taking account of the global political economic context.

The Korean Cinema in the 1990s

The period of the late 1980s and early 1990s was an important juncture for the Korean cinema industry because of the market opening to foreign distributors. Under U.S. pressure, in 1988 the Korean government allowed foreign film companies to distribute their films without passing through local distributors in Korea, which the domestic film industry fiercely opposed in vain. After this measure, poorly performing homemade flicks marked a record low of 15.9% domestic market share in 1993. While the annual number of local film productions was decreasing, that of foreign film imports was increasing. In 1984, the figures of local productions and foreign imports were 81 and 25. It changed to 87 and 175 in 1988, and 63 and 347 in 1993 (Korean Film Council, 2006). In this situation, commentators predicted the demise of the Korean cinema industry in the near future (Kim, 2003).

At around that time, the Uruguay Round (UR) trade negotiation, started in 1986, eventually concluded in 1994 transforming the General Agreement on Tariffs and Trade (GATT) into the World Trade Organization (WTO) in 1995. It meant that all member countries of GATT, including Korea, were soon obliged to open their markets in media communications and culture. This sector had been protected from foreign competition, having been considered "exceptional categories" to the free trade principle since the early days of GATT, which began in 1947. The Korean press began to write that while culture was emerging as a new sector in global economic competition, Korea was in danger of its indigenous culture being debased by foreign media, and also of dollar drain (Shim, 2002). The press also echoed Peter Drucker, Alvin Toffler and their ilk's futurological discourses on the cultural industry's contribution to national economies in the coming 21st century.

For Koreans, there was nothing that illustrated the importance of the cultural industry to the national economy better than what I would call the "*Jurassic Park* factor" (Shim, 2006). In 1994, the Presidential Advisory Board on Science and Technology proposed to President Kim Young-Sam that Korea should develop cinema and other media content production as a national strategic industry. What the proposal highlighted was the fact that Hollywood movie *Jurassic Park*'s total revenue came up to the foreign sales of 1.5 million Hyundai cars, and this "unlikely" anecdote made the headlines the next morning in Korea. It was a "paradigm shift" for the Koreans who long had strongly believed that the heavy and chemical industries, including automobile, chemical, construction and electronics industries, would lead their country through to a more prosperous future.

In this environment, the National Assembly enacted the Motion Picture Promotion Law in 1995 to replace the Motion Picture Law that had long straitjacketed the cinema industry. By the new law, the government would provide tax incentives for film production, attracting corporate capital into the cinema industry. In fact, major domestic conglomerates, or chaebol, including Samsung, Daewoo and Hyundai, which had home electronics interests, had already been planning for cultural content production taking cues from Japanese Sony Electronics' acquisition of Columbia Pictures and CBS Records in the late 1980s. Based on the concept of hardware–software synergy, these companies attempted to synchronize connections between electronic device production and areas of entertainment. In relation to this, Samsung and Daewoo started film financing or video production in the late 1980s. In addition, Samsung, Daewoo and Hyundai secured their interests in cable television services, started in 1995, as program providers (PPs).

Following these initiatives, many Korean chaebols advanced into the cultural industry ranging from video production, film import, financing and production, and theatre operation to music production. As a newspaper commented: "The *youngsang san-eop* [loosely translated into "visual industry" or "image industry"] is rising to the surface as a new field for chaebol competition" (*Kookmin Ilbo*, 1994). Table 1.1 below illustrates the five largest chaebol's involvement in cinema and other audiovisual industries as of mid-1995.

Table 1.1 Five largest chaebol's audiovisual industry activities as of 1995

Chaebol	Subsidiary	Activity
Samsung	Catch One	Pay cable channel (PP)*
	Dream Box	Film importer / home video producer
	Hoam Art Hall	Theater
	Myungbo Movies	Cinema house (Samsung leased two screens under contract)
	Nices	Film importer / producer of CDs, LDs, CD-ROMs, and films
	Starmax	Film importer / film producer
	Cheil Youngsang	Film importer / television program producer
	Audiosoft	Music producer and distributor
	Q Channel	Cable channel (PP)
Daewoo	Daewoo Electronics Video Business Division	Film importer for home video production / film producer
	Wooil Video	Film importer for video production / distribution
	Dong-woo Video	Home video producer
	Seshin Video	Home video producer
	Daewoo Cinema Network	Cable channel (PP)
	Se-um Media	Music producer and distributor
Hyundai	Seoul Production	Film producer
	HBS	Cable channel (PP)
LG	LG Media	Film importer / producer of CDs, LDs, CD-ROMs, and films
	Mediart	Film importer / film producer
	Korea Home Shopping	Cable channel (PP)
SK	SKC Video Business Division	Film importer for home video production
	Pan Production	Film producer and distributor
	Mido Film	Film importer / film producer
	Seoryung Production	Film importer for home video production

Source: *Weekly Chosun* (1995) and Won (1998)
* PP stands for program provider.

After several years of operation, these ventures suffered losses. In addition, the Korea Inc. of the mid-1990s began to show signs of economic downturn. Therefore, many chaebols were looking for opportunities to exit from the cultural industry. In a sense, the financial crisis in late 1997 gave them apposite excuses to fold their businesses. In January 1998 SK drastically reduced its video and film businesses and later that year Daewoo abandoned its cinema interests. In particular, the breakup of the Samsung Entertainment Group, which was launched in September 1995 as an integrated organization by bringing all cultural industry-related ventures within Samsung under its umbrella, in January 1999, marked the ending of "the chaebol age of Korean cinema industry" in the 1990s (Ko, 2005b).

The chaebol age of Korean cinema industry, however, did not simply end up as a passing fad but actually laid the foundation for a renaissance of the cinema industry. By holding independent film festivals and film scenario contests with considerable cash prizes, chaebol-run film companies recruited fresh talent, who infused new sensibilities into Korean cinema. In particular, the chaebols supported young directors, equipped with diplomas from prestigious film schools all over the world, who would otherwise have to wait for many years for their debut film. During this period, many competent staff members from diverse lines of business within the chaebols were put into the cinema business. By this, chaebol transplanted their advanced business know-how, including systematic planning and marketing and transparent accounting, to the Korean cinema industry which had long been caught by "mom-and-pop", "pre-modern" business practices. After the chaebols folded their film businesses, quite a number of those people remained in the cinema industry. For example, when Samsung Entertainment Group was disbanded, 30 out of 45 staff members in its cinema business team went to other film companies instead of returning to their original positions in Samsung Electronics or elsewhere. It is reported that many successful Korean films in recent years have been planned, financed or marketed by those ex-members of the Samsung Entertainment Group (Ko, 2005b).

The Korean Cinema on the Rise

Chaebol's business rationalization of the local film industry facilitated new players' entrances into the sector. When asked, "What do you think is Samsung's contribution to the Korean cinema industry?", Choi Wan, who oversaw Samsung Entertainment Group's cinema business team but is now a CEO of IM Pictures, made his answer short and clear: "Samsung made the film business transparent, making way for a new form of capital" (Kim, Min Gyeong, 2004). When chaebol were leaving the cinema industry, venture capitalists and investment firms were entering, looking for fast profits. Right after the Samsung Entertainment Group officially announced its breakup, an action thriller, *Shiri*, which Samsung had planned and funded as its final project, ironically was a big hit. By attracting 5.8 million theatergoers nationwide, it set a new box-office record in Korea. That *Shiri* was also partly funded by a venture capitalist gave many prospective investors cues to finance film productions. This new trend must be understood in relation to the revision of the Motion Picture Promotion Law in 1999 which facilitated venture capital's funding the film production (Kim, Dong Ho, 2005). Venture capitalists funded (partly or exclusively) 23 out of 58 Korean films produced in 2000 (Hwang, 2001). With the influx of capital, as of 2004 the average cost of production per film amounted to 42 billion won, a considerable increase from 0.9 billion won in 1995 (Korean Film Council, 2006).[2]

The revision of the Motion Picture Promotion Law in 1999 noted above indeed made it possible for individuals to finance film productions. What it turned out was the so-called *netizen fund*. Taking advantage of the existence of huge numbers of online film buffs based on Korea's developed broadband facilities, a film studio Bom raised a US$85,000 fund from among them. It recruited 200 investors for $425 each, later paying 200% returns (Kim, 2002). After this, many film projects employed netizen funds not only as a source of investment but also a means of marketing. In 2001, Hana Bank launched the "Hana Cinema Trust Fund No.1" of US$7.8 million (Kim, 2003).

In this favorable environment, the Korean cinema industry churned out more blockbusters. In 2001, *Shiri's* box-office record was broken by *Joint Security Area*, whose record was again smashed by *Friends* a few months later with 8.2 million admission tickets sold in Korea. 2004 saw two movies that set new box-office records by hitting 11.08 million and 11.74 million in viewership, respectively. *Silmido* revisited North-South Korean relations in the 1970s and *TaeGukGi: The Brotherhood of War* was a movie about two brothers' experiences during the Korean War. In March 2006, *King and the Clown*, a fiction film depicting a king during the Joseon (or, Choson) Period (1392–1910) falling in love with a pretty male clown, set a new Korean record by drawing in more than 12 million audiences. Upheld by these and other well-performing local flicks, the Korean cinema's domestic market share has continuously increased from 15.9% in 1993 to 35.5% in 2000, and even recorded over 50% in 2001, 2003, 2004, and 2005 (Korean Film Council, 2006).

The influx of capital into the cinema industry has facilitated not only film production but also its consumption. For one, more comfortable viewing conditions introduced by multiplex theaters, largely begun to be built in the late 1990s by some chaebol. Located in major shopping malls in big cities in Korea, multiplexes have enticed consumers back to theaters (Kim, 2003). According to director/producer Kang Woo-suk (2002), multiplexes have become a "playground" for the youth where they can spend time eating, drinking and enjoying movies. The multiplex building boom — the number of screens nationwide increased from 497 in 1997 to 1,132 in 2003 — further facilitated film production. Simply put, in order to fill those increasing screens, multiplexes, many of which were linked to production companies, funded Korean film production, which were showing signs of entertainment-quality improvement and were enjoying more audience acclaim.

In the 2000s, by making strategic alliances with film producers or through vertical integration, Korean film distributors experienced consolidation and concentration. In this regard, some observers noted that Korean blockbusters were possible because they were productions of local cinema majors which controlled distribution networks (Kim, 2003). As of 2006, Cinema Service, CJ Entertainment, Showbox Inc., and Lotte Cinema formed an oligopoly of the Korean cinema industry ranging from production and investment to distribution and theaters. While Cinema Service is founded on traditional Korean cinema industry resources, the other three are subsidiaries of mid-size chaebol. CJ Entertainment, which originally started its cinema business in 1995, has extended its business since 1999, and Showbox Inc., and Lotte Cinema advanced into the sector in 1999 (Cinema Service, 2006; CJ Entertainment, 2006; Lotte Cinema, 2006; Showbox, 2006).

Based on its domestic success, Korean cinema has even attracted larger audiences overseas. The blockbuster *Shiri* was sold to several Asian countries and received both critical and commercial acclaim. In particular, it earned US$14 million at the Japanese box office from 1.2 million theatergoers and topped the Hong Kong box office, a rare overseas achievement for a Korean film at that time (Kim, 2000). Since then, many Korean films have been released for commercial run in foreign theaters and won prizes at such prestigious film festivals as Cannes, Berlin and Venice. In 2004 a total of 193 Korean films were exported to 62 countries earning about US$58 million in marked contrast to 1995's export figure of 15 films with earnings of US$208,679 (please see the table 1.2 below). As of 2004, Japan was the biggest Korean film importer, accounting for 69.3% of all Korean film exports. Korea earned US$40.4 million from these Japanese exports. With 33 Korean films released in Japan in 2004, Korean flicks took a 10% share of the Japanese film market, a huge jump from their 3.8% market share in 2000 (please see the table 1.3 below). According to Kim Mee-hyun (2005), head of Film Policy Division at the Korean Film Council, the majority of the Japanese audiences for Korean films in 2004 were middle-aged women spurred by their fandom of television drama *Winter Sonata* and its male lead Bae Yong Jun. As such, Korean cinema's achievement overseas should also be understood against the backdrop of the Korean Wave led by the popularity of Korean television drama.

Table 1.2   Korean film export (1995–2004)

(unit: US$)

Year	Amount Exported	Increase Rate
1995	208,679	
1996	404,000	48%
1997	492,000	22%
1998	3,073,750	525%
1999	5,969,219	94%
2000	7,053,745	18%
2001	11,249,573	59%
2002	14,952,089	33%
2003	30,979,000	107%
2004	58,284,600	88%

Source: Korean Film Council (2006)

Table 1.3   Number of Korean films released in Japan as against total number of films released in Japan (2000–2004)

Year	Number of Korean films	Total number of films released in Japan	Market share
2000	14	362	3.8%
2001	13	349	4.2%
2002	10	347	3.4%
2003	14	335	4.7%
2004	33	339	10%

Source: Kim Mee-hyun (2005)

The Commercialization of Korean Television

As noted, the globally flourished "information society" discourse, upheld by advances in IT (information technology) and digital development, and citizens' demands for a more liberal public communication environment led to the media liberalization in Korea beginning in the late 1980s. In 1989, the government-assigned Commission for Broadcasting System Research suggested an idea to launch cable television in 1995 as the mainstay of digitized, integrated communication infrastructure in the coming Information Age. In 1990 the National Assembly enacted the new Broadcasting Law, by which the government granted a license to the commercial Seoul Broadcasting System (SBS) to begin operation from 1991. SBS was the first commercial television station to be established since 1980 when the then Chun Doo-whan regime forcibly reshuffled 29 broadcasters into an oligopoly of two public broadcasters, Korea Broadcasting System (KBS) and Munhwa Broadcasting Company (MBC).

In December 1991 the National Assembly passed the Cable Television Act. Based on the Act, in August 1993 the Ministry of Information selected 20 applicants to become cable television program providers (PPs) who would run their own channels. As planned, in March 1995 cable television services started across the country. In addition, four new regional commercial terrestrial television stations started operation in the same year. In 1997 another set of four regional channels started to cover their respective provinces. In 2002, satellite channels were added to this television platform, and digital multimedia broadcasting (DMB) started in 2005. In a nutshell, since the 1990s Korea has entered a multi-channel television era, marked by intense competition for audience attention (Korean Broadcasting Commission, 2006).

This competition was spearheaded by SBS, the new commercial broadcaster. Although technically a regional broadcaster covering Seoul and its vicinities, it accounted for almost half of the Korean population. In addition, by providing its programs to other regional stations newly launched in the 1990s, SBS practically functioned as a network like KBS and MBC. The advent of SBS was "threatening" to KBS and MBC which, although tagged as "public" broadcasters, had relied on advertising for their finances. In the early 1990s, KBS relied more on advertising revenue than on the reception fee by 61% to 39%. In the same period, 98% of MBC's revenue came from advertisements (Kim, 2001). Indeed, SBS publicly announced that it would compete with the established broadcasters for audience ratings in television dramas, in particular.

The television drama has always been the centerpiece of television watching among Korean audiences. For example, in the annual lists of ten television programs with the highest audience ratings, 5 or 6 are usually television dramas (Lee, 2005). By presenting the everyday lives of ordinary people, including their social relations, agony, despair, joy and victory, television dramas have entertained Korean audiences. In the 1990s, audience ratings became the matter of primary concern for broadcasters, with an emphasis on television dramas' commercialism. Spurred by SBS's "television drama offensive", characterized by increased numbers and diversified contents of television dramas, broadcasters engaged in the "drama war" by making every effort to enhance the audience ratings of television dramas (Ko, 2004). They extended into previously untouched topics, shot on locations that included foreign countries, sped up the flow of stories with better scripts and pictures. In this process, the overall entertainment quality of television dramas has also improved while chastised for their low taste and sexual morality by the elitist press.

These days, many Korean television dramas record ratings of more than a 30% share in a market where the three terrestrial networks air as many as more than 30 television dramas per week (Yi, Jiyoung, 2004). Fans' enthusiasm for television dramas is such that they often form cult-like Internet fan clubs of their favorite television dramas and provide feedback — often in the form of "pressure" to alter storylines — to television producers, and produce parodies of the dramas in the form of magazines, newspapers and posters. Because these ardent fans are leaders in opinions about the programs, and they form the guaranteed market for the dramas' sales of video-on-demand, DVD and other spin-off products, networks cannot disregard their fandom. Networks and other television drama producers often invite fan club members to locations, arrange meetings with their stars and even allow them to play minor roles in television dramas (Gu, 2004). According to Yun Seok-jin (2004), a television critic, Korean television producers have made every effort to gratify audiences.

Korean Television Drama Exports

It was around the turn of the 1990s when the Korean television industry began to export television dramas. According to Bak Jaebok, the head of the International Exchange Department at MBC, it was not until 1992 that MBC first put up its own booth at the Cannes international television programming market (Korea Culture and Tourism Policy Institute, 2005). At that time, MBC sold *Eyes of the Dawn* to Türkiye Radyo Televizyon (TRT), Turkey's national broadcaster, marking the first Korean television drama to be exported to a

European country, and *What Is Love All About* to Hong Kong's Asia Television Ltd. (ATV) (Kim and Han, 2001). With media liberalization sweeping across Asia, the scale of Korean television programming exports gradually increased.

Most observers agree that the Korea Wave, a phenomenon where Korean popular culture is enjoying fandom overseas, started in China with the broadcast of *What Is Love All About*. In 1997, China's national China Central Television (CCTV) aired it, where it became a massive hit. On popular demand, CCTV had to rebroadcast the Korean television drama in 1998. Since then, more Korean television dramas have received popular receptions from audiences in China, Hong Kong, Taiwan, and Vietnam. In particular, Korean television dramas accounted for 56% of all foreign programming imports to Vietnam in 1998 (Korea Culture and Tourism Policy Institute, 2005). About that time, boy band H.O.T. and dance music duo Clon were winning popularity in the region thanks to their pretty faces and powerful dance moves. Therefore, commentators in East Asia began to talk about the 韩流 ("Korean Wave") of popular culture (Heo, 2002).

According to Chae Jiyoung, senior researcher at the Korea Culture and Tourism Policy Institute, the Korean Wave was possible not because the government or broadcasters in Korea had certain visions or strategies for popular cultural exports. Rather, international market conditions worked favourably for the exports of Korean television dramas which were gradually improving in commercial quality based on domestic competition (Korea Culture and Tourism Policy Institute, 2005). In the late 1990s, the popularity of Japanese television dramas began to weaken in Taiwan. At this juncture, Taiwanese importers began to import cheaper Korean television dramas to fill this opening. As middlemen, they also helped Korean television dramas penetrate into markets in Hong Kong and China. In addition, the economic downturn in Asia in the late 1990s made the cheaper Korean programming a popular alternative in these media markets. Korean television dramas were a quarter of the price of Japanese ones, and a tenth of the price of Hong Kong television dramas as of 2000 (Lee, 2003).

The structural context of media liberalization in East Asia should be further taken into account. East Asia was not a region in which the television programming trade was active up until the 1980s. According to Waterman and Rogers (1994), "countries of the Asian region as a whole have [*sic*] a relatively low dependence on imported programming, and a relatively very low dependence on intra-regional program trade" (p. 107) before 1990s. Many Asian governments had for a long time been on the defensive against cultural influences from foreign countries. They, however, began to open their television programming markets in the 1990s following the global trend.

At the same time, economic development among many Asian countries afforded their citizens leisure and facilities to consume more cultural artefacts. Even the previously tightly controlled television markets in China and Vietnam have loosened their television programming import policies. For example, as of the early 1970s imported programs occupied less than 1% of total airtime in CCTV of China. In the late 1990s, the percentage rose to 20–30% according to different regions in China (Hong, 1998, p. 71).

Since their initial popular reception within what Chua Beng Huat (2004) calls the pan-Chinese pop sphere (comprising China, Taiwan, Hong Kong, and Chinese communities in Southeast Asia) and Vietnam, Korean television dramas gradually expanded their reach. A tear-jerker *Winter Sonata* was first broadcast on the Japanese NHK BS Satellite in April 2003, and was re-aired on the NHK BS in December of the same year. On popular demand, NHK aired it for the third time, this time on its terrestrial network in the summer of 2004. Although it was the third run, and despite the fact that it was aired on Saturdays at 11:10 pm, *Winter Sonata*, nicknamed *Fuyusona* in Japanese, commanded an average 16–17% share of the market. In late 2004, the Korean television drama made a fourth run, a record for a foreign programme, on the Japanese public broadcasting network. This time, *Winter Sonata* was aired with subtitles instead of dubbing (which is conventional for imported programs), in compliance with the local fans' demands to enjoy the drama with a "genuine Korean feel" (Kim, Hyeon Gi, 2004). In particular, actor Bae Yong Jun's fandom in Japan was such that when he visited the country in April 2004, about 5,000 female fans gathered at Tokyo's Haneda airport to greet him (*Korea Times*, 2004).

When the popularity of Korean television dramas was gradually weakening in the pan-Chinese pop sphere, *Dae Jang Geum* ("*Jewel in the Palace*") ignited a bigger craze for Korean popular culture. *Dae Jang Geum* is an epic drama about a real life story of a woman who rose from a lower class to the position of master chef in the royal palace during King Jungjong's reign (1506–1544) in the Joseon dynasty. In May 2005, the show's final episode became the most-watched television show in Hong Kong history with more than 40% audience ratings. Chinese president Hu Jintao and Hong Kong film stars including Andy Lau and Chow Yun-fat have publicly confessed that they are fans of *Dae Jang Geum* (Park, 2005).

One may wonder why Korean television dramas are popular among foreign audiences. I would argue that the cultural consumption is a negotiation process between consumers and cultural artefacts. In this process, consumers invest their time, money, energy and emotional allowances in cultural commodities in order to acquire pleasure and make meaning. Many commentators note that Korean television dramas touch the right chord of Asian sentiments, such as family values and respect for elders (Chon, 2001; Heo, 2002). Japanese housewives, in particular, are reported to have been attracted to *Winter Sonata* because it reminds them of the good old days when they cherished pure love (Kim, Hyeon Gi, 2004; Korean Overseas Information Service, 2004). For audiences in developing economies such as China and Vietnam, Korean television dramas are more acceptable than Japanese or American ones because the former retain traditional values while having achieved the technical sophistication comparable to that of the latter. Therefore, Korea is "viewed as a prominent model to follow or catch up, both culturally and economically" (Choe, 2001). In this sense, we can propose that Korean television dramas have provided audiences with better terms of negotiation for pleasure than other national productions.

The Korean Wave is now expanding to Europe, Africa, and the Americas (Li, 2005). It is reported that when the Korean president Roh Moo-hyun visited Mexico in 2005, local fan club members of Korean actors Jang Dong-gun and Ahn Jaewook sat in outside Roh's hotel and playfully asked him to send these stars to Mexico (Choe, 2005). According to the Ministry of Culture and Tourism (2005), the total amount of Korean television program exports dramatically increased from US$5.5 million in 1995 to US$71.4 million in 2004. The Ministry of Culture and Tourism expects that broadcast program exports in 2005 will surpass the US$100 million mark (please see Figure 1.1 below) (Park, 2005).

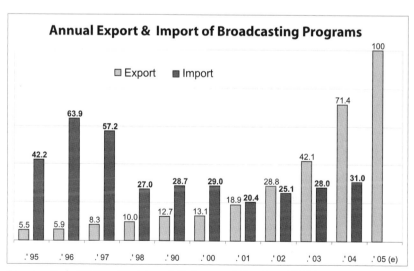

Source: Park (2005); Ministry of Culture and Tourism (2005)

Figure 1.1 Korean television program export and import (1995–2005)

Government Reaction to the Korean Wave

The phenomenon of Korean pop culture, having become the rage across Asia, had begun to hit the headlines in Korea since the late 1990s. By this, Korean policy makers saw that the export-oriented economy had found a new overseas market in the midst of the "national plight" of the International Monetary Fund (IMF)-directed economic restructuring. Motivated by the phenomenal success of Korean popular cultural products abroad, the government designated "cultural technology" (meaning the technologies that produce television drama, film, pop music, computer games, animation, etc.) as one of the six key technologies along with IT and BT (Bio-technology) that should drive the Korean economy into the 21st century, and pledged a huge amount of financial investment and administrative support to domestic cultural industries. For this cause, the government established the Korea Culture and Content Agency in 2001, with a budget of US$90 million for that year (Ministry of Culture and Tourism, 2001).

The government has also encouraged content producers to cultivate overseas markets by providing financial support. In 2004, the government subsidized 473 million won to independent producers and cable channel PPs for their participation in international content markets. Understanding the importance of such a marketplace, the Ministry of Culture and Tourism has even hosted an international content market event, BCWW (Broadcast Worldwide), every year since 2001. It was reported that about 3,500 buyers, investors and other media professionals from around the world attended the BCWW 2005. Domestic producers were reported to have made a US$15 million worth of sales during this four-day event. In particular, television dramas including *Lovers in Prague* and *My Name is Kim Samsun* accounted for about US$9 million of sales (Broadcast Worldwide, 2005).

The government support to the cultural industries is, however, not always favourably evaluated. Shim Sangmin, an expert on Korean cultural industries, argues that the government is "hypocritical" in its attitude to cultural industries. As noted above, the government announced a plan to support "cultural technology" (CT). On examination of the actual budget spending, the CT sector only accounted for 0.6% while the IT sector received 22.5% of the total amount that the government spent on the "six key technologies" after the government's announcement (Korea Culture and Tourism Policy Institute, 2005). Some even argue that the government's publicity campaigns for the Korean Wave, such as the Korean Embassy-sponsored road shows of Korean films, or the Korean Overseas Information Service's (which is under the Government Information Agency) provision of television dramas to broadcasting networks in Egypt or Mongolia free of charge, only caused backlash against Korean popular culture among some foreign audiences (Ko, 2005a; Ko, 2005c; Li, 2005).

Government policies have not always been implemented smoothly at home. The "compulsory television programming outsourcing system" is a case in point. In expectation of the commercially motivated competitive television environment in the 1990s, the government adopted a measure to ensure television programming diversity. In 1991 the government began enforcing the "outsourcing system" on terrestrial broadcasting channels so that up to 3% of all broadcasting programs should be supplied by independent production companies. Thereafter, annual increments in terms of the percentage of outsourced programming had been put in force, finally reaching 35% on MBC and SBS, and 30% on KBS in 2004 (Ministry of Culture and Tourism, 2005).

One may argue that this system contributed to an engendering of the Korean Wave since regionally popular television dramas like *Winter Sonata*, *Lovers in Paris* and *Love Story in Harvard* came from independent producers. However, there have been frictions in practicing this programming outsourcing system. While the television networks understand the government's intention of the system, they have a view that the latter is pushing the system without full consideration of the reality. In fact, most independent production companies are small-sized and ill-equipped in terms of manpower, facilities, and financial conditions. Although there were 416 independent production companies registered with the Ministry of Culture and Tourism as of May 2004, 48.1% had not produced and supplied any programs to a broadcasting network in the period of 2001 and 2004 (Ministry of Culture and Tourism, 2005). When the networks make deals with independent production companies for program provision, they have to supervise the indies from program planning to actual production and post-production stages. In most cases, broadcasters also provide production equipment to the indies. In this situation, the three television networks have resisted the compulsory programming outsourcing system itself and the government policy to push up the rate of outsourced programs on terrestrial television (Yi, Man-je, 2004).

Since the relationships between networks and independent productions are not on equal terms, it is reported that unfair "subcontracting" practices prevail between them. For example, some independent producers are forced to make a contract in which a broadcasting network pays to them an amount of less than half the actual production cost. It is also reported that the networks have even "threatened" the indies with curtailing the payment specified in a contract.[3] Further, once the indies' programs are broadcast on terrestrials, copyrights of these programs are largely transferred to the networks. As of 2004, the three network broadcasters — KBS, MBC and SBS — owned 91. 2% of outsourced programs' copyrights (Ministry of Culture and Tourism, 2005). Therefore, while KBS enjoyed a net profit of more than 2 billion won from a television drama *Full House* starring Song Hyegyo and pop sensation Rain ("Bi"), its production company is known to have put out a deficit (Yi, Man-je, 2004). In order to correct this unfair relationship between network broadcasters and independent production houses, the Ministry of Culture and Tourism is considering setting up a new terrestrial channel which will air programs exclusively produced by independent productions (Ministry of Culture and Tourism, 2005).

Conclusion and Discussion

> What the so-called Bae Yong Jun fandom (or, "Yon-sama syndrome") in Japan may cause an average Korean citizen like me to feel would be "puzzled pleasure" … . While we feel proud of ourselves, the long-time cultural importer, having become a cultural exporter, we are puzzled as to what in our culture is enchanting the foreigners. (Lee, 2004)

This statement from a current affairs magazine nicely depicts Koreans' reaction to the Korean Wave phenomenon. Korea has long waged a struggle for cultural continuity, confronted by a series of threats of foreign cultural domination. Because of a deep-seated "underdog" consciousness in terms of cultural exchanges, it was not easy for them to believe the extent of Korean pop culture being popularly consumed in other countries.

In fact, even the Korean government did not have a clear vision for popular cultural exports. Although it began to support domestic cultural industries in the 1990s, it was largely on the defensive. While the government might be credited with drawing up policies to bring new players and funding sources into the industry, many commentators and industry players in Korea tend to discount the government's contribution in engendering the Korean Wave. They even remarked that the government only jumped on the bandwagon when the phenomenon became very apparent. Rather, they gave greater credit to the roles of directors, planners, writers, actors and other production crews, avid fans, and pathbreaking traders in the growth of Korean popular culture and its international reach (*The Sisa Press*, 2005). In addition, the changing global and regional mediascape acted favourably on Korean popular cultural exports. In the end, Jeon Hyeon-taek, head of the Export

Strategy Team at the Korea Culture and Content Agency, acknowledges that the Korean Wave phenomenon is an "unintended success" (*Joong-Ang Ilbo*, 2005).

The much feared takeover of Korean culture by foreign images brought by imported media was not realized (Im, 2000). Local audiences, who had been longing for an alternative to Hollywood fare, welcomed new Korean movies and television dramas, which not only connected with their everyday lives but also achieved technical sophistication. In January 2006, however, the Korean government announced its plan to halve the screen quota for domestic movies from 146 days to 73 days from July 2006 under U.S. pressure. Domestic actors, directors and other members of film crews put up protests, arguing for the necessity of maintaining the existing level of the screen quota policy to counterbalance Hollywood blockbusters (Kim, 2006). Despite the strong opposition from filmmakers, the Cabinet passed a bill to halve the screen quota in March 2006. The original problematics which surrounded the Korean cultural industries decades ago are still around.

What cultural and political meanings can we elicit from the Korean Wave phenomenon on the international level? For most Asians, other locales of Asia have long been the unknown. As Waterman and Rogers (1994) called American culture "the common denominator" of popular culture in East Asia, most Asians have long referred to the West for melodramatic imagination as well as for modernization. However, in the 21st century, we are consuming images that originated from Japan, Thailand and Korea. The vitality of East Asian popular culture is growing, evidenced in the success of Japanese television drama and animation, Hong Kong and Thai movies, and what is called the Korean Wave. These changes are meaningful for regional cultural exchanges that have long been denied their prosperity or existence by the dominance of a hegemonic global culture. Now, the dialogue among Asians has begun.

2

Renting East Asian Popular Culture for Local Television:
Regional Networks of Cultural Production

Tania Lim[1]

Introduction

The rise of a visible circulation of East Asian popular culture from fashion, music, film, comics, to television dramas, has an impact on our everyday lives in East Asia. English-language and non-English language newspapers, magazines, talk shows, online gossip and entertainment news are often filled with stories about Asian celebrities or stars involved in various films, music videos or television drama productions. This signals both the increased marketing prowess that media corporations are attaining, mostly through 'renting' or borrowing icons or the most significant or representative figures, shows, styles or ideas, simply to turn a profit like any enterprise but also reflects how culturally relevant their output is to the people who consume them.

Concomitantly, the rise of an East Asian popular culture is a new angle to media globalization that fosters new conditions for the inter-play between local cultures and global markets in popular media products and services as never seen before. As Asian cities become exposed to more regional TV channels, newspapers, music albums, pop concerts and the regionally circulating stars that front them, cultural changes affect the mediascapes that local broadcasters operate in as well as the myriad of choices that audiences face. These changes are especially visible to broadcasters who see both structural shifts (that is, the increased impact of regional dynamics on local TV competition, the spectre of a multi-channel universe, digitalization-enabled new competitors and the problems of piracy) — and agency shifts towards greater control by consumers and intermediaries over media content (determining the shelf-life of media productions which are subject to the tensions of each cultural commodity being both public goods and commercial goods). In Asia, broadcasters now operate under the assumption of greater market fragmentation and the need to cater to niche audiences as they exhibit less consumption loyalty. Erstwhile, newer international TV channels are delivering more new titles rapidly, as governments become more responsive towards media industries, relaxing previous quotas, local content restrictions, and increasing media liberalization where these governments believe to do so would foster greater economic growth and market-oriented transformations in previously state-operated TV enterprises.

Faced with the reality of increased global media competition in the domestic marketplace and the prospect of mining a regional network of Asian media markets that have been aligned by the Internet, and international satellite and cable TV channels, local broadcasters, filmmakers, and other media producers are borrowing or 'renting' various forms of cultural capital that have popular currency in order to aggregate audiences in various ways. Television sets are historically one of the best-selling consumer products for audiences as they offer cheap entertainment. Therefore, unsurprisingly, an increasing volume of regionally popular Asian media productions have appeared on television where the most popular are often discussed and consumed both offline (i.e. video) and online as well.

This chapter will take a multidisciplinary perspective of the changing mediascape that the regional dynamics of media globalization have made on East Asian media industries. I will first discuss general trends in programming and consumption, and structural changes that have contributed to the rise of regional networks of cultural production in East Asia. Then, I will illustrate with examples how the Asian media productions form regional networks of cultural production that impact our everyday lives — culturally, politically and economically.

Next, I examine four modes of renting or renting strategies that media producers or local broadcasters use to circulate popular cultural commodities from the region, as responses to competition in the multi-channel universe of readily available international satellite TV channels, and digital entertainment. Of particular interest is how these renting strategies serve to extend the shelf-life of individual TV programmes within the networks of cultural production. Finally, the discussion will end with a brief reflection on the potential of East Asian popular culture as a mechanism for compressing space among the diverse East Asian cultures and cities as well as how a regional media culture can serve as a basis for furthering a larger and shared East Asian identity.

An East Asian Media Culture: Factors and Conditions for the Rise of Regional Networks of Cultural Production

There is clearly an impetus for change among East Asian TV industries, and every East Asian city's mediascape reflects this by the sheer output of East Asian content scheduled on their local TV channels. Some trends in Asia have become factors and conditions that contribute to the growth of regional networks of cultural production and increased intra-Asian cultural trade.

Firstly, Asia's television marketplace is huge. The CLSA/CASBAA 2004 regional report on the Asia Pacific cable and satellite TV market is indicative of its large size, raking in annual revenues of at least US$14 billion (Tanner, 2004), excluding the advertising expenditure on terrestrial television networks across the Asia Pacific. Asia makes up more than 50% of the world's population, and the region's rising affluence is attributable to the growing middleclass in these markets. With the growing expenditure carved out by urbanised and youthful demographics of an affluent East Asian region, the demand for more sophisticated productions and services will similarly increase, driving these markets to offer better quality TV productions and broadcasting services. Pricewaterhouse Coopers estimated Asian entertainment and media markets to grow on average about 9.2% per annum.[2] This modest projection is expected to accelerate as some East Asian governments have shifted their economic policies to include media communications as part of their new 'creative' economies.

While Japan and South Korea, with plenty of global brands, have the strongest media advertising and sales markets for cable and satellite TV services in North Asia and Southeast Asia to date, Singapore, China and India media markets have influenced pan-Asian advertising budgets positively.[3] This reinforces regional trends that indicate overall demand for local media content among East Asian consumers has been growing for some decades now (see Wang, 1993; Sinclair, 1998: 211–212; Chadha and Kavoori, 2000: 423–424). Combined with the rise and success of Star TV and other pan-Asian media channels throughout the 1990s and 2000s (see Chan, 1994; Langdale, 1997; Curtin, 2003) this builds a dynamic but lucrative regional cultural marketplace.

Furthermore, new deals involving media companies, owners of popular Asian cultural commodities and globalizing technology providers in the 21st century continue to be forged to expand audiences' reach across multiple platforms and territories.[4] From the growth of several pan-Asian news channels to genre-specific entertainment channels like VH1 and more recently, the successful launch of Animax, a fully dedicated Japanese anime satellite TV channel, in 2005, Asian media players are investing resources and capital to building regional production networks that offer lucrative opportunities for regional distribution.

Secondly, the somewhat organic growth of Asia-based networks of production and distribution offer great regional opportunities for trade in made-in-Asia music, TV programmes and films to local industries despite the global economic downturn over the last few years. The regional dynamics of cities linked 'geo-linguistically' to potentially lucrative markets like China, Japan and India have already begun to see results. In television, the trickle of Japanese TV drama exports in the 1980s has given way to huge waves of new kinds of idol dramas from TBS and Fuji TV in the 1990s and Korean TV drama tearjerkers from the year 2000 onwards. Arguably, one of the cultural shifts that the regional dynamics of media globalisation has brought about is the declining status of American TV programmes on East Asian TV schedules, accompanied by the rising popularity of East Asian TV programmes.

Moreover, past studies show that the Taiwanese mediascape offers similar if not more variety in not only foreign East Asian TV shows but also a large number of foreign and foreign joint-venture Asian satellite and cable TV channels from Japan and Hong Kong (see Iwabuchi, 2001; Liu and Chen, 2004) giving terrestrial local broadcasters strong competition for advertisers (see Liu, 2002).

It then follows that regionalisation and localisation appear to be favourite strategies among international broadcasters to aggregate more local audiences for their channels. For example, MTV Asia sought to galvanise Asian audiences by experimenting in the production and telecast of its first Asian TV drama series, *Rouge* (2004) which featured actresses from Vietnam, the Philippines, Singapore, and the United States as female musicians-turned-vigilantes (MDA, 2004). Others like Star TV attributed its increased viewership of its Hindi-language channel to TV formats like *Who Wants to Be a Millionaire* (TV Asia, 2005), while AXN Asia picked up the license for a pan-Asian production of *The Amazing Race* for 2006 (Sony Pictures, 2005). Often format rights cost more than ten times the price for acquiring completed programmes (Winstone, 2001). Therefore, the decision by local broadcasters to produce a licensed format has to be a strategic move to increase flagging audience ratings or beat competitors in their respective markets.

These programming and scheduling trends may also reflect larger consumer tastes and demand that speak of wider identity issues — their audiences have more diverse tastes in TV programmes and are interested in popular content that is locally relevant, and regionally accessible. Relevance, and accessibility are key criteria that broadcasters are cognizant would appeal to their audiences when promoting new TV shows to them. With short-messaging-services (SMS) and now the possibilities of online gaming, watching dramas on 3G phones, relevance and accessibility are increasingly de facto elements in new TV shows — shows with an 'interactive' component supplied by the inter-operability of digitization and mobile technologies. Therefore it is no surprise to see a cultural shift in TV scheduling and an upsurge in regional content circulating in East Asia. Many more cultural businesses have emerged to produce and (more significantly) circulate their made-in-Asia cultural commodities, offering broadcasters and audiences a wider range of East Asian popular culture.

Undoubtedly the most visible examples of Asian media enterprises creating new markets are the Japanese from the Sony group to television players — Fuji Television Network, Japanese Broadcasting Corporation (NHK) and Tokyo Broadcast Systems. The success of Japanese creative industries provide a good working model for other Asian countries seeking to develop content and reach alternative and niche markets for cultural products and services. These cities aspire to move beyond merely 'peripheral' consumption spaces to become production centres that can capitalise on, and ultimately export into, lucrative overseas and regional markets in the East and the West (see Ng, 2002; Herskovitz, 2000; Hara, 2004).

Thirdly, economic regionalisation has shifted from manufacturing to service industries as major regional hubs like Hong Kong and Singapore position themselves as regional headquarters for regional banking, telecommunications and entrepot trade. Such regionally focused and developed urban centres attract the presence of transnational firms, from NewsCorp's purchase of Star TV in 1993 (Langdale, 1997), and the proliferation of international cable and satellite TV channels focused on delivering content to pan-Asian audiences, to the onset of digital interactive services through TV and mobile phones as industry researchers indicate that mobile entertainment could generate up to US$47 billion in revenues for the Asia-Pacific by 2010 (*Electronic Engineering Times*, 2005).

While satellite television services made significant inroads across regions like East Asia and the Indian subcontinent through attempts at pan-regional programming and retrofitting smaller territories into regional markets, these external enterprises continue to face many uncertainties and limited local knowledge of various environmental and human resource limitations and constraints, banking idiosyncrasies and the complexity of building good business and social ties in these markets (Hesmondhalgh, 2002). The solutions these transnational firms adopted range from consolidation strategies establishing regional production networks with local media firms to lobbying Asian governments collectively on a range of issues from intellectual property to lowering barriers to domestic competition (see CASBAA.com, 2006).

Complementing this is the range of free-trade agreements, and the articulation of regional themes in future planning exercises by governments in East and Southeast Asia. There are significant shifts in pan-Asian TV experiment projects like *Friends* (a six-episode Korean–Japanese–Hong Kong co-production telecast in 2002), as well as the acceleration in Asian-made animation from non-traditional sources — Southeast Asian and small east Asian countries — which previously shifted from government-endorsed educational animation filmlets in the 1950s to contracted labour for foreign animation studios from Hollywood or Japan in the 1990s. Recent years have seen a few commercialised made-by-Asian (excluding Japan) TV animations become exportable (see Lent, 2000; Osaki, 2002).

Despite the continual worries of economic globalization and cultural domination of the richer G7 nations over the rest of the world, it is interesting to note that governments in East Asia like Hong Kong, Japan, South Korea, Singapore, and Taiwan have begun to take steps to engage in defining how globalization is impacting them by adopting a two-pronged strategy. Firstly, some of them have begun to form regional blocs already connected by an existing flow of East Asian popular culture, using such tools as Free Trade Agreements.[5] Secondly, even their governments have recently adopted an economic imperative over their cultural, technological and social capital, mediated by globally circulating cultures of media production. Taking on economic challenges to build a viable creative industry has become common parlance among city governments such as those of Hong Kong, Singapore and Taipei that combine the notion of developing the traditional creative arts into media businesses.

A fourth trend in Asia is the proliferation of media platforms and consumption experiences afforded by digitisation and technological innovation. Asia is quickly adopting digital technologies in media productions from radio to digital cinema to basic interactive companions to TV format gameshows such as SMS technology; to mini-cinema and broadcasting services for content on 3G mobile phones that have recently launched throughout East Asia. Broadcasting services via satellite, cable and now internet-enabled broadband services offer the experience of a 1000-channel environment. Furthermore, Japanese and other smaller East Asian producers hailing from Hong Kong, Seoul, Singapore and Taipei are also beginning to make their presence felt by offering the latest technical online and offline services as well as diverse content in Asian animations, films and television programmes. Hong Kong's blockbuster film in 2005 was *Kungfu Hustle* (2005) which relied upon similar special-effects-aided martial-arts stylistic conventions set by Hong Kong choreographer, Yuen Wo-ping of *The Matrix* fame. Meanwhile, digital and mobile TV services in Asia drew much investment after a slow start in the last few years as industry watchers expect consumption figures for 3G telephony and mobile entertainment to climb rapidly in 2007 as more than 123 million TV-ready mobile phones are to be shipped internationally in 2006 (Agarwal, 2006).

Overall, potentially huge market sizes and new niche audiences, the rise of regionally successful cultural enterprises, buoyed by governmental shifts toward developing the media sector as part of a new economic policy (i.e., of the creative and cultural industries), and conditions of multi-channel competition, have spurred popular TV programmes to become vehicles for the proliferation of regional networks of cultural production.

From all these factors and conditions, one can surmise that successfully building a sustainable media production centre or 'media capital' (Curtin, 2003) lies in developing regional networks of cultural production that can reshape the contours of media globalization in East Asia. As global media corporations expand in the East Asian region by supplying imported television programs to national broadcasters and obtaining landing rights for their foreign television channels, local broadcasters have moved towards format adaptation of game shows and transference of Asian drama serials into geo-linguistically similar markets, reflecting the creative responses of local players to global competition. The next section will discuss examples of how popular TV programmes produced in particular East Asian cities form the base for regional networks of cultural production.

TV Programmes as Regional Networks of Cultural Production

Fiske (1987: 311) argued that television (TV) programmes, like other cultural commodities, circulate in two separate but related economies — cultural and financial. However, given their short 'life cycle' and the rapid replacement of popularity by newer TV programmes (Ryan, 1992; Chua, 2004), the overlapping cultural and financial economies create a larger incentive to go beyond local borders to regional cultural marketplaces and employ networked centres of cultural production. Indeed, the more an Asian media production is able to create cultural meaning, sale and circulation of stars and related merchandise that appeal to more than one cultural market, the more likely broadcasters, advertisers, and audiences will aid the circulation of particular TV programmes within the region. Often these regional networks of cultural production increase or sustain the financial economy of not only the programme exporters but also generate financial returns for the broadcasters (who show the programmes) and social change (such as increased cultural and tourism traffic).

What are some of the examples that illustrate how progressive flows of Korean, Taiwanese, Japanese, Chinese, and Hong Kong films and TV programmes have given birth to *regional networks of cultural production*? The appearance of many pan-Asian cultural commodities and a media-centric economy from TV-land is a strong indication of cultural change.

Meanwhile, alongside every newly popular TV drama series or gameshow or reality TV format launched in Singapore, a ready supply of programme-associated merchandise (e.g., ringtones, stationary, and clothes) can be won from TV stations or purchased on Internet sites like YesAsia.com. Lifestyle products are endorsed increasingly by TV and film celebrities that have pan-Asian appeal (such as Jerry Yan of previous F4 fame as the recent 'Oral B ambassador' and Gong Li endorsing Osim's healthy living solutions, or a motley crew of China, Hong Kong, Taiwanese actors and singers who were collectively engaged to advertise in a single Pepsi campaign in 2004) rather than international runway models. Many young men and women sport fashionable hair-styles that are constantly updated to look eerily similar to current popular TV drama heartthrobs or actors, across many Asian cities. Even young children are not spared as during the *Winter Sonata* fever in 2001–2002, I spotted school-going elementary children sporting dyed-blond hair while vacationing in Seoul and Yong Pyong.

Moreover, while local TV broadcasters in Seoul, Singapore, Hong Kong, Taipei and other cities can now produce a large output of local programmes, they increasingly associate with and cross-promote programming from foreign TV industries, that is, beyond the realm of Hollywood. By offering the latest pan-Asian TV shows, Asian broadcasters are realizing that audiences prefer to watch these compared to the latest Hollywood TV blockbusters. During MIP TV 2005, one of the largest, most established international TV markets, in April 2005, press coverage hinted at the growing phenomena too:

> Stateside hits "Desperate Housewives" and "Lost" are the hottest new shows of the 2005 ratings season in Australia, but don't expect either to be anywhere near as compelling in parts of Asia, where homegrown dramas are dominant. Take South Korea, where "Lost" is relegated to a 1 p.m.

Saturday slot on free-to-air web KBS2, with a rating of around 6%. Local dramas typically reap 20%–30% of primetime auds [audiences] …

Korean dramas are racking up record sales in Asia, including Taiwan, China and Japan, says Korean Broadcasting System global strategy exec Tae Ho Sung. Last year, Korean programming exports were worth $71 million, a 70% improvement vs. 2003, and dramas accounted for 92% of the total. KBS, which had six of the top 10 local dramas, clocked $26 million in sales …

The climate for selling Japanese films and programming hasn't changed for the past few years, says Ricky Hashimoto, general manager of Tohokushinsha. "Good TV series or films always attract buyers and business opportunities."

('Local pan-Asian fare pulls big numbers', *variety.com*, 3 April 2005)

Indeed, what the above vignette reflects is that, unlike Kellner's American audiences who experience a 'media culture' that is still somewhat Hollywood-centric, the rest of the world (at least those in East Asia) may be less enthralled. These trends in programming and consumption are linked to structural changes and mindset shifts among local broadcasters and producers in East Asian media industries over the last decade. Some of these changes include: the rise of transnational television; the emergence of web 2.0-enabled multi-channel platforms; the importance of local appeal as a necessary industry factor in successful local and transnational television productions, the digitalization and convergence of both old and new information and communication technologies.

Dae Jang Geum (2003) versus *War and Beauty* (2004)

To illustrate how TV programmes that circulate successfully in the region rely upon the ability of its producers, broadcasters or distributors to create a regional network of cultural production, let us take the examples of *Dae Jang Geum* (or *Jewel in the Palace*) and *War and Beauty* which used slightly different strategies to achieve this. *Dae Jang Geum* is a 70-episode drama serial focusing on the struggles of a young woman who became embroiled in the struggles of the backroom politics of the Korean imperial court — where women served in the royal kitchens and as medicine woman to the male imperial physicians — and became the first female imperial physician.

This MBC production was not only a television blockbuster for Korean audiences in South Korea where more than half of their audiences (57.8%) caught the telecast, but it was also a media feat in Taiwan as the most popular

TV programme there. It also drew audience ratings on par with Hong Kong terrestrial broadcaster TVB's largest blockbusters in 2004 — that is, *War and Beauty* (2004), a 30-episode courtly drama of power struggles behind the throne amongst the Empress and concubines, and *To Catch the Uncatchable* (2004), a family comedy, which recorded an average of 2 million and 2.1 million viewers, respectively (TVB Annual Report 2004: 9) — with a viewership figure of 3 million in Hong Kong (TheUrbanWire.com, 2005).

Certainly, the influx of popular Korean dramas like *Dae Jang Geum* have helped to revive the declining terrestrial television viewership in Hong Kong that started in the 1990s and slid further in 2000 (see Ma, 1999; Fung, 2004), eroded by the growing draw of multi-channel and new media competitors on cable TV and the Internet. The stars of *Dae Jang Geum* were flown in for televised interviews and promotional tour with TVB Hong Kong. Meanwhile, recent press reported that a '*Dae Jang Geum* theme park was opened in Yangju, Gyeonggi province' of South Korea, drawing about 800 visitors daily. Also cited was the new appetite for Korean cuisine in Taipei where 'Korean court cuisine has become immensely popular and sales of hanbok (traditional Korean clothing) and traditional herbal medicine have skyrocketed' (*The Manila Times,* 2005).

This example illustrates East Asian popular culture is rented not only by TV broadcasters domestically, but also regionally, leading to a wider 'network of cultural production' across territories and even in tourism, fashion and food industries. This is but one example of South Korea's industry success where local TV companies using big budgets to create and market lavish drama productions are supported by their governments keen to export their culture overseas as cultural goods, trigger more intense regional dynamics for regional productions and distribution of East Asia TV programmes, music, and films. Exploiting its popularity, a whole range of *Dae Jang Geum* merchandise is easily available for purchase globally on YesAsia.com (2005) from many box sets of the series in different languages, to *Jewel in the Palace* mugs, cell-phone cases, cell-phone accessories, acupuncture case key chain-holders, and picture frames.

In comparison to *Dae Jang Geum*, TVB's post-telecast marketing efforts focused on locally issuing 3,000 copies of the limited DVD edition for *War and Beauty* after its telecast, of which 1,000 were reserved for TVB staff and selected copies with special serial numbers of 'special serial numbers of 88, 333, 888, 1388 and 1688' — numbers that reflect the Chinese cultural penchant for lucky numbers which sound like 'fortune' and 'longevity' — were auctioned at the *Tung Wah Charity Extravaganza*, a televised charity-telethon, in December 2004.[6] This was followed by TVB's closed circulation of its top-tier drama serial throughout its own distribution network of affiliated satellite and cable TV channels, and video rental franchisees in Asia, North America and Europe.

The key differences in circulation of popular drama serials between TVB and MBC lie in their structural advantages and environmental constraints. Relying on its well-established international brand name in drama serials, its familiar Hong Kong beauty-queen-turned-actresses, and its own internal content delivery system and dubbing facilities, TVB has a ready-made network of cultural markets in which to circulate easily and lucratively. However, this logic of distribution is designed to maximise profit for TVB as well as protect itself from piracy that most exported Chinese-language dramas face. Unlike TVB, MBC has to rely heavily on 'cultural intermediaries'[7] and their marketing and publicity machinery to rent out its beautiful stars and unique Korean heritage, its huge production budgets and historical authenticity to show *Dae Jang Geum* to the non-Korean speaking world.

For the moment, *Dae Jang Geum*'s publicity and marketing machinery has been very successful in extending its popularity overseas, and it joins other Korean drama blockbusters such as *All In* (2003), and *Winter Sonata* (2002) to add one more dimension to the regional circulation of East Asian popular culture. However, a quick check through the Internet on audiences' views and fans' inter-textual references to *Dae Jang Geum* reveal that its popularity is tempered by other popular East Asian drama serials that share the same audiences. For example, among avid viewers of East Asian drama serials, a mini-battle of sorts has occurred on the Internet discussion forums between MBC's *Dae Jang Geum* and TVB's *War and Beauty* where discussion of enjoyment is linked to production values (where both dramas had beautiful faces, costumes and settings), a difference of pace (where Korean drama was 'more draggy') and a sense of authenticity and loyalty. See examples of a recent discussion entered by audiences, juxtaposing the two drama serials in terms of their popularity and perceived quality on the Asianfanatics Forum (2005).

Seen in this way, East Asian TV programmes need to borrow or 'rent' intellectual property that is popular and regionally appealing in order to extend their life-cycle or trajectory when they cross to overseas territories, and in different media forms. While developing TV and film industries would feel greater pressure to rent popular culture to make their TV programmes and films on par with imports, such as in Indonesia and Taiwan (Kitley, 2004; Liu and Chen, 2004), geo-linguistic barriers and weakening global appeal would force even developed Asian media industries to co-opt popular culture in order to increase their export value.

Industrial Responses to Media Globalization: Renting Strategies

Earlier discussions about general trends across Asia argued that Asian television industries are inclined to mature as content producers and cultural businesses are sensitive to increasingly sophisticated consumers who have not only diverse tastes, but also access to a wider choice of local and foreign TV programmes, and content on alternative media platforms (such as film, online and mobile gaming, etc). Moreover, international satellite and cable TV channels that enter Asia continuously altering their programming and production strategies to tackle the competitive multi-channel environment (Moran, 2004) does spell stronger regional competition for local broadcasters in East Asian cities such as Hong Kong, Singapore, Taipei and Seoul, whose audiences can increasingly gain easy access to these international channels. What responses do local broadcasters make to these latest developments in regional dynamics of media globalization?

Acknowledging the fact that many Asian media industries share common stories, icons, talents and even histories, the tendency among media producers is to *rent* intellectual, cultural, and other forms of shared social capital that increase the chance of local (if not regional) circulation and financial success. Philip Kitley (2004) uses the concept of 'renting intellectual capacity' to describe how Indonesian television stations borrow the ideas and production process of TV formats — an industrial practice and form of strategic program development that fashions content for multiple markets systematically (Moran, 1998: 14–23) — to bridge the 'creativity gap' between training talents and producing a steady supply of popular programmes. For this article, I have extended the idea of renting intellectual capital to modes of production that can be grouped into four types of industrial responses. These responses are points in a local-global knowledge continuum that media producers can use as renting strategies: (1) localization of globally branded TV formats, (2) glocalization of local programming templates with regionally popular cultural commodities, (3) creation of media spectacles as 'must-see' television events that help market local programmes to domestic and overseas audiences, and (4) internationalisation of cultural productions via pan-Asian experiments and multi-country co-productions.

Of the four types of renting strategies, the first (i.e. localization of global TV formats) is the most conservative response, while the second and third are more ambitious as the programme-makers/broadcasters seek to sustain and circulate their content beyond their domestic borders. Meanwhile, the final response (i.e. internationalization through pan-Asian experiments or international co-productions) is the riskiest, as it requires heavy financial investments, considerable coordination and patience as international co-productions often involve different cultures of production, ethos or work habits. Cumulatively, these various kinds of cultural production not only boost the flow of Asian content regionally, but also increase the intersection of cultural identities and consumer tastes of people from different geographically bounded territories, that could form an abstract 'taste continent' that is distinctively East Asian. The following illustrates briefly each of the industrial responses with current examples.

Localization of Globally Branded TV Formats

One immediate response that East Asian local broadcasters took readily can be observed in the rapid infusion of global brand names in TV formats on local TV schedules. Formatted game shows, reality shows, and talent competitions over the last two to three years across Asia have come and gone, depending on the contexts the local broadcasters faced (see Moran and Keane, 2004). For example, the global format for *Who Wants to Be a Millionaire?* circulated quickly in the region, mostly as a stop-gap measure to increase audience ratings, boost advertising revenue for the channels and provide terrestrial broadcasters a marketing and branding exercise that could (briefly) endear audiences to the channel vis-à-vis their competitors. In Hong Kong, Asia Television Limited (ATV) used the format to pull up its viewership figures during its initial first season, jolting its competitor TVB into acquiring a global format of its own, *The Weakest Link*, in order to compete with ATV.

While the most recent examples of successful TV formats have come from the West in the form of re-invented game show formats like *The Weakest Link* and *Who Wants to Be a Millionaire* or new hybrid reality TV formats such as *Survivor* and *Big Brother*; the rapid uptake of such imported TV formats has also given rise to small experiments in 'made-in-Asia' TV formats. Some examples originating from East Asia have capitalized on popular global format ideas, such as *Discover Australia* (Singapore's answer to *Survivor*), *Enter Shangrila* (China's epic multi-provincial reality TV game show), *Everyone Wins* (Singapore/Hong Kong's answer to *Millionaire*), and more perennial variety show formats like *Super Sunday* (Taiwan's landmark variety show modeled after Japan's variety entertainment shows). In November 2005, Singapore's MediaCorp TV announced the sale of its first TV format rights, to a neighbouring TV station in Malaysia, 8TV. The programme, entitled *Project Superstar*, was a highly successful local singing talent TV show that promotes local talents employing Mandarin popular culture. Indeed, the format sale has translated into a joint production of sorts between the Singapore and

Malaysian broadcasters as they take the talent search show across three cities in Malaysia (The Star Online, 2006). It appears MediaCorp is aiming to build even larger regional networks of production, aspiring to sell the format to Vietnam and China, entertaining hopes of an 'Asian Project Superstar' (Channel NewsAsia.com, 2005).

Glocalization of Local Programming Templates with Regionally Popular Cultural Commodities

Another response is the practice of using icons of East Asian popular culture in local programmes. Iconic figures from manga to martial arts novels, stars of the latest popular Cantopop to Korean–pop-music albums, film or television series — are often used in short interstitials to full-length media cross-overs. Designed to draw audiences to watch the channels' programming, this practice enables some highly successful 'glocal' productions to be exported overseas. Some examples from Singapore can be found on MediaCorp Channel 8 which scheduled variety shows and entertainment news, where guest appearances by the hottest Korean, Japanese, Taiwanese or Hong Kong stars become familiar faces on local TV during various 'waves'. In 2002–2003, MediaCorp Channel 5 mimicked its sister Mandarin-language channel (Channel 8) and began commissioning English-language comedies that paired local comedians with famous Hong Kong TVB female veterans headlining local productions — Carol Cheng in *O Carol!* and Lydia Sum in *Living with Lydia*. In 2001, Comic Ritz Productions in Taipei adapted a famous Japanese manga into weepy Taiwanese melodramas for a new niche market — youths — and created a new genre with *Meteor Garden,* a Taiwanese teenage idol drama (Lin, 2002; Liu and Chen, 2004). Popular Japanese dramas have also been re-adapted after format sales to Asian broadcasters in South Korea. Some examples include *Yojolady (A Lady of Refined Manners) 2003*, a Korean remake of the Japanese TV drama, *Yamatonadeshiko* (see Lee, D-H, 2004), and Seoul Broadcasting System's *A Spring Day* (2005), which is a remake of the very popular Japanese TV tear-jerker, *Heaven's Coins (Hoshi No Kinka)*(1995).[8]

Creation of Media Spectacles as 'Must-See' Television Events That Help Market Local Programmes to Domestic and Overseas Audiences

Kellner (2003) refers to Debord's original work on the 'spectacle' (1967) as the starting point for his articulation of the concept of 'media spectacle': a spectacle 'unifies and explains a great diversity of apparent phenomena'.[9] A spectacle involves acts of cultural production that include the packaging, promotion, and display of commodities and the production and effects of all media. As spectacles emerge from a media culture, they reflect society's values, normalizes, dramatize, and rationalize how social norms impact everyday life. Some examples of spectacles:

> … include media extravaganzas, sports events, political happenings, and those attention-grabbing occurrences that we call news — a phenomena that itself has been subjected to the logic of spectacle and tabloidization in the era of the media sensationalism, political scandal and contestation, seemingly unending cultural war, and the new phenomenon of Terror War.
>
> (Kellner, 2003)

Kellner extends Debord's use to a more specific usage of 'media spectacles' as defining moments in a collective or society's life. Kellner further elaborates that 'major *media* spectacles of the era dominate news, journalism, and Internet buzz, and are highlighted and framed as the key events of the age'. His examples of what he refers to as 'megaspectacles' included Princess Diana's wedding, death, and funeral, the extremely close 2000 US presidential election, etc. While *Meteor Garden* (2001), *Dae Jang Geum* (2003) and other new forms of TV shows have been groundbreaking for their respective industries, they certainly became media spectacles, if not 'megaspectacles' for audiences when they made guest appearances in various East Asian cities. These further the consumption and popularity of these particular East Asian TV programmes.

Thus, as an alternative to using big budget marketing, which few East Asian media productions can compare with Hollywood 'blockbuster' television titles, some East Asian producers and distributors have developed renting strategies that allow them to create media spectacles to raise the profile of their productions. Such spectacles include staging lavish concerts and road-shows in the largest cities around the world, advertising for global brands as a signifier of their success as a pop icon, and generating lots of news and more likely rumours of love triangles, rivalry and other kinds of stories that stir the public' imagination, feelings and opinions about the stars behind the shows.

Designed to set public agendas and negotiate some importance in people's everyday lives, a classic example of how East Asian popular culture leverages on media spectacles is the phenonmena surrounding F4's good-looking foursome. Their inability to act or sing and dalliances with agents, would-be girlfriends, or rudeness in music events, are juxtaposed awkwardly against their concert tours, birthday celebrations, and celebrity appearances at mega-events and their huge fan following from 2001 to 2003. Indeed after *Meteor Garden*'s success, an F4-merchandising and advertising empire appeared briefly around the four boys that comprised the group. The hyper-capitalism that drives news and entertainment TV channels, press and Internet sites to feed on rumours, tracking the boys on their career moves (successes and failures) had the net effect of increasing F4's popularity up until recently. It also had the impact of extending *Hana Yori Dango*'s serialization in the Japanese comic book market as well as in the translated Chinese version, thus extending its life cycle as well.

Also drawing upon the earlier case study on *Dae Jang Geum*, it is noticeable how the Korean governments have used popular Korean dramas as 'media spectacles' that leverage upon their popularity as publicity and marketing drives for Korean tourist destinations. Through the aggressive promotional activities of the Korea National Tourism Organization, Korean stars are constantly linked to news of their next big TV or film appearance, and the continuous reporting of Korean popular culture in the news media of most Southeast and East Asian cities fosters an evolving network of cultural production. The network that emerges relies on virtuous re-cycling and borrowing of popular culture, resold overseas, therefore bringing more financial returns and reputation to the original producers. Besides government or overseas marketing campaigning, some TV programmes and films rely upon juxtaposing their cultural productions with significant international events, historical moments and figures, as well as associating with global branded genres, to grow their cultural marketplace abroad. The Chinese government heavily promoted Zhang Yimou's first martial arts cinematic piece, *Hero (Ying Xiong)* (2002) — set during the era of the notoriously ruthless but sympathetically portrayed the first emperor of China, Qin Shih-Huang.[10] *Hero* was clearly targeted for global release and used the successful formulaic genre that earned an Oscar for martial arts film, *Crouching Tiger, Hidden Dragon* (2000).

Internationalisation through Pan-Asian Experiments and International Co-productions

Finally, there are yet other ways in which local broadcasters have attempted to compete with international flows of culture. Firstly, they prospect talents from the region who are celebrities or regionally co-produce TV shows that garner not only local audience but hopefully regional ones too. A recent example is *Friends*, which is a joint TV drama co-production between Korean broadcaster MBC and Japan's Fuji TV Network that was shot partially in

Hong Kong, during the year of the *World Cup* in 2002 when South Korea and Japan jointly hosted the finals. Subsequently, the two broadcasters also worked on two more mini dramas, *Sonagi (An Afternoon after Showers)* (2003) and *Star's Echo* (2004) (see Lee D-H, 2005). Obviously, international co-productions are set to grow as in January 2006, the Tokyo Broadcasting System aired its first 11-part love-themed co-production drama series entitled *Rondo* (2006), starring Japanese hearthrob, Yutaka Takanouchi, and Cho Ji-Woo, Korean drama queen of tears (and of *Winter Sonata* fame).

Hong Kong's film industry is no stranger to international co-productions, as companies from Shaw Brothers to MP&GI[11] have worked with Japanese film directors and international casts across Asia and North America since the 1950s. South Korean filmmakers have been moving steadily to capitalise on the perceived benefits of international co-productions. There was *Musa* (2001)[12] involving China's Zhang Ziyi and a string of Korean film stars, but among more recent films is *Daisy* (2006), a Korean film that is directed by Hong Kong filmmaker, Andrew Lau Wai-keung of the *Infernal Affairs* trilogy. *Daisy* stars Jeon Ji-Hyun *(My Sassy Girl)*, Jung Woo-Sung *(Musa)*, Simon Yam *(Moving Targets)*, Lee Sung-Jae *(Public Enemy)*, and Cheon Ho-Jin *(The Big Swindle)* and is described as 'an urban melodrama about a woman, the police detective she loves and a killer from whom there is no escape'. Shot entirely overseas in Amsterdam, *Daisy* is produced by South Korea's Ifilm (see Giammarco and Paquet, 2006; Russell, 2005).

Earlier international co-productions and Pan-Asian productions such as the recent collaboration between Singapore, Taiwan and Hong Kong TV industries in the latest installment of Jin Yong's martial arts novel-turned-drama serial, *Heavenly Sword and Dragon Sabre* (2003). Meanwhile, Singapore MediaCorp TV's English and Chinese-language channels are focusing on including popular Asians from the region in their dramas and variety shows. In some senses, local broadcasters whether in Hong Kong, Singapore, Seoul or Taipei, all hope to move beyond a limited and fragmented regional marketplace that characterises Asia, to capture other large cultural markets. Still, as present programming trends and rising 'consumeristic' behaviour among youths in Asia suggest, the strongest dynamic for circulating their local productions overseas is the regional and East Asian.

Capitalizing on the diverse and higher demands for Asian content, all these experiments have arguably opened up new networks of cultural production for Asian producers from interactive game shows or SMS-linked game shows galore, classical imperial and martial arts drama serials from Hong Kong and Seoul, the first-ever East-West children animation show in Singapore, to the most popular teenage pop-idol drama serials to have emerged from Taipei. These TV industries are just beginning to explore the possibilities for developing tradable formats and renting within their own TV industries so as to capture new and perhaps regional/global audiences and new revenue streams.

Conclusion

This article argued that the complex processes of media globalization in East Asia are driven by localization and regionalization, mediated by the inter-operability of new media technologies. What is globally compelling about the cultural output of East Asian cities like Hong Kong, Singapore, Seoul and Taipei is that they express the nostalgia, experiences and aspirations of overseas and migrant Chinese and other geo-linguistically similar Asian populations (like the Vietnamese, and Thai) through contemporary popular culture. Furthermore, the success of a few items of East Asian popular culture can co-join with politics to break through previous political barriers between ethnic groups.

An example of the political cleansing power of East Asian popular culture is how, after generations of anti-Sino discrimination, Indonesian youths seem fascinated by *Meteor Garden* and developed F4 fever like many youths across Asia, readily watching Chinese faces on Indonesian television — normally Indonesian faces in drama serials tend to be Eurasian. It is all the more surprising because in the Indonesian TV industry, local consumers are normally prejudiced against the expression of Chinese culture in their public domain (Bachtiar, 2002). In a political economic twist, these cities' cultural output can also participate in the international television programme trade, forming part of intra-Asian and contra-flows of popular culture that articulate the cultural experiences of migrants who are globally dispersed and share common ethnic Chinese and southeast Asian origins.

Thus we see that the concurrent forces of media globalization and localization (see Wang, Servaes and Goonasekera, 2000) are reshaping how television industries operate in modern Asian cities. Setting the stage for a very crucial development in the new contours of media globalization, our everyday lives are ever so shaped by an 'East Asian popular culture' (see Chua, 2004) where East Asian music, television, film, fiction, stars, new media and fashion circulate regionally and internationally.

The increased cultural output and flows of culture in Asia are responses to: policy shifts from cultural welfare to cultural and creative industries that are increasingly defined by a new 'cultural geography of creativity' (see Flew,

2002a: 137); the identity politics of youths as they move from basic to selective but highly sophisticated consumerism (see Chua, 1998; Chua, 2000:13–14) and from elite to mass education (Flew, 2002b: 163); and the general rise in affluence of the region, driven largely by the Asian 'middle classes' living in industrialised cities like Tokyo, Seoul, Kuala Lumpur, Hong Kong, Singapore, Taipei, and recently, Shanghai and Beijing (Chua, 2000).

Such synergies of the marketplace, technological developments and changing state policies towards promoting popular culture are aided by what Harvey (1990: 240) explains as the instantaneous power of media communications. Affordable global satellite communication and the Internet offer a 'time-place compression', where the world as we know it is getting smaller and what happens in one place often has instant impact on others economically, politically, technologically and culturally.

The renting strategies described in this article suggest that local broadcasters are more than willing to leverage on substitutes or local popular icons to attract viewers and advertisers, by renting various icons of popular culture for the East Asian TV productions associated with their channels. In the process, the daily exhibition and scheduling of appearances of stars, news and talk shows that feature foreign Asian actors, actresses, and singers, directors, etc would tend to be regulated by audiences with varying degrees of cultural proximity to their own cultural identities in terms of how authentic or relevant the TV shows are to them.

This gradual and continuous network of cultural production that sustains the cultural output of East Asian programmes on local TV channels fosters a climate where individual consumers can create an imaginary and flexible East Asian identity when regionally dispersed audiences can relate to them as fans or acquire tastes that consume these hybridised popular cultural commodities as part of their everyday life. This generic identity is circulated not simply at consumption, but also increasingly at the production aspect of the network of the cultural industry. Future studies could explore the processes by which specific regional networks of cultural production are inter-connected to the wider societal processes of globalization, reflecting the complex yet inter-dependent relationships between East Asia's diverse national and regional cultures in the increasingly media-centric world.

3

Mediating Nationalism and Modernity: The Transnationalization of Korean Dramas on Chinese (Satellite) TV

Lisa Leung

News has been out recently that some kindergartens in USA are teaching Mandarin to American kids. Footage of American kids writing Chinese characters is the finest epitome of the extent of cultural global flows (and hybridity) at our era of intense media and cultural circulation. Ultra-forward-looking parents commented: 'By the time these kids grow up, China would be a world economic power, so knowing how to speak and write Chinese is a definite plus in enhancing their employment prospects.' That China is a goldmine, an untapped vast market that is set to steal the international limelight to some extent also forces China to rise to this expectation.

Amid this rampant economic growth and promise as future political and economic power, there still exists a lag in China the corresponding liberalization in political control in social life. Although political power has gradually been decentralized, there are also signs of tightening political grip on national press and flow of information. News of the authorities banning newspapers which have been more vocal about government policies, websites being forced to close down, and reporters being arrested for 'illegally leaking classified national secrets' often remind concerned audience that the one party state has never gone too far from its authoritarian roots. This disproportionate growth between economics and politics, as well as part freedom, part restriction creates potential tension and conflict, but also opportunities for manoeuvre and situational collaboration.

It is against this backdrop that this story of media globalization and transnationalization takes place. At the point of writing, the Korean wave is still sweeping strong across China, a 'western' neighbour with whom Korea has from ancient times embarked on a complex and obscure relationship, at a time when China is rapidly flexing its diplomatic and economic muscles in the international stage. The blockbuster success of 'anything Korean' in China has been in the headlines, yet little systematic research nor academic writing has been done so far. A story of why and how the Korean media *content* made it in China at this current state will not be complete without an examination of the processes involved at the site of production/industry that enabled this transnationalization in the first place.

Studies in media globalization have largely focused either at a textual level, or at the reception end of the 'global' at the site of the audience. Little has been done, however, to examine the role of the industry in bringing forth this transnationalization. Even less attention has been given to the industry at the local. Partial blame has been put on the local industry, where the latter was seen as either accomplices or dupes to dump global media products onto the local audience, thereby assisting in the brainwashing of their compatriots by the global perpetrators. Or, rationalization of the process at the industry level just naturalizes or brushes it off as a mere technical process of importing global media by the local industry, with a simple and sole objective of profit maximization, by bringing the most audience to the advertisers.

Given the fluctuating political and economic context in China, the challenge and appeal for local media industries lie in the ability to move within/exploit the space between the national and the global. This is a story of resistance of the periphery against the core; it is also a story of exhausting the provincial cultural tradition for entertainment, but more importantly the popularity of the 'global'.[1]

The relative (academic) oversight of the role/significance of the local industry in the process of media transnationalization is coupled by the assumption of the local as a homogenous whole/monolithic entity. Who is the local? How does the politics of transnationalization play in a context where there are multiple locals at play? The failure to ask these questions has resulted in the failure to recognize/problematize the complexities involved even at the reception end of media transnationalization — the site of the local — where Korean media could be used as a weapon of competition/contestation between the national local and the provincial (sub)locals. It has also led to the glossing over of the contextual elements that might affect local-global interactions.

Perhaps the question of Appadurai is poignant here at this intervention: '… . what is the nature of locality, as a lived experience, in a globalized, deterritorialized world?' (1996). Here, he was referring more to the objectives of ethnography in the study of audiences of globalized media. But while ethnography might not be applicable in the study of media industries, the same question could be asked of the challenges and problematics that the local corporation faces in the transnationalization of global media, in the local context which is 'disorganized, volatile and fluid'. How does the process of transnationalization articulate the tensions as well as the dynamics between the local, the national and the global?

This chapter, then, seeks to examine how the local media plays a role in the transnationalization of Korean wave, in the process of struggling for survival and success in a complex national and geo-political context where multiple political, economic and cultural forces converge. It also examines the tensions as well as respite along the way.[2] Despite the vast literature on media globalization, little has been focused on the role of local producers as mediators in the globalization. Still less has examined from their subject positions the interplay of diverse spaces: political, economic and cultural forces at both the national and global level. Hunan Satellite TV recently went down history with having successfully bid for *Dae Jang Geum* — one of the most popular Korean TV dramas in recent TV history to have travelled to East Asia. I hope to chart how a local TV station fishes through imperatives of government regulation as well as economic imperatives to commercialize, to rise up to being one of the 'hottest' TV station in China, with the help of 'global' (regional) media products. Through the experience of Hunan Satellite TV, I wish to throw light on the dynamics involved at the point of mediating media and cultural flows in the increasingly intensified 'globality' of the East Asian region, and whether the local has opened up new spaces within the transnationalization of the media. At the end of this chapter, I hope to contribute to the reflection of how the current rampant transnationalization of media in East Asia triggers industrial, economic, political and cultural forces at work across cultural and national boundaries.

Finding the 'Local' in Media Transnationalization

We have already reached an era where media circulating across national and cultural borders have become a habit, almost a ritual that challenged earlier approaches to media globalization studies. The perception of the local being susceptible to 'cultural imperialism' by imported 'global' media is long rendered outmoded. The flow of media products across East Asia in the recent decade has accelerated the discussion of the rise of 'geo-cultural' markets/

circuits' defined by regions, such as Latin America and Asia.[3] Having benefited from market, cultural and linguistic proximity, different (regional) circuits of production have emerged. Within these 'circuits', we also witnessed not just one, but several, national centres that dominate the flow of media and cultural products, as a result of their supremacy in financial and technological resources. The extent of transnational media circulation has already reached the stage of co-production, where the market, site locations, labour and expertise at the local/national level could be best exploited. Notions of hybridization between the local and incoming 'global' in terms of cultural content are partially based on the assumption that local industries do not just have their local markets in mind. Economic and technological advancements have strengthened local media industries so that, even though they may still be less developed than the global media, they are able to 'cannibalize' (to coin Appadurai's terminology) or consume global media for its financial gains, as well as boost its national and international status.

However, the process of importing global media is not at all smooth sailing for the struggling local industry. The biggest obstacle comes from nowhere but the national local. National media, in meeting the challenges of media transnationalization, often find themselves caught in the 'national hegemony that comes from within', including legal and regulatory mechanisms.[4] This is most prominent in authoritarian/socialist regimes where the centre legitimizes and perpetuates its political and ideological domination and economic prowess over the local as the periphery through restrictive broadcasting and financial policies. It then becomes a double risk, as well as imperative/challenge for the local to strive for its own survival, even at the political peril of winning over the national in this race for economic success. In the following, I would like to use the case of Korean wave in China to illustrate the gossamer hurdles and problematics that the local(s) encounter when importing foreign media product, because of its relative positioning, as well as the dynamics and opportunities it exploits to veer its way ahead.

Walking on a Swinging Tightrope: The 'Locals' in China

Among the extensive research on the media situation in China, Donald and Keane analyzed the challenges that Chinese media face in response to the country's rapid marketization and economic liberalization, while negotiating (uneasily) with the ideological forces at work.[5] Perhaps Zhao best explicated the current state in China where the party enmeshes political and economic prowess, accommodating private and foreign media capital, while limiting areas of operation and politically containing them through the carrot and stick strategy.

The full steam drive towards capitalist commercialization but still trying to maintain its ideological foothold has caused the Chinese media system to increasingly become a platform for profit-making, while speaking in the voice of the ruling Party elite and the rising business and urban middle class.[6] The role of the media in China has come a long way from the inception of the Communist Party. Under the new hospice of 'socialism with Chinese characteristics', there has been more obvious adoption of Western style media management techniques as well as media formats. Media outlets underwent rapid process of commercialization in the 1990s, which influenced the nature of media formats; commercial propaganda has 'rivalled, if not replaced political mobilization speech'.[7] Advertisements filled the prime time airwaves, as consumerism acquired the political and ideological overtone of supporting the state's vigorous economic marketization policy.

The 'liberalization' in media formats and management, however, has not equated a relaxation of freedoms on media practitioners. Censorship, in both active and passive terms, is still rampant. Journalists who have covered stories on the government are being imprisoned, and newspapers known for their more critical views (such as *Nanfang Weekend*) are being closed down; at the same time, news about farmer and worker protests is being suppressed.[8] These gestures go to show that while the ruling ideology might be replaced by economic (and capitalistic) state hegemony, 'socialism' might be just a synonym to justify the state's ever tightened stronghold on social, cultural and economic life in China.

While a stronger grip has been seen in the newspapers, similar structural problems prevail in the broadcasting sector. For one, television production has been central in the realization of China's experiment in authoritarian market-driven modernization, both in policy terms and in the 'making visible' of often precarious efforts to balance breakneck economic development with the social conservatism and political dictatorship of the Chinese Communist Party (CCP).[9] Television production which used to be one of the institutions under heavy surveillance by the party has gradually been relaxed as the country slowly moves towards marketization and internationalization. While television production is still heavily regulated under the State Administration of Radio, Film and Television (SARFT),[10] the 'four modernization policy' that drove the country towards more liberalized economic reforms under Deng Xiao Ping in the 1980s, translated into a gradual commercialized view on media policy.[11] In recent years, state inability to finance the growing number of TV stations at the national, provincial and city level resulted in a slight decentralization of power in broadcasting. However, these financially independent TV stations are still owned by the government at various levels.

Cable and satellite TV were put at the forefront of this media liberalization policy, at the time when state policy on TV production turned in the 1990s from 'literature and arts' to 'entertainment'. A few years on, the state even allowed independent firms to create shows for state television, giving 34 provincial networks permission to launch a satellite channel each.[12] The rapid development of cable and satellite TV was partly due to the growing technological imperatives, but despite the country's determination to modernize, there still exists an interlocking administrative-versus- state, ideological-organizational system. Power conflict between two ministries meant that the development of cable and satellite networks have always been a result of the tension between modernization (and hence more outward looking) and ideological control (satellite TVs being more exposed to 'foreign elements').[13] The conflict that prevails around satellite TV also includes the fact that satellite TV's cross-territory broadcasting clashes with government vision that the medium should assist in nation-building. The skeptical, if not suspicious, attitude towards 'foreign elements' has resulted in the STARTV incident, as well as campaigns against illegal foreign TV reception.[14]

TV stations in China, hence, are constantly in negotiation with the part-relaxed part-tightened attitude of the authorities towards TV production, which is paradoxically seen as a significant ideological apparatus, but also a symbol of China's recent modernization and liberalization. The role for the media to be the state propaganda machine might thus be even stronger. The commercialized media system is encouraged to proactively sell to the advertisers their maximized consumers, rather than create social division. Mass entertainment, therefore, assume a more important ideological role, not only serving to mobilize consumption, but is seen as politically safe and financially rewarding.

Foreign Form, Local Use: Importing and Cloning

The development of television dramas in China has been seen as central in the witnessing of China's balancing between market-driven modernization on the one hand, and social conservatism and political (and ideological) dictatorship on the other.[15] Rampant marketization and economic reforms has also rendered Chinese producers to look towards profit maximization as their prime motive in programming. Foreign programmes, thus, becomes easy target and favourites in Chinese TV stations, for a spectrum of practical reasons: 1) imports are much cheaper than local productions; 2) adopting more ideas from foreign television systems which are low budget, e.g. live talk shows, dating programmes; 3) exploiting formats of foreign TV programmes such as 'copy-catting'.[16] Cloning seems to be a habitual phenomenon for local Chinese media towards foreign media, where Hunan Satellite TV has actually been cited as a fine example of 'successful format adaptation combined with self-reliant management strategies', adopting Shanghai TV's programme to produce an apolitical entertainment show.[17] The example illustrates a growing trend in Chinese TV media of 'cloning' as 'proven formula to gain ratings, as well as introduce new technologies to appease audience desires'.[18]

It is at this juncture that Korean TV dramas entered and scored overwhelming popularity in China. The later sections of this chapter shall elucidate that the success of Korean wave is a convergence of various political, economic cultural factors (including the work of the local media industry), but for now it is worth having an overview of the extent of Korean wave in China.

Hallyu of Television Dramas in China

The 'Ha-han' fever spread like wild fire across provinces, ethnicities, and permeated different walks of life in China, at a time when the avian flu is raging in the country.[19] The first Korean drama, *Jealousy* 〈嫉妒〉, appeared on CCTV in 1993, but it was *What Is Love* 〈爱情是什么〉 broadcast in 1997 that officially announced the onset of the Korean wave.[20] Later purchases included *Stardust Love* [sic] 〈星梦奇缘〉 and *Repeated Watching* 〈看了又看〉 in 1999. Since then, a diversity of media and cultural products from Korea flocked into China, such as popular music,[21] internet technology and on-line games, and electrical appliances such as mobile phones.

The surprised success of the drama sparked off a stream of Korean imports into Chinese TV stations.[22] In 2002 alone, 67 Korean dramas were broadcast over various Chinese provinces. Among the many imports, a majority fell in the genre of romance stories in an urban setting: *Fallen Angel*, or stressing family, filial piety, friendship and loyalty, such as *Miss Mermaid*.[23] There are also variations as to the ratio between terrestrial broadcasts and those shown on provincial satellite channels. Among the figures, Guangzhou terrestrial stations have the highest broadcast of Korean dramas than Shanghai, Beijing, Wuhan and Chengdu. The amount of Korean dramas shown on satellite TV stations, on the other hand, are relatively the same, a result of government control over the percentage of foreign imports on satellite TVs.[24] While the amount of Korean dramas imported varies across provinces, the popularity of these various dramas seem to also differ across provinces.[25]

Enter *Dae Jang Geum* — and Hunan Satellite TV

A lot of discussion has been focused on the content of Korean TV dramas that succeeded in capturing the hearts of Chinese audience: beautiful settings, idolized characters, melodramatic romances, unrequited love which necessitates tragic endings. This portrayal of an urban, capitalist, modern, upwardly mobile society, however, serves only to clothe an otherwise traditional melodramatic genre about what human relationships used to be.

The above comments referred predominantly to the majority of Korean TV dramas termed as 'trendy dramas' — productions that focus on contemporary urban life. *Dae Jang Geum*, broadcast in September 2005, was the first epic drama to be broadcast on Chinese channels. Ratings for the debut reached 8.6%, and even 10% for cities like Shanghai and Changsha, which ranks first of all ratings at the same slot over the country, even topping the record made by urban based dramas.[26]

For Hunan Satellite TV, the decision to buy such an epic drama in early 2004 was a cautious one: it was largely due to the popularity of the drama in Korea.[27] But it was not until the drama became blockbuster in Taiwan that eventually caught the notice of Hunan's senior officials at the TV station that they approached Taiwan's TV8, who had copyright ownership to *Dae Jang Geum*.[28] Negotiations over buying that right was a painfully lengthy one, according to Programme Director of Hunan Satellite TV, Ms Xiao, which finally closed on 10,000USD for one episode (amounting to 10 million yuan for the whole set).[29] The reason why Hunan won the bid was largely due to the expertise and reputation of the CEO, Mr Eoyang Chang Lin, who in his six years of presiding over the station, has adopted a policy of providing 'new entertainment'.[30] After winning the exclusive broadcasting rights all over China, *Dae Jang Geum* was eventually broadcast on Hunan Satellite TV in September 2004. Ratings peaked at 180 million viewers, equating 14% of viewership in China, which was very high in terms of satellite TV ratings. High ratings also rendered unprecedented financial returns for the station, over 35 million yuan. The other immediate benefit came from advertising, where it was reported that the broadcast of *Dae Jang Geum* brought 150 million yuan of advertising revenue for the first quarter of 2005, a record 37% higher than the same quarter last year.[31] The record profits of Hunan TV made the TV station a legend of Chinese television industry, and make the station rank top among the 38 provincial level satellite TV stations.[32]

Manufacturing the Hype

The overwhelming success of *Dae Jang Geum* triggered a nationwide discussion into how *Dae Jang Geum*, the first such epic Korean drama to be broadcast on Chinese soil, managed to push the Korean wave to newer heights.[33] Before *Dae Jang Geum*, Hunan Satellite TV has been importing popular TV programmes from Korea and Taiwan, including *Gong* (宫) Taiwan's hottest epic drama 〈还珠格格〉. I will discuss at a later stage how the drama is discussed on newspapers and on the websites, and what the audience and netizens perceive of as cultural reasons for the drama's success. What I wish to focus on here is the institutional aspects involved in fabricating this *Dae Jang Geum* phenomenon. During my interview with programme directors at the Hunan Satellite TV station, I learnt that they, while feeling proud at having won the exclusive rights to the nationwide broadcast of *Dae Jang Geum*, boiled the success down to several institutional factors. One is a 'cross-programme' publicity before and during the broadcast, which involves capitalizing on other popular productions of the station. Another boxoffice/brand programme, which became another phenomenon, titled *SuperGirl*, had the contestants compete by singing the themesong of *Dae Jang Geum* (even before it was aired), thereby creating a hype for the drama. The station also planned a series of programmes paralleling the content of the broadcast, such as culinary and herbal medicine programmes, history programmes including those explaining the monarchical hierarchies in the Chosun Dynasty,[34] programmes that apply the politics depicted in the drama to real life (such as office politics), and even animation programmes further explaining the episodes.[35] Apart from publicity programmes, the station also published booklets detailing the story, cast, historical background and commentaries about the Korean drama. One of the booklets encapsulates the commodity aesthetics behind the drama: the good-looking characters, details about the main cast, anecdotes in the drama (often about romance of the leading actress and actor), or the sisterly love among the characters in the Korean palace. Cuisine was another theme brought up in the booklets, along with the shooting locations of the drama which became famous tourist sports in Korea.[36] According to Ms Liu, Vice Director of the Chief Editor Office, plans have been made to invite Liang Mei Jing (Han Sanggung in *Dae Jang*

Geum) and Lee Young Ae (the eponymous heroine) to pay a visit to Changsha, although the plans have not materialized.

Appropriating the Foreign: Importing and Cloning

Such careful marketing planning must have come from a station experienced in creating hype around popular TV programmes. Hunan Satellite TV, despite being a provincial station amid a wave of satellite TV stations throughout China, struck its mark with a more progressive and a more international outlook. With the recent nationwide blockbuster such as *Super Girl* 〈超级女声〉, *Shining Anchor* 〈闪亮女主播〉, and *The Story Behind* 〈背后的故事〉, Hunan TV has been dubbed the 'whiz-kid' of Chinese (satellite) TV industry specializing on 'popular entertainment'.[37] While *Super Girl* has become a nationwide talking point, and a trademark for the future of popular culture in China, it would be beyond the scope of this chapter to discuss the phenomenon of *Super Girl*. Yet it should be emphasized that the show is epitome to the station's drive to constructing a popular culture geared towards youth and consumerism, something symptomatic of the whole drive for modernization and trendiness.

Besides drumming up ratings boosting popular entertainment programmes, the station has also been at the forefront of importing foreign programme formats and 'cloning' them. Dating and match-making shows such as *Romantic Meeting* 〈浪漫约会〉 (2000) and *Citadel of Happiness* 〈快乐大本营〉 were remakes from the Taiwanese version *Special Man and Woman* 〈非常男女〉. The mainland Chinese version was seen to be adopting many of the 'formal characteristics' of its Taiwanese counterpart, but different in aesthetic elements, namely including more blatant self promotion.[38]

Exploiting the Indigenous: The 'Legend' of Hunan Satellite TV

The reasons for Hunan to have acquired such vision gearing towards popular entertainment are both geographical and also cultural. According to programme director of Hunan TV station, Ms Xiao (萧凭), it is in Hunan people's blood that craves for entertainment. 'We Hunan-ians have a "Sing-Song Club Culture" [歌厅文化].' Indeed, the Hunan people would recommend any foreigner to see this for themselves at any music parlour.[39] The populistic idea of public entertainment is also facilitated by the weather in Hunan, which is (relatively) warm and humid whole year round. Such practice did not seem to have died down despite the emergence of mediated forms of entertainment such as TV, films, and more recently VCDs and DVDs, which were favourite among the younger population. The former, on the other hand, have precipitated the need for, and predicted the popularity of, variety shows and song competitions like *Super Girl*.

The geographical location of Hunan might have also paved the way for the locals' reliance on satellite TV and the outward looking policies of the station. Situated in the heart of the mainland, the province would be best accessed by cable or satellite TV, which has provided an impetus for the local satellite station. The remoteness from anywhere else also prompted the station to pursue a more ambitious outward looking policy. Since satellite TVs have in theory a nation wide reach, the station has in their programme planning a policy that caters for the most general interested audience.[40]

Defeating the Central

Aside from these material benefits of broadcasting *Dae Jang Geum*, Hunan gained for itself the honour of having won over the 'big brother' CCTV. When commenting on the success of *Dae Jang Geum*, much discussion adopted a 'David and Goliath' perspective when mentioning how a 'small unbecoming provincial TV station' wins the bidding war with other stations and CCTV, and went on to win a second time over the ratings.[41] The CCTV which has also been injecting a regular dosage of trendy urban Korean dramas such as *Miss Mermaid* and *Watch Again* and had been riding high on sustaining 'Han-liu' on TV, is seen as having suffered a setback to be won over by Hunan TV, thus embarking on a TV war with the station ever since.[42] It was reported that having lost the battle over *Dae Jang Geum*, CCTV quickly bought another blockbuster from Taiwan, *Mist in Imperial Capital* 〈京华烟云〉. There was a metaphor of 'Mu Lan vs Janggeum', as the female lead in the latter was called 'Yao Mu Lan'. Although the ratings of 'Mu Lan' surpassed that of *Dae Jang Geum* at a later stage in Beijing, it still suffered a setback in more southern cities, where *Dae Jang Geum* still maintained a stronghold.

Such success over a centralized national TV station, for the peripheral media, was a victory next to being able to challenge centralized power and authority. Besides the war with CCTV was a commercial as well as a political one, as provincial satellite TVs have long been struggling through heavy handed political control which have been relaxed only recently. The sensitivity towards 'foreign elements' also resulted in the rigid policy that no foreign

TV programmes are allowed to be broadcast during prime time, hence *Dae Jang Geum* had to be shown at 10pm, outside the 'golden slot'. An indignant Ms Yao, officer of the Chief Editing Department, Programme-Purchasing and Editing office of the Hunan TV commented, 'well, as long as we comply by the rules handed down, why couldn't we import TV dramas that could sell?' (interview transcript 2005). There was also a quota imposed on the percentage of foreign imports, which amounted to 20%.

'Depoliticized, Culturally Correct' Nature of the Transnational

The distrust on foreign programmes also meant stringent measures imposed should local stations wish to buy in foreign programmes. Local stations are not allowed to approach foreign distributors directly. (Which explains the heavy dependence on Hong Kong programmes, also because of the proximity of the two places). In the case of *Dae Jang Geum*, Hunan Satellite TV resorted to going through TV8 to buy the exclusive rights for broadcasting throughout China. Ironically, this measure of 'going through back door' also puts Taiwan as an interesting intermediary for the local mainland Chinese stations.[43]

Despite its foreign status, Korean dramas managed to escape the heavy scrutiny that the Chinese authorities imposed on other foreign programmes. Apolitical sensitivity also provided another added advantage for Korean dramas. Newspapers in mainland China, besides explaining the reasons for the popularity of Korean dramas, mentioned also that the products, which focus on family values and rivalry in the commercial world, are politically de-odoured. This is confirmed in an interview with the Programme Director of the Shanghai TV Station (member of the SMG), who admitted that Korean dramas 'seem to be able to squeeze through the administrative screenings because of this.'[44] Censorship is especially strong in television stations, and among the different programmes, especially contemporary dramas seem to be one of the most closely watched types (after news and documentaries). This could explain for the uneven development in the production of epic dramas and that of more contemporary dramas in China.

Rather than their de-politicized nature, cultural proximity could be most often quoted as the reason for the success of Korean dramas in China. This is even more pronounced in the case of discussions around *Dae Jang Geum*, which is seen to have caused 'a new Han-liu' (Korean wave).[45] In another study, I discussed at length the cultural reasons behind the success of Korean dramas in China.[46] What I wish to focus here, is how the local TV station gets caught up with the discussions around Korean dramas. The vast popularity of *Dae Jang Geum* seemed to reflect and be fueled by the torrent of discussions on newspapers, on-line discussion groups and blogs. The avid fans tend to embrace the drama for the universal virtues it depicts: 'the characters of *Jang Geum* [*sic*] bring out the highest of human virtues, her toughness, courage, and perseverance. TV producers should follow the example of *Dae Jang Geum* to fulfill their social responsibility to give our kids a bit more sunshine and fresh flowers.'[47] Others commented about the 'all-roundedness' of the drama, satisfying the ideals of different segments of the audience: 'To everyone the spirit to strive, love and compassion to humanity; to women the ideal man, to men the ideal woman; to housewives the finest cuisines, to young audience pretty faces and glamourous fashion; to white collar workers the innuendoes and bickering in everyday office politics.'[48]

More supportive comments, however, focused on the elements that pertain to cultural proximity between Korean and Chinese cultures, such as the use of 'Han characters', the similarity of Chinese and Korean cuisine, as well as the development of herbal medicine, including acupuncture.[49] As one critic commented, 'The identification Chinese audience has on *Dae Jang Geum* reveals a recognition of Chinese culture, an acknowledgement of the Chineseness in the Korean culture depicted in *Dae Jang Geum*.'[50]

Mediascape versus Ethnoscape: Cultural Ownership and Patriotism

It is at this point that the broadcast of *Dae Jang Geum* courts a wave of criticism. The 'anti-*Dae Jang Geum*' voice was started off by a producer who collected fame with his production of epic dramas in mainland China — Zhang Kuo Li.[51] Zhang criticized *Dae Jang Geum*'s content as 'boring, slow tempoed, and lack of creativity.'[52] He did not only lay his criticisms on the drama itself, but also on those who watch them, calling them as 'favouring the foreigners at the expense of local productions'. Most importantly, he accused the drama of 'cultural theft', having claimed as Korean what should be originated from China — acupuncture, herbal medicine, culinary methods. As one netizen, obviously in favour of Zhang's criticisms, remarked:

> what *Dae Jang Geum* is doing is stealing others' cultural heritage and claiming them to be one's own! And somebody has the nerve to praise *Dae Jang Geum* as having preached goodness, kindness and beauty. This is absolute deception! Koreans deceived themselves, and think they can

fool the world. They think they can use a kind and innocent Janggeum to construct an illusion (and easily accessible cultural products) for what was used to be China's subordinates — Korea! They even went on to try to convert the world's belief and identification that China is the core of Asian traditional culture, forcing one to think that the Koreans are in fact the finest, in order to satisfy their own ethnic self esteem and vanity.[53]

Patriotic responses on the web went to the extent of accusing all Ha-ru and Ha-han fans as having 'singlehandedly tarnished the face of Chinese traditional culture', laying the few thousand years of national prestige that China earned onto the shoulders of popular culture fans. These waves of patriotic protests were responded with equally vociferous defense for *Dae Jang Geum*, which retorted that nowhere in the drama was acupuncture, herbal medicine and cuisine claimed to be Korean.[54] Others criticized the meaninglessness of raising the discussion of a mere (fictitious) television drama to such ideological and patriotic levels, but pointed out the (ironically) growing xenophobia of the Chinese, at a time when China has entered the WTO.[55] The critical voice, coming mainly from the industry, is seen to contradict that of 'lao bai xing' (the common folks), who in the majority tend to embrace the Korean dramas, bypassing the nationalistic sentiments churned out by some industry people. Some comments even called on those hardline patriots (with their vested interests) not to go against the wishes of the public.[56]

Arguments like these exemplify what has been discussed as 'cultural nationalism' that are engaged in popular culture. Caught in the midst of these arguments was Hunan TV (and all the other Chinese TV stations), who have been condemned by Zhang as the panultimate 'traitor' who ushered in this cultural invasion. Zhang's calls were somehow echoed by Hong Kong-turned-Hollywood megastar Jackie Chan, who in his latest Hollywood blockbuster, *Legend,* also had Korean bombshell Kim Hee Sun co-star with him, called on Hong Kong audience to 'resist Korean wave'.[57]

Bearing the brunt of 'selling China to Korea', indirectly encouraging the latter to plunder and loot China of its national cultural treasures, Hunan is almost accused of bringing China back to its dark age in late Qing dynasty — the invasion by eight foreign powers. Except that this time the loss of face is even greater, that the perpetrator was once the 'grandson' of China.[58] Amid the surprise over the wave of criticisms that *Dae Jang Geum* attracted, Ms Xiao and Ms Liu somehow welcomed the responses as 'helping to boost the publicity of the drama'. While defying the claims that they were being 'traitors', they seemed affected by those claims, and throughout the interviews, I had the impression that they would try to be more cautious in selecting and promoting Korean dramas, at least for the time being, to let the voices die down.

However, one side-product of this war of words was the wave of critical reflection on the local TV industry. On one camp were people like Zhang (and Jackie Chan), who called on a ban against Korean imports; on the other, critics and industry figures urged an immediate step up on the cultural industry in China. Even more so, some others called on the country to embrace popular culture as a response to impending globalization. Producers, clearly inspired by the Korean drama formula, had the following four suggestions.

Address the 'Cultural Deficit' between China and Korea

Some discussions focused on how the Korean wave results in the uneven trade balance between Chinese and Korean media products. The recent marketization and liberalisation of Chinese trade led China to be riding the trade surplus wave with other countries. However, China suffers a trade deficit in terms of cultural products, which is as low as 10:1 in terms of the I/O of media products to foreign countries.[59]

Improve the Quality of Local Production

National Chinese TV production is seen as formulaic, often featuring complicated power struggles, multiple relationships, innuendoes, which bring out the worst in human beings.

Fully Exploit One's Cultural Heritage to Promote One's International Image

The success of *Dae Jang Geum* is seen as exhibiting the 'creativity of the (Korean) cultural industry', which, as exemplified by the Korean case, is able to turn something as mundane, rigid and bland as historical facts, into something so 'attractive, virtuous and affectionate'.[60]

Find a Way of 'Getting Closer to the People'

In an article titled, 'Let Cultural Products head towards the World', the contributor accused local productions as not being able to capture the hearts of the audience. 'At an age of massive economic and social transformation, people succumb to mounting stress, they lose their sense of balance. What they need is some channels of escape and relief through popular entertainment, and a reminder of the virtues of traditional values.'[61]

Liberalizing National Policy on Foreign Imports

Seen from the above, there have been mounting calls within the industry of the impending need for local TV production, in order to be more competitive, not just internationally, but nationally. With the immediate pressure from many national TV stations, individual TV channels resort to buying in foreign dramas to boost ratings and thus sales. At the outset, there was also a need for local channels to redress the 'cultural deficit' as a way to combat the ensuing 'invasion' by Korean media and cultural products. CCTV, which has always played the dominant role in national TV industry (bearing the status as the top party mouthpiece and opinion leader), was taking the lead to expand its 'foreign drama hour' at 10 pm into the 'variety show hour' at 11 pm. This enhances the flexibility of extending the broadcast of (Korean) dramas, and bringing in more diverse variety shows, in a move towards expanding its popular entertainment.[62] The station was also importing serials from the US, such as *Desperate Housewives*, in a pioneering bid to increase foreign imports. The war over foreign imports looks set to wage on among different stations.

Parallel with the extension of foreign imports, there is also competition in terms of 'modernizing' the station.[63] CCTV, for example, was publicizing their 'three modernizations': professionalization of the channel, characterization of items, and glamourization of programmes. In the bid to 'streamline' the structure of the station, more 'modern' programmes are designed, for example programmes about business, or fashion. Programme designs were especially geared towards garnering advertisements.

Conclusion

What I have been trying to do through the case of Hunan Satellite TV is to illustrate the many forces the local media has to negotiate in the place of transnational media circulation, at a time of shifting political, economic and cultural paradigms in the local and the regional. The case of importing Korean dramas revealed the process of how the local 'transnationalizes' foreign media products to enhance its local national status: exploiting the indigenous, negotiating the political and the national, and fabricating the modern. Situated in a local political context where state policy over TV production is obscured and unpredictable, the local is faced with the daunting task of cautiously juggling with state policy. This is also a time and space where the state itself is juxtaposed uneasily between the rhetoric of marketization and economic liberalization (hence internationalization) on the one hand, and maintaining political and ideological control on the media on the other. Where the media is gearing towards modernizing its programming policy, increased foreign imports are often made the symbol for trendiness and modernization. Conversely the local media's outward looking policy could be charged as cultural traitor.

The insight gained from the case of Hunan Satellite TV, that might benefit a rethinking of transnationalisation in East Asia, is twofold. First, it revealed how the political, economic and cultural could be so entwined in the habitat of the local; the ideological role of mass entertainment, plus the multifaceted use of foreign media in this process. When consumerism and economic progress could be elevated to the level of national ideology, the use of mass entertainment and importing (as well as cloning, in this case, Korean TV dramas) of 'healthy' foreign elements might serve a dual political function of appeasing the authorities as well as advancing the national and financial status of the local station. Second, the case exposes the multiplexities of 'the local' which is far from monolithic. It shows the intricate interplay of politics between the provincial and the national local. While the latter assumes the constant support of the central authorities, the former as a satellite medium attains national (and international) success by toeing a popular entertainment direction, and internationalizing its television content and format. The success of Hunan Satellite TV has sparked off a trend of 'one-off broadcast drama' (独播剧)[64] which puts it in direct competition with CCTV, which is so far the only station which could afford the purchasing expenditure needed to acquire this exclusive right. However, the intensified rivalry has also sparked off fellow provincial satellite TV stations to form alliances (mainly pooling financial resources) to combat 'the hegemony from strong stations'. The 4+1 alliance includes Zhejiang Satellite TV, some Shanghai terrestrial stations, and another 3 satellite TV stations.[65] As the competition between the national and provincial local, and amongst different locals, exacerbates, the tightening of political control over the stipulation of more stringent media regulation, would be juxtaposed with unrelenting import of foreign media, ideological debates over cultural nationalism, and economic liberalization. Appadurai's notions of the conflicts and dynamics of the different 'scapes' are well demonstrated in the case of *Dae Jang Geum*. Tension among the ethnoscape, mediascape and ideoscape are wonderfully explicated here, when modernization is becoming an ideological imperative in a continuously paradigm shifting context in China. Amid the shifting planes, the local seizes/capitalizes on the gaps and fissures, exploiting the 'transnational' as the epitome of modernization, with Korea as the more short-term goal in terms of economic development, as well as advancement of cultural economy.

II
Transnational-Crosscultural Receptions of TV Dramas

4

Structure of Identification and Distancing in Watching East Asian Television Drama

Chua Beng Huat

Flows of television drama series across national, cultural and linguistic boundaries in East Asia are by now a routine affair. The presence of imported TV programmes in every urban location within the region is now so ubiquitous that they are no longer 'remarkable' as they have become part of the daily diet of television audiences throughout the region. This 'East Asian' media space has been 'characterized as a self-aware but non-consensual force field articulated by the region's mixed postcolonial experiences, negotiation with globalization, and interacting media cultures' (Tsai 2005: 102), with uneven and unequal directions of flows. The predominantly ethnic-Chinese locations of the region — Taiwan, Hong Kong, mainland China and Singapore, which has a 75% ethnic Chinese population — has its own long history of exchanges of pop cultural products in different Chinese languages, constituting a subset that may be called 'Pop Culture China' (Chua 2000). There is scant flow of TV programs from Pop Culture China into Japan and Korea. For example, Hong Kong TV dramas have never been shown in Japan.[1] In the 1980s, the main current was of Japanese trendy dramas flowing into the rest of the region. Since the mid-1990s, with the South Korean government's conscious economic strategy of transforming pop culture into an export industry (Shim 2002), the Korean current has become more prominent. Given the, albeit, uneven flows of TV dramas I want to address in this chapter the question, 'How does an audience watch/read an imported cultural drama series?'

It is common place to suggest that meaning of a text of print or other media is not transmitted straightforwardly from the author to the reader/

audience. The consumption of a text is not simply the direct apprehending of the author's intended meaning. This does negate the fact that the author intends and encodes certain meaning in the text; the encoded meaning may be said to be the 'dominant' meaning of the text. However, in 'decoding' the text to derive meaning from it, a reader/audience brings one's own context to bear on the text and, in the process, the intended meaning may be appropriated, modified and resisted.[2] Furthermore, it is necessary to note that the text is not consumed exclusively as a coherent whole, but also in a fragmentary manner, i.e. different textual components may be treated differently by the same audience. Analysis should therefore be sensitive to this fragmentary reading.

In the present analysis, an additional dimension needs to be added to the general reception process, namely, the 'foreignness' of the TV drama programme to the audience. Significantly, the by now canonical texts on audience reception have paid almost no attention to the 'foreign' elements of imported programmes.[3] Considering the global domination of American TV programmes, this is rather surprising, since American programmes would be technically 'foreign' in all locations but the US. Yet, this foreignness is seldom problematized in Western audience analysis, perhaps because of the absorption under the generic sign of the 'West' or the idea of 'English' as the global, universal language. In contrast, the 'American-ness' of American pop culture is a constant source of public discourse in Asia, with reference to the effects of 'Westernization' and 'cultural contamination' of the local (Chua 2000).

Conceptually, the 'foreignness' is central to the idea of border-crossing of cultural products. Substantively, 'foreignness' is very much foregrounded by the audiences as part of the reason and pleasure for watching imported programmes. The 'foreignness' of imported TV drama series for different East Asian audiences thus motivates the research question, 'How does an audience watch / read an imported cultural drama series?'

Circulation Paths of Imported TV Programmes in Pop Culture China

Before we examine the reception of imported drama series, one significant peculiarity of their circulation in Pop Culture China should be noted. Different Chinese languages dominate in different ethnic-Chinese dominant locations: Mandarin in the mainland China and Singapore, especially in the latter because all Chinese languages other than Mandarin are banned from the mass media; Cantonese in Hong Kong; and Mandarin and Minnan (闽南) / Taiwanese, a language of Fujian (福建) province in southern China; the three main Chinese languages may be mutually incomprehensible to a monolingual ethnic-Chinese. This accounts for the 'peculiar' phenomenon of subtitling of Chinese films and TV programmes for Chinese audiences; if a viewer does not understand the particular dialogue on screen, one might be able to read the subtitles, but if one was never schooled in the Chinese script, one would neither understand the dialogue nor the subtitles.[4]

Things have become more complex in recent years, as the once relatively shared standardized idiographic written script becomes differentiated across the different 'national' boundaries with substantial ethnic-Chinese populations. Mainland China simplified the ideograms radically in the 1960s, to make it more accessible to the masses; Singapore has adopted this simplified script. Taiwan, for the obvious political desire to differentiate itself from mainland China, has retained the old, complex script and with the gaining strength of the Taiwan independence movement through the 1980s, also adopted Minnan as a 'Taiwanese' language. Hong Kong has also continued to use this older script; furthermore, since 1997, has adopted Cantonese as the language of instruction in schools. Secondly, the Hong Kong Cantonese have always used what might be called 'Cantonese' script; an ideogram might be used just for its 'sound' to be read in Cantonese and its appearance in a specific location within a line of dialogue might be nonsensical for non-Cantonese speakers / readers. Alternatively, a new ideogram could be constructed that does not exist in the standard Chinese dictionary; these are therefore strictly speaking 'Cantonese' words. Consequently, there are many written Cantonese words that are not comprehensible to non-Cantonese speakers / readers. The same is happening in Taiwan, as the Taiwanese begin to use Mandarin ideograms for their sounds in the Minnan language.

As a consequence of language differentiations, it is entirely possible to be watching a drama series that is dubbed in one Chinese language, with subtitles in another. For example, in Singapore, one could watch a programme with dialogue dubbed in Mandarin but the subtitles have to be read in Cantonese. This presents a puzzle of the route that a non-Chinese drama series has travelled within Pop Culture China: It could have first been imported to Taiwan, dubbed in Mandarin and subtitled in complex script. A copy could have then be re-exported to Hong Kong, where the dialogue is re-dubbed in Cantonese but subtitles remain in the complex Chinese script. Another copy could be re-exported to Singapore, where the Mandarin dialogue remains and the subtitles are rendered in simplified script or even erased. Alternatively, the drama series is first dubbed in Cantonese and subtitled in complex script in Hong Kong, or in simplified script in order to capture the increasingly number of Mandarin-speaking PRC citizens on the island. Or, the series could be first imported to Singapore, dubbed in Mandarin and subtitled in simplified script, then re-exported to PRC, where no changes in dialogue or subtitles need to be made or to Taiwan, where the dialogue remains but subtitles change to complex script.

Due to the complexities of language differentiation within Pop Culture China, Korean and Japanese drama series tend to be dubbed and subtitled in different Chinese languages, depending on where they were done; Cantonese dialogue in Hong Kong, Mandarin dialogue and complex Chinese script of subtitles in Taiwan, Mandarin and simplified Chinese scripts in Singapore and the PRC.[5] Two general observations can be made: first, there is no way for an ethnic-Chinese audience to ascertain the route the drama series has travelled and, second, with dubbing and subtitling, the possibility of circulating the film throughout the very large market of Pop Culture China is one of the primary reasons why Korean and Japanese programmes are more likely to be translated for ethnic-Chinese audiences than vice versa. Conversely, it also accounts for the unequal flows of pop cultural products between Japan and Korea and Pop Culture China.

Dubbing as Domestication

Now, let us examine the question of dubbing and its effect on the audience. At the most immediate level dubbing is the translation of on-screen dialogue from its original or 'source' language to one that is common among the 'target' audience, such as from Korean into Cantonese for Hong Kong audiences.[6] Technically, however, dubbing is not simply the replacement of the words in one language by another.[7] Constrained by the need to synchronize lip-movements (lip-sync), particularly in close-up shots, of the characters on screen, the translator 'must move away from literal conceptions of translation and build up confidence in his or her abilities to put forward alternatives that move away from the source text to focus on the function of the text and on the viewer' (Varela 2004: 35). In short, some changes to the original dialogue to suit the cultural context of the target viewer is unavoidable, indeed necessary. In creating the belief that it is a 'local' programme, 'visual synchrony' between the translated words and the lip-movements[8] is the most important aspect in creating 'the impression that the actors on screen are pronouncing the translated word'. Where synchronization fails, the programme loses much of its 'reality effect'.

Beyond the issue of lip and visual synchronies, there are political and cultural concerns in dubbing. In the translation process, often terms, expressions and contextual references of the source language have no equivalent in the target language. Faced with such problems, translation is generally oriented to the cultural context of the target language and expressions are changed accordingly (Agost 2004: 71). At its most extreme, 'fidelity' to the original is so relaxed that target 'oral colloquial language' is utilized 'to provide the viewers what they are used to' (Agost 2004:68–69) rather than sticking to the greater demands of written norms. Elements of the culture of the target consumers are thus introduced into the dubbed text. With lip synchronization, these insertions of the culture of the target audience may remain unnoticed by the latter.

An interesting example of how the different on-screen social and cultural elements work together with dubbing to produce a successful transnational drama series in East Asia is the very popular Korean period drama series, *Jewel in the Palace, Dae Jang Geum* (大长今). The period drama series 'chronicles' the ascendancy of a royal cook in becoming the first female imperial court medical officer to the Korean Emperor in the 16th century. It was dubbed into Mandarin in Taiwan in 2004 and into Cantonese in Hong Kong the following year. The series was subsequently broadcast to very high rating in the PRC and in Singapore in 2006.[9] In this particular instance, consistent with the actual practice during the 16th century, all written documents on the TV screen, from reports to the imperial court to personal letters, were written in Chinese characters, rather than in contemporary Korean alphabets. This contextual element further enhanced the 'Chinese-ness' initiated by the dubbing into Chinese languages.[10] Further domestication is achieved by direct interventions of Hong Kong TVB in providing additional 'explanations', in Cantonese voice-over, the Chinese equivalents to the Korean recipes and medicinal items featured on screen. All these efforts were further supported by the relatively similar physiognomy of East Asians as a given factor that facilitates domestication of each other's films and TV dramas.

The popularity of *Dae* is something of a breakthrough. Although every East Asian location, with the exception of Singapore, produces a very substantial amount of historical-costumed drama series, very little of these are exported successfully.[11] This is because historical drama series require audiences to have at least a rudimentary knowledge of the historical period depicted to comprehend the narrative. In the case of *Dae*, there is actually very little Korean history content. History merely serves as a frame for a story of court intrigues, a story of personal growth, of greed versus righteousness and finally, of romance, dressed in period costumes, narrated consistently in close-up focus of the main characters. No historical knowledge is demanded of the audience at all.[12]

Dubbing and the contextual Chinese features of the series collaboratively transformed the series into a 'local' 'Chinese' drama, making *Dae* easily consumable for ethnic Chinese throughout East Asia. Dubbing is thus not only a 'translation' but also a process of 'transmutation' (Varela 2004:39); a dubbed drama is equivalent to a locally produced one. Through dubbing audiences are 'induced' into consumption of the familiar, which facilitates real-time identification with the characters on screen. This combined with the relatively similar physiognomy undoubtedly contributes greatly to the popularity of East Asian drama series that circulate within the region.

Foreignness Preserved: Clothes and Urban Icons

However, the target audience of a dubbed series is also attracted to the imported drama series by its 'foreignness' as a source of viewing pleasure. The ethnic-Chinese audiences in Pop Culture China want to be watching a Korean or a Japanese drama series; they are attracted by this foreignness and the 'difference' it implies — the 'not us' — which are preserved in the various visual elements of the TV drama, particularly costumes and images of the foreign locations; foreignness is visual rather discursive.

'Ethnic' costumes are a convenient and efficient vehicle for signalling difference between groups; they are thus common signifiers of culture. Difference is especially inscribed on the female body dressed in 'traditional' costumes. This is very apparent, for example, in the case of the above mentioned *Dae Jang Geum*; as the narrative is centred on the life of female servants in the Korean imperial court, there are scenes upon scenes of groups of traditionally dressed female actresses. It is, therefore, unremarkable to single out ethnic costumes as an element that preserves the foreignness in a TV drama series. However, as mentioned earlier, *Dae* is an exception, as generally the drama series that are successfully exported and circulate within locations in East Asia are urban, contemporary drama series. In urban stories the characters on screen don international fashion, thereby eliminating the one single most convenient carrier of foreignness. Another vehicle needs to be found and used.

In the urban drama series, if one turns off the sound, the relatively similar physiognomy of East Asians renders it difficult for an audience to distinguish the product of one location from another. This is especially so in indoor close-up shots of the on screen characters, unless the audience is able to identify the specific actors and actresses. 'Foreignness' is shifted to 'iconic' images that metonymically represent the city in which the scenes on screen are unfolding: the Tokyo Tower, the needle-tower in Shanghai, the Hong Kong ferry; and more generically, as in Korean dramas, street scenes where the neon signs are in local language, because Korean cities, including Seoul, generally lack internationally recognizable icons. The success of locations as markers of foreignness is reflected in the fact they are marketed and visited as tourist's sites by fans of the TV stars. TV sights have become tourist sites; the exoticism of watching the 'foreign' is materially realized in the 'exotic' gaze of the tourist.[13] The 'exoticism' of the foreign — the 'not us' — allows the audience to distance themselves from the on-screen events, characters, attitudes and behaviours which dubbing tries to indigenize.

Taking the translation/dubbing practices and the visual-foreignness together, it is apparent that consumption of imported TV dramas and other visual media products is a process of identification and distancing, simultaneously or as a series of intermittent moments of one or the other. This identification-distancing is replicated in the different modes that audiences of different locations within East Asia watch/read TV drama series imported from elsewhere in the region.

Capitalist Modernity: Distance and Desire

As in every communicative instance, TV drama narratives construct a reception space and position — a subject position — for their audience; this is the space of identification with the on screen character that is preferred by the producer. However, as audience reception studies have repeatedly shown, audience actively interpret what is going on in the screen and develop preferred meanings of their own. In so doing, acceptance of the assigned audience space is but one of the many possibilities that an active audience can take up. Rejecting the messages and/or behaviours on screen is also a possibility.[14] Conceptually, where the audience accedes, consciously or otherwise, to the subject position offered by the drama script, he/she would be identifying with the character and action on screen; conversely, where one resists the subject position offered, one would be distancing oneself from the character and the action on screen. Obviously, the watching/reading of a TV drama involves both processes. Alternating moments of identification and distancing, where and when the on screen characters are 'like me/us' or 'unlike me/us', are generated during real-time watching. When identification/distancing takes place is thus entirely contingent on who is watching and what is being watched. Again, in the case of watching/reading an imported programme this identification/ distancing process is complicated by the audience's awareness of the foreignness of the programme which raises hurdles to identification and facilitates distancing.

Pioneering work on trans-Asian consumption of pop culture by Iwabuchi shows that there is a 'national' level of the 'like us/unlike us' at work. Two broad responses have been identified through analysis of the way other parts of Asia are presented in Japanese media and interviews with Japanese audiences of pop culture from those parts. Since the nineteenth century, Japan has consistently seen itself as 'being in Asia but not part of Asia'.[15] It has a tendency to place the rest of Asia at a culturally-historically 'backward' position vis-à-vis itself, a cultural-historical temporality defined by the level of development in capitalist modernity. This attitude appears to underpin contemporary Japanese audience responses to imported pop cultural products from elsewhere in Asia. Iwabuchi found that Japanese audiences have a tendency to appreciate media-mediated cultural representations — 'visualization of society' (Hartley 1996: 210) — of other parts of Asia with a sense of 'nostalgia', as a sense of 'loss' of its own past, especially in the post-bubble economy period when the Japanese economy was stuck in the doldrums.

For example, referring to the representation of Vietnam in the popular 1996 Japanese TV drama series, *Doku*, Iwabuchi argues that, 'Because they are still not quite modern, Vietnamese are energetic and can afford dreams of a bright future; hence, they are expected to unilaterally afford Japanese people spiritual nourishment' (2004: 156). In these and other instances, Japan's past is inscribed by the Japanese on other Asians' present. To the extent that nostalgia is always simultaneously a critique of the present — dissatisfaction with the present creates the longing for a mythical golden past — identification with the less developed capitalist-consumerist development in the rest of Asia might motivate Japanese pop culture consumers to attempt to recover their lost vigour, energy and drive.

Since the arrival of the Korean wave, particularly the TV drama series *Winter Sonata*, to Japan in 2004, Iwabuchi has had the opportunity to further specify the sense of nostalgia among Japanese audience. According to him, it is the drama series' depiction of 'pure, simple-minded love, affection and caring interpersonal relationships' that attracted the audience of largely middle aged housewives, who are nostalgic and try to recuperate their own lost sentiments of love and interpersonal relations.[16] Taken together, nostalgia is evoked in the Japanese audience of 'media texts' imported from elsewhere in East Asia at either or both the personal and the societal levels.

Significantly, the Japanese view of the 'belatedness' of other locations in Asia in terms of capitalist-consumerist modernity appears to dovetail with the self-projection of the youths from the latter locations, where the representation of present day Japan in Japan TV dramas 'signifies prosperity and sophistication and engenders longing, a longing for a richer consumer world, for technical expertise and creativity, and for societies that foster these elements' (Thomas 2004: 186).[17] Although Thomas was referring to Vietnamese youth, findings from young Taiwanese Japanese TV drama fans suggest similar desires. According to Ko, these fans latch on to the well crafted representation of the contemporary urban landscape as the index of 'realism' of Japanese TV dramas:

> Japanese idol dramas provide a *real imaginary*, and the imagery is manifested beautifully into a spectacle of modernity. Therefore, the metropolitan Tokyo is re-presented as the locus where the individuals pursue freedom, love, and careers; the imagery of 'Tokyo' is a *visual place* that mediates between reality and dreams. These dreams have not yet been realized in Taipei, but are already presented on screen … not the Tokyo in Japan, but the "Tokyo" on screen. (2004: 123, original italics)[18]

The dovetailing of Japan's assumption of its placement ahead of the rest of Asia and the Vietnamese and Taiwanese youths' imagination of Japan as their 'future' suggests that Asians from different locations may share a similar orientation towards capitalist-consumerist modernity. This is further attested to by the brutally direct Singaporean Japanese pop culture fan:

> Interviewer: Could you elaborate on why you would not want to be like the mainland Chinese?
>
> Respondent (a 24 year old, Singaporean ethnic-Chinese male): Okay, I am not trying to be nasty here but I do not really think well of the mainland Chinese. The images that they portray are not as good as the Japanese and even if the mainland Chinese try to be fashionable, the results can be quite disastrous. In school, I see the Mainland Chinese with long and dyed hair and although they do not look good, they are still okay but once they open their months, that's it, because everything is ruined. They talk loudly in Mandarin with a weird accent. My impression of the mainland Chinese is that they are rough, loud and crude people and I am glad that neither the Japanese nor I (in some sense) look and behave like them. (Chua 2002/3: 38)

This Singaporean ethnic-Chinese self-conscious discriminatory exclusion of the mainland Chinese, in spite of potential ethnic affinity, and his identification of 'sameness', with Japanese pop-TV idols is obviously articulated along the single dimension of capitalist consumerism. Along this dimension, mainland China, having only opened up to capitalist consumerism since late 1970s, remains 'backward' and thus, a distant and denied 'Asian' to the self-perception of the media consumers in developed economies in East Asia.

However, as parts of East Asia become economically develops and consumerism expands, Japanese 'advanced' status becomes more untenable and cracks in the Japanese assumption of ahead of the rest begin to appear. This appears to be the case with Japanese fans of Hong Kong pop culture who consider themselves to be 'a community of taste', in an environment where Hong Kong pop culture is not part of the mainstream and thus not readily available in Japan. Such fans appear less Japanese-centred or Japanese-chauvinistic and see Hong Kong's capitalist modernity as one that is 'different', even 'preferred', to that of Japan's own path to its own modernity. Quoting a Japanese fan: 'Hong Kong has also achieved a high economic development, but retains the vitality that Japan has lost' (Iwabuchi 2004: 165). Contemporaneity — different but equal — along capitalist modern temporality is granted to Hong Kong.

The research that problematizes the 'foreignness' of media products to audiences in different parts of East Asia foregrounds an emerging consciousness among audiences: A self-characterization as 'Asians' who are differentiated by different placements on the single dimension of capitalist, consumerism-driven modernity. Along this dimension, Japan remains at the front, while less economically developed countries, such as Vietnam and mainland China, take up the rear. The general structure of respective audiences' gazes is as follows: The nostalgic gaze of the Japanese audience: the present of the rest of Asia is the past of Japan, thus enabling the Japanese fans to retain their self-centredness. Singaporean and Taiwanese audiences' future-oriented gaze in watching/reading of Japanese TV dramas: the present of Japan is the future of the rest of Asia where capitalist consumerism is less developed, thus enabling audiences from the rest to desire, identify and embrace Japan as a representation of their future. Finally, this linear temporality of capitalist-consumerist modernity has also enabled pop culture fans in developed capitalist economies — Japan, South Korea, Taiwan, Hong Kong and Singapore — to distance themselves from their counterparts and media products from less developed economies as the 'backward' Others who are nevertheless also 'Asians'.

Real-time Identification and Difference

Beneath the 'national' level, audience identification with the characters and activities on screen are more immediate and direct, especially within actual viewing time. This enables further specification of identification and distancing processes among East Asian audiences. At the most immediate level, identification is disclosed in audience comments such as 'I can understand the character and why she acts the way she does. I would do the same if I were in her position because we are all humans.' However, identification is often rendered indirectly. Drama fans' reworking of on screen events, activities and characters into their own everyday lives is a commonly observed phenomenon among researchers. For example, this Hong Kong audience member:

> Many times in life I encountered obstacles, or often I feel frustrated at nor being able to utilize my capabilities, hence I do identify with the male lead in *Long Vacation* [Japanese drama series]. But I find one thing quire reassuring in the drama. When Kimura Takuya summoned the determination to win the piano contest and eventually won it, it seemed that his 'vacation' had ended. I hope my 'vacation' will end like his. (Leung 2004: 94)[19]

Another instance is a Singaporean audience member:

> Such things can happen anywhere in this world. It's just that it is filmed in Japan and the characters are Japanese. But when you are talking about love, sex, and marriage, it happens anywhere in the world where someone, out of a situation, has sex with someone else on a fateful night and then thinks about it and, your know, wonders, "Why did I do it?" (MacLachlan and Chua 2004: 147)

A less inclusive mode of identification than 'humans as such' takes the form of 'I identify with the character and his/her actions because we are Asians'. Behind the 'we are Asian' response is the ideological consciousness that 'we are not like non-Asians', thus generating and affirming a sense of 'Asian-ness', despite the fact that the culture of the production location is different from that in which the audience is located. This idea of 'being Asians' has been conceptualized by Iwabuchi in terms of 'cultural proximity'.

Significantly, in both 'we are human' and 'we are Asians' identifications, the factual foreignness/difference of the imported TV drama is never erased but merely displaced and substituted with and by more abstract identities.

This is a conceptually and substantively crucial point. Foreignness and difference is always just beneath the surface of such abstract identifications. As soon as on screen characters and actions are contrary to an audience's sentiment, the foreignness/difference surfaces immediately to enact a distancing from what is on screen. For example, a Singaporean audience of married women apparently have a tendency to resist Japanese dramas' representations of sexual relations:

> [The Japanese] want to be first in everything. Their technology is first and this may affect them. They want to be advanced in everything … And unconsciously, it may influence their thinking, their attitude towards sex, their values. (MacLachlan and Chua: 2004:164)

'Difference' between 'the Japanese they' and 'Singaporean us' is emphasized repeatedly and unmistakably. Another Singaporean example:

> I have a wish. I wish these Japanese dramas would not encourage our youths to accept those one-night love relationships so easily, sleep with each other and that's it. This is very unacceptable. (MacLachlan and Chua: 2004:165)

Here, in contrast to generalized, abstract categories of 'human' and 'Asian', the specificities of the 'culture' of production location, represented by the TV dramas, are evoked to create 'difference' and the basis of distancing. Obviously, if foreignness is a source of visual pleasure, as mentioned earlier, it is also a source of disdain for an audience, who moves between the two at will. That identification/distancing is an intermittent process rather than consistently sustained throughout the duration of the watching/reading of an imported TV drama series and has a consequential implication on the formation of a stable identity of the audience vis-à-vis the TV programmes.

Consumption and Community

A common concern for academic analysts of popular culture is the possible emergence of a 'collective identity' among the consumers. In East Asia, this is not only of academic interest but also, perhaps more ominously, of nationalist and regional interests. Given US dominance in global media entertainment, almost every location in Asia has its version of 'anti-Americanism' in local media-and-ideology debates. The possible exception is Japan which sees itself, simultaneously, as being able to absorb all things

Western and make them its own (Iwabuchi 2002:265). In addition to anti-Americanism, the popularity of Japanese pop cultures in Korea and Taiwan are often seen as cultural 'neo-imperialism' by Korean and Taiwan nationalists who remember their colonization by Japan. Such xenophobia is obviously intentionally simplistic.

An individual's cultural identity formation may be conceptualized as an unending process of interactions of a constant stream of cultural knowledge acquisitions, each time adding a new layer to one's personality and identity. It is fashionable to say that the 'identity' of an individual is always multiple and complex and open to changes with each new knowledge input. Nevertheless, it cannot be denied that the culture(s) acquired in the early formative years of life might be dominant and deeper and serves as a reservoir of cultural repertoires that absorbs, and is changed by, each new knowledge input.[20] One of the identities acquired early in life is, of course, a 'national' identity. Although national identity is essentially one of political convenience necessitated by the administrative logic of a world organized in terms of nation-states, it unavoidably slides into a never specified concept of 'national culture'. This 'national' identity-culture is constantly reinforced by social institutions that regulate a very large part of the necessary services in the everyday life of citizens, under the auspices of the nation. Individual citizen's dependency on the state for their daily need for public goods and services constitute the material basis for the inscription and internalization of the national identity-culture as technologies of the self. Thus, in the context of East Asian pop culture consumption, we see the tendency of audiences to assume a 'national identity-culture' as a main frame from which to identify/distance themselves from on screen characters and actions. In each individual citizen, however, the national identity-culture is complicated by the other culturally salient inputs to identity formation, namely, gender, ethnicity, profession and age, the standard sociological package of 'social economic status'.

In the constellations of inputs to identity formation, leisure activities are largely residual and volunteered, engaged in only after the necessary routines are done, with no social institutions that enforce compliance and payoffs. This, of course, does not preclude the possibility of 'obsessive' consumption of a particular form of leisure; however, it remains residual unless one turns 'professional' and makes it part of one's occupational identity. As a leisure activity, the consumption of TV dramas has some additional features that are likely to dilute its effects on stable identity formation. Like all pop culture products, TV dramas are short-lived. The affection of consumers, even fans, is ephemeral, changing rapidly with the latest trends and icons, both in terms of objects and artistes. Any suggestion of 'lasting' effects on identity formation based on pop culture consumption is therefore difficult to establish, far-fetched; although, ex-consumers and ex-fans can readily recall, often fondly, the period of life when such consumption was an important part of their everyday life.

An artiste or a drama series is 'popular' because there are large numbers of consumers of the artiste's work or the drama series. The question is through what processes can this statistical presence constitute itself into a 'community', however ephemeral. The most conventional manifestation is the 'fan club' as a community of consumers who share affections for a particular artiste or pop culture programme. Indeed, they are often established by the artiste or the production companies as means of sustaining consumer interests so as to extend the longevity of an ephemeral phenomenon. However, the audience for a popular TV drama series far exceeds fan club members, making it necessary to conceptualize the idea of 'community of consumers' beyond the restrictive boundaries of fan clubs. As consumption is largely a private affair, consumers need not be aware nor consciously seek to be members of any imaginable community, although the act of consumption potentially disposes them to one. A 'community of consumers', if constituted, would be even more of 'imagined' than a nation state as it would be transnational and transcultural because the consumers are as widely dispersed across a geographic space as distribution and market radius of the TV drama or artiste.

In the contemporary world, the Internet is a medium and instrument for the organizing of geographically dispersed consumers, especially for avid consumers who are looking for ways to intensify the pleasure of consumption through active engagements with others similarly disposed. This is the case, for example, for Japanese TV drama fans. Japanese TV drama producers are often disinterested in marketing their products in the rest of East Asia primarily because the domestic market is sufficiently profitable but also because of the weakness of intellectual property rights protection in the region. This frustrates the regional fans impatient in their desire for the latest episode of a popular series broadcasted, leading them to find alternative means to the programme.

Take the example of the popular drama series, *Pride*. According to Hu, 'In January 2004, a Hong Kong fan, R, who is a skilled Japanese speaker, did the Chinese subtitling for *Pride*, a few days after the original broadcast in Japan' (2005: 177–178), with an immediacy that even defied the piracy business and a circulation that threatened the latter's business.[21] Hu further elaborates,

Attention should be paid to the stylistic injection of R's personal enthusiasm in her Chinese translation. Her subtitling is an individual display of her mastery of language in articulation of her love for the drama … She thanks T and A for their supplies of the raw material, and online fans for their support and suggestions by constructing herself a fan persona, which interacts with those of other fans. Even when she made a mistake in the subtitling, she took care to insert a correction by thanking another fan for pointing out the mistake.

R and N's initiative in subtitling *Pride* in Chinese has been a great success among Chinese fans. Many thanks to them from fans are posted online. The inner passions for drama, fan friendship and performance/ self-expression are displayed in the context of this Chinese translation/ subtitling; being 'acknowledged by a community of like-minded is a characteristically romantic structure of feeling'.[22]

Obviously, there is nothing accidental about this East Asian online community. The consumers/participants/members are initiated by the passionate involvement of a few multilingual and technologically savvy individuals, taking the lead in constantly doing the painstaking work of initiating and amending translation/subtitling of their favourite drama series. These are done for the benefit of the other members of the fan community, beyond the clutches of profit-oriented market players and the copyrights and censorship constraints of the nation-state. All these are done in cyberspace, without face-to-face interactions that are essential to the life of a conventional community. That there is a community is indubitable. However, membership will always remain unstable and ever changing, voluntary through consumption of pop culture products, with no other qualifications required. As one fan grows out of it, a new one will induct him/herself, in quick succession, often following the rise and fall of a particular artiste as personal 'idol'. For many, the duration of fandom is often too short and culturally ephemeral for it to contribute significantly to the long process of self-identity formation.

In contrast to the almost 'hyperactive' Internet community, most consumers of TV dramas are passive. They either wait for the weekly instalments to be screened on television as part of their free time at home or impatiently sit in front of the TV set in marathon sessions of DVD watching, getting the entire series over with quickly. Yet, even these consumers are not without the possibility of realising that they are part of a community. A sense of 'community' is often engendered by other component members of the media-culture industry, such as the print media of newspapers and lifestyle magazines. Take the entertainment section of any newspaper in an urban centre in East Asia as an illustration. The entertainment pages can be conceptualized as a 'community' space for the entire East Asian pop culture industry. Geographically, 'East Asia' is defined by the places that appear regularly in the daily entertainment pages; namely, the production centres of East Asian pop culture, Seoul, Tokyo, Shanghai, Beijing, Hong Kong, Taipei and very occasionally, Singapore. The page-space is peopled daily with images and information of artistes from these urban areas: Bae Yung Joon in Seoul, Faye Wong (王菲) in Shanghai, Wong Kar Wai (王家卫) in Hong Kong, Jay Chou (周杰伦) in Taipei. East Asian artistes inhabit these page-spaces at unpredictable intervals, more frequently in the rising phases of their careers and their presence diminishing when they are on the way out. These pages are read by an unknown number of readers, unknown to each other. A 'community of consumers' is instantiated should two or more readers happen to be co-present at an occasion/event, during which they participate, as part of free flowing conversation, in exchanges concerning one of the artistes or a TV programme reported in the pages. Such instances materialize the 'community of consumers' of East Asian pop culture as 'occasioned' and 'occasional' community, befitting the practices of the overwhelming majority of consumers, where consumption is leisure and entertainment, rather than as a primary focus of everyday life.[23]

Conclusion

The presence of an East Asian pop culture is empirically indubitable. Regional marketing of pop cultures is now configured into their production cost. The consumption of these cultural products has become part of the daily diet of media consumers throughout the region. The result is the emergence of transnational communities of consumers, variously constituted through their collaborative practices and modes of consumption, through a body of shared knowledge about the East Asian pop culture scene and at a less involved level, through the less attentive consumption of East Asian pop culture as leisure and entertainment.

An overwhelming number of potential consumers in the region are ethnic-Chinese. The predominantly ethnic-Chinese locations constitute a subset within East Asia and can be conceptually designated as Pop Culture China, with histories of established networks of production and consumption of Chinese language based genres of pop culture. The size of this potential market of consumers has resulted in an uneven flow within the larger region. Korean and Japanese media cultural products, especially TV dramas, are regularly translated and dubbed into different Chinese languages, and the translated products routed through different paths but eventually reaching all the major locations of Pop Culture China. The reverse flow of Pop Culture China cultural products into Korea and Japan are very much less frequent, largely because of lower production qualities, in addition to the smaller market sizes in these two countries.

It is now common place to point out that the 'meanings' of media cultural products to its consumers are dependent on the latter's contextual situation; the analytic task is to detail out these 'contextual' elements. One significant element that frames the context of consumption of pop cultures within East Asia is the placement of the consumer's location on what may be called the linear trajectory of capitalist consumerist modernity. The East Asian locations can be placed, relative to each other, along the line of development of capitalist consumer culture, with Japan in the lead and mainland China at the rear, and Korea, Hong Kong, Taiwan and Singapore in the middle with relatively equal levels of development. Location on this trajectory has very significant effects on the attitude of the consumers: Japanese consumers have a tendency to read the pop cultures from the rest of East Asia as representations of 'Japan's past', evoking nostalgia for a 'Japan that was', while the rest of East Asia has a tendency to read Japanese pop culture as representations of an 'imaginable' and 'desired' future. However, as the locations in the middle of the trajectory ascend to the level of the consumer culture of the Japanese, the framing and attitude of Japanese consumers will become more contested.

Finally, the emergent reality of an East Asian pop culture is juxtaposed against the presence of Hollywood and other American media cultures, defying easy suggestion that the media world in East Asia is being 'Americanized'. This has provided the discursive and ideological space to challenge the simple xenophobic scream of 'American media imperialism' by Asian cultural moral gatekeepers who seek their own political and financial gains through such shrill accusations. This is an aspect of the politics of East Asian pop culture that remains to be analysed.

5

Re-Imagining a Cosmopolitan 'Asian Us': Korean Media Flows and Imaginaries of Asian Modern Femininities

Angel Lin and Avin Tong[1]

1. Introduction

The new millennium witnessed increasing transnational flow of Korean popular cultural content including TV dramas, movies and pop songs and Korean stars have been remarkably well received in China, Taiwan, Hong Kong and other East and Southeast Asian societies. This sudden frenzy about Korean pop culture in Asia has been regionally dubbed 'the Korean Wave' ('Hallyu'). While Hallyu has aroused critical response from both public and intellectual discourses, pointing to legitimate concerns about the potential rise of Korean cultural domination in Asia (alongside the long-existing popular cultural influences of Japanese and Western media), Lin, Kwan and Cheung (2004) pointed out the Koreans' unique contribution to contemporary exploration of Asian modernities — exploring different ways of being modern, and being a modern woman in Asian societies, especially in the areas of familial relations, gender relations and sexuality ethics. In the first section of this chapter, we will review some of the major studies on Korean media flows, particularly the consumption of Korean TV dramas. In section 2 we shall present our audience studies of Korean drama fans in Hong Kong and Singapore. In section 3 we shall discuss imaginaries of 'Asian' modern femininities that seem to be emerging from these women's drama consumption practices. In the final section we shall discuss both potential uses and dangers of the 'Asian values' discourse when women located in different Asian societies try to imagine and negotiate their own ways of being modern women in Asia.

1.1 The Korean Wave: Rising Transnational Popularity of Korean TV Dramas in East/Southeast Asian Societies

In cosmopolitan cities in East/Southeast Asian societies, many people are consuming globally circulated, trendy cultural products, regardless of their origins. This seems to be a kind of transnational cultural flow that highlights both cultural resonance and asymmetry, with Japan as the leading source of cultural media flows in East and Southeast Asia, replacing or coexisting with Western media influences, under what Iwabuchi (2004) called the decentering processes of globalization. Robertson (1995) emphasized both the global production of the local and the localization of the global: this cultural dynamic refers to the (often commercial) appropriation of local culture in transnational cultural adaptation and commodification, which results in constant interpenetration of the global and the local through cultural hybridization. The success of Japanese dramas in the 1990s in many Asian societies reveals the importance of this (cultural industrial) strategy of transnational cultural adaptation and cultural hybridization. According to Iwabuchi (2004), the most appealing elements of Japanese dramas include the subtle use of music, superior organization of plots, and sympathetic representation of urban youths' experiences. The Japanese TV dramas' depictions of stylish, cosmopolitan lifestyles readily invoke cultural resonance among audiences (particularly urban youths) in many fast urbanizing Asian societies.

Negotiating with Japan's influence on drama production styles, Korean and Taiwan television industries have developed their own genres of youth trendy dramas. Their representation of the 'here and now' in Asian urban contexts has transnational appeals in a different way from those of Japanese dramas (Iwabuchi, 2004). Korean television culture began to develop in the 1960s when a full-scale modernization project was started by the government. From the early 1970s, Korean TV dramas began to experience a boom in popularity in the domestic market. In the early 1990s, a new form of TV drama genre called 'trendy drama' emerged. It became an active agent in creating a craze for South Korean pop culture across Asia since the late 1990s (Lee, 2004). In the early 2000s, concerns about Korean dramas as cultural phenomena have arisen. 'Hallyu', or the transnational circulation and consumption of popular Korean cultural/media products (in particular, women's genres such as melodramatic soap operas), has swept across Asia, i.e., regions and societies that share a socio-cultural history of having been under some form of influence from traditional Confucianist familial, social and cultural values (e.g., China, Taiwan, Hong Kong, South Korea, Singapore).

1.2 Pleasure of Drama Consumption: Audience Studies on Korean Dramas

Among different themes of TV dramas, romance is one of the few populist issues that tugs at the hearts of the majority, and it enables the viewers to take temporary flight from the routine and ordinary (Leung, 2004). In the case of most exported Korean dramas, the recurrent theme of romance allows viewers to give themselves up temporarily to enjoy the feelings of love without regard for consequences or practical concerns, deriving vicarious pleasures in their consumption of media. While the above theorizing about what happens when women consume Korean dramas seems persuasive and popular among both public and academic discourses, there has been little systematic research conducted on women's consumption of Korean dramas. An ethnographic study conducted by Lee and Cho (1995) found that the middle/upper-middle class female Korean drama fans in Madison, USA preferred Korean dramas to American ones for what they called the 'Confucianist' values (especially regarding sexuality ethics). Another study by Wu and Tseng (2002) found that women constitute the majority watching Korean dramas in Taiwan and most of them were aged 25 to 30, or 37 to 42. They found viewers generally expressed positive attitudes towards the modern consumerist life styles portrayed in Korean dramas.

In Hong Kong, Lin and Tong (2007) have conducted a study on Hong Kong male viewers of Korean dramas, and most of these viewers pointed out that Korean dramas situate women at the centre of the story and tell the story from the female's perspectives, which surprisingly, is a feature they said they enjoyed. For female audiences, Lin and Kwan (2005) reported what some Korean drama fans described and saw as 'Asian subtlety' in the portrayal of romance and love relationships in the Korean dramas that they watched. Despite apparent social and cultural differences, the women interviewed in Hong Kong, Singapore and Japan (see Lin and Tong, 2005) were all attracted to the 'fairy tale' storyline of the Korean dramas that they watched (note that this is the feature of the exported Korean dramas that they are exposed to and these dramas seem to constitute only a biased sample of all the Korean dramas produced in South Korea and thus cannot be taken as representative of all Korean dramas; Doobo Shim, personal communication, July 2005). In the fantasyland created by these Korean dramas the 'perfect prince' is ultimately there for the virtuous 'Cinderella', and the female protagonist typically can achieve both career and family success, and despite much hardship they are invariably rewarded and pampered by a perfect man's love in this drama/dream world.

1.3   Commonality of Cultural Experience: Imaginaries of Asian Modernities

The TV drama is considered by some media scholars as the most powerful medium of proposing a framework for representing the world as a world with meaning and order, and redefining the context of the world (e.g., Mamoru, 2004) in projecting a social imaginary (Poovey, 2002) . One of the reasons for the popularity of Korean TV dramas among women in East Asian cosmopolitan cities (e.g., Taiwan, Shanghai, Hong Kong, Singapore) might be that Korean dramas tend to dramatize conflicts and tensions between Confucianist socio-cultural values and modern cosmopolitan living, working styles or conditions — tensions that many women in East Asian cities can readily identify with (Lin, 2002; Lin and Kwan, 2005). Besides, local language dubbing enables transnational viewers to treat the imported drama almost as a local drama, enhancing realism (Chua, 2004), but at the same time they can also enjoy the fantasy elements as both possible and plausible since the story happens in a different city in Asia and thus offers some room for imagination or fantasy.

Before the arrival of the Korean Wave, the Japanese media industry had played an important role in cultural globalization (or Asianization of Japanese culture/media), which articulates a new phase of transnational cultural flows (Aksoy and Robins, 1992). Iwabuchi (2004) suggested that the popularity of Japanese dramas in Asia is driven by the perception of 'cultural proximity', as Japan and other Asian societies may share certain cultural values and Asian viewers often refer to this cultural affinity as a reason for their preference for Japanese TV dramas. This refers to the commonality of cultural experiences shared by Asian viewers, and this similarity is based upon a consciousness that we all live in the same modern temporality. Mamoru hypothesized that the 'simultaneous progression of modernization and postmodernization boosted the commonality of the cultural experiences of each area, and pushed forward the "cohesion" of the cultural interpretative code' (Mamoru, 2004: 40). The development of these increasingly shared 'cultural interpretive codes' has aroused our interest in the question of how women might consume Korean TV dramas in rapidly modernizing and globalizing East Asian cities.

2.   The Study

The present study aims at comparing female Korean drama fans' drama viewing practices in Hong Kong and Singapore. Using the snowballing method (Brown, 1994) the second author of this chapter successfully contacted and interviewed 30 Chinese females in Hong Kong and Ms. Hung Lihuan, a native Singaporean serving as a research assistant for this project, conducted similar interviews with 30 female Chinese Korean drama fans in Singapore during the year of 2005. The two authors of this chapter and Hung worked closely as a team and held Internet (Skype) meetings regularly. Tables 5.1 and 5.2 show the demographic background of the informants. Pseudo-names are used to protect the informants' privacy. The criteria used for selecting the informants as Korean drama fans is that they like very much one or more of the Korean drama series that they have watched. Each informant was invited to participate in a one-to-one, in-depth, semi-structured interview and to fill in a standardized questionnaire at the end of the interview. All the interviews were audio-taped, transcribed and coded for recurrent themes (using the qualitative data analysis software, MAXQDA).

During the interviews, the following major areas of questions were covered directly or indirectly: conditions and habits of Korean drama viewing, the main sources of pleasure derived from viewing, views of the status and situation of modern women in Hong Kong/Singapore, and current challenges faced by modern Hong Kong/Singaporean women. All of the interviews in Hong Kong were conducted in Cantonese, the everyday language of the Hong Kong informants, while all of the interviews in Singapore were conducted in Mandarin Chinese, the preferred language of the Singaporean informants, except for Silvia whose interview was conducted in English (the quotes from the informants in this chapter have been translated into English). The fact that the Korean drama fans that we came into contact with in Singapore were mostly Chinese-language oriented suggests potentially an attachment to Chinese cultural values.

As can be seen in Tables 5.1 and 5.2 the demographic backgrounds of the informants in Hong Kong and Singapore are similar. Both groups comprise a wide age range (from 22 to 73 in Hong Kong, and from 19 to 80 in Singapore) but the majority of the informants in both cities are in their thirties or forties. Most of the informants in both cities are white-collar workers or professionals. There is also an even distribution of marital status in both cities with approximately half of the informants in each city being married. In the next section we shall present the findings and analysis of the study.

Table 5.1   Background information of the informants (Hong Kong)

Pseudonym	Age	Occupation	Education Level	Marital Status
Lau	20	Accounting clerk	Secondary school	Single
Irene	22	University student	University	Single
Kat	22	University student	University	Single
Stephy	22	University student	University	Single
Pam	23	Property management trainee	University	Single
Gillian	24	Sales executive	University	Single
Kelly	25	Property management trainee	Secondary school	Married
Pauline	25	University student, teaching assistant	University (postgraduate)	Single
Vivian	25	TV reporter	University (postgraduate)	Single
Kin	26	Marketing executive	University (postgraduate)	Single
Sharon	27	Social worker	University	Single
Suzanne	28	Accountant	University	Single
July	30	Social worker	University	Single
Winkie	30	ICAC investigative officer	University	Single
Angel	32	Bank manager	University	Married
Elly	39	Senior clerk at university	Secondary school	Married
Monica	40	Senior management	University	Single
Alice	40+	Senior lecturer at university	University (PhD)	Married
Emma	40+	Magazine editor	University	Married
Sally	41	Retired	Secondary school	Married
Ceci	42	Banking	University	Married
Ng	42	Housewife, part-time shopkeeper	Secondary school	Married
Fung	43	Primary school teacher	University	Single
Jenny	43	College teacher	University (PhD)	Married
Anna	49	Secondary school teacher	University (postgraduate)	Married
Becky	50	Accountant	University (postgraduate)	Single
Lilly	50	Retired	Secondary school	Married
Chan	65	Retired	Primary school	Married
Leung	65	Retired	Secondary school	Married
Mary	73	Retired	No formal education	Married

Table 5.2 Background information of the informants (Singapore)

Pseudonym	Age	Occupation	Education level	Marital status
Leslie	19	Cashier	Secondary school	Single
Niki	19	Student	Secondary school	Single
Zen	20	University student	University	Single
Sisi	22	Primary school teacher	University	Single
Tina	23	Administrative work	University	Single
Yan	24	School assistant	University	Single
Anita	26	Administrative executive	University	Single
Jessica	26	Travel agent	–	Single
Joey	28	Public relations manager	University	Single
Minnie	29	Language teacher	University	Single
Hua	30	Teacher	University	Single
Charlene	30+	Reporter	University	Married
Katherine	31	Artist	Secondary school	Single
Tani	31	Kindergarten teacher	University	Single
Neon	32	Part-time clerk	University	Married
Ling	33	Supervisor of sales department	Secondary school	Single
Silvia	33	Researcher and teacher	University (postgraduate)	Married
Polly	35	Housewife	Secondary school	Married
Bena	36	Language teacher	Secondary school	Single
Anson	39	Housewife	Secondary school	Married
Law	39	Primary school teacher	University	Married
Candy	40	Language teacher	Secondary school	Married
Jan	40	Editor	University	Married
Tammy	40+	Private tutor	University	Single
Queenie	48	Editor	University (postgraduate)	Married
Yanny	48	Reporter	University	Married
Gigi	50	Housewife	Primary school	Married
Sophie	51	Dentist	University	Single
Mia	52	University hostel manager	University	Married
Monique	80	Housewife	Primary school	Married

3.   Findings and Analysis

We shall present the findings and analysis in three main subsections. The first subsection will discuss the kinds of values the informants said they appreciate in Korean dramas. It seems that these Korean dramas appeal to them because the dramas preserve what the informants called traditional ('Asian') values while packaging them with attractive modern and trendy aesthetics. Section 3.2 describes the imaginaries of Asian modern femininities that seem to be emerging in the informants' consumption of Korean dramas, as the informants seem to identify with the female characters who possess both some of the conservative/traditional values and some of the new/modern qualities. Section 3.3 compares and contrasts the views of the informants in Hong Kong and Singapore, particularly in their stances toward tradition and modernity.

3.1   Hybridization of Traditionality and Modernity

Portrayal of Different Kinds of 'Qing', Family and Traditional Values

Comparing TV dramas from different countries, most informants said they liked Korean dramas most, as they found them 'more subtle', with more emphasis on 'qing' (a Chinese word referring to compassion for family members, friends, spouses, colleagues and people of different relations). Some informants pointed out that Korean dramas tend to focus on a wide range of topics including love, friendship, family relationships and moral values, issues that they said are not seriously dealt with in local productions in both Hong Kong and Singapore. One of the informants in Hong Kong, Vivian (aged 25, TV reporter), said she appreciated the description of 'qing' in Korean dramas (e.g. *Dae Jang Geum*), which was not confined to heterosexual love but also extended to 'qing' of a family, 'qing' between friends, and 'qing' between teacher and student. Another informant in Singapore, Polly (aged 35, housewife) also made a similar remark. She found that Korean dramas could express 'a strong sense of human touch'. This kind of 'love', she said, is 'multi-dimensional' and can touch the very bottom of her heart.

Many of the informants said they liked the very realistic and sophisticated portrayals of what they called 'Asian' ways of expressing various kinds of relationships and emotional attachments among the characters. One of the relationships they appreciated most is the deep connection among family members, and the virtues of filial piety the characters possessed. Many of them said they were drawn by the 'family warmth', 'strong sense of family', and 'traditional family virtues' depicted in the dramas. For example, a Hong Kong informant, July (aged 30, social worker), said that Korean culture is 'very close to Chinese culture', in terms of a sense of cultural proximity and self-perceived 'closeness' in people's qualities. Originally she was interested in Japanese culture in the mid 1990s, but later the Korean Wave drew her to Korean culture, which she described as 'very Chinese' and 'closer to Chinese values'. In her words:

> I think the humanist values and the behavior [of people] in Korean dramas are somewhat like the Chinese, very straightforward, a bit coarse … I think [they are] very straightforward, very direct, and they also value the family, and I think this is warm and sincere.

On the other hand, Tammy (aged 40, private tutor) in Singapore pointed out, 'Although the family members (in Korean dramas) sometimes have quarrels, they will be united when faced with problems; this fully shows the cohesion of a family'. Another Singaporean informant, Tani (aged 31, kindergarten teacher), found that Korean dramas often portray brotherhood and fatherly love, which led her to conclude that Korea is 'a nation of strong sentiments'. This also gave her a sense of closeness and intimacy, and invoked a sense of 'resonance' in her heart. Candy (aged 40, language teacher), also an informant in Singapore, appreciated the daily rituals portrayed in the dramas, like bowing to seniors, being polite and showing respect to the elderly, and she considered all these to be examples of 'traditional values' and 'the traditional Confucianist style' which she thought people should treasure.

As mentioned above, different types of 'qing' and moral values depicted in the Korean dramas are often interpreted as 'Confucianist values' by our informants. These informants seem to see these values as originating from Confucianism and see them to be at the heart of what they conceive to be the 'Asian worldview' which embraces different aspects of life: family relations, gender relations, romance and sexuality ethics. In this case, informants in both cities seem to identify with these so-called 'Confucianist cultural values', which, in fact, can also be found in some non-Confucianist, non-Asian cultures. They also revealed their deep-rooted (sociocultural) desire for 'qing' (compassion). For instance, a Singaporean informant, Silvia (aged 33, researcher and teacher), pointed out, 'The plot is, I think it's Asian, the theme is very Asian, but it's very new in the way it deals with the scripting. And I think the way it's dealing with characterization, the way they, they filmed … and the unfolding of the themes, and all that was very new, very subtle.' A strong sense of 'Asian-ness' seems to be constructed (in contrast to what Silvia implicitly set up as 'Western cultures') and at the same time affirmed and re-affirmed through consumption of Korean dramas. However, Silvia's appreciation of the 'new' way of scripting seems to point to another major appeal of Korean dramas — global cosmopolitan aesthetics.

Cosmopolitan Packaging: Globalized Cityscapes and Glamorous Consumerist Lifestyles

The informants pointed out that Korean dramas also possess 'modern qualities', side by side with the 'Asian', 'traditional' elements that they valued. There are lots of Korean dramas featuring romance of young, heterosexual individuals in contemporary urban settings. The fashion, music, beautiful sceneries, and the pleasures and plights of city life form the building blocks of the stories, and present images of a glamorous cosmopolitan city living, which stimulates global consumerist desires. These dramas combine both existing and idealized (consumerist) lifestyles into the storylines. A Hong Kong informant, Gillian (aged 24, sales executive), described Korean dramas as offering an aesthetically appealing 'package' to viewers — wonderful music, beautiful scenery and backdrops. Another Hong Kong informant, Kin (aged 26, marketing executive), liked the 'beautiful people, beautiful sceneries and beautiful clothing' that could be found in Korean dramas.

Beautiful scenery is frequently considered to be a key factor in the success of Korean dramas. Monica (aged 40, senior management), a Hong Kong informant, believed that the drama producers know that 'the plot is not important', and that the most useful tool in attracting the viewer is 'beauty'. She pointed out that many scenes have become tourist spots. Most of the scenes in Korean dramas, particularly outdoor scenes, are outcomes of sophisticated cinematographic design. According to the results of our end-of-interview questionnaire survey, 95% of the Hong Kong informants and 93% of the Singaporean informants reported 'the scenes are beautiful' as a reason for viewing Korean dramas. One of the Singaporean informants, Candy (aged 40, language teacher), is strongly attracted to the theme parks, snowy grounds (e.g., winter skiing resorts) and beautiful lakes. She described Korean dramas as 'using the best camera angle, shooting the best scene'. Another Singaporean informant, Polly (aged 35, housewife), said that Korean dramas stimulate viewers to go traveling and sightseeing in Korea. After watching the wonderful sceneries, she had a strong desire to join the 'special tours' (i.e. taking tourists to the filming locations of the dramas).

Korean stars have also made a big impact on consumer culture, including food, fashion, cosmetics trends and even plastic surgery (Shim, 2004). Many of our informants appreciated the beautiful fashion of the famous stars. For instance, Anna (aged 49, secondary school teacher) from Hong Kong described the fashionable clothes of the characters in *Winter Sonata* as 'very attractive' and 'never out-of-date'. The new generation of Koreans is believed to be more hedonistic and materialistic, and the trendy drama producers have intentionally targeted the new generation by breaking away from traditional dramatic conventions (Lee, 2004). In our study, all of the informants are attracted by the scenery, fashion, music, stars and other cultural commodities in the dramas. These Chinese female viewers seem to be very much attracted by the cosmopolitan city lifestyles and consumption patterns depicted in Korean dramas. In this way, Korean media texts embody (and perhaps 'Asianize') global consumerist cultures, and Korean dramas both project and promote a kind of mediated globalized consumer lifestyle. This matches the spread of global consumerism and expansion of the middle class in many modern Asian cities.

Modernity promises mobility and metropolitanism, and it is said to be a cultural rupture from the experience of yesterday (Harvey, 1990: 12). The imagination of modernity usually refers to a certain image of city life (Ko, 2004). In many Korean dramas, the portrayal of modern career women and their working conditions and social mobility point to the emerging realities of modern city life for women in Asian cities. Many informants recognized the 'realism' of working scenes in Korean dramas, especially those of modern career women who are tough and capable, and bold enough to express their feelings and desires. In some stories, change in the gender hierarchy is observed, as some women can occupy relatively high positions in the workplace, or achieve personal success with their own efforts. There is a mixture of cosmopolitan pursuits of success and individuals' struggles for true love and happiness, and in many Korean drama stories, personal choices, efforts and pursuits for individual freedom are taken as keys to personal success.

The emphasis on individual choice (e.g., of one's love partner and career), social equality and personal efforts and achievement constitute important concepts in modern society. They provide a source for viewers' identification and personalization. For example, Silvia (aged 33, researcher and teacher) in Singapore identified with concepts such as 'free love' and 'social justice' which she considered 'very modern'. She appreciated the ways the characters tried to break away from traditions and strive for personal happiness, as she said:

> In the dramas it seems that [they] are upholding values which upset the cultural norms. And I thought that's very brave and very modern. Through a medium of expression, their concept of free love, freedom

to love someone, and other concepts of justice ... I admire this, the modern sensibility that they have, they try to break away from certain traditions that don't make sense. (Interviewer: Right, like the parents controlling one's love and marriage.) It's the value system that I admire, the new sensibility that they are trying to craft out of agentic actions.

(Interviewer: Agency?) through this medium, they are expressing this new attitude.

In short, the representation of cosmopolitan city life, individual pursuits of free love, social justice and modern consumerist desires can go beyond national boundaries, attracting viewers in many parts of Asia and creating a shared desire among them. This helps to articulate a sense of cultural resonance as female viewers across Asian cities personalize these (modern) ideas of Korean dramas, to 'consume' both kinds of traditional (e.g., family values) and modern lifestyles (with some individualistic elements such as the pursuit of free love) through drama viewing. The inherent contradiction between respect for/ obedience to parents (e.g., springing from family values, values of filial piety) and pursuit of individual freedom in the choice of love partners and careers has often been used as a plot device to create dramatic tensions in Korean dramas but very often the two are ultimately happily reconciled (e.g., the parents finally accept the young people's choices), constituting an imagined reconciliation (in the drama world) of contradictory values of new and old experienced in many rapidly globalizing societies in Asia (Lin, 2002).

Yearning for 'Pure Love' and Family Love, and Constructing Cultural Dichotomies: Viewers Comparing Korean Dramas with Japanese/Western Dramas

The informants often quoted Japanese dramas in comparison with Korean dramas. Some of the informants had been 'fans' of Japanese dramas before (and more accurately speaking, Japanese culture). However, almost all of them had shifted to Korean dramas in recent years. Some of them said Korean dramas 'have more depth' than Japanese dramas in portraying 'characters' and 'emotions', and the actors/actresses can express their emotions in a realistic way (e.g., constructing a sense of 'emotional realism' as suggested by Ang, 1985). One of the Hong Kong informants, Pauline (aged 25, university student/teaching assistant), criticized most Japanese dramas as 'just shooting pretty/handsome faces of popular artists' and made the charge that the story is 'superficial' sometimes. A Singaporean informant, Silvia (aged 33, researcher and teacher), also made a similar remark, when she compared the 'depth' of Korean dramas with that of Japanese dramas:

The real thing that attracted me to Korean dramas is absent in the Japanese dramas. Everything to them [Japanese dramas] is very cartoon-like, even in (the) way they present the relationship. (Interviewer: Cartoon-like?) Yes, the same character. Yes, their values are appealing, but the way they deal with it lacks the depth that the Koreans deal with human relationship ... the ways they played it out is very two-dimensional, no complexity in their characters. [Sylvia was referring to the recent Japanese drama, *Good Luck*.]

According to these Chinese female viewers, the root problem in Japanese dramas is what they see as their difference from 'Chinese values'. In the audience study conducted by Maclachlan and Chua (2004) in Singapore, it was found that Chinese female viewers disliked what they called 'Westernization' as reflected in Japanese dramas. Some Chinese Singaporean viewers said that the Japanese dramas lack 'traditional values and "are more open towards sex"', in contrast to "our tradition from China (where) there should be no premarital sexual behavior"' (Maclachlan and Chua, 2004:164). Many informants labeled Japanese dramas as 'more liberalized' while Korean dramas are seen as much more 'traditional'. For example, Polly (aged 35, housewife) described Japanese dramas as 'too frivolous', 'lacking the correct moral values for youth' (e.g. a girl dedicating herself to a man just to gain his love, a concept she regarded as 'absolutely wrong'). She felt that Korean dramas are more concerned with 'traditional values'; for instance, 'children should respect their parents and seniors' and 'a married woman should respect her mother-in-law, help her husband and teach her children'.

Romance depicted in Japanese dramas might be 'too explicit and too sex-oriented' for some viewers in Chinese societies. For instance, one Hong Kong informant, Emma (aged 40+, magazine editor), suggested that the relations in Korean dramas are very 'simple' and 'pure', particularly when compared to Japanese dramas. As she put it,

Those Korean dramas I watched ... [are] very different from Japanese dramas; Japanese dramas always have sexual scenes! And then you discover, there has been no such restrained love [in TV dramas] for a long time, and [you finally] find it in Korean dramas! That is, just a kind of eye contact, just a little touch, [one] still gets very excited ... [I'm] so surprised to find an ethnic group [referring to Koreans] who possesses such qualities!

Another Hong Kong informant, July (aged 30, social worker), regarded Korean dramas as 'a fresh spring' in the current complicated society. Another

Hong Kong informant, Kat (aged 22, university student), described the love shown in the stories as 'spiritual love' rather than 'physical love', involving a process of 'sublimation', and she said she has been longing for such kind of love. Anita (aged 26, administrative executive), a Singaporean informant, appreciated the 'pure love' depicted in the drama. '[The guy] will not stay with a girl just because he wants to possess her. I like the pure feeling, purely falling in love, holding hands. Engage first, and then get married. Not sustained by physical relationship, but nurtured by time.' Many of the informants in both cities considered 'no sex before marriage' a sign of respect for women.

It can be seen from the informants' remarks that these Korean drama fans in both cities seem to subscribe to the dualistic division of love versus sex, which insists that 'sexual fulfillment without love is false' (Belsey, 1994: 33). 'Pure love' is seen to be the necessary precedent of and condition for sex and they desired to see the portrayal of 'pure love' rather than 'casual sex'. Our informants said that they were searching for 'true love'. For these Chinese women, love is more important than, and is a precondition for, sex. Some of them compared the Korean drama shooting styles with those they found in Western television serials, saying that romance depicted in Western dramas (at least those that they are exposed to) tends to be too explicit. Here is a comment by a Hong Kong informant, Irene (aged 22, university student):

> It [romance in Korean dramas] is very ideal ... When I watch [the dramas], I find Western ones start [having sexual relations] very quickly, and have some stimulating scenes [sex scenes]. I do not feel that the two characters really have deep affection for each other. But in Korean dramas, they at most give each other a hug, and will not do anything [further]. I feel it is real affection rather than [desire for] physical contact.

Apparently, the lack of 'intimate shots' in Korean dramas is highly appreciated by most female viewers, both in Hong Kong and Singapore. Hayashi (2005) also found that many Japanese middle-aged female viewers admired the 'perennial theme of pure love' in Korean dramas. They emphasized the absence of physical contact, and reserved (or restrained) expressions of sexual desire. Culture involves a set of practices which are the outworking of a worldview (or social imaginary), which develops a sense of belonging and identity. In our study, some informants described the romance in Korean dramas as a kind of 'Confucianist culture' and 'Asian culture', although as Belsey (1994) showed, this dualistic view of love and sex also has a long tradition in Western romance literature. It is interesting to note that the cultural dichotomy of 'Asian-ness' and 'Western-ness' is artificially constructed when some of our informants believed that the Korean dramas gave them a 'heart-warming feeling' which they considered to be lacking in Western dramas. As a Singaporean informant, Silvia (aged 33, researcher and teacher) said, 'It's a feeling that I get from Korean dramas, and I seldom get this feeling when watching Western dramas like *Desperate Housewives*.'

To conclude, Korean dramas are preferred to Japanese/Western dramas for their cultural proximity (i.e., Confucianist familial, social and sexual values). A recent study by Lee (2004) contrasted the production values and styles of Japanese and Korean TV dramas. She found that while Korean TV drama producers have drawn on the modern production values of Japanese TV dramas, and both kinds of dramas portray cosmopolitan globalized consumerist lifestyles, Korean TV dramas are different from Japanese TV dramas in its greater emphasis on the portrayal of familial relationships, family values and sexual morality. In our study, Korean dramas seem to provide an important space for fulfilling and reconciling the conflicting desires of the informants as they explore the contested issues of modernization and Westernization by dramatizing the tension between the pursuit of personal freedom/happiness (e.g., in the choice of spouse and career) and the traditional Confucianist sociocultural value of emphasis on responsibility to the family, fulfilment of traditional gender roles and the observance of different types of moral values regarding sex and romance. Interestingly the sexually repressed or 'restrained' (in the words of our informants) feature of Korean dramas (c.f., the more 'liberalized' feature of Japanese/Western dramas) seems to be precisely what is appreciated by these Korean drama viewers and this feature seems to be readily drawn upon by viewers to construct cultural dichotomies and 'Asian' cultural identities (e.g., an 'Asian us' vs. a 'Western/Westernized they').

3.2 Imaginaries of Asian Femininities: Modern Asian Women with Both Old and New Qualities

Reproducing and Reaffirming Traditional Qualities of Ideal Women

One of the important interpretive practices of drama audiences is personalization; that is putting oneself in the drama scenario and identifying with the situation and characters (Baym, 2000). This process of identification, or personalization implies a sense of fantasy. This fantasy expresses the desire for fullness, which bridges the gap between reality and wish (Hinderman, 1992). Dyer (1986) proposed that the media stars represent how our experience is or more often how we would love it to be. The characters in Korean dramas seem to embody some idealistic femininities desired by the fans, even though they also explicitly acknowledged that these qualities are difficult to find in the 'modern' world. In our study, it is discovered that despite their 'unrealistic' nature of the 'nearly perfect', the female characters still constitute a kind of identifiable image of the female that many viewers long for.

The gendered nature of modernity in the European Enlightenment tradition has naturalized and institutionalized an essentialist, binary system of masculinity and femininity (Marshall, 1994, 2000; Felski, 1995). A similarly hierarchicalized, binary system of gender role relationships also seems to underlie the Confucianist social order in East Asian cultural traditions (Lin and Tong, 2007). Deeply inscribed in our culture and language are the Confucianist sayings regarding women's subordinate position to men. Confucianism defines women's social positions according to the submissive relationship with their male family members, the principle of 'Thrice Following' — a woman should follow her father when young, her husband when married, and her son when old (Ko, 1994). In order to perform their caretaker roles, they should be soft, tender, persevering, hardworking and obedient.

However, there has been an increasing number of women receiving higher education and participating in the labor markets in many Asian cities, even taking up professional and managerial work (just like many of our informants in Hong Kong and Singapore). They have increased socioeconomic mobility and financial independence, and some of them are no longer satisfied with the traditional division of labor. Many modern-day Asian women are seen by some of our informants to be losing some of the 'traditional virtues' (e.g. too strong, too independent). It seems that the binary of women's traits/roles as domestic subordinates and men's traits/roles as leaders promoted by Confucianist ideals/ideologies has been somewhat destabilized in the modern workplace, especially in fast cosmopolitanizing Asian cities such as Hong Kong and Singapore. The identities of modern women are not just dependent on or derivative from men's identities and they have developed many new qualities beyond the 'traditional Confucianist framework' (this will be further discussed in the latter part of this chapter).

At the same time, our informants seem to be able to recover the lost traditional feminine virtues in the female protagonists in Korean dramas. In terms of personal qualities, most of our informants pointed out that the female characters in Korean dramas have an 'attractive appearance', and that they are 'soft', 'tender', 'humble', 'considerate', 'delicate and touching'. Tammy (aged 40+, tutor) in Singapore could easily identify with the tender disposition of the female protagonist, and she felt that 'it will be great if I can be her'. In terms of working attitudes, the heroines tend to be depicted as less aggressive and more submissive in Korean dramas. A Hong Kong informant, Anna (aged 49, secondary school teacher), found them very obedient and polite in the workplace; for instance, she noted that women frequently nod their heads in the dramas, like those female news anchors in *All about Eve*.

In terms of love relations, many informants described the female protagonists as 'single-minded', 'faithful to love' and 'willing to sacrifice' for their partners. They always put their lovers as their first priority and orient themselves around their male partners. A Singaporean informant, Sisi (aged 22, primary school teacher), said that many female characters have their own careers, but 'love seems to be more important to them', and 'they can give up their careers for love.' The above qualities — tenderness, softness, obedience, indulgence in faithful love — are considered to be 'traditional' (and some informants labeled them as 'Asian' as well). One of the Hong Kong informants, Becky (aged 50, accountant), described most female protagonists as having a 'traditional mind'. In contrast, women in modern-day society, especially Hong Kong women, may not possess these qualities. For example, a Hong Kong informant, Leung (aged 65, retired), described most Hong Kong women as too 'ferocious' and 'blatant', and preferred women to have a good temper and to be more obedient to their partners, like the female characters in Korean dramas.

It should also be noted that traditional femininities are affirmed and rewarded by the qualities of the non-traditional (but desirable) qualities of the male characters in Korean dramas. They seem to fulfill the criteria of 'good men' in TV dramas. 'Good men' in TV dramas are 'caring', 'nurturing' and 'verbal', who are rather feminized and seldom express their masculinity in direct action (Fiske, 1989). Our informants showed their appreciation of these male qualities using adjectives like 'gentle', 'handsome', 'faithful', 'kind-hearted', 'caring', 'good and able', 'perfect in every way' to describe the male characters in the dramas. One of the Hong Kong informants, Kin (aged 26, marketing executive), pointed out women's desire to be treasured by men. She believed that the portrayal of the considerate male character was an essential factor for the success of Korean dramas.

> Because it [Korean dramas] always portrays the male characters as very understanding. Japanese [dramas] will not do that to such an extent. Frankly, girls want to be treasured, to be loved, just because they want men to understand them, to take care of them, and to protect them! I

think Korean dramas are very successful; they successfully portray such kind of male characters!

One of the very important functions of Korean dramas is their provision of a fantasy world. They offer channels where women can express their desires — desires for a pure society, for pure romance, for being pampered and loved by men — this can also be seen as an escape from everyday stress (e.g., full of struggles at work with men). Many informants agreed that Korean dramas projected 'a fantasyland which does not exist in reality'. In this dream world, the heroines and heroes are idealized females and males. Our informants were deeply impressed by the beautiful sceneries and perfect characters of the series, even though they realized that these were unrealistic and cannot be found easily in real life. For instance, a Hong Kong informant, Kat (aged 22, university student), described the leading actress in Korean dramas as 'Snow White', i.e. an ideal woman. Another Hong Kong informant Kin (aged 26, marketing executive) held a similar view, 'Watching Korean dramas really makes you feel that you are a princess, and then think that this world is very beautiful ... even if it is a tragic story ... sickness and some things like that, you still feel very sweet after viewing [the drama].'

New Qualities of Modern Asian Women

Though the female protagonists are described as 'beautiful', 'tender' and 'humble', they are not 'conservative' in the eyes of our informants. Despite the traditional ('Asian') qualities they possess, they are also 'strong' and 'open-minded' in certain aspects. Many informants found the female characters quite 'tough' in general, as they 'have their own ideas', and they will take the initiative to strive for happiness (especially in love affairs). For example, one of the Singaporean informants, Niki (aged 19, student), recalled the story of *Beautiful Days*, which features a poor orphan (the female protagonist) who is very hardworking and tough, and who never gives up but strives to achieve her goals. She appreciated this character very much. Emma (aged 40+, magazine editor) in Hong Kong found women in Korean dramas 'very traditional' but 'not stupid'. They need to work for their own living, and to face problems by themselves, which she believed, can 'reflect the modern situation'.

We can see that these female images possess some new/modern women qualities: tough, with working abilities and independence. On the other hand, they are willing to express their wishes and desires, particularly in love relations. Most female protagonists in Korean dramas insist on finding 'true love'. They are eager to take the initiative in a relationship and even fight for their love. For instance, a Hong Kong informant, Sally (aged 40, retired), appreciated the toughness of the female character in face of love troubles in the drama *Autumn Tale*. She described the female leading actress, Eun Suh (Song Hae Gyo), as a 'strong' girl who can 'put forth new life with her own efforts' (e.g. Eun Suh in *Autumn Tale* always tells the male protagonist Joon Suh how important he is to her, while Joon Suh seldom does the same thing). Combining the traditional virtues and new women qualities, our informants seem to identify with a 'hybridized modern woman's image'. A Hong Kong informant Becky (aged 50, accountant) said that her favorite love storyline is about a 'talented', 'career' lady meeting a man who is willing to protect her (e.g. *All about Eve*). She believed that a 'happy modern woman' should be career-minded while dedicated to a man/a relationship at the same time.

Similar to the substantive transformations brought by socioeconomic developments and feminist movements in Western societies (Bourdieu, 2001), the conditions of women in many developed Asian societies, such as Hong Kong and Singapore, have changed in many different social and economic arenas; for instance, increasing access to higher education and waged work, and increasing participation in the public sphere. The level of education attained by Hong Kong women has improved continuously over the past decade. In 1991, the proportion of women with tertiary education (9.4%) was much lower than that of men (13%) but by 2001, the proportion increased to 15.1%, which was closer to the 17.8% of men.[2] The situation is similar in Singapore, as the proportion of women graduating from institutions of higher learning increased dramatically from 37 (per 10,000 female population) in 1986 to 68.5 (per 10,000 female population) in 1996.[3]

Another dramatic social change in the twentieth century has been the entry of women into the workplace. Better education, more favorable attitudes and ample job opportunities have resulted in a substantial rise in the labor force participation rate of women. During the past two decades, the female labor force increased while that for men decreased in both cities. The female labor force participation rate in Hong Kong increased from 49.5% in 1981 to 51.6% in 2001.[4] In contrast, the male labor force participation rate in Hong Kong substantially decreased from 82.5% in 1981 to 71.9% in 2001. In Singapore, the female labor force participation rate increased from 24.5% in 1957 to 52.2 % in 2000, while that of males dropped from 85.7 % to 70.6% in the same period.[5] Many women in Hong Kong and Singapore have become outstanding performers in the labor market. Some of them have entered the professional/associate professional ranks and have taken up important positions that were previously reserved for males. (See Tables 5.3 and 5.4).

Table 5.3   Proportion of working population by occupation in Hong Kong (%)

	1991		1996		2001	
	Male	Female	Male	Female	Male	Female
Managers and administrators	11.8	4.9	15.4	7.1	14.1	6.5
Professionals	4.1	3.0	5.5	4.3	6.3	4.6
Associate professionals	9.7	11.3	11.0	13.9	14.6	16.2
Clerks	8.0	28.8	8.5	29.5	8.2	26.6
Service workers and shop sales workers	13.7	12.5	14.0	13.5	14.5	15.7
Craft and related workers	20.9	4.4	17.9	3.7	16.2	1.9
Plant and machine operators and assemblers	13.9	12.7	11.6	4.0	11.4	2.2
Elementary occupations	16.6	21.7	15.3	23.5	14.3	26.2
Others	1.2	0.7	0.9	0.5	0.4	0.1

Source: Hong Kong Statistics Department

Table 5.4   Proportion of working population (below 40) by occupation in Singapore

	1987		1997		2000	
	Male	Female	Male	Female	Male	Female
Administrative and managerial	7.4	13.1	13.1	6	44.9	41.5
Professional and technical	16.6	33.4	33.4	29.2		
Clerical	6.2	6.0	6.0	32.8	17.6	40.5
Services and sales	13.8	10.9	10.9	10.4		
Production and related workers	43.8	27	27	21.4	31.1	17.6
Others	12.2	9.7	9.7	0.2	5.8	0.4

Source: Department of Statistics, Singapore

With their increasing educational attainment, economic independence and financial contribution to the family, traditional gender role boundaries between men and women have become increasingly destabilized, both at the workplace and in the family. Korean dramas seem to act as sites of hegemonic discursive practices, through their projection of imaginaries of 'Asian modern femininities' — a combination of both traditional virtues and modern sensibilities. This kind of 'ideal perfect modern Asian woman' seems to embody the deepest desire of many Asian women — to have the best of both worlds (i.e., career and love/family). This matches the 'role-play' tactics mentioned by a Hong Kong informant, Lau (aged 20, accounting clerk), who emphasized that women need to take up different roles depending on the context. She said, 'I think she needs to get a balance in the middle! Under certain situations, [women should be] as tender as a little bird [in a romantic relationship], but sometimes [they] need to be brave and fight for their own rights [in a job situation]! Yes, that's it! Be strong when you need to be strong, and be weak when you need to be weak!' These discourses of the strong-and-weak, tough-and-gentle ideal woman have many inherent contradictions. We shall turn to a discussion of these contradictions in the next section.

Conflicting Discourses of Femininities

As mentioned in the previous section, more highly educated career women have been entering the labor market in Hong Kong and Singapore. Some of them occupy professional positions and have proved themselves to have the same ability as their male counterparts, if not higher. Most Hong Kong informants agreed that women should try to show great ability in the workplace and to achieve financial independence. For instance, Jenny (aged 43, college teacher) found most Hong Kong women to be very 'independent' and 'tough'. She described them in this way, 'thinking independently, earning [money] independently, [doing] everything independently'. Some Singaporean informants also supported this viewpoint, like Tina (aged 23, administrative work), who believed that modern women should be independent and be able to maintain their own living, 'No matter man or woman, only if he/she has a pair of hands to work, how come he/she needs to lean on others?'

Some of our informants are examples of such kind of 'strong and capable' modern working women (as accountant, manager, professor, teacher, editor, etc.), who are breadwinners in the family. These modern Chinese women are no longer confined to the domestic sphere, and they have established their own financial independence. Some of these so-called 'superwomen' work harder than men, gaining higher social prestige as well as making more money than their partners. However, the emergence of capable, independent career women also results in dilemmas and conflicts in everyday life. One of the serious problems faced by modern Asian women is heavy burdens, as they need to take up multiple roles, both within and beyond the family. All of our married informants found themselves in a dilemma of double burdens, and they admitted that taking up two jobs (taking care of family and having a paid job) made them lose most of their personal time and space. Below are some tensions expressed by some informants:

- I think if you are a career-minded woman, then how can she strike a balance between her family and her work? That is I think you go out to work nowadays, it's impossible to come back early, [get] off duty at five o'clock, and have to cook when you get back to home! You get back to home at eight or nine o'clock, then I think it will certainly affect your family life. The time you spend with your husband, children, family will be less, and there will be communication problems! (Becky, aged 50, accountant, Hong Kong)

- If we want a career, if we want [a] family, and all that, then it's up to you to balance it all out … For me, it's like … only when he [her husband] is extremely tired, when he, when both of us are extremely tired, then he will say let's not do anything. But the thing is I feel compelled to do them … that's [it's] women [who] do all these [household chores]. Because if not, how [can] all these things [be] left undone? I'll have to do it. He can still, when both are extremely stressed, he can take the position that, the more comfortable position …' (Silvia, aged 33, researcher and teacher, Singapore, interviewed in English)

Faced with all the dilemmas encountered in the real world, our female informants seem to gain some pleasure in consuming Korean dramas. Within the realm of everyday life, they need to work very hard in their job on the one hand, and to fulfill the perceived social expectations of women as primary care-takers in the family on the other. However, the fantasyland of Korean dramas is completely different. As mentioned by many informants, most of the male characters are 'born to be rich', and they do not need to worry about money. This allows them to take care of the females and provide them with a comfortable life. Besides, the perfect (tough-and-weak) female figure offers an important source of identification, which allows the viewers to take a break from the tough and harsh everyday world by going into the dream world created in Korean dramas.

Despite the phenomenon of more women entering the labor force and taking up important roles in both Hong Kong and Singapore, many informants (especially those in Singapore, and this point will be explored in the next section) believed that establishing a happy family is their 'ultimate goal' in life and only this will bring them 'ultimate happiness'. Lee (2004) found that many Korean dramas finally return to traditional gender relations, and these happy endings conform to the traditional ideology of marriage which sustains the traditional values underlying the relationship between men and women. In our study, the Chinese female viewers in both cities dreamed of such 'happy endings' in their real life. They identified with the social realism of women portrayed in the dramas, who appear to be strong and career-minded on the surface, but in fact they cherish the wish of being a happy housewife, and to have a husband to lean on.

One Singaporean informant, Minnie (aged 29, language teacher), defined a woman's happy life as one with a 'complete family', and she said, 'A family should have a father and a mother, then it is completed and happy ... and also a son and a daughter; that will be good.' A Hong Kong informant, Kin (aged 26, marketing executive), admitted that she wanted to be 'the woman behind a successful man'. One of the reasons that she worked very hard is to be 'smart and beautiful', so that she could find a good husband. 'I think that working makes me beautiful, and working makes me smart. Getting more beautiful and smart, then my husband will love me more.' A married Hong Kong informant, Emma (aged 40+, magazine editor), suggested that many Hong Kong women are still bound by the 'traditional framework'. She quoted herself as an example, as she believed that 'family is much more important than career', and her most important goal in life is to 'maintain a healthy and harmonious family.' Though she is also a career woman, she secretly wished for an ideal life like this — 'having a man to take care of you financially, then no need to work, you can sleep till very late and wake up whenever you like!'

Most of our informants admitted that family/love is an essential part of their lives. The romance depicted in Korean dramas are particularly attractive to female viewers and thus constitutes an important source for identification. For example, a Singaporean informant, Anita (aged 26, administrative work), enjoyed the ever-lasting love in the stories, and she pointed out that 'a lover' is more important than 'a career' in a woman's life. However, in the harsh reality, many women (and particularly the career women, like some of our informants) fail to find such love and so viewing Korean dramas becomes a form of vicarious pleasure for them. The comment of a Hong Kong informant, Winkei (aged 30, ICAC investigative officer), is illustrative:

> This kind of life and death love story will never happen to me ... in Hong Kong, especially our job, really makes people exhausted. Therefore, those things that are too tiring to me, I may not do that! Especially this kind of life and death [love relationships], wastes me too much time, I will not do that definitely ... all are things that will never happen to me, and I feel that they have happened [to me] through viewing the drama world.

Ang (1985) pointed out that there is no punishment for whatever identity one takes up in the fictional world, and it offers a safe space of excess in the otherwise ordered and restrained social life. In this case, Korean dramas seem to offer an idealized buffer space to reconcile the conflicting discourses (and desires) of femininities in reality — traditional women who are soft and family-oriented, completely dependent on men at one extreme; and superwomen who are tough and career-minded, completely independent at another extreme. The 'almost perfect' female characters and 'romantic love mixed with social realism' help these Chinese female viewers to construct an imaginary of Asian modern femininities, which seem to form a main source of pleasure in Korean drama viewing. Consumption of Korean dramas seem to provide temporary relief from the irreconcilable tensions created by both kinds of femininities (traditional and modern) which seem to constitute their contradictory subjectivities. These Chinese women seem to be located at the crossroads of tradition and modernity and experiencing intense tensions between contradictory values regarding what count as being a good woman and a good life for a woman amid the many contradictory demands of modern societies.

3.3   Differences between Hong Kong and Singaporean Viewers: The 'Asian Values Discourse' and Patriarchal Ideals of Femininities in Singapore

Singaporean Viewers' Identification with the 'Asian Values Discourse'

As mentioned above, both groups of audiences recognized and appreciated the happy hybridization of traditional values and modern images in Korean dramas. On top of this common cultural appreciation and personal identification, the female viewers in Singapore seemed to be more inclined towards traditional values and Confucianist ideals, such as traditional virtues related to family relationships. According to the survey results (see Table 5.5), 28.5% of our Hong Kong informants (19% agreed and 9.5% strongly agreed) adored Korean dramas because 'they can reveal the importance of family'. For the Singaporean informants, 46.7% of them (36.7% agreed and 10% strongly agreed) adored Korean dramas for the same reason.

Table 5.5   Reason for viewing Korean dramas: 'They can reveal the importance of family'

	Hong Kong informants (%)	*Singaporean informants (%)*
Strongly disagree	4.7	6.7
Disagree	23.8	23.3
Neutral	42.9	23.3
Agree	19.0	36.7
Strongly agree	9.5	10.0
Total	100	100

First of all, our informants in Singapore seemed to pay more attention to moral values in the family (e.g. filial piety) in Korean dramas, and they could easily identify with the storylines and characters. One of the favorite Korean dramas of Ling (aged 33, supervisor of sales department) is *The Gift*, which features children's love for their parents in a subtle way. She enjoyed the love provided by parents of the female protagonist, as she recalled this scene — the father cooks for her after work, and her mother takes care of her when she is sick — she believed that all these were instances of 'love in daily life'. Another Singaporean informant, Charlene (aged 30+, reporter), was deeply impressed by the family warmth in the dramas, and she pointed out that family is 'the most important thing' in one's life. She said, 'In case of emergency or (in a) risky situation, family is the best support. No matter how successful you are, family is still the most important thing.'

The ethical principle of filial piety in Confucianism emphasizes kinship networks as the focus of Chinese culture. The Singaporean government has promoted a certain version of Confucianism as an ideology for political and social control, emphasizing that individual views must be subordinated to the common good (Wilen and Wilen, 1997). Its notion of 'Westernization'/ Western choices refers to 'wrong' or 'bad' choices, including values, attitudes and ideas that pit the individual and his/her concerns over and above societal concerns (PuruShotam, 1998). One of the common good that Singaporeans are concerned with is the family good — harmony among family members. For instance, one of the Singaporean informants, Silvia (aged 33, researcher and teacher), placed great importance on family values and she considered this an indicator of 'Asian-ness'. She pointed out her personal feelings on 'traditions' and 'family values' in this way:

> The tensions between, the traditions, the family values, the Asian-ness, okay? I do not know, I think that is very relative. I related to it. I am very Chinese, I am very family-oriented, kind of person, the more I grow up, the more I realize. I watch myself, and I realize that I am, I am very attached to the family … I probably admire [the] Asian, or the Chinese that I think I was. When I watched these [Korean dramas], I found myself relating very deeply to that family values, very, very deep. (original in English)

Her claim of 'Asian-ness' reveals that family values are seen to be at the heart of the 'Asian worldview' that she seems to be constructing for herself as she watches Korean dramas. In addition to family values, some informants claimed that their conservative attitudes toward love/sex are also characteristics of Asian people. The Singaporean informants seem to be more inclined towards traditional values in love affairs and sexual relationships. As indicated in Table 5.6, about half of the Hong Kong informants agreed/strongly agreed to the statement 'I will be faithful to my partner unto death', while over 70% of the Singaporean informants reported with the same answer. Women in both cities, particularly those in Singapore, seem to affirm faithfulness and loyalty to love. Similar to the practice of 'learning family values from Korean dramas', some Singaporean informants considered Korean dramas 'educative materials' for youth in terms of love/sex relations today.

Table 5.6   Response to the statement 'I will be faithful to my partner unto death'

	Hong Kong informants (%)	Singaporean informants (%)
Strongly disagree	0	0
Disagree	4.4	3.4
Neutral	43.5	23.3
Agree	39.1	50.0
Strongly agree	13.0	23.3
Total	100	100

Singaporeans are in a very controlled environment and most people are still very conservative towards sex (Maclachlan and Chua, 2004). In our study, many Singaporean female viewers emphasized that they cannot accept pre-marital sex, and they preferred more 'restrained' and 'pure' expressions of love. For instance, Minnie (aged 29, language teacher) has been in love with her present boyfriend for ten years, and both of them cannot accept premarital sex. Another informant, Jessica (aged 26, travel agent), suggested that 'the good thing is worth waiting for; waiting till marriage will be more valuable'. When talking about 'one-night stands', most informants showed a strong opposition; for instance, a Singaporean informant Bena (aged 36, language teacher) said, '(I) can accept it mentally, but cannot accept it physically'. Polly (aged 35, housewife) believed that Korean dramas could deliver a positive message to youth in modern Singapore (in contrast to Japanese dramas), which she said fits the traditional mindset of East Asian people. As she puts it,

> I prefer encouraging those (youths) to watch Korean dramas. The love attitudes depicted in Japanese dramas are not good, and the trend is not good, either. For example, the female protagonist (in a Japanese drama) is willing to dedicate her body to a man, just to gain his love; the feeling is so frivolous. It's less conservative than our thinking, (different from) the traditional mind of East Asian women.

It seems that Korean TV dramas have offered these Chinese women a useful alternative to some sexualized Western productions (e.g., *Sex and the City*), as they seem to use Korean dramas to negotiate alternative forms of Asian modernities and femininities. As illustrated above, our Singaporean informants appeared to be more attached to the 'traditional' notion of family and conservative ethics of love/sex, with some claiming that these attitudes belong to 'Asian values', which the Singaporean government constructed as the basis of an Asian modernity (Wee, 2002). Langlois (2001) believes that Asian values are used as political tools by the state to carry out the so-called authentic Confucian governance. Our Singaporean informants seem to have internalized this government-promoted 'Asian values discourse' and Korean dramas are appealing as the dramas appear to re-affirm their values as 'Asian' rather than just Singaporean.

Modification versus Preservation of Patriarchal Ideals of Femininities

Though women in both cities are confronted by similar family-job dilemmas their attitudes in dealing with role conflicts seem to be slightly different. It seems that female viewers in Hong Kong preferred a more liberalized/ Westernized notion of femininities, while those in Singapore held a rather conservative/conventional definition of femininities. Leon and Ho (1994) argue that under the influence of Westernization and modernization, the patriarchal traditions of Chinese culture have gradually been modified in Hong Kong to adapt to urban city lifestyles. Many Hong Kong informants believed that Hong Kong women were quite different from those in Korean dramas, as they now occupied a much higher social status than before and tended to be more career-minded. One of the indicators is the relatively high proportion of female government officials in Hong Kong as compared to other Western and Asian societies.

In many Western societies there seems to be a general movement of the two genders toward each other, a movement towards common occupations, common interests and common ideals in modern societies (Felski, 2000). Many Hong Kong women seem to accept and welcome this trend, and they embrace a more liberalized discourse on femininities, which grants women more freedom and allows them more room for self-development. Some informants found that Hong Kong women could be very independent and aggressive (e.g., in their careers), and that they always made decisions on their own without negotiating with their partners. In contemporary Hong Kong, it is generally accepted that women's social status is very close to, or even the same as, the social status of men. Many of them have become dissatisfied with gender stereotypes and rigid role boundaries, and they cannot accept males' superiority over females. Most of our Hong Kong informants disliked the kind of 'male dominance' depicted in Korean dramas, both in the workplace and in love relations.

According to the results of our end-of-interview questionnaire survey (see Table 5.7), 20% Hong Kong informants believed that there was no discrimination against women in Hong Kong, while only 6.7% Singaporean informants held the same belief. On the other hand, nearly half of the Singaporean informants reported that 'there is some discrimination', but only 29.6% of the Hong Kong informants reported the same view (also see Table 5.7).

Table 5.7   Self-perceived discrimination against women in one's country

	Hong Kong informants (%)	*Singaporean informants (%)*
There is no discrimination at all	22.2	6.7
There is little discrimination	44.4	36.7
There is some discrimination	29.6	46.7
Not sure	3.7	10.0
Total	100	100

The Singaporean government has particularly strong feelings about a woman's social role as a mother, and Singaporean men still prefer wives who are controllable (Wilen and Wilen, 1997). In our study, though many of the Singaporean informants are independent career women, most of them still adhered to the ideological discourse that stipulates that women have to put family matters before her career, that the identity of 'mother' is more important than that of 'worker'. According to our survey, the 'maternal love' expressed by the female characters constitutes a major element of appeal to the Singaporean female viewers. A larger proportion of Singaporean informants than Hong Kong informants agreed to the statement that they watch Korean dramas because they can reflect the maternal love possessed by traditional women, and also a larger proportion of them agreed that 'I have to be married to be happy' (see Table 5.8). This seems to point to their strong identification with the social role of mother/care-taker.

According to many Singaporean women, families and mothers are their main sources of values and identities (Wee, 2002). Although the median age of first marriage has kept increasing from 23.3 in 1970 to 26 in 1997 for Singaporean women,[6] the tendency towards getting married remains relatively strong for Singaporean women (Saw, 1999). The general marriage rate only

Table 5.8 Response to the statement: 'I have to be married to be happy'

	Hong Kong informants (%)	Singaporean informants (%)
Strongly disagree	4.3	6.7
Disagree	39.1	10.0
Neutral	26.1	46.7
Agree	30.4	26.7
Strongly agree	0	10.0
Total	100	100

Table 5.9 Response to the statement: 'It is natural to have children when married'

	Hong Kong informants (%)	Singaporean informants (%)
Strongly disagree	11.1	10
Disagree	48.1	16.7
Neutral	18.5	33.3
Agree	14.8	26.7
Strongly agree	7.4	13.3
Total	100	100

decreased slightly from 11.5 (per 1000 population) in 1970 to 10.7 (per 1000 population) in 1997.[7] On the other hand, the divorce rate for Singaporean Chinese indicates a recent deterioration in marital harmony. From 1980 to 1997, Singaporean Chinese divorce rate increased steadily from 55.3 (per 1000 marriages) to 159.8 (per 1000 marriages).[8] As a result, the Singaporean government has promoted the 'happy marriage discourse' with greater effort. Despite the steadily increasing divorce rate, Saw (1999) believes that most Singaporean women are inclined to see 'marriage' and 'motherhood' as two of the crucial goals in their lives, which shows that they seem to have retained Confucianist notions of femininities in their modern lives.

4. Conclusion

In this concluding section, the implications of Korean drama watching culture among Chinese female viewers in Hong Kong and Singapore will be explored, with a critical discussion of the pleasures and imaginaries offered by Korean dramas. We shall start with a critical discussion of the construction of conservative ideals of femininities by the Singaporean government, followed by the largely government-led projection of Asian cultural identities as packaged in the 'Asian values discourse'. Then we shall end on a discussion of imaginaries of Asian modern femininities that seem to be emerging in the Korean drama consumption practices of these Chinese female viewers.

4.1 *'Masculine' Singapore: Construction of the Happy Family Discourse and Conservative Ideals of Femininities*

Most of our Singaporean informants are more attached to the traditional discourses of femininities than the Hong Kong informants. They affirm many of the so-called 'Asian'/'Confucianist' virtues of women — conservative, restrained, obedient, family-centered. The 'traditional virtues' possessed by the female protagonists in Korean dramas seem to provide them with resources to re-affirm what they construct as their 'Chinese and Asian cultural identities'. With increasing education and job opportunities, many Asian women have begun to realize their potential and have started to make independent judgments. For example, women in Hong Kong and Singapore seek more education and treat careers seriously, sometimes refusing marriage and children. There are public discourses lamenting that working mothers do not spend enough time with their children, causing family breakups. As the former Prime Minister of Singapore Lee Kuan Yew said, this might have posed 'real dangers to the transmission of our traditional values, our cultures' (Lee, 1984).

As compared to the Hong Kong government, it seems that the Singaporean government has been more active in promoting the 'happy family discourse' to stabilize the gender role boundaries between men and women. Today the Singaporean government's official discourses still promote marriage and childbirth, and the 'happy family discourse' divides women by conferring status to those who have conformed to the state-set ideals — married mothers, while those who have not (i.e. single females) are identified as potentially problematic (Maclachlan and Chua, 2004). The promotion of traditional and pro-family values (e.g. filial piety, sexual restraint and marital fidelity) aims at restoring families and mothers as the sources of values and identities (Wee, 2002). This helps preserve the patriarchal culture and paternalistic governance in Singaporean society. Singaporean women thus have to strive to organize their lives amid the conflicting demands of (1) the traditional caretaker role of women, (2) the exigencies of an industrial economy that encourages and rewards female labor force participation, and (3) the modern values of gender equality.[9]

Even with a more sophisticated and nuanced approach to Confucianism, there is no denying that some Confucianst sayings regarding women's subordinate position to men have been deeply inscribed in the culture, language, and lived experience as Asian women. This Confucianist/traditional version of femininities constructs women as caring, submissive and obedient, attending to 'qing' (compassion, attachment), and dependent on men for protection. Their ultimate goal/happiness is to get married to men, which turns out to be the recurrent kind of happy endings offered in Korean dramas (Lin and Kwan, 2005). In our study, many Chinese female viewers, especially those in Singapore, seem to readily endorse the Confucianist/traditional version of femininities. This may provide the most comfortable subject positions for them, which consist of modes of femininities that are most culturally acceptable/legitimate in many Asian societies (in this case, particularly the Singaporean society).

Although we have reservations in labeling these traditional version of femininities 'Confucianist values', they seem to be part of the lived cultures that many Asian women (e.g. our informants) have experienced. Our informants seem to find value and re-assurance in re-affirming their traditional cultural roots and cultural identities through re-affirming their traditional/ Confucianist cultural ways of caring and expressing love as depicted in Korean dramas. Unwittingly, this also reproduces the Singaporean government's 'happy family discourse' and the relatively conservative ideologies of femininities. It should be noted that the Singaporean informants might be re-voicing the discourses of the government (i.e., drawing on the state discourses to narrate their own stories). However, their stories might also reveal their lived experience and perceived status of women in Singapore, which deserve closer attention and deeper analysis.

4.2 'Neo-Traditional Modernity': Constructing an Asian Cosmopolitan Imaginary with the 'Asian Values Discourse'

As described earlier, Korean dramas are attractive in their ways of packaging traditional values with modern aesthetics. Korean dramas affirm the commitment to certain traditional values in a globalizing and Westernizing modern Asian society. It is interesting to note that these Chinese female viewers identify these 'traditional elements' (e.g. conservative attitudes towards love and sex, female chastity as a natural quality of women, family-orientedness, respect for seniors and the elderly) as being 'Asian'. They try to construct their own 'Asian' cultural identities (in contrast to Western cultural identities) through the personalization of the subtle ways of expressing love, romance, care and respect as depicted in Korean dramas. It seems that this is a very important part of the pleasure that these female Chinese viewers seem to be deriving from their consumption of Korean dramas.

At the same time, the representation of cosmopolitan city life, love affairs and global consumerist lifestyles in Korean dramas is appealing. One of the Hong Kong informants, Irene, found that the Korean cityscape in the dramas remains in a developing stage, which she said is 'more developed than China, but less developed than Hong Kong'. She liked this stage very much as it represents a mixture of tradition and modernity. This leads to a hybridization of two seemingly conflicting discourses — traditionality and modernity — which together constitute a kind of 'neo-traditional modernity'. The term 'neo-traditional modernity' includes a simultaneous homogenization and differentiation, which originally refers to harmony among different ethnic groups (Wee, 2002). However, its meaning can be extended to embrace both traditional and modern values/virtues, and can be constructed to represent some form of cultural coherence/solidarity in a trans-border Asian cosmopolitan imaginary.

The term 'modernization' has often been used as a code word for 'Westernization' although recently 'globalization' has replaced the term, 'modernization'. However, Asian societies have their own economical, social and cultural contexts, and we cannot emulate the practices of Western societies without considering our own needs. Ang points out the uniqueness of Asian modernity in this way, 'Modernization may unavoidably involve a fundamental element of Westernization, especially in a structural sense, but Asian modernity — as a way of life — is by no means a simple replication of Western modernity.' (2004: 306). She believes that Asian idealized cultural modernity is associated with material affluence, consumerism, female emancipation and individualism. Our study shows that the kind of 'Asian modernity' desired by Chinese women seems to be based on a hybridization of both modern (e.g., pursuit of choice in love and careers) and traditional values (conservative family and sexuality values). It represents a dream of alternative modernities that can embrace both modern and traditional values, and the term 'modern' becomes more fluid and also ambiguous.

However, one of the dangers of the Asian values discourse is the government's use of it in imposing conservative ideologies for political and social control, including the control of women's bodies and aspirations. Wee (2003, 2004) suggested that the Singapore state's Asianization attempt is now in abeyance, given the criticism of 'Asian values' to be nothing more than bad values like collusion, corruption and nepotism after the 1997 Asian economic crisis. It is possible that this 'Asian values discourse' can be manipulated by the government to continue its authoritarian and paternalistic rule, and to reject liberalized ideas from the West. In fact, 'Asian values' are extraordinarily diverse, ranging across the political spectrum and drawing on religion, tradition, politics and culture (Mamoru, 2004). Owing to the diversification, it should be noted that there is no such thing as a monolithic Asian modernity (Ang, 2004). The term 'Asian values' should be considered a representation of a set of cultural and moral norms, which are not exclusively good or bad, and diverse within itself. Future studies may analyze the changing 'Asian values discourse' in correspondence to the economic, social and cultural development of different societies in Asia.

4.3 Escape or Agency? Transnational Korean Drama Flows and Imaginaries of Asian Modern Femininities

Despite the fact that informants in both cities seem to identify with these so-called 'Confucianist cultural values', some of them (mostly Hong Kong female viewers) actually practice 'selective' identification with the traditional femininities depicted in Korean dramas (as well as in everyday discourses). This ensures that a more fluid subject position can be adopted by modern Asian women, which preserves the 'good qualities' of what they labeled as an 'Asian' tradition while keeping up with demands of the rapidly changing society. The modern/Western feminist discourses construct women as increasingly more assertive, rational, independent of men and equally capable of handling their tough everyday management work just as men do. Some of our informants, especially the career women in Hong Kong, recognized and appreciated the 'realism' of workplace scenarios in Korean dramas (e.g. modern career women who are tough and capable, willing to express their wishes and desires). They rejected a complete and blind acceptance of all traditional gender values that are considered to be 'Confucianist virtues'.

While a non-critical acceptance of the 'Asian values discourse' (including traditional gender ideologies) seems to be rather regressive, it should be noted that some of the traditional values are not necessarily 'bad things'. Some of these 'traditional ideals', such as the emphasis on 'qing' and commitment to a love/sex relationship, constitute a social imaginary with compassion and love, which is very important to women suffering from the alienation and rationalist discourses in modern society. Many modern working women need to fit into the tough masculine workplace culture on the one hand, but would also like to retreat to a safe fantasy space where they no longer need to put up with the struggle and return to a more traditional/Confucianist femininity on the other (Lin and Kwan, 2005). As illustrated by our informants, we can see that many working women are yearning for 'qing', for pure and absolute love in a society that privileges rationalist efficiency discourses and non-compassionate approaches to work. A Hong Kong informant, Irene, said that she loved the warm feeling offered by the dramas. She believed that Korean dramas were a response to rapidly changing Asian society:

> In reality, the relationship[s] between people are getting more and more distanced, [Korean drama] wants to give people a space for reflection, something like that, to represent the kind of warm love, warm feeling, such kinds of things.

In the identification process, the Chinese women may feel that they are bonded with other Asian women who also cherish lost traditional values/ virtues. This shows the social imaginary constructed and consumed by the Chinese women through viewing Korean dramas. Poovey points out that 'social imaginary is not simply a social theory developed by specialists but 'is at least partly generated by ordinary people for use in life, and it reveals itself in stories, myths, and commonplaces as well as theoretical narratives' (2002: 131). What we will like to propose in this chapter is that Korean dramas seem to constitute an important imaginary space which portray a social universe with compassion, as embodied in the Chinese saying 'you-qing tian-di', which can be translated as: 'a sky and earth with compassion', and this is alternative to the Western modern imaginary of objectification and abstraction (see Poovey, 2002). Nevertheless, it is by nature an imaginary re-creation of the social world, and there is always a tension between the realism and idealism offered by a drama.

To conclude, this study reveals the complexities and contradictions inherent in the modern living conditions and subjectivities of women in the rapidly modernizing, Westernizing and globalizing societies of Hong Kong and Singapore. Korean dramas seem to re-affirm the traditional discourse of femininities on the one hand, and provide a potential imaginary space for alternative (hybridized) modernities and femininities on the other. Modern Asian women need to recognize that the 'Asian values discourse' (including the 'patriarchal ideals of femininities', 'happy family discourse' described in this chapter) is a modern–day construct that different parties (e.g., the government, the media, politicians, and also ourselves) have participated in creating and maintaining. What counts as a good life for a modern Asian woman and what counts as ideal femininities in modern Asian societies? As Asian women continue to experience conflicting demands exerted on them by various structures and discourses in the modern society, Korean dramas would seem to continue to have a role to play in these women's simultaneous consumption, construction and exploration of different modern Asian femininities.

Whether this role is largely progressive or regressive (or mixed) would seem to turn on how women use the dramas rather than the narratives of the dramas per se. We believe that agency is one's socioculturally mediated capacity to act (Ahearn, 2001). The agency of the women consumers can be enhanced if their consumption practices are taken seriously to generate critical discussion of the different kinds of social imaginaries emerging from women's reading (interpretive) practices when they consume different media texts such as Korean dramas. And perhaps in the process both the consumers and the analyst shall also be acquiring critical media literacy (a kind of sociocultural and interpretive resource) that enables us to use Korean dramas (and other media texts) in ways that are more an expression of our agency than an escape.

6

Winter Sonata and Cultural Practices of Active Fans in Japan:
Considering Middle-Aged Women as Cultural Agents

Yoshitaka Mōri[1]

Introduction

On the day before Christmas Eve in 2003, I visited my parents in Tokyo. My mother, 65 years old, suggested that we should watch a TV drama together, by saying cheerfully that the hero was so handsome and the story was so romantic and so on. This was my first encounter with a Korean drama, *Winter Sonata*.

I was a little bit confused by her suggestion, as I have not watched any TV dramas with her since I left home at the age of nineteen. To my knowledge, she has never been a big fan of TV home dramas, as she has always complained about the uncultivated taste of home dramas. Moreover, she had a strong prejudice against Korea and Korean people. This had often created an unhappy tension between her and me in the past. When I had a part-time job teaching Japanese to Korean residents in Japan during my university days, she was not happy about it and told me to quit as she was worried that my students might seduce me, though they were only primary school students! After we had a bitter argument over her prejudice, I decided never to talk about Korean issues with her again. The fact that she disliked Korea and Koreans made me sad and even embarrassed, as I had many friends who were Korean residents in Japan, *zainichi* 在日.[2]

During the 2004 New Year's holidays, I watched the whole series of *Winter Sonata* with her. The drama was, in fact, more interesting than I had expected. However, what interested me more was the way in which she talked, like a young girl, about the drama and the hero, Bae Yong Jun (nicknamed *Yon-sama* in Japan), as if she were a girl. I found that she had exchanged information about the drama through the Internet or over tea meetings with her friends. She became interested in Korean culture and even traveled to Korea. I started to wonder why *Winter Sonata* fascinated her so much, why Bae Yong Jun could change her ideas about Korea, and what would eventually happen to her during and after the Korean Wave? This essay is motivated by my personal experience in relation to my mother; however, I believe that our situation is exceptional.

Puzzled by the prevailing Korean Wave in Japan, I started to ponder why middle-aged women like my mother were so attracted to this particular Korean melodrama, *Winter Sonata*. The following argument is based on interview research with twenty female fans, which I conducted in August and September 2004 at the peak of the *Winter Sonata* phenomenon. The face-to-face, unstructured interviews took mostly one or two hours. Three group interviews were also organized. Throughout the period, ideas were exchanged on the Internet after the interviews. In this essay, I will not ask why *Winter Sonata* became so popular in Japan, as the mainstream media including TV, newspapers and popular journals have already discussed this often in a generalized way. I will ask, instead, how *Winter Sonata* was being watched and talked about by the individual fans. This is because I want to avoid the risk of overgeneralizing individual fans' activities, and would rather look at the differences among them.

The Korean Wave and *Winter Sonata* Phenomenon in Japan

Let me start by summarizing what the Korean Wave has been like in Japan and try to situate the *Winter Sonata* phenomenon within a Japanese context before entering into detail examination. There are different levels of definition of the Korean Wave in Japan. It is roughly defined as a cultural and social phenomenon in which Japan accepts Korean contemporary popular culture. Called either *Kanryu* or *Hanryu* (韓流) in Japanese, it initially appeared around 2004, and is still prevalent today (though it may have peaked already). Bae Yong Jun, Lee Byung Hun, Won Bin and Jang Dong Gun were the most successful Korean actors, and were called 'the Big Four of the Korean Wave', *Hanryu Shitennoh* (韓流四天王). The Korean Wave often includes the popularity of Korean films, although some of them, such as Park Chan Wook's *Oldboy* and Kim Ki Duk's *Bad Guy* succeeded not only as part of the Korean Wave, but as experimental films that attracted enthusiasts who are always seeking cutting-edge films. It may also include Korean contemporary music, such as Paik Yongha, Rain (Pi) and BoA. However, their impact was relatively limited in the Japanese market. Moreover, BoA is likely to be seen as a Japanese pop star as she often sings in Japanese, and an 'Asian' star rather than as a Korean. Consequently, Korean music (K-Pop) is not always understood as part of the Korean Wave in the Japanese context. The Korean Wave in Japan is primarily the popular movement of Korean TV dramas. Therefore, *Winter Sonata* should definitely be located at the center of the Korean Wave.

It should be noted that *Winter Sonata* was not the first drama that was introduced into Japan, though it might be the first mega-hit Korean drama in the Japanese market. The Korean Wave was not the first entry of Korean culture into Japan either. It needs to be situated in the history of the cultural exchange in Japan. Looking back, it was during the 1988 Seoul Olympics that the image of Korea changed dramatically in Japan. It created a new representation of Korea, a more developed and urbanized one than was previously supposed in Japan. But it was not until the late 1990s that mutual exchanges in the field of popular culture were clearly activated. The delay was because while colonial memories had been kept alive in Korea, Japanese politician's repeated blunders over issues that arise from the memories of the period, often severely damaged diplomatic relations. In addition, a Korean cultural policy that banned the import of Japanese popular culture made it difficult to establish mutual understanding through cultural exchanges during the 1990s. The 2002 FIFA World Cup was definitely a crucial turning point. Although both countries had initially reluctantly accepted co-hosting, it eventually resulted in creating unexpected mutual cheering for each national team and created a friendly atmosphere, particularly among young people.[3] The new cultural exchange was also accelerated by the gradual abolition of the Korean government's policy of banning Japanese popular culture imports.

In the early stage of the Korean Wave, films had been more successfully promoted than TV dramas: *Shiri* was a moderate hit in 2000, followed by *JSA* in 2001, *My Sassy Girl* in 2003, and by *SILMIDO* in 2004. All the films gained their own popularity as part of the 'Korean New Wave' cinema. An increase in popularity of Korean culture and South Korea as a tourist destination could also be noticed in Japan. Kusanagi Tsuyosi, a member of the hugely popular Japanese idol group SMAP, learned Korean and introduced Korean culture on his TV programs in a rather oblique way. As for TV dramas, in 2002, a Japan-Korea collaborative drama *Friends*, featuring Fukada Kyoko and Won Bin was broadcasted by TBS in Japan and achieved a certain degree of popularity and received a lot of attention mainly because it was one of the first 'collaborative' effort; the program was not particularly impressive in terms of ratings. Since then, some Korean dramas were shown mainly by BS (Satellite TV); *Autumn in My Heart, Kashikogi, A Wish Upon a Star, All about Eve,* but it is difficult to say that they were widely supported as they were welcomed only by a small number of avid fans of Korean culture. Nevertheless, taking films and TV drama together, it could be said that there had already been a pro-Korea sentiment before the *Winter Sonata* phenomenon began.

Winter Sonata was first broadcasted at 10 pm every Thursday from April 2003 by NHK BS.[4] The average audience rate was about 1.1%. This was not that bad as it was on satellite, but the viewership was limited due to the nature of the satellite broadcasting. However, it rose gradually in popularity by word of mouth and in the end, NHK received considerable inquiries about re-broadcasting. Following popular requests that were sent to the station, NHK BS decided to air the drama again during the 2004 New Year week. The DVD was also released and available at rental shops before the re-broadcast. The media had slowly started to report the start of *Winter Sonata*'s popularity by that time.

A critical moment in the *Winter Sonata* phenomenon came on 3 April 2004. On that day Bae Yong Jun arrived at Tokyo International airport. Five thousand fans, mostly middle-age women, gathered to welcome him. This was exceptional, considering that five hundred fans came to the airport when footballer David Beckham arrived in Japan. This particular news shocked the Japanese people and the *Winter Sonata* and *Yon-sama* phenomenon drew great attention as a new boom. In the same month, NHK started to terrestrially broadcast the drama at 11.30 pm and gained more than 20% of the audience rating at the highest and about 15% on average. Considering that it was aired around midnight and that average audience ratings were about 10% even during prime time (7 pm–10 pm), the rating was incredibly high. The drama series also contributed financially to NHK which earned about 3,500 million yen ($3.5 million) from *Winter Sonata* related products. It also sold 330,000 sets of DVDs and 1,220,000 copies of a novelized book. In the end of 2004, NHK broadcasted a complete, original director's-cut version of *Winter Sonata* again.[5] This was the first subtitled version on TV broadcasting which had been dubbed in Japan.

Winter Sonata is unique in the history of Japanese culture's relationship with Korea in three senses. Firstly, it has played a crucial role in reconsidering the cultural relationship between Korea and Japan. It may be true that the relationship was getting closer over the 1990s because of the success of the FIFA Korea-Japan World Cup, and increasing popularity of Korean films and other popular culture among young women, such as travel and food.

But it was the mega hit of *Winter Sonata* and the subsequent *Yon-sama* phenomenon that changed a stereotypical image of Korean people and culture in Japan in an unprecedented way. This seemingly took place out of the blue. It was something that most of those who had been sincerely involved in Korea-Japan cultural exchange were unable to fully understand; some even warned that this may be merely superficial and ephemeral. Of course, it is still too early to conclude what the lasting effects of *Winter Sonata* would be, but I would like to take this phenomenon positively rather than critically, as it definitely made a crucial change in the cultural field.

Secondly, *Winter Sonata* is important because it made middle-aged women, roughly between 30 and 70 years old,[6] visible as its audience. They have often been marginalized and invisible as cultural practitioners in both journalism and academia. Academic studies of popular culture have looked at youth culture, subculture, girls' culture, ethnic culture and working class culture, but have marginalized and/or ignored middle-aged women. The *Yon-sama* phenomenon and its relation to middle-aged women has been reported in the mainstream media seriously, as well as contemptuously, almost everyday. For instance, on 29 August 2004, some TV chat shows reported pejoratively that fans organized birthday parties in different Korean BBQ restaurants in Tokyo to celebrate *Yon-sama*'s birthday. This is one of the examples that show how the media deal with *Winter Sonata* and the *Yon-sama* phenomenon, focusing on fans that were sometimes described merely as a stupid audience. On the other hand, there are other media which look at middle-aged women in a more sympathetic way. A weekly journal *AERA* analyzed more seriously what was happening to middle-aged women through detailed research and concluded that *Winter Sonata* provided a new sensation to women who were not happy in Japanese patriarchal society.[7] In any case, the drama made middle-aged women a central topic in popular television culture for the first time.

The third issue is related to the second one. The *Winter Sonata* phenomenon goes beyond just watching a TV drama. It created more social and cultural practices in its fans' everyday lives. As we will see, many fans have started to show a general interest in Korean culture, to organize fan meetings, to participate in *Winter Sonata* tours in Korea, and even start studying Korean language and culture. Some Japanese fans even suggested *"Winter Sonata* has changed my life!" It may sound exaggerated, but when one interviews the fans, one finds them to genuinely believe so. This broad influence on their life is a characteristic feature of the impact of this drama. This is hardly surprising. Studies of TV drama fan culture in the US and the UK consistently suggest that fans are neither merely passive nor poor audiences who are manipulated by the media industry, but complex agents who actively decode and re-interpret media products and eventually create their own culture by themselves.[8]

In the mainstream media, the middle-age women *Winter Sonata* fans are often seen as passive, manipulated and poor 'consumers'. This pejorative perception is often uncritically reproduced both in academia and in the circle of critical leftist intellectuals. I would suggest that, on the contrary, once their activities are examined in detail, a lot of complicated and interesting cultural, social and even political possibilities can be discerned. *Winter Sonata* has given me a good opportunity to discover the importance of middle-aged women as active cultural agents. My research interest is fandom of active audiences and the cultural and political potential within it.

How Do Audiences Watch *Winter Sonata*?

To examine how audiences watch *Winter Sonata*, I should reiterate that due to the limited number of fans interviewed, I do not intend to generalize the activities of all fans. It has to be emphasized that ways of watching differ between interviewees of different genders, ethnicities, ages and cultural backgrounds. For instance, as I interviewed those who thought of themselves as *Winter Sonata* 'maniac' fans, I found considerable differences in the extent to which they are 'fans' in the fandom. The relationships between Bae Yong Jun, *Winter Sonata*, and Korean culture are complicated in various ways. Some are very crazy about Bae Yong Jun, some love only Lee Min Hyung (a character played by Bae in *Winter Sonata*) but do not like Bae very much, others only like *Winter Sonata*. Generally speaking, younger fans in their twenties were more interested in Korean culture than *Winter Sonata,* while older fans favored exclusively *Winter Sonata*. As above, I must emphasize again that we should not over-generalize their tendencies.

I would like to point to three characteristic features that I have found through my interviews: repetitive ways of watching, the intertextuality of *Winter Sonata,* and active fans as performers. I would also like to highlight the complicated relationship between the experience of *Winter Sonata* and postcolonial memories expressed in the interviews.

Repetitive Watching

It is surprising that most interviewees repeatedly watch *Winter Sonata* either by recording it on video or by buying DVD sets. Some of them have watched it more than ten times, while the others did so at least a couple of times. As the series consists of twenty 60-minute episodes, it takes twenty hours to watch the whole story. There were two interviewees who did not remember how many times they had watched it because they are continually watching it in an almost addictive way.

Ms A (60+) had watched the drama twelve times. She began to watch it when she was asked to record it for her friend. She did not know what it was like, but once she watched it, she quickly got 'crazy' about it. She started to make her own recordings and watched them almost everyday. She watched *Winter Sonata* from the beginning to the end and then from the beginning again. When I asked if she watched other dramas or programs, she answered that she wanted to watch *Winter Sonata* again and again, rather than to watch a different one. Ms A is not an exception. I guess that those who did not remember how many times they had watched it might have watched it more than ten times.

Not only housewives, full-time workers also watch it repetitively. Ms C (40+) watched the series at the end of 2003 and then bought the DVD set. She did not know how often she watched it but do so regularly after she came home from work. It is interesting that she would play the DVD even when the drama was broadcast on NHK, because she did not like the dubbed version on the NHK broadcast. However, after enjoying the subtitled DVD version, she would switch to NHK in time to watch the TV broadcast of the original program — she could not ignore it even if she did not like the dubbed voices.

Winter Sonata may be seen as having the same form and style as other melodramas, but people's way of watching it is quite different. Ordinary dramas are consumed only once or twice at most while repetitive watching was a characteristic feature of *Winter Sonata*. Similar patterns of repetitive watching can possibly be found among animation or cult sci-fi fans, known as *otaku*, a Japanese term which means a nerdy maniac who is crazy about comics, animation, video games and computer media entertainment. While most audiences of animation or sci-fi programs are young or recently young males, most of *Winter Sonata*'s audiences are female and middle-aged. One may say that *Winter Sonata*'s audiences were the first middle-aged female group who had practiced an *otaku*-styled way of watching it.

In fact, most of them said that it was the first time that they had watched a TV program in such a repetitive and even addictive way. But there were three interviewees who said that they had done this once before, when they were in their twenties. These three were fanatical supporters of the Japanese idol group SMAP. It should also be pointed out that most of *Winter Sonata* fans used be big fans of other entertainers, like Elvis Presley, James Dean, or Queen. It would therefore be wrong to assume that they had been culturally poor before the *Winter Sonata* phenomenon. On the contrary, the different cultural practices had given way to an *otaku* style of watching, after 'discovering' *Winter Sonata*. As we will see, the practice of watching *Winter Sonata* is not a passive exercise but a very active one.

As part of their active consumption practices, most interviewees, particularly the younger ones, use media technology adeptly to gather information. For example, a university student, Ms G, watched Korean dramas by internet-streaming services of Korean TV stations such as KNS, MBC and SBS. Because her Korean was not good enough, as she had only just started to learn the language, she downloaded Korean drama scenarios and translated them into Japanese by using an OCN translation service on the Internet. Likewise, most interviewees often use the Internet in different ways to get information on Korean dramas because information was limited in the mainstream media. Apart from the Internet, four out of twenty interviewees purchased a region-free DVD player to watch Korean dramas because Japanese players do not play Korean DVDs, though a region-free DVD player is very difficult to find. This use of new technology is also a good example of the similarity between these middle-aged women's way of enjoying the drama and *otaku* culture.

Intertextuality of Winter Sonata

The obvious question is, why do fans repeatedly watch *Winter Sonata*? Significantly, some fans did not like the drama at the beginning. Two interviewees said that they gave up watching during the first episode. Ms D (40+) watched the first couple of episodes but gave up following the series because she found it somehow 'vague', and not well-made. She started watching it again after one of her friends, returning from China, told her that the drama was popular in Shanghai. Ms C could not watch through the first episode in April 2003, because she found it strange that actors and actresses spoke Korean even though they appeared very Japanese, and because she thought that the filming technology was not good enough. By the end of the year, she started to watch it and was gradually carried away by it. The same is true in the 'Bae Yong Jun syndrome'. For instance, Ms E (30+) did not think that Bae was attractive at first sight. She thought that he was chubby and not her type. But as she got into the drama, she slowly came to like Bae.

These examples show the process through which the audiences are gradually attracted to *Winter Sonata*. Most interviewees suggested they constantly discovered something new while watching it. Ms. A pointed out that the most attractive point was that *Winter Sonata* made her understand the cultural background to the drama, sometimes by reading mail fanzines circulated through the Internet. Apparently, 'discoveries' were made not only by watching the drama, but also by reading magazines, by surfing websites, and by discussing in meetings. Many agreed with Ms A, and said that they were learning about Korean culture while enjoying the drama. Ms. F (40+) found it intriguing to see cultural differences in the way of having dinner, or even sitting together. Ms. C was interested in the changing way of calling characters' names according to the degree of intimacy. These nuanced changes in address were not translated into Japanese because Japanese has only a couple of words *san, chan* and *kun* as a title. She said that she discovered the nuances as she watched a subtitled version and could hear the Korean. During group interviews, once someone started to talk about their discoveries, others responded with their own, and eventually the overall discussion continued with enthusiasm, sometimes for more than an hour. The space for interview was often so transformed into an opportunity for the women to exchange information.

How can we understand this particular way of watching the drama? A Japanese cultural critic, Otsuka Eiji, suggested that in the late 1980s, children who were eagerly collecting hundreds of stickers from the packets of *Bikkuriman* chocolate wafers (a huge phenomenon in Japan then), were not only consuming the fragmented stickers, but also creating, editing and then consuming a 'big narrative', what *otaku* called *sekaikan* (world view) through the practice of collecting.[9] I would argue that fans of *Winter Sonata* also actively produce their own narratives even if at a first glance they were seen to be passively consuming the drama. They associated the story of *Winter Sonata* with other Korean stories, culture, history and even their personal experiences and memories by reading and watching other media. Their narratives were very much varied. The narrative's productivity and re-productivity was a key for understanding the repetitive practices of watching and thus the distinctive success of *Winter Sonata*. It added addictive attraction to the drama. What Otsuka called *sekaikan* may be seen as ways of understanding Korean culture and history, but they are, however, never singular but plural because they are being produced through the practices of different audiences.

Fans as Performers, Not as Consumers

The Japanese mainstream media depicts the stereotype of a *Winter Sonata* fan as a rich, middle-aged (fifty-something) housewife who obsessively and even shamelessly loves Bae Yong Jun, goes wherever *Yon-sama* appears, and buys anything related to *Winter Sonata*. My question is how the fans themselves see this often over-exaggerated and pejorative stereotypical media image of the fans of *Winter Sonata*?

In contrast to the media representation, I found almost all the fans whom I interviewed to be, in fact, very frugal. Certainly most had *Winter Sonata* DVDs but only full-time workers bought the DVDs themselves, while housewives and part-time workers had them only because their husbands or relatives bought it for them. This was also the case with the *Winter Sonata* tour in Korea. Virtually all who went on the tour were full-time workers. Some of them traveled with their daughters as part of a family outing. It was clear that they spent money only with agreement from their families, in particular their husbands. Even full-time workers just spent reasonable amounts of money, compared to the expenses of men on alcohol, cars, and golf.

Some, particularly young interviewees, disliked the stereotyping. For instance, Ms G, who likes Korean dramas in general rather than just *Winter Sonata*, said "Well, they [the middle-age fans] are not in our generation. I am impressed by how much they spend on *Winter Sonata*, but I am totally different from them. I do not want to be seen in the same way as they are". Ms H (40+) told me, "I do not understand why they put Bae's poster on the wall. I have never done it." However, it should also be noted that more than half of the interviewees had more sympathy with stereotypical fans than was originally expected. For example, Ms E and Ms K (20+), whom I interviewed together, said that they would call the fans in the media their 'sisters'! In fact, Ms E, who was fortunate to get a press pass as she works in the film industry, went to Tokyo to attend a press meeting with Bae Yong Jun. Another said, "We do not do what the maniac fans are doing in the media, but we do understand why they do it". However, their sympathy did not mean that they totally identify with the way fans were represented in the media. Even Ms E told me that she was scared of her 'sisters' when too many 'sisters' turned up as a mob, and that they seemed to believe that all women should love Bae Yong Jun. How should we understand this complicated relationship between fandom and the representation of fandom in the media?

Ms D's self-analysis may be suggestive. She said that fans loved not only *Winter Sonata*, but also themselves as they uncritically love *Winter Sonata*. According to her, fans loved themselves because they were like someone who can be 'crazy' with a pure, romantic love story even when they are middle-aged. She said that fans want to be on the news; they are happy to hear, for instance, their husband sighing 'my wife is crazy about *Winter Sonata*' or their daughter complaining 'my mum loves Bae Yong Jun too much'. In the same vein, Ms C said that she enjoyed it when she asked herself what a seemingly stupid thing she was doing in her midlife. This complicated sentiment was also seen in group interviews when they talked both proudly and bashfully about what kind of 'stupid' things they were doing, for example, letting others listen to *Winter Sonata*'s theme music set as their mobile telephone ringtone. This combination of 'pride' and 'bashfulness' was one of the characteristic features shared among the fans. When I asked Ms D if it meant that the fans were manipulated by the media, she replied, "No, no, we believe that it is 'we' who manipulate the media!" In fact they were 'performing' as fans, as if they were actresses. Pretended 'stupidity' was a performance, a game.

It should be added that Ms D's reply contained an intellectual sense of humor. It should also be noted that most fans believe that the *Winter Sonata* phenomenon was created by the fans, not by the media. As we have seen, the fans gather and exchange information through independent media, especially the Internet. They are critical of the mainstream media as they think that the latter only report what the fans already know. This imbalance between what the media see in the fandom and what the fans see in the media is characteristically interesting in the phenomenon. I would argue that we should see the fans as performers, not merely as consumers. While they are fans, they also perform as fans, acting as fans.

Winter Sonata *and memories of colonialism*

Finally, I would like to look at the way in which the image of Korea and Korean people in the fans' minds has changed through watching *Winter Sonata*. In the interviews, I found that the most common comment is that Korea had become closer to them. For example, for many, Korea was a 'close but far' *chikaku te toi* country, a conventional Japanese description of Korea. Although the phrase 'close but far' was repeatedly heard, there were very different nuances in the expression, when examined in detail.

For example, Ms I, a middle-aged woman in her fifties, said that she had not learned anything about Korea before. She reluctantly said that women in her generation knew only a few things about the Korean War and about the 38th Parallel North,[10] because school did not teach anything about contemporary Korea. As she had not been interested in any other aspects of Korean culture, such as football in the FIFA world cup, watching *Winter Sonata* was truly her first contact with Korea. Ms L (50+), a big fan of Bae Yong Jun who both proudly and bashfully showed me her *Winter Sonata* mobile phone strap, told me that she knew almost nothing about Korea. She had believed that all Korean women still wear Korean traditional dress even today, until she watched *Winter Sonata*. What surprised her most was that Koreans live their lives in the same way as the Japanese do. She said that she was also impressed by the development of technology, such as mobile phones. By and large, middle-aged women in their fifties have a sense that they have not learned about Korea in the existing education system. They also feel that their access to Korean cultural has been very limited.

In contrast, interviewees in their thirties and forties already knew about Korea to some extent, while they also think *Winter Sonata* had dramatically changed their image of Korea. Ms M (30+) had Korean resident friends in Japan, *zainichi*, when she was a child. She traveled to Korea with her professor when she was a university student. What she felt in that trip was that Koreans were 'rough', and their fashions were ten years older than the Japanese. She also had good relationships with Korean friends when she studied in Mexico. Now she realized that she likes Korea and its culture, in particular the fashionable style of the characters in *Winter Sonata*. Ms H (40+) thought that she knew Korea, as she had been taking care of Korean students in a Japanese university as part of her work. They were always polite and kind, as were the characters in *Winter Sonata*. However, the drama had changed her impression of Korea, too. She certainly recognized through the drama that the Koreans live their lives in completely the same way as the Japanese do. Until the drama, she thought Korea remained behind Japan. She had started to study the Korean language to know more about Korea.

It is difficult to summarize how the fans thought and think about Korea before and after the drama as I had the impression that they found it difficult to talk about how they felt about Korea before *Winter Sonata*. This might be because of the lack of language of how to speak about Korea in Japan. Generally there have been two 'official' ways of speaking. The first is a comparatively liberal one which says that Japanese need to understand colonial history properly, to apologize sincerely for Japan's past and to establish a new relationship with Korea. This is an official postwar discourse shared by liberal and even leftists, often in education institutions. I believe that though most of us academics share this perception, it sometimes sounds too moralistic and even authoritarian. The other is an exclusively patriotic, nationalist discourse often expressed as *honne*, a hidden but real consciousness. It justifies Japan's colonial past and never shows any regret or apology. This discourse has been more or less repressed in public, therefore ironically it sometimes sounds 'radical', so it attracts followers, particularly young people. Increasingly, these nationalist sentiments are seeping into even more casual conversations and articulations.

I would argue that the fans did not like to speak about their perceptions of Korea before they watched *Winter Sonata*, because they thought that these two discourses were not only too official and too authoritarian, but too superficial, merely produced from a male governmental perspective. To express their own ideas from their heart, they could not choose either of the two official discourses. *Winter Sonata* is important because it has provided for them a set of new, personalized and realistic vocabulary. I would like to introduce two examples.

Ms A (60+) said to me in the interview:

> As I grew up in Omura city, where a camp for illegal migrants was located, I had a certain image of Koreans. They often had quarrelling with each other. They were always loud. Honestly, I looked down on them. But *Yon-sama* changed everything. I have learned about Korea through *Winter Sonata* and now understand that a large part of Japanese culture came from Korea. This reminded me that I was born in Manchuria [during Japanese colonial time] where my father worked.

It is interesting to see how she associated *Winter Sonata* with her own personal experience during the war. She had her own stereotypical image of Koreans, based on her childhood experiences in Japan. Through watching the drama, she re-organized and re-constructed her personal history including her colonial experience.

Ms C (40+), who participated in the *Winter Sonata* tour in Korea, said to me:

> Korea was very far from me. I thought that they just copied us. I was only thinking what we could give to them, but I thought there was nothing I could receive from them. After watching *Winter Sonata*, Korea got closer, but a strong gap still exists: it is in our history. We can easily say that we love *Yon-sama*, we love Korea, but they cannot. I have Korean Japanese friends and Korean American ones, but not real Korean friends. I was confused when I saw, during my tour, what the Japanese military authority did in Korea. But now I believe that women like me can be a good breakthrough, by loving Korean dramas and actors, even if Korean people may be surprised at us.

Ms C, unlike Ms A, does not have any memory concerning the war as she was too young to experience it. Being a big fan of American culture before *Winter Sonata*, she was not interested in Asian culture at all. But as she was disappointed with the US, in particular after the Iraq War of 2005, she turned her eyes to Asia. During her tour, she found a history of more hardship than friendship between Japanese and Koreans. This made her reconsider how she should understand history, and eventually led her to believe that her fandom is necessary to overcome it.

I found it very intriguing to see the way in which these women spoke about Korea in their personalized vocabularies. They were persuasive, although different from the two official discourses, liberal or nationalist. The emergent vocabulary provided by the *Winter Sonata* phenomenon opens up the political potential of re-constructing and understanding an old and new Korea-Japan relationship in different ways.

Conclusion

It is still too early to evaluate what the *Winter Sonata* phenomenon and the Korean Wave means. It is difficult to judge whether *Winter Sonata* will produce better political relations between Korea and Japan. However, it is clear that a significant number of middle-aged women, who have often been marginalized and even looked down upon as merely media consumers, have started a variety of interesting cultural practices after the phenomenon.

I would like to end the chapter with an experience that I had during my research. After the publication of the book, *Nisshiki Hanryu* (Japanese-Style Korean Wave), which I edited, I was sometimes asked to give talks at symposiums. In January 2005, I was invited to speak on the Korean Wave in Akita prefecture by a local civil organization. When I discussed the matter with them, I learned that the organization was a women's support group for female immigrants in Akita. I wondered why they wanted to know about the Korean Wave and *Winter Sonata?*

They answered that in Akita, there are many new brides from other Asian countries, in particular from China. These brides are one of the effects of globalization. The widening gap between metropolises and rural areas, north and south, and advanced countries and developing countries promotes the mobility and fluidity of labor forces at a global level. Even the family, which used to be regarded as a basic unit of community and as the foundation of a nation-state, is getting fragmented by the effects of globalization. National boundaries are gradually invading even into private spheres such as the family.

In Akita, an agricultural prefecture, as in all rural areas, finding Japanese brides is increasingly difficult because farming is hard work and men are getting old. As a result, some Japanese farmers chose to find brides from other Asian countries, especially from poor rural areas. These women came expecting a better life in Japan, but in reality they are often trouble, disillusioned with rural life and isolated from the local community due to language problems and cultural gaps. *Winter Sonata* and other Korean dramas are one entertainment which they can enjoy at home. The women's organization in question supports language education for 'Asian brides' and finds Korean dramas a good communication tool, because some of them have both Japanese and Chinese subtitles. This is why they invited me as part of the educational program.

It is interesting that Japanese and Chinese housewives share an experience of watching the same program and utilize it to establish new relationships among themselves. It can be said that the local organization, most of whose members are housewives, is intervening in their everyday practices of culture. Watching Korean dramas at home is not political in a traditional sense. It may be a small but definitely an important step which we should continue to be concerned about. How can we perform new transnational identities, through enjoying transnational cultural production and consumption?

Today, neo-liberal and post-Fordist modes of production in the late capitalist society are now trying to incorporate all people, including women workers, housewives, students and even children, as flexible and mobile labor force, within the globalizing market. In order to respond to this shift, an urgent task is to find different ways of understanding politics and of organizing people. Popular culture may not be an answer, but it helps us to rethink a new way of understanding politics for those who have been historically marginalized in politics. Considering the *Winter Sonata* phenomenon definitely enables us to examine the transnational potential of middle-aged women's politics in the age of globalization.

7

Touring 'Dramatic Korea': Japanese Women as Viewers of *Hanryu* Dramas and Tourists on *Hanryu* Tours

Yukie Hirata[1]

Korean pop culture has been spreading since the end of the 1990s, and the big boom of the Korean drama, *Winter Sonata*, brought a cultural and social phenomenon called the Korean Wave, or *Hanryu*, to Japan in 2004.[2] As of 2005, Korean pop culture seems to have definitely taken root in Japan, and it is diversifying and changing. Examination of the Korean Wave indicates that media goods as well as people are moving across borders. The number of Japanese who traveled to Korea in 2004 recorded a growth of 35.5 percent compared to the previous year; people who are traveling to Korea, or "moving people," are in the spotlight along with media products. The number of Japanese tourists who travel to the shooting locations of *Winter Sonata* have rapidly increased, particularly since the end of 2003, and most are women. Transnational drama consumption is causing women to move transnationally to visit these locations. Such transnational cultural traffic indicates changes in gender dynamics and inter-Asian cultural flows, relative to the imbalanced flows of mainly male travelers from Japan to the rest of Asia just a few years ago. It is emblematic of cultural traffic in Asia that is becoming more complex and diverse.

This chapter examines the effects of the Korean Wave, particularly in the field of tourism. First, it discusses gender politics and the postcolonial situation of Korea as a historical tourist destination for the Japanese. Second, it deals with the question of why women in particular are now traveling to Korea, facilitating and intensifying the Korean Wave. Thirdly, the change in Japanese tourists' view of Korea following the change in gender dynamics and the boom in Korean popular culture since the 1990s will be discussed. The research is based on fieldwork and interviews[3] with Japanese women who visited or planed to visit Chunchon, Seoul, Nami Island and Yonpyon, which were shooting locations for *Winter Sonata*. Moreover, this chapter focuses on the transnational consumption of dramas by Japanese women and what occurs in the process of a viewer turning into a tourist. Finally, this work discusses conditions concerning *Hanryu* tourism and its place in the history of Korean tourism from the perspective of gender.

Nostalgia, Gender and Tourist Gaze

Saying tourism is the satisfaction of curiosity without considering socio-historical context risks guest-centered or tourist-centered thinking. When sociologists like Rojek (1985) and Wang (2000) argue generically for "the satisfaction of curiosity" in tourism or leisure theory, they do not take into account the tourist's socio-economic status, such as ethnicity, class, or gender. In postcolonial situations, such as between Japan and Korea, subjects who are moving are often romanticized as steeped in "imperialist nostalgia" (Rosald 1989). In addition, such moving subjects were mostly men or masculinized, intentionally or otherwise. Women travelers were long ignored or their travels equated with consumption. However, many works by feminist scholars argue that women's travels and their gaze, including their contact with others, differ from those of men because of women's position in a male-dominated patriarchal society (Kim 2003; Ghose 1998). The 'tourist gaze' is thus closely related to the subject's identity and position in time and space, including gender.

However, the tourist's gaze includes complex contradictions that cannot be simplistically grasped as a dichotomy, i.e. by whether the gaze is male or female. For instance, Laura Mulvey (1975) discussed the relationship between gaze and media using psychoanalysis as a political weapon in her classic study titled "Visual Pleasure and Narrative Cinema", exposing the gaze in Hollywood movies as the male gaze. Her argument was criticized because it denied the subjectivity of women viewers and ignored their complex positions. Subsequently, Mulvey modified her argument, taking into consideration the possibility of an active female gaze. Bobo (1988) studied black female groups as viewers of *The Color Purple* and revealed how they were empowered through the text and in turn restructured the text. Mulvey's modification and Bobo's argument show that the subjectivity of media viewers is not just structured psychoanalytically but that there are moments in which it is actively constructed through various readings. Such feminist arguments have been raised in the field of media studies. What about in the field of tourism sociology?

In John Urry's (1990) *Tourist Gaze*, an important text in tourism study, who specifically is gazing and his/her relationship with what is glimpsed were not discussed in detail. The identity of the one who is gazing was not problematized or, one might say, was unconsciously assumed as male. Indeed, in both existing literature and in itineraries, subjects who were moving had been presumed to be male, white, and heterosexual; static women emphasized against dynamic men (Leed 1991). In contrast, Ghose's (1998) study of the gaze of English women who traveled to India in the 19th century find that their 'gaze' was very complex, ambivalent and fraught with contradictions, rather than a specific female gaze. She further argues that the 'gaze' of English women in India at the time was no different from that of men. Such arguments provide many useful suggestions when discussing the Japanese history of Korean tourism. In the historical context of Korea and Japan, what does 'tourism' to Korea by Japanese tourists mean and what kind of social impacts (including conflicts and frictions) does it cause? Moreover, what kinds of gazes do Japanese women construct?

Why Do Japanese Women Travel to Korea?

Winter Sonata, a Korean romance melodrama, starring Bae Yung Jun and Choi Ji Woo, was aired in Korea in 2002. In Japan, it was aired four times from 2003 to 2004. It dramatically changed the image of Korea in Japan. Viewers started to travel to the locations in Korea where the drama was shot. Most were women. Japanese women audience came into the media spotlight because of all the related activities that resulted from watching the drama.

Until 2003, Korea had been 'male space' for Japanese tourists. The first Japanese package tour took place in 1906. It was a colonial tour that belied the story of Japan territorial expansion in Manchuria and the Korean peninsula. One of the purposes of this imperialistic tour was to observe how Japanese superiority and empire would reveal themselves as the best of Asia. Therefore, the participants of the tour most likely tried to be rulers rather than tourists (Ariyama 2002). An 'imperial gaze' remained in Japan after the 1945 defeat in the Second World War. Within a gender dynamic, it emerged in the form of sex tourism by Japanese men, throughout Asia. *Kisaeng*[4] tours of Korea were very popular among Japanese male tourists in the 1970s to 1980s. Kisaeng tours were characterized by an "international division of labour" (Mies 1986) that regards Japanese women as consumers or as a means of reproduction, and Korean women as commodities or workers. This was a period that displayed gendered imperialistic desires.

To the Japanese, Korea at the time was, according to Natsuo Sekikawa, "not a foreign country. That doesn't mean Korea was our colony. Korea was just … an ambiguous place that is colored brown or khaki. It had no specific form. No one could envision the specific demeanor of Koreans. Although they are sensitive to the name Dae-Jun Kim, they have no idea about typical Koreans. Korea was a place where baser men went secretly in groups" (Sekikawa 1987, quoted in Chong 1995). So Korea was a men's space haunted by guilt. Most Japanese women maintained an indifferent attitude towards this situation. However, they were not spared from such social and historical contexts. For example, one interviewee (40s) mentioned this image of Korea before seeing *Winter Sonata*:

> My husband went to Korea numerous times on company trips and had Kisaeng parties. Because of that, my image of Korea was really negative. I knew nothing about Korea, but I didn't have a positive image.

In this historical context, Korea was perceived negatively, particularly by Japanese women who now are in their 40s. Their experiences were very different from women in their 20s and 30s who, comparatively free from such historical context, gradually made inroads to Korean tourist destinations, encountered Korean pop culture, and came to know Koreans while studying abroad in the 1990s. An interviewee (30s), who consumed Korean pop culture since her college days in the beginning of the 1990s, vividly expresses this point:

> People who are shocked by *Winter Sonata* now have previously had no interest in Korea or Asia at all. So I can understand that most of them are our mothers. They are greatly touched by the drama because they have different feelings [about Korea] than our generation. I remember being surprised like them when I was attracted to Korean pop culture. … So I don't feel that *Winter Sonata* is very special. I think that Korean pop culture has finally become popular [in Japan].

This statement is targeted at women of comparatively older age groups, implying that the latter having become viewers of *Winter Sonata*, it seems logical that they would become tourists to Korea, as past ignorance and prejudice toward Korea are changed into a kind of 'desire' by dramas like *Winter Sonata*. However, the generalization or dichotomy that young generations have consumed Korean pop cultures and older generations did not have the opportunity to do the same should not be taken categorically. For example, one interviewee in her 50s said:

> I didn't start liking Korea with *Winter Sonata* but had liked it before. It is so interesting for me to travel to Korea. I have been to Korea with my daughter three times. So I watch *Winter Sonata* as one part of Korean culture.

Feminization of Korean Tourism and the Image of 'Women's Consumption'

Indeed, after the 1945 defeat, Japanese women started to make actual inroads in tourism to Korea but only did so in earnest around 1988, during the Seoul Olympics, an event that drew tourists generally. The proportion of women, which had not exceeded 10% prior to 1988, increased to 22% of all Japanese tourists arrivals in Korea in 1989. The number of Japanese women tourists continued to increase gradually in the 1990s. There are several reasons for this increase. First, it was partly directly connected to changes in social moods, i.e. the regional economic boom in Asia of the 1990s, which in turn engendered a boom in tourism in Asia. Second, Japanese women had gained upward social mobility through greater employment participation and economic power. Third, the approval for Japanese tourists to enter Korea without a visa in 1994 spurred tourism.

That the main target of Korean tourism shifted from Japanese men to women cannot be overlooked. To prepare for the Olympics, the Korean government strived for greater urbanization and modernization. As part of this effort, the Korean government tried to sweep away the image of Kisaeng tours, the dark side of modernization. By that time, Japanese women were beginning to be noticeable in Korean tourism. Posters and guidebooks published by Korean National Tourism Organization (KNTO) often depicted Japanese women shopping and in beauty salons in Korea. These images of Japanese women contributed to the removal of the negative image of Korea associated with Kisaeng tours. However, such representations obscured the realities of Japanese women tourists, of their ambivalent and complex attitudes and positions, and also obscured their gaze that was in a sense newly formed.

In my research on Japanese women in their 20s and 30s who live in urban areas and who traveled to Korea from 1994 to 2002, most toured Korea as a way to further their interests in Korea and things Korean, including visiting Korean friends they met abroad (Hirata 2003). Seen in their 'gaze' are the state of everyday life and temporal coevalness in which they recognize Korea as a contemporary. Such a new 'gaze,' noticeable among women, overcame the male-dominated imperialistic historical context, reflected new tendencies created by global consumer culture in the 1990s.[5] This nascent trend of Japanese women traveling to Korea ballooned after the screening of *Winter Sonata* in 2003 and 2004.

The rise of Japanese women tourism was not only the result of the achievement of economic power or a sharp decrease in domestic work through mechanization. There were other reasons, including the difference and gendered inequalities between men and women in work and leisure. According to Baudrillard (1998), as leisure is constrained by time spent working, it is therefore not autonomous but defined by the absence of time spent working. A questionnaire survey in 2002, for instance, revealed that women could take more annual paid holidays than men because of men's higher position in the bureaucracy.[6] On the other hand, women who have economic power and are able to readily take holidays become a good target for tourism promotion; the lower social status of working women apparently motivates them to go abroad. The same can be said about women who have part-time jobs or who are full-time housewives. Significantly, Felski points out, the culture of consumerism, of which tourism is a part, "may undermine rather than simply consolidate certain forms of male authority." Women's desires and the culture of consumerism "reaches into and disrupts the sanctity of the private sphere, encouraging women to indulge in their own desires in defiance of their husbands and of traditional forms of moral and religious authority" (1995:74).

Touring the Shooting Locations for *Winter Sonata* and Japanese Women

Japanese Women 'Reading' Winter Sonata: *Fiction or Reality?*

This section looks at the reception of drama by Japanese women based on interviews. Almost all of the interviewees mentioned 'closeness' and 'diversity' as the attraction of the drama. Korean dramas, as Dong-Hoo Lee points out, were influenced by Japanese dramas, consciously or unconsciously; often with stories embodying global culture of consumerism.[7] But of course at the same time it includes a local Korean context. Then how do Japanese audiences interpret the 'closeness' and 'diversity' mentioned? In other words, how do audiences receive and gaze at media texts in a transnational context?

First, Japanese women audience acknowledges that cultural differences between themselves and Koreans are reflected in a perception and acceptance of a 'sense of oddness': "All of the characters are very kind to each other, and I was also touched after watching the drama. Japanese drama represents too much 'reality' but Korean drama is really beautiful" (interviewee in her 30s). Foreignness of the Koreans was preserved.

Older interviewees often mentioned 'family relationships' in the drama as an attraction of Korean drama, in contrast to Japanese dramas targeting younger generation. In fact, parents of the main characters play important roles in *Winter Sonata*.[8] A woman in her 50s who has two children said:

> I really envy the family relationships in *Winter Sonata* because children take care of their parents … I was in awe of the family relationships in Korean dramas. It's a really wonderful culture. Besides, there are no such dramas in Japan. I don't know if there were in the past.

'Family relationships' represented by the Korean drama were seen as those which had been lost in Japan. Seeing Korean as Japan's past evokes 'nostalgia' among the interviewees.[9] This reflects a level of cultural intimacy that Japanese women derived from transnational consumption of Korean dramatic texts; Korean 'other' is uncannily consumed as the 'same' as the Japanese us (Iwabuchi 2001).

Interviewees who are over 40 years old, who longed for and were nostalgic for what Japan had lost, also longed for the specific 'class' that Bae Yong Jun, the main male character in *Winter Sonata*, represents. These women audience see him both as a person as well as the role in the drama. A fan in her 30s visited Korea to meet her Korean friend and stayed at the Plaza Hotel, one of *Winter Sonata*'s shooting locations. She expresses her attraction to Bae:

> There is no man like him in Japan. Have you ever met a man like him? He is like a prince. But he might not be. We might be able to meet him somewhere. I feel very close to him.

The heterosexual attraction felt by the audience of the romantic story discloses simultaneously, a sense of intimacy and a sense of distance: "there is no one like him in Japan" yet "we might meet him somewhere [in Japan?]". Such ambiguous feelings toward the dramatic text lead the audience gaze beyond the drama to 'Korea'.

A woman in her 70s who had fled Korea in 1945 had intentionally kept her distance from Korea. She came to encounter Korean pop culture through *Winter Sonata*. Subsequently, she participated in small meetings once a month to study Korean culture, after being invited by a Korean woman living in Japan. In 2004, she visited Seoul and traveled to the place where she had lived in her childhood. Like this woman, many Japanese women noted that their prejudiced gaze towards Korea disappeared or softened once they encountered Korea's cultural context beyond dramatic texts. Before moving on to examine such travels to Korea, it should be noted that the younger audience do not necessarily share the same attractions to the centrality of family in Korean dramas. For a woman in her 20s:

> The family relationships are too deep. To be blunt, such relationships would be impossible in Japan. Of course I don't want to be in such a deep family relationship. But it's kind of attractive in that it is possible in Korea but not in Japan. Because it's a foreign drama, the deep relationships are good and the fact that they aren't possible [here] is a master stroke, eclipsing today's Japanese dramas, which have no sense of "ooh, what's going to happen", no surprise, and no depth.

This type of audience in their 20s felt that such intense family relationships were 'not possible' in Japan, and more significantly they do not want it anyway. They seemed to be attracted to Korean drama by the 'surprise' that such relationships appeared to be possible in Korea.

The Discovery and Reproduction of 'Images'

Reflecting the popularity of the drama, *Winter Sonata* tours were a great hit from the end of 2003 to 2005. KNTO organized a Hanryu marketing promoting team in 2003 and sought to profit by packaging and extending Hanryu from a media cultural phenomenon into the tourism, fashion, and shopping. The main targets were Japan and Chinese-speaking countries. In addition, there were women who traveled to the Hanryu locations by themselves. What do Japanese women gaze upon in their trips to Korea? And how are their gazes related to the shooting locations of Korean dramas?

> Are there such beautiful men and women in Korea? Are there such fashionable places in Korea? Are there such beautiful scenes in Korea? Before watching the drama and visiting Korea, my image of Korea was "anti-Japanese sentiment, inferior goods, poverty, and filth", but I didn't know anything about Korea.

This is from a woman in her 50s who started her own website after participating in a *Winter Sonata* tour from Japan. In the website, she listed information about *Winter Sonata* shooting locations, as well as information about Korean traditional culture and customs. Her comments were indicative of the sea change in attitude towards Korea among the Japanese middle-age women audience of the drama.

There were three ways to tour shooting locations, and the audience/tourist gaze can be influenced by the method the tourist selected. One was to travel by oneself without a tour guide and scheduled plans, which is for tourists mainly in their 20s and 30s. Another was to participate in local tours, which is for tourists in their 20s to 70s. There were many local tours to Chunchon and Yonpyong, the two primary shooting locations, organized by city tour companies in Seoul. And lastly are the full package tours like 'Loving *Winter Sonata* Tours' organized from Japan; this is mainly for tourists over 40. My analysis will focus on local tours and individual tours to one location, Chunchon. The town held the symbolic position as the very beginning of Hanryu and had come to be called the 'Mecca of Hanryu.' Its image has been reproduced repetitively on the Internet by tourists who wrote about their experiences and magazines and newspapers constantly link it with Korean TV drama.

Local tours to Chunchon from Seoul were the most popular tours because there were one-day trips. There were still many tourists doing the day-trip in October 2005, though the peak had passed. Local tours to Chunchon and Nami Island start from Plaza Hotel to Nami Island, where Yu Jin and Chung Sang, the female and male lead characters respectively in the drama, dated. It then moved to Chunchon: Chunchon Station, where lead characters met their friends in their high school days; Chunchon High School which they attended; Chunchon Myongdong Street where Yu Jin waited for Chung Sang; the edge of Gonji River where they met for the first time; Chung Sang's house; and Yu Jin's house. Regardless of the tourist's choice to travel individually or in a group, the route was the 'standard' tour, with little or no variation.

A woman traveling by herself before tours started in 2003 wrote her feelings of the trip:

> I went to the shooting locations in Chunchon and Seoul. I was very satisfied with my trip. My plan was just to travel to *Winter Sonata's* shooting locations and to feel the attractions of the drama. But I had the valuable experience of interacting with Koreans. I never felt 'anti-Japanese sentiment' from Koreans, but I met very kind ajossi and ajunma [Korean men and women], and also junior high school students who were interested in Japanese pop culture. I talked with a student on the train from Chunchon to Seoul. People I met were really attractive. (Yatabe 2003:154–155)

Another woman (40s) who had watched *Winter Sonata* and participated in a local tour to Chunchon in April 2004 said:

> I am crazy for Bae Yong Jun. I participated in the local tour with my family. A full-package *Winter Sonata* tour [from Japan] does not include the shooting locations of other dramas like 'Hotelier' that Bae Yong Jun acted in. So I chose the local tour [that included the latter locations]. I didn't know anything about Korea. Korean food is spicy. To know about a culture that I was unfamiliar with is interesting to me.
>
> I had visited Seoul before but I didn't know anything about Chunchon. If I hadn't watched *Winter Sonata* I would have never known about or visited rural cities in Korea. I really wanted to visit because the scenes were really impressive in the drama. I didn't know that there were such beautiful places in the country of Korea.

The first of these two women was a college graduate who had quit work after marrying and had one son. She started to learn how to use the Internet because of *Winter Sonata*. She also liked Shin Sunhoon (Korean famous singer) and went to his concert in October 2004, and since then she has become a fan of Korean pop music. The second woman, in her 30s, had visited Seoul before but did not feel drawn to it. However, she became interested in Korea again after watching *Winter Sonata*, and visited Korea with a friend.

Another fan in her 20s said:

> Korea has conscription, doesn't it? I think Korean men are attractive and have good bodies because of conscription. Bae Yong Jun is also good-looking and attractive. I have read that conscription is really long.

The woman's statement disclosed a mixed image of Korean men derived from the drama and the reality she saw while traveling. Indeed, all Korean men are conscripted into military service for 2 years. Her statement suggests that she sees reality through the drama, while showing no concern or even awareness of a divided Korea in a state of military standoff.

A woman who visited Chunchon in September 2005, which was relatively late in terms of the popularity of the tours, said:

> I visited Chunchon for the first time, and felt nostalgic in comparison to Seoul. I wanted to go Chunchon once because Chunchon is so popular in Japan. A few years ago, I heard that Koreans called themselves a developing country and had the impression that it was inferior to Japan. But now such an image has completely disappeared. I feel affinity for

Korea. I think this is because of *Winter Sonata* as well as what I can see in the faces of Koreans. I do not feel such affinity for England even though I lived in England for a year. (in her 30s, interviewed in 2005)

This woman who had visited Korea five times before had been interested in Korean pop culture since the mid-1990s. Her statement shows the changes in her attitude towards Korea and the changes in Korea.

Interviews in 2005 differed from those in 2004; those in 2005 used Korean words like 'ajunma' or 'momchan' naturally in their conversation. An interviewee in her 50s from a group of women studying the Korean language said:

Now time has passed *Winter Sonata* by, and Korean pop culture is becoming popular. In our group, E is still crazy for Bae Yong Jun, and we keep meeting with a Korean wife from the neighborhood to study Korean and Korean culture once a month. (interviewed in 2005)

This woman closed her website in the summer of 2005 but remains interested in Korea. I met her and her group in Seoul on March 2005; she was traveling on a local package tour so she could enjoy her free time even though she participated in a full package tour from Japan in 2004.

The changes in attitude and awareness of these women audience, of course, deserve analytic attention. The Japanese women audience-turned-tourists gaze upon Korea 'symbolically' while visiting the scenes they had seen on television. Such audiences do not remain within the framework of the drama; rather, the boundaries of the drama, everyday life, and tourism are blurred. Moving transnationally because of *Winter Sonata* had caused changes not only in their gaze of Korea but also in their everyday lives. This is apparent from their attitudes of comparing their everyday lives with Korean culture (i.e. family relationships), and their concerns about Korea beyond the drama. They had read the dramatic text differently from its original context and reconstruct its meaning. Also noteworthy is that the 'space' they use to exchange information about Korean culture and learning Korean is a 'women's space' resulting from *Winter Sonata* and tours to Korea. Such were the dynamic processes by which Japanese audiences/tourists localized *Winter Sonata*, and other Korean drama. There is a double process at work: If audiences of Korean drama discover and rethink 'Korea', then as tourists they rediscover Korea.

The famous Japanese director, Kitano Takeshi, whose remarks about Korea were sometimes discussed by Korean netizens, suggested that Japanese women who traveled to Korea had certain similarities to Japanese men who traveled there to hold Kisaeng parties in the 1970s and the 1980s.[10] His remarks showed a lack of consideration of the changed social and historical contexts of Korea and Japan, and the relations between the two nations. Moreover, unlike Japanese men's sex tours, the drama/tourism cultural phenomenon did not consist only of a heterosexual desire for pure love on behalf of women, even if it is part of Hanryu. Neither was the relationship between a specific drama actor and his fans, as many Japanese female audience/ tourists to Korea are not fans of particular Korean stars. Unlike the singular interest of Japanese male tourists, Japanese women who travel to shooting locations have a complex and varied gaze with respect to 'the drama' and 'other aspects' of Korea.

Incidents Surrounding Japanese Women as Viewers/Tourists

Tours to Korea were significant not only at the level of individuals but had also caused many social and political events, positive or negative, in which Japanese audience/tourists are sometimes unintentionally involved in postcolonial situations between Korea and Japan. There is no end to such cases; only one instance will be mentioned here.

In March 2005, the Council of Shimane Prefecture in Japan enacted a bill that designates 22 February as 'Takeshima Day'; this was a symbolic gesture to lay claims on a set of islets, the Tokto Islets in the East Sea, that are under the control of South Korea. The Prefecture's gesture raised anti-Japanese public opinion in Korea, leading the city of Chunchon, the 'Mecca of Hanryu,' to announce to its sister cities in Japan that formal exchanges were halted for an indefinite period. The staff of KNTO said with a distraught expression that "Japanese women who don't know Korea well have no choice but to ask 'why?' But Chunchon's response is necessary considering the historical facts about Korea and Japan." However, the city simultaneously announced that political and private exchanges should be kept separate and Japanese tourists are very welcome; furthermore, public opinion suggested that "Hanryu tourism should be continued" for economic reasons in Korea. In the following month, about 2000 Japanese tourists visited Chunchon as part of tours to shooting locations for a Bae Yong Jun movie called *April Snow*, and the city and Gangwon Province extended a warm welcome to them. In this instance, the transnational space of Korean television drama confronted and was able to transcend or subvert the continuing uneasiness in international relations between Japan and its ex-colony, Korea.

Conclusion

Urry (1990) argues that the tourist gaze is based on a system of social behaviors and social symbols and that it "naturally includes the fantasy and expectation of new experiences". However, fantasy and expectation of new experiences were not sufficient to explain the changes in the gaze of female Japanese tourists. Their tours of the shooting locations embraced a fiction concerning *Winter Sonata*, as they experienced directly the physical reality that is Korea. Given the history of colonization which had left a negative perception of Korea among the Japanese, the reality they see in Korea had severe consequences on the audience/tourist's everyday life and on their approach to political and cultural problems between Korea and Japan, which transcended the space of tourism.

In the history of Japanese tourism to Korea, tours to shooting locations in *Winter Sonata* meant the diversification of Japanese tourists to Korea, following the feminization of tourism in the 1990s. The gaze of the Japanese women tourists can be characterized by as a process of encounter which included criticisms of Japanese attitudes of discrimination, prejudice, and ignorance with regard to Korea. In this sense, it included an approach to a shadow of Japanese modernity, regardless of whether it consciously included a large measure of colonial discourse. In a broader sense, it created a chance to reconsider the relationships between tourism and gender in a postcolonial situation.

8

Popular Cultural Capital and Cultural Identity:
Young Korean Women's Cultural Appropriation of Japanese TV Dramas

Dong-Hoo Lee

Introduction

In 2004, the Korean government finally wrapped up the program that it had begun in 1998 of unlocking its doors to Japanese popular culture. It removed restrictions on Japanese movies and songs that had been previously banned to those under the age of 17, especially Japanese TV dramas that can now be accessed via cable or satellite TV channels. It took six years for the Korean government to completely generate its policy of openness towards Japanese popular culture, reversing a decades-old ban that had been in place since its liberation from Japanese colonial rule in 1945.

Although the inflow of Japanese popular culture had been officially restricted until 2004, it had been informally imported into Korea. While Japan's popular culture has profoundly affected the narrative forms of Korean television via informal routes of copying (Lee, 2004), there have been informal circulations of Japanese popular cultural products in Korea, which have generated spontaneous acts of fandom. In particular, since the spread of computer- mediated communication in the late 1990s, many young Koreans have shared their information and experience about Japanese popular culture, and have actively formed numerous fan communities.

With widespread information communication technologies (ICTs), the consumption of Japanese popular culture has transformed from a small number of private acts to a larger number of leisure activities. For instance, in 2004, at Daum, the largest Internet portal site in Korea, there were 549 Internet communities related to Japanese TV dramas. The largest community, called "Ilbon TV," had 820,000 members (*Hankyoreh*, 29 June 2004). Japanese TV fans can share information about and instantaneously consume recent Japanese dramas, and dramas aired on cable TV channels. They have constructed a consumption space where they can interpret and appropriate foreign cultural products regardless of the marketing purposes or intentions of their producers and distributors. Meanwhile, they have witnessed that with the wave of enthusiasm for Korean pop culture that started in 2003 in Japan, popular cultural flow between the two countries is no longer one-way, and that Korean pop cultural products are transnationally circulating in Asia.

In order to understand the ongoing multi-layered, complicated sites of production, circulation and consumption of popular culture in Asia, it is necessary to examine a local site of transnational cultural consumption. This research attempts to ethnographically study the transnational TV consumption articulated in young Korean women's everyday lives. Specifically, it intends to understand how they have viewed and related Japanese TV dramas to their daily lives and what kinds of popular cultural capital have been created by these enthusiasts' appropriation of the cultural codes found in Japanese TV dramas. While Bourdieu's (1977) notion of cultural capital suggests that the financial and cultural economies have a similarly top-down operation, Fiske (1992) argues that the cultural economy and the financial economy do not work in the same way, saying, "popular cultural capital can maintain its relative autonomy because the financial economy can exercise control over only a fraction of it." Further, Fiske suggests that the audience can reinterpret cultural products in terms of the needs and desires in their own lives. With easy access to Japanese TV dramas via the Internet, one can accumulate popular cultural capital beyond the control of formal production or distribution agencies and utilize them for his/her own pleasure. Thus, this research tries to look at how young Korean female fans have accumulated popular cultural capital via viewing practices and what it has meant to them.

Rather than generally mapping out Korea's consumption of Japanese TV dramas or investigating the reception of a specific type of Japanese TV drama, this research makes an attempt to examine in both an experiential and microscopic dimension how young Korean female fans between their late teens to early thirties, whose social conditions have been changed but still constrained by conventional gender systems, have received and appropriated Japanese TV dramas in their daily experiences. By examining their consumption of Japanese TV drama, this study will discuss not only the ways in which young Korean female fans have created or experienced transnational consumption space, in which they have negotiated their cultural or gender identities in an age of globalization, but also the degree to which their reception experiences have been hybridized.

Transnational Media and Fandom

To study the viewing practices of young Korean female fans of Japanese TV dramas from an ethnographic perspective, this research has considered two bodies of scholarship. The first body of scholarship is global media studies, particularly those studies that have focused on the concurrent formations of various Asian media cultures. As globalization has proceeded, production has been decentralized and multi-centralized, and circulation has become more multi-directional; the global and the local are not opposite but inter-constituent (Robertson, 1995; Morley and Robins, 1995). In the age of 'glocalization,' transnational media productions and receptions in East Asia have challenged established research dichotomies in global media studies, namely, the Western dominance versus peripheral vision, and globalization versus regional diversity. East Asian cultural traffic cannot be fully explained by the notion of unilateral globalization, or by the concept of 'Third Way' globalization. Transnational popular cultural flows in East Asia have tended to elude the constraints of nation-state and the intentions of global media giants, and to form new intra-cultural traffics beyond national boundaries. Studies on intra-East Asian cultural traffic, especially studies on the consumption of Japanese popular culture in East Asia, have shown the ways in which East Asians have received, interpreted, and appropriated transnational popular culture, and have exemplified the dynamic relationship between global convergence and local specificity (Iwabuchi, 2001; Iwabuchi et al., 2004).

Studies on intra-East Asian cultural traffic have been led by those who have made an inquiry into the ways in which or the reasons why Japanese popular culture has been so popular in Asian countries since the 1990s. They have argued that the modernization of Asian countries, intra-Asian post-colonial power relationships and political economy, the emergence of a metropolitan consumer culture in Asia, and the construction of a local cultural identity, especially by young people, have been articulated in the popular receptions of Japanese popular culture (Chua, 2004; Iwabuchi, 2001; Iwabuchi et al., 2004; Kim, 2003; Leung, 2004; Yoon and Na, 2005; Thomas, 2002). They have shown how Asians, young people in particular, have appropriated Japanese popular culture and have felt a shared 'contemporaneity' through its consumption.

Intra-Asian cultural traffic has become more complicated with a surge in the popularity of Korean popular culture, which has made transnational cultural space in East Asia more hybridized. In addition, the widely-adopted new digital technologies such as VCD and high speed Internet have accelerated the flow of transnational popular culture, and at the same time, have empowered users by providing them with more efficient tools for consumption and appropriation (Hu, 2005). Recent developments of transnational media flows in East Asia and 'technoscapes,' have made us think about whether the transnational popularity of certain popular cultural products can be explained in an inclusive and essentialist way; whether transnational media consumption in East Asia would lead to an East Asian popular cultural bloc; and whether as a consequence of this intra-cultural traffic, the boundaries of a local culture sustained by a nation-state would be easily dismissed. To extract and assert certain elements of 'East Asianness' in transnational cultural flows, to celebrate the cultural power of transnational media consumers, or to disregard multi-layered contexts that situate a local reception of transnational popular culture would be problematic for understanding the concurrent processes of transnational media flows in East Asia and their cultural consequences. A study to conduct a close investigation of a local site where various media cultures have plurally (not evenly) coexisted and their consumptions have been hybridized is still needed.

The second body of research consists of subcultural studies that emphasize young media consumers' tactics, resistance, and pleasure in their media consumption. Young media consumers have been considered the spearheads of cultural globalization, those who most actively come into contact with cultural products without regard for the physical boundaries of nation-states. Recent 'post-subcultural studies' have outgrown the Birmingham School's resistance theory to concretely approach the interactions and receptions of pop cultures in terms of the formation of 'neo-tribalism' and the expressions of postmodern, alternative sensitivities (Muggleton and Weinzier, 2003). Fandom studies, as a part of sub-cultural studies, have taken notice of the productivity of fan cultures (Kim and Lee, 2003). Rather than limiting fan activities to textual interpretations, they have paid attention to fans' cultural practices that appropriate the original texts and produce second or third texts for their own pleasure, in addition to their making of an 'affection economy' by projecting and sharing their feelings, and their accumulation of cultural capital and knowledge.

In particular, studies on female fandom have looked not only at the ways in which women have consumed and appropriated popular media products but also at the ways in which the consumption of popular media products have constructed and reconstructed women's cultural identities, which are typically confined by the existing gender system (for example, Lin and Kwan, 2005). Female fans have often transformed the Internet into their playground where they share experiences, produce their own cultural texts out of the original text, and form a cultural power of their own (Bury, 2005; Mazzarella, 2005). By translating popular culture in their own terms, female fans have deterritorialized and reterritorialized a popular cultural media space, and at the same, have negotiated their cultural identities. They have shown that cultural practices and the affection economy, are not fully won over by mainstream media culture. And their subjectivities have become further diversified along with their class, age, locality, and sexuality.

Along that line of thought, this particular investigation tries to contextually examine the ways in which young Korean female fans of Japanese TV dramas have consumed or appropriated these dramas. It tries to look at the subcultural characteristics of their transnational media consumptions and cultural practices, and to study how they negotiate their cultural or gender identities along with these consumptions and cultural practices. Their diverse experiences reveal that there are multi-layered contexts which have situated their reception practices, and that intra-cultural traffic in East Asia has become far more complicated.

Ethnographic Approach to Japanese TV Drama Consumption

In order to investigate young Korean women's practices of viewing Japanese TV dramas in the context of the current intra-Asian cultural flows, this research has taken an ethnographic approach. From January 2005, the author has paid close attention to two Japanese TV drama online fan clubs, which have been operated by women; one of these clubs has about 70,000 subscribers and the other has about 10,000 subscribers. I had subscribed to and made participatory observations on their online fan activities, and has exchanged emails with their web mistresses who have become the informants for this research. Moreover, to have basic knowledge of Japanese TV dramas and better understand fans' cultural practices related to interpretation and appropriation, I had downloaded the dramas, via peer-to-peer services, and watched the Japanese TV dramas, sharing viewing experiences with the online fans.

Additionally, I had contacted two informants, an undergraduate student and a graduate student who have identified themselves as Japanese TV drama fans. With the help of these four informants, two web mistresses and two students, I recruited 20 Korean female fans by the snowballing sampling technique. These included three high school females in their teens, 10 females in their 20s, and seven females in their early and mid-30s, living in Seoul and neighboring cities. I conducted in-depth interviews with them individually or in groups from August through to October 2005 (see Appendix). While I was searching for female fans who could share their viewing experiences, their demographic backgrounds were not considerations, although with the exception of three high school teenagers and three undergraduate students, they all held bachelor's degree. They were employed, graduate students or searching for jobs, and were all single.

The interviewees have had different histories of viewing Japanese TV dramas; some had watched them since the 1990s, and others from the early 2000s. However, all of them had consumed Japanese TV dramas before they were officially shown on Korean cable or satellite TV channels. They told the author about their motives for viewing Japanese TV dramas, their favorite dramas, characters, and stars, their likes and dislikes about the dramas, the contexts and contents of their receptions, the significance of these viewing practices in their everyday lives, and their methods of appropriation. Rather than posing structured questions on their viewing practices or urging them to talk about their responses or interpretations of a specific drama, the author let individuals or groups talk freely or share their histories of viewing Japanese TV dramas (J-dramas) and their pleasures. All the interviews were transcribed for analysis.

Modes of Consumption

Interviewees made contact with Japanese TV dramas for the first time through various routes. Some became interested in J-dramas after they consumed other Japanese popular cultural products such as manga, animation, J-pop, or films. Sometimes their fondness for a specific star led them to J-drama consumption. As Kim (2003) argues, fans of Japanese popular culture have expanded their consumption practices by moving around the related cultural products; many J-drama fans discovered their interest in J-drama while consuming other Japanese popular cultural products. The highly intertextual nature of the Japanese media made these transfers easy. A cultural product often becomes a node linked to other products. The familiarity of other cultural products allows fans to view the drama intertextually and to have the pleasure of reading its subtext. With this ability for intertextual reading, they distinguished themselves from other general audiences.

We enjoyed a kind of story like *Manhattan Love Story*. Although we have fun watching such a story, people in general would be embarrassed. … While we can find all the Japanese codes in there, they would be very, very bored and wouldn't know when to laugh. Therefore, we cannot have conversation with them. We get to be talking only with people here (on the fan site). [MH, 26, editor of fan webzine]

While their peer group's shared culture often played a great role in introducing Japanese popular culture to the interviewees, the Internet provided an accessible consumption space that allowed fans of Japanese popular culture to extend their tastes for a specific product or genre to similar and related others. The consumption space of Japanese popular culture has been markedly expanded by the wide spread of high-speed Internet. ICTs have provided an environment where J-dramas can be actively circulated and consumed. A fan can easily find a drama that she wants to watch as well as other like-minded fans.

This media environment had made possible immediate and simultaneous consumptions with no delay from the original airing time, and at the time, had provided a vast archive of J-dramas. J-drama fans can search J-dramas synchronically and diachronically, and have the pleasure of selecting a drama according to one's own taste. Each interviewee created her own lineup of J-dramas as she pleased, and downloaded and watched her selections at convenient times. One's lineup would consist of recent dramas or would be a mosaic of the old and the new. Most of the interviewees had experiences with 'immersive' viewing, as they watched their own lineup of dramas within a short period of time. With 'immersive' viewing, they formed more emotional attachments to J-dramas.

When I had a flight to Japan on Thursday and returned on Friday, I was pleased that I could watch *Trainman* on air time. … Although by watching it on airtime I would differentiate myself from others [other Korean fans], I enjoy watching video files. While I cannot concentrate on the drama when I watch it on air, I can see all the details when I watch in computer file. (KJ, 27, flight attendant)

The interviewees have shown different usage patterns of ICTs for their J-drama consumption. Although all the interviewees identified themselves as J-drama fans and used the Internet for the pleasurable viewing of J-dramas, some were actively uploading, creating subtitles, providing related information, publishing webzines, and leading fan communities. Others were read-only fans, downloading and watching J-dramas, and (what the online community calls) "lurking" on bulletin boards. Those who worked as web mistresses and fan-site managers, played the role of cultural producers who create and maintain consumption spaces where fans can obtain and share various information about J-dramas, including knowledge about drama narratives, characters, stars, producers, writers, Korean subtitles, program scheduling and ratings in Japan, and other related subjects. They were willing to devote their time for fan communities without earning any financial and cultural rewards; they were just pleased with their role as benefactors. According to Fiske (1992), "fan cultural capital, like the official, lies in the appreciation and knowledge of texts, performers and events," and "the accumulation of knowledge is fundamental to the accumulation of popular cultural capital" (42). Those web mistresses and fan-site managers not only accumulated knowledge but also shared it with other fans to facilitate community interactions. They identified themselves as 'pyeoin' or manic fans, distinguished from 'otaku,' who, they said, didn't know how to share cultural capital but know how to accumulate it. To create texts such as subtitles and webzines, and to maintain communicable fan sites, they had to become technologists who have a good command of ICT languages, skills which are usually assumed to belong to the male domain.

On the other hand, those read-only fans cannot be necessarily assumed to be passive, inactive J-drama fans. Although they were lurking on J-drama fan sites, they actively shared their viewing experiences with their offline peer group, and made their media pilgrimage to drama sites and star concerts in Japan. One interviewee — JH, 33, graduate student (interviewees are denoted by their initials, age and occupation) — indicated that "to become a Japanese fan, one should have a financial ability," the spending power to go on media pilgrimages and buy related cultural products such as OST and concert tickets.

The transnational drama consumption has encouraged these women to move around transnationally. While high school and undergraduate interviewees hardly had a chance to make a media pilgrimage, and could only dream of one, others in their mid- to late 20s and their 30s had actually made trips to Japan to pursue their pleasure as fans, which in turn contributed to their accumulation of popular cultural capital in the fan economy. These media pilgrims extended their consumption of J-dramas to that of other related Japanese cultural products, as well as the drama's imaginary spaces, and have built their distinctive subjective positions as fans.

Pleasures and Flexible Subjectivities

Most of the interviewees took pleasure in J-dramas primarily because J-dramas provided diverse narratives different from Korean drama conventions. They were intrigued by imaginations and cultural resources that they had rarely seen in their local popular culture. Rather than foreignness and exoticness, or 'cultural proximity,' the narrative conventions of J-dramas are different from Korean dramas, and this is a main draw or attraction. These differences that they mentioned include diversity in generic forms and themes, drama quality, refined commercialism, a larger pool of actors and actresses, and so on. In particular, they indicated that J-dramas were relatively free from the conventional dichotomist gender imagery that they found often in Korean TV dramas. Their inclination towards J-dramas didn't come merely from the charms of J-dramas themselves. Their viewing practices were implicit acts of resistance against Korean drama conventions.

As they were intrigued by differences in generic forms and contents, they came to develop a flexible subjectivity. They sometimes identified with a character in the drama, and yet, at other times, they only celebrated, and did not necessarily identify with the character. And sometimes, they adopted a position outside the text, criticizing the drama's "exaggeration" and "extremity." At other times they maintained a position of a relatively detached onlooker and took a voyeuristic position over what the drama showed. Rather than criticizing expressions of sexuality or themes such as adultery, incest, sexual intercourse between teacher and student, which were suppressed in Korean TV dramas, they kept a certain distance from the text, and remained as onlookers.

For example, when they talked about *Witch's Conditions,* which described sexual intercourse between a teacher and a student, or *A Hundred Million Stars from Heaven,* which suggested incest between a brother and a sister, the interviewees merely confirmed cultural differences rather than rejected them or expressed displeasure. Most of the interviewees didn't resist themes that violated conventional sexual norms, and accepted them as cultural differences. And yet, a group of interviewees felt great displeasure when a Korean drama portrayed adultery between a heroine's husband and her friend. They couldn't accept it because it was Korean. A sense of cultural distance formed their double standards in tolerating J-dramas' unconventional settings.

According to Chua, the marker of the location of production in an imported program such as scenery and language "enables a Singaporean audience to maintain a stance of watching, in a voyeuristic manner, the lives of others elsewhere in East Asia," and to differentiate oneself from other East Asians "in spite of sharing a similar urban and familial disposition" (Chua, 2004, 213). However, for Korean J-drama fans, the markers that put them in the position of a relatively detached onlooker didn't seem to come from the exterior signs of scenery and language. Rather, generic specificities or unprecedented dramatic settings and social norms signified in the text enabled them to maintain a voyeuristic position. And these cultural codes were not perceived as utterly foreign and peculiar but as possible codes that Korea would adopt in the near future.

Viewing Practices and Gender Identity

Korean women still face disadvantages in social positioning and economic activities. Although Korean women's social and economic participation has increased, gender equality has not yet been achieved. While among the unmarried, women's economic participation rate is 53.3 % compared to men's 53.6%, among the married, women's economic participation rate drops to 48.7% compared to men's 84.3% (National Statistical Office, Economically Active Population Survey 1990–2004). Marriage and raising children, as well as social conditions adverse to women, have kept women out of the labor market. However, regardless of these disadvantageous social conditions, a growing number of single women tend to delay marriage in order to pursue their career goals: the median age of women's first marriage rose from 24.8 years in 1990 to 27.5 years in 2004 (Choi, 2005). These so-called 'contra-sexual' women, who value their self-realization and wage-earning capacity more than conventional gender roles, have become more visible. A recent survey has reported that 51.3% of surveyed single women in their 20s and 30s do not mind remaining unmarried, whilst 40.8% of them do not mind remaining childless (*Yonhap News*, 22 November 2005). In recent years, many young Korean women have revealed a collective desire to get away from fixed gender roles and to lead their own independent lives. This desire is reflected and projected in the interviewees' television viewing practices.

Interviewees in their 20 and 30s talked about their fascination with the portrayal of urban single professionals in J-dramas (Japanese TV dramas). They said that while Korean TV dramas (K-dramas) depicted the professional world as a mere backdrop, J-dramas illustrated it in a detailed and realistic way. In showing their liking for the generic diversity of J-dramas, they said that they had had enough, and thus had got tired of 'romantic stories only for romance' and typical gender relationships in Korean dramas. Along with their liking for generic diversity, they showed more interest in the depiction of both an individual's personal growth in the professional world and one's social and organizational life; they appreciated characters who were more than merely heroine and hero in a romantic relationship.

In addition, the dramatic reality delineated by J-dramas appealed to them more than that of K-dramas. They were critical of the depiction of class issues which are often used by Korean dramas to highlight an obstacle to the consummation of a hero and heroine's love and to maximize the dramatic effect. They were also critical of the depiction of gender identity. Although J-dramas portrayed both independent women with their own subordinates and subservient, feminine women, most interviewees recalled the roles of self-determining female characters. They also felt the relatively unrestricted sexual expressions in J-dramas truthfully reflected reality. Although the interviewees had different moral positions concerning these sexual expressions, they agreed on their probable occurrence in real life.

On the other hand, the interviewees were attracted by their favorite male stars' masculinities. While they thought Korean heroes were too perfect, and therefore too unrealistic for them to be approachable, Japanese male characters illustrated less typical and more diverse masculinities. They felt their images were more realistic and individualized, and different from traditional gender stereotypes, which they often found in Korea dramas. In her analysis of SMAP members' characters, Daring-Wolf (2004, 367) writes that the hybrid identities of male/female, macho/sensitive, and Asian/Western, and the characterizations were antithetic to the emotionless salaried man, "deconstruct(s) the essentializing notion of masculinity," and appeal to young people's "increasingly questioning traditional gender roles defined by a workforce relying on overworked male workers and full-time housewives." The interviewees perceived a more diverse and hybridized masculinity from the Japanese male characters with whom they could be emotionally and safely engaged. Their favorite male characters were sensitive, emotional, possessing a human frailty, and eccentric. As these interviewees were discovering or attempting to discover new types of masculinity, they took pleasure in consciously or unconsciously resisting conventional gender imagery.

> Compared to [masculine] Korean male characters, there have been two types of Japanese male characters; one is a neutral or feminized style, and the other is a typical salary-man. J-dramas have only shown these two types. However, Tomoya Nagase seemed to provide a new style. He is tough, funny, with personal charms, quiet, and so on. I have been very amused by such an odd style. I guess he has an attractive personality in reality. (KA, 34, journalist)

Viewing practices were more than just the pursuit of pleasure as fans. They were cultural lessons for young women to help overcome the pressures of an idealized romance or marriage to 'the boy next door' and to display their independent individuality. Since viewing practices as well as other fan activities were time-consuming activities, the interviewees had to devote a significant part of their lives to them. In particular, those who worked as web mistresses and managers spent most of their leisure time viewing dramas and contributing to the fan sites, sitting alone in front of PCs; physically, they simply didn't have time to date. These viewing practices allowed these single women to build their own fantasy world. Having such an obsession and living in these fantasy worlds, they constructed their own independent identities. Such obsessions often buffered social pressures on their single status, and were sometimes used strategically to escape from socially determined gender roles. And these female fans were happy to find they were not alone in their obsession.

The following excepts reveal what their viewing practices meant in real life terms:

BH   (26, designer/systems operator): My boss only talked to me about brand names, saying, "Buy some clothes for yourself." My schoolmates told me about their boyfriends. If they have had a taste in romance, I have had mine in this [J-drama]. ... I wanted to talk about my taste and yet, they only talked about their boyfriends or brand names.

MH   (26, webzine editor): And having a baby ...

BH: I couldn't talk. Last time when I bought a Japanese album at 50,000 Won, I heard, "Are you crazy?" ... They said, "Pull yourself together! At your age, you should save up money for your marriage."

JM   (29, office worker/operator of women's bulletin board): At this marriageable age, I don't get married, and I am staying at home and watching TV [J-dramas] all day long while others go out on dates. That's why my mom has told me to turn off my PC and to go out.

MH: I've heard that nagging from my younger brother! He said, "How old are you, Sister?" If I bought a magazine, he would say "Come on! Won't you get married?"

BH: When I watch TV [J-dramas], I see good-looking guys. However, when I went to an arranged marriage meeting, I met a man with 'pumpkin skin,' trying to strike a manly pose. Alas! I wanted to go back to my TV world and return to the front of my monitor. How Korean men are so ugly!

JM: Many members [of the fan club] want to have an offline meeting on the National Holiday. Next New Year's Day, I am planning to hold a meeting.

Since during the National Holiday they would face more pressures and expectations from gathered family members, JM suggested an offline meeting in order to be freed from these social burdens imposed upon single women. Their tastes in J-dramas have enabled them to construct their own independent cultural identities. With these tastes, they have come to confirm their desires. As they were investing much of their time in their own interests, and they were discovering a professional world, an individual's ordinary life, or diverse masculinities from J-dramas, they could have their own imaginary world where they were released from the gendered social pressure to define women's lives in terms of marriage and domesticity, and even make their single lives more viable.

Hybridized Consumption

Although young Korean women have been enthralled by the charms of transnational TV dramas, their viewing practices and fan activities are affected by cultural contexts in Korea. As deeply rooted sentiments against Japan still prevail, to identify oneself as a J-drama fan in public can attract negative attention. For example, when BH, a J-drama fan website's systems operator, swapped its front web page with that of an American drama fan site on April Fool's Day as a harmless joke, her site was called a "traitor's site." When the newspapers headlined the conflict between Korea and Japan over the controversial Tokdo issue, many bulletin boards related to Japanese popular culture had to be shut down for a while because of strong protests. While the interviewees are fairly open to Japanese popular culture and willing to defy narrow-minded nationalistic sentiments, they keep insisting that their consumption is not a pointless activity. According to Yoon and Na (2005), Korean teenagers have adopted several strategies to appropriate Japanese popular culture without coming into conflict with the maintenance of their Koreanness. These strategies include one which separates Japanese popular culture from its nation or its politics and another in which they maintain a critical distance. While the interviewees in their teens tended to consider J-dramas as separate from their Korean identity, and were critical of people's narrow-mindedness, the interviewees in their 20s and 30s tended to be more insightful about their fandom. Some interviewees critically pointed out imperialistic nuances embedded in some texts such as *Kokusen* and other school dramas. Others took care to differentiate their fandom from that of teenagers. They said they were not such blind followers as the teenagers. The interviewees in their 20s and 30s condemned the act of receiving Japanese popular cultural symbols decontextually. They not only distinguished themselves from the blind pursuers of Japanese popular culture, but also took precautions against ultra-nationalism, not only in Korea but also in Japan and other Asian countries. The context of politics in the real world still matters in the context of transnational cultural consumption.

An individual can watch a different selection of J-dramas according to her personal interests, peer group mechanism, and local context. As the Web and new media environments have enabled access to dramas from various countries, one can adopt nomadic viewing practices, following a drama's enjoyment value and quality, regardless of its national origin. Unlike interviewees in their teens, the interviewees in their 20s and 30s had consumed not only J-dramas but also American dramas, both on the Web and via cable TV. Acknowledging this phenomenon, MH, the editor of a J-drama club webzine, once posted a special issue on American dramas. Its introduction, as follows, shows clearly the ways in which their viewing practices have been recently formed:

> Have you enjoyed your life with J-dramas? It seems that many of those who have encountered Japanese dramas for the first time would have been surprised by their peculiarity and diversity and have become indulged with their charms to become 'Paiyin' [manic]. But there's been always a slump after one year of viewing J-dramas!!!! How do you overcome this slump?? … Thus we have prepared this issue. "Those who are tired of J-dramas, take a break in the world of American dramas!!" Most of those who like J-dramas would also like American dramas. I am also watching J-dramas at the same rate as American dramas.

Many interviewees said that although they currently had a 'feel' for J-dramas, depending on the drama type, they also watch American and Korean dramas. Amongst their lineup of J-dramas, American dramas and Korean dramas had also become strong candidates for viewing. Moreover, the great enthusiasm that Japanese female fans showed for Korean dramas had made J-drama fans rethink the dramatic power of Korean dramas, and heightened their interest in them. As a result, their drama readings had become more intertextual. As one consumes different cultural products simultaneously, one develops more hybridized consumption. While the origin of media products or their nationality still works as a criterion to make the consumer feel a cultural distance, the consumption space has become more hybridized. In this hybridized space, these women have acquired the cultural power to select and appropriate more specific cultural products.

Concluding Remarks

Although Korean female fans of J-dramas physically reside within the boundaries of their nation-state, they have created a transnational imaginary space through their consumption of J-dramas. This consumption is closely related to their life conditions in their home area, and leads to the creation of various cultural practices. Through new information and communication technologies, these consumers can acquire, archive, annotate, appropriate, and re-circulate transnational cultural products. These young women are not merely consumers. They can also be cultural producers, distributors, community members, media pilgrims, critics, and popular culture capitalists. They control their own conditions of reception, create their own consumption patterns, and share experiences with like-minded people who enjoy a similar obsession. Also, their fan activities can be cultural practices used to resist the social and economic conditions imposed on women in Korea.

Although these women have been attracted to the specific cultural codes and symbolic systems of J-dramas, they can turn their attention to other entertainment contents appealing to them. With globalization and new media technologies, media space becomes more hybridized and thus, so does consumption. Repertoires of consumable cultural products can be flexibly constructed, depending on one's taste. From these repertoires, a woman can select what she wants to consume. However, local contexts, including social norms and ideologies, gender systems, media systems, and one's own social and economic conditions, are still important references points for understanding this consumption.

Korean women have managed their own identity politics by viewing and appropriating J-dramas. It is noteworthy that they have discovered and also envied diverse generic forms, modes of life, and types of masculinity. These experiences and adoration of diversities or differences have often been projected onto their daily lives. They have also found possible the fulfillment of women's desires across nations, even under local gender constraints. Whether their consumption leads to a transnational alliance or a cultural identity across East Asia, it forms a local subculture that precedes its own cultural politics.

Appendix

Profiles of Interviewees

Names	Age	Occupation	Year started watching Japanese TV dramas	Other consumptions	Remarks
MK	17	high school student	2001	manga, animation	
SR	17	high school student	2002	manga, animation	
ME	17	high school student	2003	TV talk shows, J-pop	plans to study in Japan
YR	21	undergraduate student	2000	animation	
JY	23	undergraduate student	2003	animation, TV shows	
HS	22	undergraduate student	2002	variety shows, concert DVDs	translator (creating Korean subtitles)
HJ	24	graduate student	2001	films, J-pop	
JE	26	graduate student	2002	J-pop	
BH	26	designer	1999	manga, animation	systems operator
MH	26	none	2002	J-pop, films	webzine editor
SM	26	office worker	2001	J-pop	bulletin board master
JM	29	office worker	1994	J-pop	bulletin board master
KJ	27	flight attendant	1990	J-pop, concerts	systems operator
KH	31	web designer	1998	animation, J-pop	
SY	33	office worker	1995	animation, J-pop, concert DVDs	
MY	31	none	1990	manga, J-pop	
JH	33	graduate student	1994	J-pop	
SJ	33	none	2003	none	
KA	34	journalist	1998	J-pop, manga	
SS	34	TV scenarist	1998	variety programs	

* Interviewees are represented by their initials.

III
Nationalistic Reactions

9

Mapping Out the Cultural Politics of "the Korean Wave" in Contemporary South Korea

Keehyeung Lee

Introduction: Hanryu, What's in a Name?

This chapter deals with the so-called "Korean wave" or Hanryu as a highly complex and multilayered formation that is composed of real, imagined, and hybrid cultural practices, a diverse range of lived experiences, and sets of powerful discourses which exist at national, translocal, and transnational levels. By Hanryu or the Korean wave, I refer to the varied and uneven reception process of South Korean cultural/media products and images in Asia as well as particular forms of media and cultural representations in the transborder flows of South Korean popular culture in South Korea. Although Hanryu texts and images are produced and exported by South Korean culture industries, the Hanryu phenomenon is hardly a unitary and coherent process. It entails a complex range of transnational or translocal concerns and connections which unfold unevenly. Put differently, Hanryu texts — television dramas, popular music, and film — travel to different geocultural zones and contexts, resulting in many differentiated forms of reception, responses, and re-appropriation across Asia.

This chapter aims to outline a diverse range of issues regarding the rapid diffusion and growing popularity of South Korean cultural products across Asia by employing a critical and culturally nuanced approach. Indebted to Haejoang Cho (2002), Koichi Iwabuchi (2002; 2004a; 2004b) and other cultural studies practitioners' pioneering studies on the historical formation of, and the transborder flows of South Korean and Japanese popular culture in Asia, this chapter situates the Hanryu phenomenon in the larger context of transnational cultural formations in the making. It also discusses the implications of the Korean wave from several interconnected angles, and seeks to suggest alternative ways of envisioning South Korean popular culture across Asia for furthering inter-regional cultural understanding and dialogue. Admittedly, my aim in this chapter is limited, but focused: though I will not provide a detailed analysis of dominant discourses that surround the Hanryu phenomenon, nevertheless, I will raise several thought-provoking issues and problematics on the emergence of Hanryu. By doing so, I believe that we as concerned scholars and cultural critics in translocal cultural traffic can come to illuminate the Hanryu phenomenon and other related issues through a more balanced, panoramic, and self-reflexive prism.

The Emergence of Hanryu, the "Boom," Bandwagoners, and Skeptics

The Korean wave or Hanryu phenomenon and discourses on the highly visible reach and flow of South Korean cultural products across Asia have started to grab wider popular attention since the late 1990s. The term Korean wave was coined by the Chinese mass media in 2001 responding to a rise in popularity of South Korean pop culture products and stars (Jang 2004). This trend later spread to countries in Southeast Asia, in particular Vietnam, and other parts of Asia. South Korean popular culture has recently had a strong impact in Japan with the broadcasting of popular South Korean TV dramas like Winter Sonata and the emergence of active fandom surrounding its main characters. It is almost a customary experience in South Korea to see Hanryu-related reports and events in print and broadcast media (Hirata 2005).

Looking back, the rise to fame of South Korean dramas in the Asian region is indeed quite an interesting saga: up until the late 1990s, South Korean dramas and popular music were produced mainly for domestic audiences. At the same time, they had only a limited foreign fan base and potential to appeal to audiences in Asia. Thus it can be said that South Korean popular culture's influence on neighboring Asian countries was minimal. Across Asia and in the western market, Japanese popular culture — popular music, manga, and animation — was conceived collectively as the dominant cultural force in Asia with wide appeal to youth and urban professionals (Iwabuchi 2002). Although the South Korean government had firmly closed its cultural market against Japanese cultural products until the late part of the 1990s, they were often smuggled into, and copied in

South Korea. This presence of relatively widespread popular desires and appetites for Japanese popular culture among youth in South Korea in spite of strong nationalistic sentiments and deeply entrenched memories of Japanese colonialism merits its own critical analysis.

Hence, in the late 1990s when the reports started to pour in about the impressive and unexpected surge of South Korean television dramas and popular music in some parts of Asia, many local cultural critics were puzzled at first, and took to the Korean wave in a belated fashion. Hanryu emerged rather suddenly and local media institutions, culture industries, and governmental branches on culture and tourism took an active role in defining, capitalizing, and generating Hanryu-related discourses, whereas many cultural critics, progressive academics and experts on popular culture took a more cautious or wait-and-see approach. For most of them, the Hanryu phenomenon was regarded as a temporary or extraordinary phenomenon or fad that was expected to either submerge in due time or decline eventually.

Things have drastically changed since then. It seems that the Korean wave is more than a passing fad and is now here to stay. For the past couple of years, the South Korean media has continuously provided a number of telling signs and symptoms that the Korean wave is indeed a real thing. A number of empirical observations and personal experiences, albeit mostly episodic and one dimensional, have been regularly reported by the local media on the heightened status and increased visibility of South Korean cultural products in China, Vietnam, Taiwan, Singapore, Hong Kong, etc. It was suggested that starting with the Korean TV drama *A Star in My Heart* in 1997, Hanryu's popularity began to be detected in China, subsequently including various cultural genres: popular drama, music, film, games, etc (Jang et al., 2004; K. Lee 2004). It was reported that the exporting of Korean pop culture reached new heights in 2004 with the *Winter Sonata* boom in Japan and another boom with *Dae Jang Geum* in Hong Kong this year. In particular, the so-called "Yonsama phenomenon," a sudden highly active fandom centered on the South Korean drama *Winter Sonata* and its male lead Bae Yong-jun, carried out passionately by middle-aged Japanese women, is perhaps the most mediatized and celebrated example of the reach of Hanryu products in Asia in recent years.

Surely this "boom" in South Korean popular culture across Asia has generated significant economic gains and profits which had never been the case in the past. The South Korean government and culture industry provide information on the economic effects of Hanryu in a seemingly convincing fashion, and the Hanryu boom is often predominantly framed by its commercial potential and monetary gains: according to the Korea

International Trade Association, in 2004, Hanryu created 1.4 billion won in added value. It is suggested that Hanryu is responsible for raising Korea's gross domestic product by 0.2 percent. In particular, South Korea amassed $1.87 billion in three sectors that are largely related to cultural contents and activities: products, tourism and film and television programs (*JoongAng Daily*, 4 May 2005). According to the Ministry of Culture and Tourism, as of 2004, exports of Korean TV programs abroad brought in $71.5 million, more than two times the imports of foreign TV programs into South Korea, which marked $31 million (*Korea Times*, 15 April 2005). According to the Korea International Trade Association, cultural products, mainly television programs, movies and recorded music, showed notably brisk export growth owing to the Hanryu phenomenon. The figures contrast starkly with an 8.9 percent rise to $230 million in 2003 and a 4.0 percent drop to $211 million in 2002. It also said as much as 76 percent of South Korean exporters responded to its inquiry that they benefited positively from the increasing popularity of Korean pop culture across Asia (*Korea Times*, 23 February 2005). It was also reported that the national tourism income posted a turnaround for the first time in six years thanks to the boom in South Korean popular culture in Asia. According to the Korea National Tourism Organization (KNTO), the success of South Korean dramas have an positive impact on tourism: in the January–October period, a record high of 4.79 million foreigners visited Seoul, and in October alone, the number reached a monthly high of 574,690. KNTO officials said tourists from Japan and Southeast Asia accounted for the majority of the visitors. A number of these tourists are attracted to Korean celebrities such as Bae Yong-jun and Won Bin and the locations where Hanryu films and dramas are shot (*Korea Times*, 29 November 2004).

As a result, at the current juncture in South Korea, Hanryu has been increasingly framed as a legitimate and highly publicized cultural phenomena to be reckoned with, by many social groups with varying interests. By now Hanryu has gained both currency and legitimacy not only in popular cultural spheres and business circles, but also in South Korean scholarly communities. Again this is mainly inspired by seemingly omnipresent signs and kaleidoscopic images presented by the local media that continuously characterize the reach of the Korean wave across Asia. In Asia these days one is bound to see a dramatic increase in things Korean from television dramas to pop stars: there are successive news stories and enough media coverage of popular Korean stars visiting neighboring countries for promotional tours, having concerts and performing in joint productions, and appearing on foreign TV ads; and of Asian youth chanting the Korean names of these stars during their visits or creating online and offline fan clubs, etc.

Local politicians and governmental agencies have jumped on the "Hanryu bandwagon" by presenting various policies and suggestions related to the Hanryu phenomenon. For example, the Kyonggi provincial government recently announced a plan to build by 2008, a 2-trillion-won ($1.95 billion) entertainment and exhibitionary complex named HanryuWood — a compound word of hanryu and Hollywood — in Ilsan, a satellite city near Seoul (*Hankyoreh Daily*, 17 April 2005). Recently the Ministry of Culture and Tourism announced that it would take concrete measures to support and promote local culture industries after the prime minister's meeting with cabinet officials during a National Image Committee meeting. The ministry said it would create a graduate school in cooperation with local universities to provide specialized programs in culture technology within this year, and an academic program to develop expertise on the development and exportation of South Korean cultural contents. Other institutional measures are currently being suggested: an online database of well-known Hanryu stars, named the Hanryu Portal Information Center, under the supervision of the Korea Foundation for Asian Culture Exchange (KOFACE), a further increase of cultural exchange programs with neighboring Asian countries, and the education of manpower for cultural content industries have been planned (*Korea Times*, 16 February 2005).

With the steady rise and diffusion of Hanryu across several Asian zones, there have emerged groups of business experts, media personnel, and policy makers, especially in government and culture or "creative industries" in contemporary South Korea, who have insisted that Hanryu can create a number of positive and constructive outcomes and lucrative rewards. For instance, Yi O-ryong, former minister of culture and tourism, famed essayist and cultural critic, defines Hanryu as a manifestation of the country's emerging "soft power" which is a new kind of highly competitive, innovative, and adaptive cultural power in an era of accelerated global cultural traffic under the rubric of glocalization and the rise of information and a culture-driven economy. For Yi O-ryong, Hanryu certainly signals and symbolizes a particular example of the glocalization process which can enhance the positive image and new cultural identity of South Korea, from a former colony and culture importing nation to a main cultural exporter in Asia (Yoo et al., 2005:17–18). He also emphasizes that the Korean wave must overcome its "parochial" character to go mainstream: "To become the global mainstream, the Korean wave must die. As South Korean digital technology spreads around the world, it also causes social and civilizational phenomena. But rather than trying to prolong the Korean wave, we must create a new Hanryu based on universal and natural values — a sort of digital Oriental wave" (cited in *New*

York Times, 30 June 2005). Notwithstanding his problematic hyperbole on the significance of Hanryu phenomenon in civilizational terms, Yi is one of the most vocal supporters of mainstream Hanryu discourses in which the strategic merger between information technology and cultural contents is strongly accentuated as a crucial means of not only enhancing the collective image of South Korea as a new cultural powerhouse, but also translating the surge of South Korean cultural products in Asia into financial gains (*JoongAng Daily*, 7 January 2005; also see Yoo et al., 2005).

According to Yi and other cultural entrepreneurs in creative industries, the promotion of the IT (information technology) industry can demonstrate Korea's capabilities as an advanced nation. In addition, South Korea's surging cultural sector led by the booming film and television industry can demonstrate Korea's dynamic cultural qualities and forward-looking national character. Recently, Prime Minister Lee Hae-chan also emphasized a similar view: he stressed the pressing need to expand and manage the gaining popularity of Korean pop culture abroad which could cement the image of the nation as a formidable "IT Power." On this kind of IT and cultural policy-related agendas were measures to connect an improved image of the nation with increased investment opportunities and exports. Accordingly, various government agencies are encouraged to create more diverse events in cooperation with private companies to spread the slogan "Dynamic Korea," and for that purpose, promotional ads for South Korea's IT power, IT promotion booths, series of Hanryu-related conventions, and investor relations meetings are being proposed and implemented. (*Korea Times*, 4 February 2005). These mainstream views, steeped in culture-flavored economism and boosterism are actively formed and supported by leaders of business communities, cultural intermediaries, politicians, and state officials (Kang 2000). Collectively they have vocalized that the surge and growth of South Korean popular culture is a golden opportunity to export cultural contents as well as demonstrate the power of "culture made in Korea." Let me further elaborate on the implication of these mainstream views on the Korean wave below.

Defining Hanryu Alternatively: Mainstream versus Minor views

In this relatively short analysis, I am unable to provide a detailed discursive analysis of Hanryu-related discourses in South Korea though I have provided a thumbnail sketch in the preceding section. According to several cultural studies practitioners in Korea, Hanryu-related discourses are, in large part, shaped by three positions: that of neoliberal thinking, cultural nationalism, and the culturalist position (Cho 2002; Paik 2005).

First of all, powerful discourses formed by governmental, cultural and media institutions have attempted to define and explain Hanryu and its success across Asia through a neoliberal view of culture and in nationalistic terms. In this mainstream views on Hanryu, culture or popular culture is, above all, associated with its "market value" and potential in the highly competitive transnational cultural cum media market. In this vein, Hanryu is often promoted and accentuated as the very evidence that South Korean creative industries have a competitive edge over their counterparts in other nations. Furthermore, it is often emphasized that the Korean wave both demonstrates and embodies the so-called soft power and spirit of innovation which is argued to be essential in the 21st century — a "century of culture and limitless competitions" (*muhankyungjjang*). In addition, this position, which readily associates culture with knowledge and economy, is often merged with hegemonic or covert forms of renewed cultural nationalism: that the recent rise of South Korean cultural products across Asia embodies the impressive adaptability and creative cultural capability of the Korean people (Yoo et al., 2005).

From a related but slightly different angle, the mainstream approach to the Hanryu phenomenon in the cultural sector tends to utilize several by-now familiar frames: that the Hanryu phenomena, spearheaded by such a well-known drama as *Winter Sonata* or *Dae Jang Geum* and popular dance music of, say H.O.T., a local boy band, demonstrates relative generic strength, innovative strategy, and the vitality of South Korean cultural products. According to this dominant explanation of Hanryu products, suggested by cultural producers and critics in the mainstream, Korean dramas have highly attractive stars, sophisticated visual schemes, and absorbing narratives that revolve around emotion-ridden family relationships, love interests and other interpersonal matters among the characters. According to some media scholars in South Korea, these dramas have "common" elements — such as Confucianism and family as master thematic tropes — that can appeal to the audiences in East Asia in terms of "cultural proximity" — sharing of certain powerful social norms, in particular Confucianism, and traditional values centered on family relations (Lee 2004; Yoo and Lee 2001).

Again, from a more genre or style-related angle, Korean popular dance music usually deploys a formulaic structure of its own: idol bands with good looks and superb dancing ability who can digest and perform different forms of music, including hip-hop, rhythm 'n' blues, and popular ballads, have become a reigning norm. To put this differently, it has been argued that Korean popular dramas and music have the specific quality of relatively high production values, well-crafted textual and visual strategies that can appeal to a diverse range of audiences, especially youth and urban professionals in Asia, who live in an increasingly modernized, image-conscious, de-traditionalized, and urbanized context (Iwabuchi 2004a; Jang 2004; Lin et al. 2004).

Mainstream approaches to the Hanryu phenomenon are also adopted or shared by journalists at major media organizations, government officials and policy makers who tend to embrace cultural essentialism willingly or unproblematically: according to them, the Korean wave demonstrates the "superiority" of modern Korean popular culture and collectively it can be the very core of local cultural contents for export and profits. This essentialized use of cultural nationalism in the Hanryu phenomena is also widely supported and adopted by conservative cultural critics and some members of the academia who often function as allies or cheerleaders of South Korean cultural industries. Simply put, these groups of opinion leaders and scholars are closely associated with the production of annual reports, cultural analysis, and journalistic editorials which often exaggerate the economic effects of Hanryu-related cultural contents. They also tend to overemphasize the role of Hanryu products as the source of national pride and empowered collective images for South Koreans, as well as a new means of "cultural diplomacy."

What is seriously lacking in dominant discourses on the Korean wave is a more historicized and nuanced understanding of culture in general and the "hybrid" notion of Korean popular culture as an ensemble of heterogeneous elements. From the viewpoint of cultural studies, dominant discourses on the Hanryu phenomenon in South Korea tend to utilize a predominantly essentialistic, homogenized, and reductionistic sense of culture, which is highly problematic and, at best, one-dimensional. Moreover, they often hide a desire to utilize culture instrumentally as a key, yet a reified ingredient of what is often known as "cultural economics" [*munhwa kyungjaeng*], a new breed of emergent scholarship in the era of "the culturalization of economic life" (Hartley 2005; Miller and Yudice 2002). The mainstream version of cultural economics has been constituted through the articulation between capital and culture, creative activities in the cultural sector — such as film, television, popular music, and IT — and economic enterprise. In this kind of hegemonic cultural economics approach, creative activities embodied through the promotion of cultural contents and culture-related services are increasingly being seen as a formative part of key national strategies of innovation and survival. Increasingly culture and creativity have become market assets and new sources of wealth. It seems that this kind of new trend which prioritizes culture and knowledge emerged during the Kim Dae Jung government when it selected and publically advertised the so-called "new intellectuals" [*shinjisikin*] as a forward-looking visionaries and "venture specialist" in creative industries who would lead the development of the knowledge-based new economy. It was no accident that Shim Hyong-rae, a former comedian who became a science-fiction filmmaker was selected and promoted as South Korea's first new intellectual. Indeed, the status and stock of culture and cultural contents have risen enormously with such an endorsement. The state has started to implement neoliberal policies not only in economic areas, but in media and cultural sectors. Thereafter cultural contents industries have been in the public spotlights and gained recognition. At the same time such a heightened visibility of, and attention to culture and culture-related areas have been shaped by commercially minded cultural boosterism and rampant promotionalism.

At this point, one can point out the very fact that culture, in South Korea, was historically long regarded as a second fiddle to economy in South Korea's bulldozer-style phase of developmental capitalism. Or culture was often considered as key ideological means to boost ruling ideologies and to mobilize the popular masses by the state. Under authoritarian rule in the 1960s to the late 1980s, elements of Korea's traditional and patriotic culture are selectively reinvented and utilized in the disciplinization and "education" of the popular masses. At the same time, popular and youth cultures are often the target of severe official repression for their association with "foreign[ness]" and moral decay (Kang 2000).

Such an attitude toward culture started to change in the 1990s with the rapid growth of local culture industries and the expansion of consumer cum popular culture in everyday South Korean life. What the emergence of youth culture and the rise of Hanryu accompanies, is a radically changed outlook where culture, especially popular culture, has become *the representative* culture of modernized and "dynamic Korea." At the same time, as is mentioned above, mainstream Hanryu discourses are increasingly merged with, or submerged into econocentric and statecentric discourses on the knowledge-based "new" economy, national branding strategies, and national competitiveness, are the newly emphasized names of the game South Korea must play and actively pursue.

Against this kind of instrumentalistic use and redeployment of culture for neoliberal economic entrepreneurship, self-conscious local cultural critics and progressive cultural workers have begun to intervene. By challenging the reification of culture and cultural exceptionalism often attached to dominant discourses on Hanryu, the culturalist approach presents a much more sober and balanced view which resituates the Hanyru phenomenon through a non-state-centric and counter-nationalistic counter-discourses. Put differently, the culturalist position at one level challenges the deeply embedded nationalistic and essentialist claims often utilized in mainstream discourses on Hanryu, though it certainly recognized the power of the state and culture industries as main agents of cultural production.

From the standpoint of the culturalist approach, the mainstream views on Hanryu disregard or willfully forget the very fact that South Korean popular cultural products are hybrid in their very nature, and relatively new cultural constructions. As a matter of fact, Hanryu-related cultural products have little to do with traditional Korean culture or collective popular sentiments (Shim 2004). For instance, they are mostly a mixture of western cultural genres and formats, and they also convey cosmopolitan imaginaries and sophisticated urban styles (Kim and Yang 2005). Here, one of the most telling examples is that of South Korean pop and dance music which utilize a complex array of generic and stylistic forms and beats — for instance, hip-hop, techno and dance music, rock and rhythm and blues — selectively borrowed or sampled from their dominant others, either American or Japanese popular music. In this respect, South Korean cultural products — such as films, television dramas, music videos, and popular music — are relatively refined, but not so original "copies of copies" or commercially creolized or bastardized texts that have similar "clones" or counterparts in other geographical regions. Progressive cultural critics argue that in reality, South Korean popular culture should be considered as a subcategory to transnational popular and consumer culture which operates through the commodification of diverse (multi)cultural differences. Borrowing a local cultural critic's words, South Korean popular culture is "a regional variant of [commodified] global pop culture" which in reality was "nothing uniquely Korean" (Shin 2005).

Instead, the culturalist position traces and resituates the emergence of Hanryu as a complex transborder cultural phenomenon and formation in the era of polycentered cultural production by using nuanced historical and comparative approaches. In this alternative position to Hanryu phenomenon, the making of Hanryu is interpreted both comparatively and critically through its historical predecessors – the Americanization of Asian popular cultures in the post Word War II years and the surge of Japanese popular culture as a dominant cultural force and form in the region for decades. In this position, Hanyru is regarded as an accidental event that came to emerge due to the unexpected convergence of multiple — institutional, cultural, and political

— factors and conditions. As cultural critic Shin Hyunjun aptly puts (2005:23):

> the so-called "Hanryu (the Korean Wave)" is neither Japanese pop culture nor something like a common culture shared by Japanese and Korean audiences. It is a hybrid culture from its very inception and formation... K-culture [Korean popular culture] is a concept that is defined according to its relationship with others [American and Japanese pop culture], this relationship includes a "hierarchy."... when K-culture stars perform in China or Southeast Asia the [local] media often uses such slogans as "going out to conquer Asia." This (groundless) pride in the superiority of Korean culture is defined not in terms of original creativity but rather through the establishment of hierarchical relations with [hegemonic] others.

Hence, progressive intellectuals and cultural studies practitioners in South Korea criticize the mainstream views on Hanryu for their lack of due cross-cultural sensibility and concern for inter-regional dialogue, as well as their emphasis on the willful commodification of culture and cultural differences. Instead, they approach and evaluate Hanyru more cautiously through a series of contextualizing efforts. For instance, the culturalist position takes the Hanryu phenomenon as a relatively recent wave of transnational cultural flows and traffics which have historically existed for decades in Asia. Before and even with Hanryu, the flow of Japanese popular culture as a prototype of transnational culture created by a non-western other has been a strong presence across the Asian region. In the 1980s, Hong Kong cinema was a defining element of a particular form of transnational cultural flow especially in Asia before its popularity somewhat died out in the following decades.

In this fashion, the culturalist position attempts to bring in a much more critical and politicized reading of the Hanryu phenomenon by foregrounding the issues which are often disregarded or downplayed by mainstream discourses on Hanryu: the possibilities of cross-cultural or transborder dialogues from below that can be mediated through Hanryu texts and their audiences in various geopolitical regions. Moreover, the culturalist position looks into and traces other agents and players who are bracketed or marginalized in dominant versions on the flow and reception of South Korean cultural forms. There are multiple audiences including women and youth as well as cultural workers in different geographical regions and sites who consume, receive, use, and interact with South Korean cultural products differentially. These audiences have created multiple forms of symbolic spaces and identities — kinds of translocal cultural zones and "pan-Asian identities" in the making — that have emerged with the negotiated receptions of Hanryu texts and contents.

For instance, Angel Lin and her colleagues (2004) did a qualitative analysis of the reception process of South Korean media texts in Hong Kong. To summarize, their findings indicate that local audiences approach these "alien texts" through pre-established cultural repertoires and sets of cultural meanings of their own. That South Korean media texts as travelling cultural forms convey urban and modern ways of living and images did appeal to the local viewers in Hong Kong. There seemed to exist common structures of feeling and lived experiences. Nevertheless, due to the highly syrupy and melodramatic storytelling and expression in South Korean media texts, the viewers responded that they tended to hide their following of South Korean melodramas in public settings. What has emerged through Lin and her colleague's analysis is that Hong Kong viewers demonstrate the negotiated reception process of South Korean dramas by both challenging the limitations of some values embedded in these texts and acknowledging the emotional or affective power of the texts they watch. In doing so, the viewers adopt different socio-cultural values, including feminist and established ones, in reading and utilizing South Korean dramas in their own lives. By ushering in much differentiated and location-specific reception modes of South Korean cultural texts in Hong Kong, their research testifies to the fact that the Hanryu phenomenon has multifaceted dimensions, connections, and ramifications which are often not properly dealt with in the mainstream discourses which are circulated in South Korea.

Koichi Iwabuchi (2004b) brings in an equally important perspective which is not shaped by nationalistic frames or essentalistic claims on the Hanryu phenomenon. Upon charting the emergence of South Korean popular texts in Japan and Korea-related popular themes in Japanese television dramas, Iwabuchi focuses on the problematic status of Korean Japanese whose presence and identities are often sidelined or disregarded in both South Korea and Japan's mainstream approaches to the Korean wave phenomenon. Among other things, Iwabuchi sharply points out the fundamental flaws in the statecentric celebration and admission of Hanryu as a means of bringing about mutual understanding in each country. What is missing in this kind of dominant — and seemingly benign — argument is that the much complicated social issues surrounding Korean Japanese people and their particular history of identity formation and the problem of their oppressed status as marginalized ethnic others in Japan are often erased in the name of celebratory rhetoric which claims that Hanryu brings both Japanese and Koreans much closer.

There is yet another exemplary piece of research on the Hanryu phenomenon which utilizes a much balanced and inclusive analysis. Recently, a research team at Kwangwoon University in Seoul, led by Professor Soohyun Jang and other faculty members (2004), has explored the reception of South Korean cultural products in China. It is one of the most organized and detailed studies which interrogates the Korean wave phenomenon in China. According to their multidisciplinary work, the mainstream portrayal of the lived realities and reception processes surrounding the Hanryu phenomenon in China is much exaggerated and lacks a balanced as well as context-specific understanding. By using institutional, quantitative and qualitative research, they have found out that Hanryu is not a widespread cultural phenomenon in China. It is revealed that Hanryu-related products and images are consumed and received by specific groups of people: predominantly urban-based youngsters and urban dwellers. In other words, Hanryu certainly seems to have a niche market in China: some groups of followers or loyal fans in mostly urban areas indeed follow and consume Hanryu-related cultural products. According to the research team, the wider exposure to South Korean popular culture among Chinese viewers and users does not necessarily enhance the national image of South Korea. In their collaborative research, for instance, Chinese viewers' responses to Hanryu texts varied. Some viewers tended to perceive urban imagery, lifestyles, and images related to consumption in Hanryu texts as much desired elements and were the reasons why they pursued Hanryu texts. By identifying with the characters who have to deal with family and interpersonal relations in a modernized setting in Hanryu texts, some Chinese viewers could connect the social world depicted in Hanryu texts with theirs. In other words, Hanyru texts functioned as cultural and symbolic cultural vehicles through which the Chinese viewers could project and engage in their own lived experiences and "emotional realism" shaped by the compressed and uneven process of modernization.

An equally important matter Jang and his colleagues' research found is that Hanryu should be perceived and located in the institutional and political context: the relative success of South Korean cultural products has been attributed to the rapid growth of Chinese media industries and the following demand for relatively cheap and appealing forms of popular entertainment from abroad. It should be also pointed out that the Chinese government allowed and regulated the flow of South Korean popular cultural products through its intervention and management of the domestic cultural market (Jang 2004:385). Jang and his research team diagnosed that Korean cultural products have representational strategies and thematic elements that can certainly appeal to, as well as attract a particular structure of feeling in Chinese audiences: their desire for relatively well-crafted cultural products and images, consumption and modern life styles. Their research findings challenge the mainstream views on Hanyru in South Korea which are often steeped in rosy forecastings of Hanryu's enormous economic potential, market edge, and cultural creativity. In a way, what is emerging from this exemplary research is that a more cautious, self-reflective, and modulated approach to the Hanryu phenomenon is needed.

In Lieu of Conclusion: Towards Inter-Asia Cultural Dialogues: Where Is Asia in the Dominant Discourses on Hanryu?

In contemporary South Korea, many cultural studies practitioners would agree that Hanryu-related phenomena have (accidentally) brought about important issues surrounding the role of transnational cultural traffics and border crossings embodied through cultural forms and images to the forefront of public concerns and agendas. This can be considered an enabling opportunity for those who take (transnational) cultural politics seriously and people who want to utilize Hanryu as a new opportunity for constructively engaging with translocal and transnational forms of popular cultures shared through Inter-Asian channels (Kim and Yang 2005; Lee 2005).

Unfortunately they still belong to the minority. What is often missing in the mainstream discourses on Hanryu in contemporary South Korea is any self-reflexive understanding of Hanryu as one of the potential conduits for cross-cultural sensibilities and inter-regional dialogues, and eventually as an opportunity for taking steps towards cultural regionalization (Paik 2005). What makes such alternative imagining and networking hard to materialize is the kind of pervasive and rampant neoliberal market thinking and state-centric thought that tends to shape and dominate the discourses and representations surrounding the flow of South Korean popular culture into other regions in Asia and elsewhere.

Looking at the recent circulation of Hanryu discourses through the cultural studies lens presents new forms of explanation of translocally consumed cultural texts as well as new problematics that need more than critical discursive intervention. To say the least and emphasize the obvious, more concerted and collaborative efforts are necessary for South Korean cultural workers, intermediaries and critics in order to lay the groundwork for more open, non-hierarchical, and reciprocal cultural understanding and exchange among South Korea and its neighbors. Especially for concerned cultural practitioners, the next step seems to be to put more interventionary and institutional measures into the existing alternative approaches to the Hanryu phenomenon beyond the usual informed criticism of mainstream approaches. Such attempts seem to include, to name a few, more concrete institutional level interventions in the name of "critical cultural policy," politico economic analysis of local culture industries as a main producer of Hanryu texts and their strategies, and more self-reflexive ethnographic and comparative analysis of the discrepant reception processes of Hanryu texts in specific geographical locales through the collaboration between South Korean and local scholars.

10

Rap(p)ing Korean Wave:
National Identity in Question

Fang-chih Irene Yang

The recent popularity of Korean dramas in East Asia in recent years has been described by the media as the "Korean wave," and in Taiwan as "the invasion of the Korean wave" (*hanliu laixi*). This chapter unpacks the meanings of "the invasion of the Korean wave" by examining three genres of public discourses on the Korean wave. Public discourses presume different addressees and adhere to different cultural, rhetorical, and stylistic conventions to evoke affect and assemble different publics. In this chapter, I point out that the most dominant genre of the public discourse on the Korean wave articulates globalization with economic nationalism, which derives its legitimacy from disembodiment, rationality, calculation, and competition for self-interests. The second discourse on the Korean wave is articulated as cultural nationalism, with the Korean drama and the Korean man as the other. This discourse operates through body and affect, using scatology to assemble national citizens. The articulation of scatology to cultural nationalism, and later, economic nationalism, elevates the powerless male public from disgrace to serious, esteemed academic conferences and (elite) cultural circles. These two discourses, despite their hierarchically structured publics as a result of their bodily (in)visibility, are predicated on a masculine conception of the nation, with women as the other, prone to invasion and manipulation. Contrary to these masculine discourses of the nation, the third discourse on the Korean wave takes on a feminine form, addressing to female readers/consumers how women consume affectively Korean dramas, and particularly, that of the body of male stars. Though the three discourses co-exist in the same public space, they are ordered according to gender hierarchy, with the first two "citizen" or "nation" discourses excluding women from participation and the third fan/women discourse functioning as a "mode of containment" which marginalizes women's speech to "female complaint" (Berlant, 1988). But as the "complaint" itself is both resistant and containment, self-expressive and self-confining, this chapter ends with a re-reading of the fan discourse through Heidegger's notion of "technology" in the hope of transforming the existing public sphere which leaves women no place to speak.

Text-based Publics

Warner (2002) proposes a theory of text-based public in response to the much criticized masculinist, bourgeois rational public sphere that Habermas idealizes. In Warner's formulation, publics are self-organizing through their encounter with texts, that is, the assembling of publics is necessarily mediated through cultural forms. The bourgeois public sphere denies the mediation of cultural forms and misrecognizes discussion, information, and will formation as such rather than the effect of particular cultural forms — the rhetorical dimension of a public context which regulates individual's relation to the public (1992: 379; 2002). This misrecognition is what Warner calls "ideologizing," and it is the ideology of print that informs, conditions, and constitutes the rational, abstract (from body) bourgeois public sphere (1992; 2002).

In denying the mediation of cultural form as its founding ideology, bourgeois publicness denies its own historicity and specificity. This "dehistoricized self-understanding guarantees at every step that difference will be enunciated as mere positivity, an ineluctable limit imposed by the particularities of the body" (1992: 384). Coding itself as universal allows the bourgeois public sphere to minoritize difference by marginalizing or excluding those who are constrained by bodily particularities. This minoritizing strategy becomes a tool of domination. Hence, claims Warner, that the public sphere is inherently contradictory: on the one hand, it delivers promises (for universal good); on the other hand, it cannot fulfill its promise as bodily differences (race, gender, sexuality, class) are minoritized. For the minoritized bodies, consumption becomes one of the venues to engage with their publics as consumption offers promises of difference and promises unfulfilled by the bourgeois public sphere (Warner, 1992).

The bourgeois public sphere's minoritizing strategy is a strategy of ordering. As Foucault makes it clear that "in any society the production of discourse is simultaneously controlled, selected, organized and redistributed by a certain number of procedures, the role of which is to ward off the powers and dangers of discourse, master its chance events, evade its weighty, fearsome materiality" (1981: 52). The ordering of discourse in the bourgeois public sphere minoritizes women's public speech to a marginalized, cramped space (Morris 1988; Berlant 1988; Deem, 1996), which "makes speaking difficult or impossible for women" (Morris, 1988: 7). Warner (2002) and Berlant (1988) contend that it is through the (ab)uses of cultural forms that women's speech is ordered to the lower rung of the cultural hierarchy. For Warner, the bourgeois cultural form allows it to operate through abstraction, rationality, neutrality, and universality through the denial of body; while a mass cultural form for mass subjects (mostly and especially women) offered through consumption operates through bodily difference and affect. For Berlant, women's genre (such as melodrama, soap opera) functions as a "mode of containment" which contains women's speech as "female complaint" — a mode of speech which addresses to the public of the complainer's suppressed injuries while circumscribing that expression to a failure for transformation (1988: 243).

As such, Warner calls for the necessity of understanding the rhetorical dimension of public discourses for it is through style, language, mode of address, and poetics — the particularities of cultural form — that publics are led to imagine themselves as belonging to a particular public. Any cultural form, though called public, is contradicted by "both its material limits — the means of production and distribution, the physical textual objects themselves, the social conditions of access to them — and by internal ones, including the need to suppose forms of intelligibility already in place as well as the social closure entailed by any selection of genre, idiolect, style, address, and so forth" (2002: 55). That is, for a particular text to function as public, to assemble and call upon its own constituents, it must be available to the public. Availability includes two dimensions — materiality and stylistics/poetics. The cultural form in question needs to be available to its subject only when the subject can afford it, has access to it, and through his/her cultural capital, can understand it and be sutured into its subject position. The material aspect is a matter of political economy, the stylistics/poetics, is a matter of culture. It is about the cultural capital of the addressee, the shared knowledge of the addressee's community, and the style of language used within that community. The style of the cultural form performs an affective function, calling into community its own addressees.

If the production of any cultural form presumes preexisting knowledge of certain communities, that preexisting knowledge should be seen as "dialogic imagination," "a context of interaction" (Warner, 2002: 62) — as responses to and encounters of many discourses from the "multigeneric lifeworld" and as the infinite encountering of citations and characterizations. The public space is a space of ongoing encounters of discourses, it is intertextual, but is always conditioned and constrained by the members' access to it. The dialogic aspect of the public space is most compelling for it enables us to analyze cultural texts as composed of multiple voices, and the combination of which allows the formation of a particular kind of community of belonging.

Warner's proposal of a text-based public has several advantages in understanding the formation of publics: it avoids the pitfalls of the bourgeois public sphere which evicts its own cultural/historical/bodily particularity. As such, it particularizes the bourgeois, rational public as one of the publics, rather than the Public, and allows for the theorization of subaltern or counter publics. By paying attention to the particularities of cultural form in the formation of public subjectivity, it allows us to take into account both the material and the cultural/linguistic aspects of communication. Moreover, it enables us to analyze not only the communicative but also the affective function of language in shaping human belonging, as well as the complexity of subject formation as overdetermined by different discourses and affectivities.

One way to start with analyzing cultural forms is through genres, as genres are negotiations of forces among institutions, texts, and audiences. Here, I analyze three genres of public discourse that articulate the meanings of the Korean wave — the discourse of economic nationalism, cultural nationalism, and fan discourse. In analyzing these genres, I will pay particular attention to these aspects: intended addressee, institution of production, textual "poetics" (including the performative and affective dimension of the texts), and the multiple discourses that are adopted to characterize the world. However, as discourses are ordered hierarchically in the service of mostly the male elite, it is significant to call attention to the gender dimension of the discourse which "leaves a woman no place from which to speak, or nothing to say." As feminist intervention, this piece takes it that "to write, to read, or to speak is first of all to turn other texts into discursive material, displacing the enunciative position from which those materials have been propounded" (Freadman, quoted in Morris, 1988: 3) in the best hope of creating and expanding the cramped female space of public speech.

Korean/Cold Wave in a Competitive Economy

The first discourse on the Korean wave is an economic discourse. Most of this discourse is produced by magazines or journals centered on economics and finance, such as *Commonwealth, Cheers, Digital Weekly, Wealth Magazine* and the politics and economics pages in newspapers. This discourse addresses itself to the elite of the society, namely, the professional managerial class, the corporate leaders, and the upper-middle and middle class ("About Commonwealth"). As *Commonwealth* states, its goal is, "together [with the Taiwanese to] create sustainable development for a fair, harmonious, livable and good society" ("Declaration for A Beautiful Vision of Taiwan in 2020"). It appeals to "gentleness and rationality" as the basis for "adopting caring and practical action, in the hope of lifting the quality of its people, solidifying social consensus, and progressing forward together with Taiwan" ("About Commonwealth"). On the one hand, the target readers are to be informed of worldly affairs so that they become cosmopolitan citizens; on the other hand, this worldly knowledge in turn positions the readers as the elite who are then endowed with the responsibility in shaping the future of society. Positioned as both global and national citizen, this reader identity is mainly defined through its relationship with the economy. Issues that are repeatedly addressed include "what is going on globally?" "How does this global process affect our nation?" "What should we do as a nation to survive in the global world?"

Informed by middle-class morality and decorum, the economic/citizen discourse produced and circulated for this class emphasizes rationality and places itself in the sphere of "civil society" whose position is to regulate the state of its economic and political policies, as in "During the past, we have played a significant role in shaping the government's decision-making process" ("About Commonwealth"). The role of the "civil society" should be marked as it is only through the use of the rhetoric of civil society — that is, the rhetoric of social responsibility as citizenship — that allows the (economic) speaking subject to mask himself as national citizen/subject. The rhetoric of social responsibility — such as "create a ... livable and quality society" and "lifting the quality of its people" — functions as a veneer, masking the hidden abode of production/exploitation. As Stabile comments, "the marketing of social responsibility works mainly for those more distant from economic necessity — those more likely to buy into the ideology of the corporation as global citizen" (Stabile, 2000: 199). The "consumerist caste" being addressed here — the managerial professional class — uses this self-presentation as socially responsible, as gentle and rational, to legitimize the superiority of their position not only in the realm of politics and economy, but in the domain of culture. As such, this economic discourse has become the most legitimate and respected discourse — a discourse of and about national progress and national future, hence, national identity.

A typical example of this economic discourse on the Korean wave can be found in the conclusion of "Because of Qing, We Can Step Forward," originally published in the *Economic Times* and *Commonwealth Magazine*:

> Qing refers to amicable relationships and ethical relationships. It includes relationships among family members, friends, teachers-students, and even love for the nation and humankind in general. It is qing ... that gives new strength to Korean dramas and films and gives birth to the "Korean Wave" in the world. It also gives Koreans "dream[s] and hope[s]," enabling them to challenge the world ...
>
> Looking into the Korean experience necessarily leads us to reflect on our own. The conditions for us to achieve success is not as appalling if we possess a little more qing and tolerance, develop a little more cultural depth and courage for participation [in the world] as well as a strong will to achieve the best. Among the four little dragons in Asia, Taiwan's GDP ranks the third, and Korea, the fourth. At the present moment, it's a tie, but who will win out in the future? (Preface to *Rising Korea*, 2005: 14)

This text on the Korean wave employs existing discourses in order for it to make sense to its middle-class readers. However, despite its uses of various discourses, all of them narrate Taiwan as a nation in crisis because of its economic situation, and that mode of address, as I will demonstrate later, is masculine and militaristic.

First of all, there is a shared assumption among its addressees that Taiwan and South Korea occupy the same temporality in the global march toward modernization. This "coevalness" (in Fabian's terms) comes from the addressees' understanding of their shared historical background with Korea, which refers to both nations' past histories as influenced by China (Confucianism) and colonized by Japan. Most significantly, the sense of simultaneous temporality is recognized in economic terms, that is, both nations are known as members of the four little dragons, namely, the NICs (Newly Industrialized Countries). This particular way of understanding national history through economic modernization reflects these two nations' postwar nation-building projects: both use economic development to define the essence of their national identity, thereby legitimizing and masking undemocratic practices. This economic understanding dictates popular thinking about their relations with other nations, with the U.S. and Japan as more advanced, and South Korea as standing in a "tie." If Japan is the "mother" who gives birth to Taiwan's modernization project, South Korea becomes a sibling, but this sibling relationship is based, not on mutual care and help, but sibling rivalry, competing for GDP ranking. Hence, the last sentence, "at the present moment, it's a tie, but who will win out in the future?"

The second discourse adopted here is the discourse of globalization — that the sibling rivalry between Taiwan and Korean has intensified as a result of the recent processes of globalization. The discourse of globalization deserves a whole chapter; here, I will briefly map out how and what globalization discourses get localized as popular memory and how it is articulated through the Korean wave to warn the Taiwanese public of the urgency to join the globalization march. Globalization is a transnational discourse which travels through multi-channels for its dispersal and effective performance. In addition to establishing management firms and workshops which translates Western, capitalist ethos to discipline local subjects and subjectivities (Ong, 2006), there is a proliferation of translation of books written by Western economists. In this type of discourse, globalization is endowed with an agency of its own — it moves by itself and is inevitable and irreversible:

Like [unstoppable] water flowing through natural geographies, corporations and capital also flow with natural trends in the global economy. The government's responsibility is to create a good environment for corporate investments. If you stop the corporations from leaving [the nation], everybody will eventually die on this boat. If you help the corporations to invest abroad, maybe they will come back and save the economy (Wu, 2001a:61).

Here, globalization is metaphorized as a natural process — as "flowing water," "sea wave" (Wu, 2001a:54), or even as "the invasion of the third wave of the tsunami" (Song, 2005: 107) — beyond human control. What humans can do is to follow wherever capital flows, to go against "nature" is to look for death. The flow of capital as a product and process of human labor, as a man-made flow sustaining unequal relationships between the rich and the poor is constructed as a natural process which cannot be changed or stopped. It is "not a choice, but a reality" (Chu, 2005: 148).

While the globalization discourse travels cross national boundaries like a "wave," globalization as an economic process also "flattens out" the world (Chu, 2005:142). It deterritorializes and reterritorializes, namely, it breaks down all national boundaries and reconstitutes new boundaries along monetary lines. Globalization flattens the world into a space of equal competition, with the result of dividing the world into winners and losers. "'Flatness' characterizes the recent globalization trend. It allows people in every corner of the world to cooperate or compete at a new level. Technological, economic, and political revolutions are breaking down all kinds of barriers and boundaries, a flattened world is a world of equal competition" (ibid: 142). In this competitive world, successful businessmen become the heroes of this age — their wealth and power can surpass that of a nation (Wu, 2001b: 59). This individualizing rhetoric works on two levels — on one level, it makes business a site of spectacle; it makes ordinary, boring business activities and tradings an exciting space where major action takes place (Grace, 1993); on another level, it demands that individuals be solely responsible for their success or failure in the global economy. Thus hundreds of articles are about how to manage and produce a self that is conducive to the use of the economy. To survive the global economy, one must compete with others. Military metaphors are used to describe the business world as a "battlefield" (Wu, 2001b: 61) and the end result is only a matter of "winning and losing" (Wu, 2001b: 62). Military terms such as "deployment," "control," "management," "new strategic thinking," "invasion," "bravery," "mobility," "monopolize resources", "competition," "competitive power," and "risk-taking" (Wu, 2001: 48–49) are often invoked to describe the business world, making it a spectacle of warfare where heroes win out with honor and enemies die hard. The use of military metaphors intensifies the urgency for competition and turns it into a matter of survival: "The globalization wave makes a stranger thousands of miles away a competitor, vying for the same rice-bowl [job]" (Lu, 2005).

While winners are singled out as the exemplars of the new age, ordinary people constantly walk on the fine line between success and failure. Many articles discuss the dim future of ordinary people as a kind of cautionary tale to warn them to ameliorate themselves with new technical know-how and to engineer themselves into a new kind of corporate individual. These cautionary tales include objective and subjective survey of the economic reality in Taiwan, such as "The Rise or Disappearance of Your Jobs?" (Wu Wang-yu, 2005), "How Do Your Jobs Disappear?" (Lu, 2005), "There is No Future for the People" (Li: 72), and "Globalization? Emptification?" (Wu, 2001a). In these articles, the downside of globalization as experienced by the majority of the middle class is depicted: "Our economy is declining and life becomes more and more difficult, the gap between the rich and the poor is increasing, as well as the intensifying ethnic conflicts and the worsening of life quality. Moreover, Taiwan is being isolated from the world, it is disappearing from the world map" (Li, 2005: 72–74). This grim "reality" of Taiwan's economy is likened to "a swordsman without Kung-fu [another military metaphor] in the chilly winter." "Its competitive power deteriorates in the blink of an eye … Faced with the competition from around the world, what kind of strategic deployment can Taiwan's corporations use?" (Wu, 2001a: 52)

The globalization discourse circulated in Taiwan creates a new kind of belonging centered on corporations and corporate leaders, transforming the previous state-centered national belonging. The story presented here makes corporations and corporate leaders the agents of history, rescuing the Taiwanese from the sinking boat/nation and leading them to the next century. As such, ordinary individuals are responsible for making themselves useful for corporations in a competitive world, as in "increase in one's 'lifetime employability'" (Song, 2005: 113) — one has to actively make oneself wanted by the corporations so that one can participate in the corporate war to save the nation. However, this organization of new belonging does not work through eliminating the nation-state, but laterally through transforming the nation-state to the service of corporations. This new corporate belonging as national belonging does not meet much resistance from the nation-state or the people as Taiwan's national identity has been built upon its economic development as a way to suppress political dissidents during the KMT ruling. As such, economic nationalism lives on, now via the heroic lives of those corporate leaders.

One way to find the global niche to save the economy is through developing cultural creative industries. The development of the creative industry, or the use of culture as a resource for the development of the economy is not specific to Taiwan's economic strategy in the global economy, but as part of, albeit a significant part of the transnational globalization discourse. In this discourse, "culture is invested in, distributed in the most inclusive ways, used as an attraction for capital development and tourism, as the prime motor of the culture industries and as an inexhaustible kindling for new industries dependent on intellectual property" (Yudice, 2003: 3–4). One special feature of contemporary globalization is its transformation of the meanings of culture as uplift, tradition, distinction, or a whole way of life to culture as resource for profit-making (Yudice, 2003). Following capital flow, this concept of culture travels speedily to many countries, changing their cultural policies, including Taiwan and South Korea.

In the context of Taiwan, the turn toward the cultural economy marks the shift in the state's direction of cultural policy from the Cultural Production Industry (*Wenhua Chanyie*) in 1995 which views culture as central to identity politics to the Cultural Creative Industry (*Wenhua Chuangyi Chanyie*) in 2000 which treats culture as an economic resource. The former defines culture as rooted in the local community and the traditional way of life, and thus is seen as central to the formation of Taiwanese consciousness. This view of culture coincides with, and is part of the Ben-tu-hua (Nativization) movement in the early to mid-1990s. However, as the velocity of globalization intensifies, culture is emptied of its original meaning, and replaced by the sign economy — any sign that can be traded with surplus value is defined now as culture (Wang, 2005). The Korean wave takes place in Taiwan at a time when the meaning of culture is in the process of shifting toward an economic-based definition in framing new cultural policies. Hence, many of the discussions used the Korean wave as a reference point to think about the cultural policies in Taiwan.

In this discourse, the popularity of Korean dramas and movies is not only seen as the successful product of the government's cultural policy but also as Koreans' use of traditional culture to sell. Cho points out that around 1994, the Korean government and businesses began to engage in a process of "understanding" Korean culture through new narratives of "Korean-ness" as a response to globalization. These narratives include the revival of Confucianism and the revival of popular folk culture through the concept of "han" (Cho, 1999). These two narratives have also informed how media narrate Korean-ness in Taiwan. In general, the Confucian tradition is constructed as a part of Korea's roots, a root that Koreans carry into the future. The rediscovery of Confucian tradition is seen as a "consumer need" in a lost, modernized world where tradition and filial piety have lost their values. Hence, "qing" and "filial piety" are seen as Korea's traditional philosophies which give Korean dramas an edge in the global economy: "Koreans have a lot of qing and they are not afraid to express it, they are willing to sacrifice for love and family without regret" (Li and Sun: 193). "Han" — a product of colonization — has also shaped Koreans' persevering, tenacious, aggressive, and competitive personality (Li: 140): "when you are determined to do something, you will always do everything you can to achieve the best result ... This is the Korean spirit — never give up easily, never stop in the middle, always persevere and be optimistic (Di, Li, and Lyu: 74–75).

These two narratives about Korean-ness — Confucian tradition and Han — are constructed as the key ingredients of Korean culture which lead to the economic success of the Korean wave. These discourses of Korean-ness are employed in the quote above not only to inform Taiwanese middle-class readers about the reasons of Korean's success, but also to situate them within the frame of economic globalization where competition is the rule of the game. By combining these three discourses in the quoted text above — Korea as a rival sibling nation, Korea as a competitor/enemy in the global economy, Korean-ness as competitive, persevering, and tough — a new sense about self and (Korean) other is created. Through the creation of a picture of the global economy as a place for winners only and Koreans as tough competitors with the knowledge of soft sell, we, the Taiwanese, facing our own economic decline, need to unite as a nation (with corporate leaders as the guiding light) so that our national/economic place in the world map won't be replaced by Korea.

In theorizing about the emotion of belonging (to a community, a nation), Ahmed points out that any form of belonging requires, first, the creation of an imagined other who threatens the lives of ordinary subjects (hate); second, the creation of a community through the mobilization of hate via a process of difference and displacement — a process of expressing love for the community. Such emotions of love and hate, dis-identification and belonging are economic — "they circulate between signifiers in a relationship of difference and displacement" (Ahmed, 2001: 11). The creation of a sense of a nation in crisis poses the ordinary subjects, the middle-class readers, as under threat. Their jobs are in danger of being restructured and replaced as in "There Is No Future for the People" (Li, 2005). With the use of military metaphors in creating an enemy as anybody outside the boundary of the nation, and Koreans as tough competitors in the battlefield, the sense of masculine competition becomes intensified. Further colored by a historical understanding of sibling rivalry, the Korean wave is now being marked as a threatening other, endangering the future livelihood of the nation, as in "Taiwan Drowned by Korean Wave" (Lin, 2001:98). Hence, the adoption of the term "the invasion of the Korean wave" in popular use, which also puns with "the invasion of the cold wave" — a cold front threatening the security of Taiwan's economic position in the world. These notions of "cultural invasion" (Lin, 2001: 100) inspire many articles to encourage a "fighting back" attitude: "If Koreans Can Do It, Why Can't the Taiwanese?" (Li, 2004: 116); "The War to Fight Back Korea [against economic deficit] Awaits Our Effort" (Wang Chun-rui, 2004)

Despite the rhetoric to interpellate national citizens with global vision, the citizens who are being addressed are gendered and class-based. The mode of address — "gentleness and rationality" — is abstract(ed) (elite) male speech which denies bodies and emotions. Its rhetoric, though "rational" and "moral," often employs military metaphors to legitimize a competitive way of life in the global age. This masculine discourse, through middle-class decorum and social responsibility, constitutes the majoritarian discourse in the elite, male-centered public sphere, with national citizens as its addressees. Coexisting with this discourse, but situated in the less privileged public sphere is another masculine discourse which articulates the Korean wave as cultural nationalism. But this cultural nationalism is soon subsumed under the economy. I will use the rap song "The Invasion of the Korean Wave" performed at Tai-ke Rock Concert to mark Bae Yong-jun's visit to Taiwan as the primary text of my analysis.

Rap(p)ing Korean Wave

Tai-ke (*Taiwanese Guest*) Rock Concert made their debut performance on the day Bae Yong-jun came to Taiwan to promote his new movie, *April Snow*. While the media entertainment pages were filled with Bae's fans welcoming him at the airport and wildly following him everywhere he went, another headline, though much smaller, hit Taiwan's intellectual circle: "Tai-ke Rocker Chang Zhen-yue Swears at Bae Yong-jun" (*Liberty Times,* 20 Aug 2005); "Tai-ke Pissed by the Korean Wave, Singling Out Bae Yong-jun as the Target of Foul Language" (*China Times,* 20 Aug 2005). These headlines immediately triggered a cultural debate on the meanings of Tai-ke and Taiwaneseness. As such, the discussions soon moved from the entertainment pages to newspaper forums, editorials, literary supplements, and literary/intellectual magazines such as *Eslite Book Reviews*. Workshops and academic conferences were also organized to discuss this Tai-ke phenomenon. These debates are articulated into two domains — economic nationalism and cultural nationalism, though both of them converge at the end under the logic of economy. In elevating itself to a debate about economic, cultural, national identity in the public sphere, vulgar bodies and languages that were central to this phenomenon were erased from discussion. I will start with the lyrics of the rap which triggered the event.

> *The Invasion of the Korean/Cold Wave*
> When I come to Taiwan, I ask myself whether there is hip-hop made in Taiwan for export, the answer is no. Why? When I turn on television, there is various hip-hop music which looks like Chinese but sounds like an-ya-ha-sa-ya [the incomprehensible sound of Korean language]. Strange! Why do you buy Korean music when it is just incomprehensible s**t
>
> Recently, I get colds easily with running noses because of the frequent invasion of the cold/Korean wave. Taiwanese are fools. Korean singers in Taiwan earn easy money. Pop idol singers only need to have sunny smiles and charms like the boys from next door. Their lyrics are like farts. Tell me why you like them. Bae Yong-jun is not even half as handsome as Wu Bai ["the king of Tai-ke"]
>
> F*** your mother's c***, f*** your mother's c***, f*** Bae Yong-jun, F*** Bae Yong-jun.[1] Yuki, A-mei, Coco Lee, s*** s*** s*** ... . s*** my d***

Refrain
The beautiful faces on the screen are killers, easy rhythm and superficial lyrics putrefy the heart. Painting peace as a veneer of the world, indulging in romantic love, [the lyrics] can't mask the world's injustices. The so-called great love is nothing but whining which makes me a rapper angry with you (Korean singers) like an enemy. Listening to you [Korean singers] sing provokes me to kick you. Your presence/face crosses me just like mine crosses you. Underneath your glamorous appearance, there is no depth. Audiences rush to you without any sense of integrity and distinction. They blindly take whatever you offer just like eating s**t. Are you [Taiwanese audience] willing to be a foolish grandson/scum? ...
> F*** f*** f*** f*** f*** f*** ...

What you see on television is only superficial, are you pretending to be a fool or are you a real fool? It's all about love, it's all too fake. Can't stand it. So I have to come forward and swear ... you eat guava/trash everyday, surely someday you'll be fed up with it, you must s**t, your excrement should be from your a**, but for the singers, s**t from the mouth
> F*** your mother' c***, f*** your mother's c***, f*** Bae Yong-jun, f*** Bae Yong-jun
> Yuki, A-mei, Coco Lee, s*** s*** s*** ... s*** my d***
Refrain

A series of binaries, with the subordination of the first term to the second term, are employed here as the underlying structure which allows the audiences to make sense of the song: Korean vs. Taiwanese, pop vs. rock/rap, love vs. politics, surface vs. depth, and women vs. men. Korean music is love/pop music without substance/depth and Korean singers only have beautiful faces. But Taiwanese women are fools who fall for appearance and love. Taiwanese rappers, on the contrary, use music to reveal social injustices, but their space as true and serious music is invaded by these superficial, sappy Korean singers. To take back their territory, they assert their masculine authority by f***ing the feminized Korean pop stars: Bae, Clon, and H.O.T. and demanding Taiwanese female pop singers to "s*** my d***" as a proclamation of female pop's submission to male rap/rock, of love to politics.

Through existing gender hierarchy, the Korean wave here is framed as a cold front invading foolish Taiwanese women, employing the weapon of love, smiles, and good looks, and causing Taiwanese men to sneeze with running noses. The addressees of this song are obviously those discriminating male audiences (mostly young men) who know the differences between good rap and bad pop. Scatology (the use of obscene words) is intentionally employed to convey rap's masculine power over feminine pop. The employment of scatology, however, can be read as the weapon of the powerless to speak against bourgeois norms of rationality. Kipnis (1992) and Stallybrass and White (1986) point out that there is a "transcoding between bodily and social topography, a transcoding which sets up a homology between the lower bodily stratum and the lower social classes." "The transcoding between the body and the social sets up the mechanisms through which the body is a privileged political trope of the lower social classes, and through which bodily grossness operates as a critique of dominant ideology." If the power of disgust is "predicated on its opposition from *and* to high discourses, themselves prophylactic against the debasement of the low (the lower classes, vernacular discourse, low culture, s**t ...)" (Kipnis: 376), then the transgressive power of this rap needs to be situated in its opposition to and from the "gentle and rational" mode of address (including gender civility) that the middle and professional managerial class set up as the norm.

To understand the transgression of this song as powerless against bourgeois rationality, I will route through the context of the alternative music scene in Taiwan. Alternative music in Taiwan emerged in the late 1980s with the hit compilation "Song of Madness" by Blacklisted Workshop. "Song of Madness" was seen as the product of the "golden ten-year social movements" in Taiwan — the burgeoning of women's movements, environmental movements, and democratic movements in 1980s Taiwan. Directly attacking the KMT government for erasing Taiwan's history and language, the compilation used Taiwanese, the forbidden language before the lift of martial law, rather than the official Mandarin, and adopted the genre of rap, to explicitly criticize local politics and address the concerns of the lower class (Lin, 2002).

The critical spirit caught the attention of the intellectual circle and soon was expanding its market to the young generation. In the early 1990s, Lin Chiang's hit song, "Marching Forward," marked the mainstreaming of songs in the Taiwanese language. However, unlike the previous alternative scene which emphasized its critical spirit toward politics, this song expressed the young generation's spirit of marching forward. Wu Bai followed Lin Chiang and became the next popular singer by incorporating rock to his music. Wu Bai's Taiwanese accent and his masculine stage performance, as opposed to the gentle, sappy, Mandarin pop performance, marked him "the king of Tai-ke." However, as songs in the Taiwanese language have gone into the mainstream, their alternativeness — using the Taiwanese language as a tool of political critique — which is central to this genre has also changed. Instead, alternativeness is characterized by its anti-mainstream, that is, anti-pop, ideology. The "alternative mainstream"[2] music expresses disdain for Mandarin pop through rocking, rapping, and celebrating "individuality" or "self-expression" (*ziwo zhuzhang*).

The recent singers, such as M.C. Hot Dog and Chang Chen-yue (the singers who rapped "The Invasion of the Korean Wave" at the Tai-ke concert), belong to this alternative mainstream scene. Tailored for the younger generation, these singers mix languages — English, Mandarin and Taiwanese (Holo) — to sing about the life experiences of urban male teenagers, such as taking on part-time jobs, the pressure of entrance exams, the desire and fun of "getting chicks" (*ba mei*), male bonding, street life, and so on. Unlike their counterpart rappers in the U.S. who address the poverty and crime of the underclass, these bands emphasize the spirit of "individuality" — in particular, teenage rebellion against conformity to parental and school authority, but keeping the misogynist attitude intact. In the case of M.C. Hot Dog and Chang Zhen-yue, they intentionally take on the Eminem-style in-your-face confrontation as their expression of individuality (Li Shan, 1998). They swear at pop singers and anything that is considered "mainstream" commercial success, including bourgeois ideal beauties such as Lin Chi-ling and Peggy Chen.

If the employment of scatology is read as transgression, its transgression is mostly about middle-class youths' rebellion against parental and school authority. However, that transgression has also to be framed within the previous discourse of globalization and economic nationalism which sets up Korea as a rival in the global economy, taking up resources and thus, threatening Taiwan's future. With the circulation of the discourse of the nation in crisis, teenagers are uncertain about where their future lies. Rather than taking the advice of studying hard and equipping themselves with the ability of "lifetime employability" as middle-class adults inform them, they use their only resources — their bodies and penises — to assert their symbolic power through f***ing the Korean stars and those women who fall for them. And the f***ing intentionally takes on a form of noise — as opposed to the gentle and rational mode of address that requires the abstraction of the body — shouting, screaming, sweating, wild dancing, rowdy clapping. Instead of "reasoning," f***ing (Koreans) becomes an affective mode of collective bodily movement, an affective mode of collective belonging.

However, as part of the Tai-ke concert, with Wu Bai as the organizer, this low discourse on the lower body stratum with much excrement and fluid gets eliminated and recontextualized within a high discourse of national identity. Because of the historical roots of alternative music which is associated with the rediscovery of Taiwanese consciousness and the political critique of the KMT ideology, the cultural debate triggered by the f***ing of the

Korean wave gets articulated to a discussion on the meaning of Tai-ke — what it means to be Taiwanese and what Taiwanese culture is — within domestic ethnic/class conflicts. The North Club (*Bei She*) points out that Tai-ke is a debased term for the Taiwanese because it carries the historical trauma of denigration that the mainlanders (*waishengren*) had imposed on the Taiwanese in subordinating them through culture (W.C Yang, 2005; C.Z. Yang, 2005). Wu Bai and many other critics, on the other hand, argue that with the commercial success, Tai-ke's negative meaning is subverted and is now given a positive touch to mean "coolness" and confidence (Wu, 2005). The two opposing groups represent two kinds of national imagination, with Wu Bai's economic nationalism taking center stage.

Scatology here, in particular, the rhetorical employment of male sexual organs, is constructed — through the eradication of vulgar language in public forums and the use of rational, analytical language — to symbolize the lowliness of the Taiwanese (guest) as opposed to the highness of the mainlander (hosts), and that lowliness is considered as the product of the KMT ruling which privileges mainlanders through the exploitation, politically, culturally, and economically, of the Hoklo and Hakka groups. As such, scatology is established as the essence of Taiwanese culture — something that needs to be redeemed through the subversion of its historically associated humiliation.[3] The redemption of scatology as a form of national culture is made through its articulation as economic nationalism — the dominant discourse of the bourgeoisie. I will use the definition made by "the king of Tai-ke," Wu Bai, to explain the process of "subversion" (a term used by many critics in Taiwan) or "redemption":

> I have always hoped to dance my soul on the world stage, and the soul here refers to the Tai-ke spirit. Its essence is to stand on our land and ground ourselves in what our land supplies us. [This is like] doing stretching exercises. On the one hand, my feet stand tightly on the ground; on the other hand, I let my hands stretch upward and try to transcend my own limitations ... The Tai-ke concert is trying to create, discover ... the special characteristic and essence of our own culture ... . We hope to transform it into a new Cultural Revival Movement ... .
> (Wu Bai, *China Times,* 17 Aug 2005)

This quote characterizes Tai-ke music as the direct expression of national culture which is grounded on land and tradition while stretching out to incorporate new elements. This definition reflects the discourse of cultural nationalism since the 1970s which uses "land" to locate Taiwanese consciousness (as opposed to Chinese consciousness). This land-centered discourse allowed the DPP to develop a new discourse of cultural nationalism — "community of fate" in the late 1980s and early 1990s to incorporate all ethnicities into the nation in order to deflate ethnic conflicts. Since then, this discourse has become the dominant discourse of cultural nationalism — a discourse of multiculturalism, of the fusion of different cultures, grounded in the land of Taiwan (Hsiau, 1999; Hsiau, 2000). However, the attempt to find one's own culture, as Wu states, is a "pure market concern" to find one's own niche within the current music market (Wu Bai, *Eslite Review*). Liu's analysis of the Tai-ke phenomenon, which gains much support among the public, also frames it within the discourse of globalization discussed in the previous section:

> The emergence of the concept of Tai-ke … is a brand-name promoted by the market forces … . Multiple media participated in defining this brand-name … it is the product of their promotion … What we need to face is competition from Korea, Japan, and India's culture industries in the Chinese market. The critical winning point is not about the definition of Tai-ke or Taiwaneseness, but about the creation and maintenance of more capital, distribution and promotion … (Liu, *China Times* 22 Aug 2005).

Here, scatology and Taiwaneseness are articulated — scatology as the essence of *ben-tu* (local) culture — as such, it becomes an asset to be used as a surviving strategy in the global economy. Consequently, the original ethnic/class conflicts are subsumed under this economic urgency as the editorial on "Tai-ke and Korean Wave" advocates: "Tai-ke should avoid ethnic conflicts and learn from Bae Yong-jun, a symbol of qing, which transcends all ethnic conflicts and transforms it into economic advantage" (Editorial, *China Times*, 20 Aug 2005). The potential use of scatology in the rap, "The Invasion of the Korean Wave," as transgressive of bourgeois public speech, of parental authority, of ethnic/class boundaries gets subsumed under the logic of the economy in the name of national culture. As Yudice observes, "the turn to creative economy evidently favors the professional-managerial class, even as it trades on the rhetoric of multicultural inclusion. Subordinate or minoritized groups have a place in this scheme as low-level service workers and as providers of 'life-giving' ethnic and other cultural experiences" (2003: 20). In other words, it is through the buying and selling of minoritized groups' life experiences in the name of multiculturalism that the creative industry thrives, to the benefit of a few.

Not only is Tai-ke's experience as a powerless group in the society being traded in the cultural economy, women's powerless experiences as unhappy housewives are also managed and channeled into profit — the cause of the popularity of the Korean wave. However, before I delve into the third discourse on women as the consumers and participants of the Korean wave, I would like to emphasize the gender politics of these discourses of economic and cultural nationalism. The elite discourse uses a rational and gentle mode of address as its norm, a masculine mode of address that abstracts itself from the lower body stratum (which leaves the brain as the only part allowed in the public sphere) and universalizes itself as the voice of truth. Under the guise of rationality and gentleness, military metaphors are employed to construct a nation in crisis, hence, the urgency for the reformation of national heroes and national citizens. And this urgency is made through constructing Korea as the other — a tough enemy competing for limited global resources. The second discourse on the Korean wave operates within this framework but deliberately uses the lower body stratum — Taiwanese men's masculine power to f***/fight the Koreans — as its mode of address. However, the use of bodily excrements and fluids as a mode of speech can only circulate in a sub-public sphere, subordinated to the rational public sphere (hence, its appearance on entertainment pages). However, this mode of address gets elevated to the rational public sphere when rappers, rockers and critics articulate this event to cultural nationalism and economic nationalism, making invisible the use of misogynist language which constitutes the core of this "low" genre. This "low" genre, however, depends upon its subordination of women/pop/love to position its high-ness in the consumption/ entertainment space. This means that, both these nationalistic discourses in the rational public sphere and the consumption space leave women with no legitimate place to speak as higher beings.

But it is women who, through their participation in the consumption of Korean dramas, create the Korean wave. How are they positioned in the (sub-) public sphere? How are they spoken about? And how do they speak as subjects? In the next section, I will analyze the third discourse on the Korean wave, mainly, the fan discourse. I will first analyze how they are spoken about in the entertainment pages in the public sphere and then, discuss their own form of address within fans themselves. I argue that this feminine fan discourse is contained to the genre of complaint in the public sphere, disturbing but at the same time affirming the dominance of the masculine rational public sphere.

Korean Drama Fans Speaking Out and Spoken About

Warner (1992) points out the inherent contradiction within the bourgeois public sphere — that with its minoritizing strategy through the abstraction of the bourgeois body, the bourgeois public sphere always fails to keep its promises, leaving minoritized bodies to seek consumption for the fulfillment of these promises. However, in the case of Taiwan, as discussed in the first section, the rational public sphere itself speaks the language of the economy; that is, there is a conflation of the public sphere with the economic sector. Within this context, the commercial sector actually plays a double role — on the one hand, through the rational mode of address, it constructs Korean drama fans as a spectacle — a surface, a carnivalesque image — to be watched and consumed by the rational public; on the other hand, it provides fantasies and dreams for those Korean drama fans whose frustration comes mostly from the failed promises of the rational public sphere. Debord discusses the spectacle as a "social relationship among people mediated by images," which provides legitimation for the domination of the ruling classes over the masses (Debord, 1994:12). What Debord proposes is that images are ideological tools which play a double function — on the one hand, as pure surface, they mask their mode of production which produces unequal social divisions; on the other hand, they channel proletariats' real interests into the consumption of images and commodities. Taking this double notion theorized by Warner and Debord, but re-reading it through Mulvey's (1992) women-as-spectacle (which emphasizes woman as the object and man as the subject of gaze), I want to emphasize the gendered dimension of spectacle which, on the one hand, constructs Korean drama fans as the other — a spectacle for the consumption of the general public; on the other hand, a spectacle that serves as an ideological tool that channels women's gendered harm into consumption.

I will first provide an account of the Korean drama fans being spoken about in the public space as spectacle of the Other to be consumed by the general public. I will use the media coverage of Bae's visit to Taiwan to promote *April Snow* as an example to illustrate this point. On 20, 21, and 22 August in 2005, all the major newspapers in Taiwan, including *Apple Daily*, *China Times*, *United Daily*, and *Liberty Times*, used the bulk of their entertainment page to cover this event. The coverage was image-centered. Different sized brightly colored pictures were arranged disorderly to create a sense of uncontrollability and excitement, like a noise disrupting the banality of everyday life. Even the headlines were colored bright red, blue, green, and yellow (as a contrast to the sobriety of the serious economics and politics pages). These noisy pictures, which are about and of the body, can be divided into two categories. The first category contains the bodies of the irrational and overjoyed fans crowding and squeezing, even stepping on each other, competing for Bae's attention, or better yet, his physical touch. Headlines such as "Fans Thrilled Out of Control to Have Handsome Bae's Hugs" (*Liberty Times,* 22 Aug 2005), "Crossing the Ocean to Pursue Bae Yong-jun, Fans Offer Loads of Gifts "(*Liberty Times,* 20 Aug 2005), "People Wall Crumbled Down with the Arrival of Handsome Bae: 66 Year-old Grandma Tripped in the Crowds at the Bottom of Human Pyramid but Still Insisted on Chasing after Bae" (*China Times,* 20 Aug 2005). "Come and Take a Picture with the Water Cup that Bae Just Drank From" (*China Times,* 20 Aug 2005). "Hard to Say Good-bye to Handsome Bae, the Airport Is Wild and Chaotic" (*Liberty Times,* 22 Aug 2005). These headlines, with the use of different colors, while describing the popularity of Bae, convey the craziness and childishness of these Korean drama fans. Both the headlines and pictures make these fans and their behavior into a spectacle for the consumption and entertainment of the general public. However, with the spectacularization of these images as out of control, these female Korean drama fans are also constructed as the Other of bourgeois rationality — a bunch of brainless bodies driven by desires, fantasies, and illusions.

The second category of pictures are mostly of Bae's body — his close-ups, his clothes, his handshakes with fans, his every gesture and movement, and most important of all, his smiles. Captions which facilitate the anchoring of the meanings of images emphasize fans' carnivorous desires for Bae's body. A few examples will suffice. The first example is a series of pictures and corresponding captions demonstrating the fans' ecstasy in gazing at Bae's body. The first picture is a close-up of Bae pouting: "God! Handsome Bae's small pouting mouth." This is followed by another close-up of his legs and ankles: "Look, without wearing socks, Bae is still very cute." The third picture of the series is a close-up of his torso, with a bit of his belly exposed: "Wow! Wow! Wow! Handsome Bae exposes his small belly" (*Liberty Times,* 20 Aug 2005). The second example also comprises of a series of pictures: the first one is full-length photo of Bae, with an inset featuring Bae's calves and shoes, with the caption reading: "Oh, oh, the shoelace is loose! Wish I could tie it for him." Following this picture is a close-up of Bae drinking water, with the caption: "His pose for drinking water is 'super-elegant'!" This is followed by a picture of him eating: "Look at him eating, it's / he's delicious." The final picture in this series is also a close-up of him, making with a V sign: "Handsome Bae reveals his secret code!" (*Liberty Times* 22 Aug 2005).

Here we have to pay attention to the addressee of these images as these images play the double function of subordination and satisfaction. While these entertainment pages circulate along with the serious pages among the general public, they are also pitched toward women. Hence, the chaos the first category of images creates — through the descriptive modes of address, coupled with frivolous visual and verbal languages — produces the effect of this page as subordinate to the seriousness of political and economic affairs, and women as subordinate to men because of their irrationality and their concern about triviality. The second category of images speaks of intimacy among women. It draws from the genre of female fan speech — confessions of bodily sensations in encountering their idols.[4] In this type of speech, bodily touch and sensations are emphasized such as body contact, hand-shakes, exchanges of eye contact, throbbing and pumping heart ("my heart pumps from *putung putung* to *bang bang bang*," as one fan confesses), or the feeling that the brain is blank, or that things are out of control. Through their direct mode of address (confession) and their emphasis on bodily sensations, these images speak directly to the desires of female Korean drama fans — particularly their sexual desires for men — like women's pajama party talk. This private speech, while satisfying women's private desires, is also relegated to the space of the low in the public sphere because of its violation of the convention of female respectability/morality — the only mode of address allotted to women in the rational public sphere.

However, rather than the "f***ing experience" that the minoritized men invoke as the expression of their transgression through their masculine power, the female fans, on the other hand, frame these bodily talks within heterosexual romantic longings, as in "He [Bae] smiles at me, just like Joon-sang [the male protagonist] in *Winter Sonata*." This particular framing emphasizes that women's emotional needs have to be attentively looked after, to be cared for with love and gentleness by men — a desire that emerges out of men's "f***ing" carelessness. A female complaint channeled into escape through the vicarious living of a Korean dramatic fantasy.

In fact, unlike the rational economic discourse on the Korean wave which uses qing (interpreted through the frame of Confucian ethics) to explain the popularity of Korean dramas, many popular discourses (including television news which is the exemplar of Taiwan's lowness) and fan discourses acknowledge that it is gender injury that triggers the Korean wave. However, this gender harm is used as a form of economic resource for capital gain — a point echoing Yudice's observation on how minority's experiences of subordination get used for capital gain as a way of managing populations. I will use one example to illustrate how gender injury is contained to a form of female complaint through women's genre of romance.

ET Mall (the largest television shopping channel in Taiwan) recently shot a commercial, "The Blissful Smile" (*xingfu weixiao*), inviting Bae to be their channel's spokesman. This commercial, a co-production between Korea and Taiwan, claims ET Mall, demonstrates Bae's "brand-name smile and amorous gaze" (*shenqing yanshen*). "Combining all the elements of Korean dramas that Taiwanese women desire, this is a mini-Korean drama which transforms Bae into a persistent lover who silently and quietly cares about his first love. As long as he sees his girl friend smile, he feels contented" (ET Mall, "The Blissful Smile Blog"). Starting with Bae's smile, followed by daisy fields and then sunlight shining through tree leaves onto his face, the commercial sets its tranquil and romantic tone while at the same time fulfilling its promise of giving "warmth" to their audience through their delivery of Bae's sunny smile. Accompanied by Michael Jackson's "Too Young" as its theme music (sang by a female vocalist), the commercial uses a man's voice — Bae's monologue of his interior desire — to narrate a love story. The story emphasizes loving and caring at a distance. Through the secret delivery of daisies to his first love every week (who is now married and has one little girl), Bae is contented, from a distance, to see his first love's smile, and because of her smile, his love persists as well as his delivery of flowers. The commercial ends with Bae's narration: "For the past four years, as long as I can see her happy smile, I feel blissful. I don't need any reason, for the [love] of her smile. I will see you again next week, for the next ten years, with determination and persistence. Just like we are determined, with all our heart, to see your smile – ET Mall."

That "love at a distance" — of being cared for from a distance — is the safest kind of love that women can afford without disrupting their marriage or the normality of their lives — taking care of children, cooking, cleaning, working, and shopping. Moreover, this family space which is safe-guarded by the distance of love is also a national space — with a Korean man's love at a distance, the sanctity of male domination within the "domestic" space is also preserved. This commercial, reflective of the "essence" of Korean dramas, transforms women's unhappiness with their husbands in the space of the family — the foundation of a nation — to an imaginary world of love — which, of course, can be obtained through consumption (of ET Mall commodities). Berlant (1988) calls this the mode of containment which transforms women's speech about their rage into the genre of complaint. The female complaint exemplifies the social contradictions that women face in a phallocentric culture — that culture channels women's sexual and emotional desire and allegiance to men (especially about the promise/lie that marriage is the end and means to women's happiness) while at the same time denies women power and privilege in the public sphere. The female complaint serves as a mediation of this contradiction — that women use this cultural form to speak out their rage against the patriarchal lie in the public sphere while at the same time this rage gets circumscribed as a speech not to be taken seriously. This female complaint is an "aesthetic witnessing to women's injury":

> To the extent that women employ the complaint as a mode of self-expression, it is an admission and a recognition both of privilege and powerless: it is a powerful record of patriarchal oppression, circumscribed by a knowledge of women's inevitable delegitimation within the patriarchal public sphere. The a priori marking of female discourse as less serious is paradoxically the only condition under which the complaint mode can operate as an effective political tool: the female complaint allows the woman who wants to maintain her alignment with men to speak oppositionally but without fear for her position within the heterosexual economy — because the mode of her discourse concedes the intractability of the (phallocentric) conditions of the complaint's production. (Berlant 1988: 243)

The Korean drama fans, when spoken about in the public sphere, are represented as wild and irrational for the consumption of the general public. At the same time, their private talk in the bedroom — with an emphasis on the language of bodily sensations and sexual desires — is also spectacularized, with the effect of reinforcing the myth of women being controlled by bodies — a brainless being. With this antinomy between women and rationality, women's outrage against gender injury gets channeled and translated, through the genre of romance, into female complaint which at the end, safeguards patriarchal order.

Conclusion: Creating a Space for Women in the Public Sphere

In this chapter, I have tried to demonstrate the gendered nature of the public sphere which leaves women no place to speak as authorities. Through deconstructing the meanings of the Korean wave articulated in Taiwan, I point out that, the most dominant discourse of the Korean wave is the discourse of economic nationalism which uses a rational and gentle mode of address to legitimize its domination through the rhetoric of the nation. However, this national space belongs to a few elite men only. The second discourse of the Korean wave, despite its employment of scatology, is elevated to the debate about cultural nationalism and circulated within the respected cultural space for (male) intellectuals. Male vulgarity is redeemed through its articulation as the essence of Taiwaneseness and is subsumed under the logic of the economy when articulated to the discourse of economic nationalism.

These two discourses on the Korean wave, articulated through the logics of the nation, the economy, and their convergence, leaves women no place to speak. The third discourse, a discourse about women spoken about and speaking out, unfortunately, relegates women's speech to a genre of complaint. Unlike male vulgarity in the public space which uses the nation as its redemption (either cultural nationalism or economic nationalism), women's injury gets circumscribed within the national space of the heterosexual family, which excludes them as active participants of the nation. Hence, they are deprived of the hope of redemption as national citizens, except through consumption.

But if feminists' work is to "transform discursive material that, in its untransformed state, leaves a woman no place from which to speak, or nothing to say" (Freadman, quoted in Morris 1988: 3), what can be done here? Morris speaks of this transformation of existing masculine discursive material as a problem of "rhetoric," of thinking about "the production of a speaking-position as a matter of strategies of reference" (1988: 7). If so, what speaking positions or references can feminists offer on the Korean wave for transformation?

Heidegger's reading of technology might be a starting point to think about the strategies of transformation. Heidegger defines technology as "enframing" (Ge-stell) which embodies two paradoxical meanings. The first essence of technology refers to a kind of instrumentality which orders every way we live, driving out any other possible way of living, thinking, and revealing. "Enframing means the gathering of that setting-upon which sets upon man, i.e., challenges him forth, to reveal the real in the mode of ordering, as standing reserve" (1977: 20).[5] At the same time, Heidegger also reminds us of the other essence of technology as located in the realm of poiesis which "lets what presences come forth into unconcealment" (1977: 21). That is, through the second essence of technology — of bringing forth that which is already ordered into appearance/unconcealment — that the instrumental nature of the first essence of technology can be undermined. He situates that space of transcendence in the realm of art. Yudice uses the first notion of technology to describe the way culture is made into "standing reserve," always available for ordering, for instrumental use. He argues that "culture as a resource" has become the episteme for the postmodern times, even art itself has become a resource for economic ordering. As such, there is no transcendental space to speak against such ordering. Given technology's double meaning, rather than look for a transcendental space for its subversion, that space should be immanent within technology itself. Hence, Berlant, though coming from a different perspective, argues for a kind of critique within technological space: "Rather, feminist populism will be [sic] emerge from the engagement of the female culture industry with the patriarchal public sphere, the place where significant or momentous exchanges of power are perceived to take place" (1988: 240).

I argue that female complaint should be the space for us to think about transforming existing discursive material in order to open up speaking positions for women. In my analysis, it is the logic of the economy — the space of technology, of instrumentality — that dictates what the public sphere should be while at the same time providing a safety valve for its failed promises. As such, this is the space that we need to work with to bring forth into unconcealment what has been ordered. The logic of the economy plays two hands. On the one hand, it constructs a hierarchy among different discourses circulated and addressed to different publics. Through the rhetoric of the nation, the logic of the economy, in the name of the bourgeois public sphere, elevates itself to the national space, designating itself as the guiding light of the nation. This self-designation is made through the employment of a particular mode of address — rationality and gentleness — which it also constructs as the superior speech mode in the public sphere. Male/masculine vulgarity, as such, is excluded from this mode of speech. However, as a form of private locker room talk made public, male bodily vulgarity is elevated to the rhetoric of transgression in the national space of conflicting ethnic/class interests. The logic of the economy exploits this male scatology as transgression for commercial gains while at the same time elevating its status to the space of the national — it turns the debate into a debate about cultural nationalism while using economic nationalism to circumscribe this space of cultural nationalism. Female intimacy/vulgarity, however, takes a very different route. The logic of economy, through the adoption of rationality as the standard public speech, subordinates female vulgarity into irrationality which cannot be redeemed in the national space; at the same time, it exploits women's gender injury as a result of subordination (which the masculine national space fails to address) and circumscribes it into the genre of female complaint.

But as I demonstrate, via Berlant, that female complaint is female outrage and injury made public. Women's resistance potential lies in this outrage. However, if feminist's work is to create speaking positions for women, female complaint as it is can not be the form to operate through. Rather, it is through the demonstration of the logic of the economy — the ordering of culture into hierarchy and the ordering of minority culture into standing reserve — via different rhetorical modes that subordinates women's speech to triviality.

While minority culture, in this case, women's culture gets technologized into standing reserve, it is this technologization of minority into minority that exposes rationality's façade.

At the same time, feminists need to rewrite women's genre, to open up women's injury to a space exceeding its current enframing within the national space of heteronormativity. The genre of complaint, exemplified by the ET Mall commercial, incorporates women's gender injury into the national space of family — a space of phallocentricism, with the Korean man as a savior only looking and caring from afar while women are commanded to the "s***ing" job! A feminist intervention would have to expose the gender hierarchy that structures the nation and national family, turning women's injury into outrage, breaking apart the national family and extending it to the transnational space. While the national family gives rise to women's emotional attachments to men, women's pajama talk offers the potential for breaking apart the sacredness of the national family which functions as the conditions of its production. In fans' pajama party talk, gender injury and romantic longing (which are two sides of the same coin within the commercial space) get to be expressed through the cutting up of foreign male bodies into fragments (such as Bae's legs, pouting mouth, hand gestures, exposed belly, and so on — as shown in the newspaper entertainment pages analyzed above), but this cutting up of male bodies also functions as a form of sharing and exchange of intimacy among women. For example, a Korean drama fan spoke about her obsession with Bae to me (also a fan of Bae) in an interview: "there is nothing to say about him [my husband]. In reality, [Taiwanese] men can never be like Bae Yong-jun, this is why I like Korean dramas so much … If you get to see Bae in Korea, touch him for me! Oh, his smile melts my heart … I can't wait to see more of his body [in the movie *Scandal*], oh, his naked body is so sexy!"[6] Within this fan space of pajama talk, the national space of men gets eliminated (out of women's rage for their own men) from the picture, however, the foreign men also get cut up into pieces to be shared (as in "touch him for me") — something that undermines the one-man-one woman romantic ideal that heternormativity relies on (men are exempt from this though). This subversion of normative heterosexual desire (through dispossession and sharing of male bodies) can be more powerful if we also emphasize the other function of pajama talk — as a space of female intimacy and bonding. This reading of fans' private talk, accompanied by the exposure of the logic of the economy in subordinating this talk to triviality, hopefully, can create a new script for women's speech in the public sphere which challenges the existing discursive references around the Korean wave.

11

Existing in the Age of Innocence: Pop Stars, Publics, and Politics in Asia

Eva Tsai[1]

> What the star does can *only* be posed in terms of the *star doing it* [original emphasis], the extraordinariness of difficulty of his/her doing it, rather than in terms of the ostensible political issues involved. (Dyer 1979, p. 79)

Although it is not without historical precedences, the 1990s and 2000s have seen a heightened effort by cultural promoters in Asia to bring together big and familiar names from the region to make and market a variety of media and cultural commodities. In 2004, Pepsi put nine popular Hong Kong and Taiwan stars in a multi-market, region-wide advertising campaign. Around the same time, *hallyu*, or the Korean Wave, marshaled a new breed of Asian-Korean celebrities. The entertainment pages in Asia's major newspapers and magazines contain a flurry of stories and images of pop stars from close and distant neighbors making "hurricane-style" visits. The omnipresence of Asian celebrities — made possible by trans-Asian cultural traffic and constituencies — becomes, inescapably, a matter of public culture. While the star still draws attraction by a self-sustaining logic as noted by film scholar Richard Dyer, political issues are moving to the foreground, especially in the inter-Asian context.

In this chapter, I strategically juxtapose two Asian pop stars who both became "grounded" amid trans-border politics in 2004. Aboriginal-Taiwanese pop diva Chang Hui-Mei (A-mei) faced "patriotic" protesters in China and unpatriotic charges "back home" from Taiwanese politicians. Song Seung-Heon, the leading man in the *hallyu* hit drama, *Autumn Fairytale*, admitted to draft-dodging by illegal means and began mandatory military service despite efforts by fans to keep him on a highly anticipated drama about to begin production. Treating pop stars as accessible sites of contentious public meanings in inter-Asia, this research experiments with an inter-referential approach by examining analogous experiences in which much valued transnational stars became implicated in public debates about national loyalty. The discourses and experiences of the diverse publics (e.g., the press, authorities, and fans) who claimed a stake in the predicaments of Chang and Song illuminated an intimate relationship between politics and entertainment in Asia. Chang and Song are hardly the only celebrities coping with the respective dynamics of cross-strait politics and the morality behind South Korean conscription in times of globalization. But their explicit and difficult entanglement with the official definitions of patriotism and the subsequent affective engagement of their cross-strait and transnational fans underscore issues of irreconciliation in border-crossing, from stars' resistance to politicization, the infantilization of popular culture and its participants, to the inappropriateness of criticizing across the national and gender border. Stardom and fandom in this chapter re-politicize the "politically correct" ambassadorial function of popular culture in the transnational context and recast notions of East Asian publics through affective terrains.

Pop Stars as an Oblique Site of Inquiry

A site of inquiry rather than proof of fame, the phenomenon of trans-Asian pop stars allows ordinary participation in the trans-Asia cultural traffic. It also raises questions about the public meanings of "Asia" because of celebrities' capacity to involve multiple publics in intimate ways. Building on the political concern in star studies, this section situates pop stars in Asia's politicized contexts and raises signposts for dealing with the un/popular[2] mixture of pop stars and politics.

Traditionally a contingency of film studies, research on celebrities and stars as "intimate strangers" (Schickle 2000) has grown over the years in media and cultural studies with a focus on Asia. Some studies draw a relationship between the star texts and cultural identities along lines of gender, ethnicity and sexuality (Chou 1997; Gallagher 1997; Martin 2003; Lee 2004; Darling-Wolf 2004). Others focus on contextualizing the star persona in specific industrial, cultural and historical conditions (Raine 2001; Tsai 2005; Fung and Curtin 2002). Transnational stars in these studies become de-centered, "oblique" venues for discussing a range of converging issues like cultural formations and identity politics.

Understanding the social embodiment of stars is a classic agenda in film-originated star studies. The ideological criticism put forth by Dyer (1979) is concerned with how ideological work in contemporary, mass-mediated societies helps settle the contradictory values and meanings around certain constructed personalities. This explains why certain individuals effectively appear "larger-than-life." Yet in most of the film-based star analysis and western celebrities studies, there has been little interest in making explicit or contesting the national borders. Other shifting borders within the nation, such as sexuality (DeAngelis 2001), race (Dyer 1986; Nakamura 2002), and gender (Stacey 1994) have formed the basis of analysis. But there is no reason why the "at-large" cultural influence of stars must be national in scope when cultural borders are being rapidly remapped today. As Meaghan Morris reminds us, "… when cultural goods are trafficked, we are entitled intensively to study their *uptake* in any of the contexts in which they circulate, without always following them back to a 'source'" (2004, p. 252).

The "uptake" of pop stars in Asia is, precisely, their politicization in a region where nation-states still figure actively and prominently into the identities of people. There are a variety of circumstances in which entertainers become part of politics. Chang's and Song's involvement in politics was publicity of the unflattering kind. Both entertainers faced a career crisis and a media feeding frenzy. The perception of stars being victimized by politics may even produce the illusion that entertainers can somehow remain apolitical. Indeed, a politicized view of a pop star can be unpopular unless it is couched in the politically correct (still political!) language of cultural exchange.

But in Asia, ideological changes and divides in the region have yielded opportunities for pop stars' involvement in political affairs. An example would be Kao Jin Su-mei (a.k.a. May Chin), former actress known for her role in Ang Lee's *Wedding Banquet* and a legislator in Taiwan since 2001. With her newly claimed Ataya heritage, she has become a representative of the disenfranchised aborigines, leading famously the descendants of the former Takasago people in several protests to demand that Japanese government remove the names of volunteer soldiers from the Yasukuni Shrine.[3]

Meanwhile, as vibrant public expressions and political society emerge in Asia and contend with the nation-state's narrow definition of what is political, the inability and unwillingness of pop stars to handle political issues can be seen as a failure to perform their duty as citizens. The recent one-man protest initiated by Korean film stars like Jang Dong-gun against the South Korean government's plan to reduce screen quotas under the pressure of the United

States prompted a Hong Kong critic Ip Iam Chong (2006) to lament the political apathy of Hong Kong film directors and stars.

Inspired by the outspokenness of some stars from other countries, the expectation for pop stars to develop a political voice seems to be gaining ground.[4] The perspective that politics and entertainment do interpenetrate has its merit — a position this chapter is siding with. But it also opens a can of worms, that is, a political game that can be quite ruthless and hierarchical, preserving certain positions of substantiation — often more alternative, anti-establishment — while excluding other questionable "political" practices. The place of fans as politicized publics, for instance, seems to have been overlooked given their association with the "depoliticized" stars.[5]

Doing Inter-referential Research in Asia

Since I have already trotted into the area of inter-referencing, let me use this opportunity to elaborate my inter-referential approach toward the politicization of trans-Asian pop stars and the perspectives that have informed this experiment. But first, inter-referencing is hardly mimicking, like demanding that pop stars adopt certain political causes. If political consequences are inevitable in Asia's public culture, it becomes necessary to identify and differentiate between ways of politicization instead of assuming safety in a prescribed solution. It does not seem productive to ask why stars in one nation (particularly "our nation") cannot be as gutsy as the outspoken movie stars in another nation.[6] Getting to the circumstances in which the celebratory language of pop stars is burst open and pluralized beyond the control of publicity — like Chang's and Song's reluctant engagement with cross-strait and transnational politics — can be equally illuminating, if not more so because it is only then that we have successfully undone the "superlative" rhetorical catch identified in Leo Lowenthal's (1962) critique of celebrities.

The year 2004 was a demoralizing year for Chang's and Song's fans. It was supposed to be a glorious year for both stars. Chang had planned a concert in China, which was the most anticipated event since her Beijing concert in 1999 and Shanghai concert in 2002. Song was riding high on the tide of "hallyu" owing to the popularity of *Autumn Fairytale* and *Summer Scent*. All eyes were on his next starring role in *Sad Love Story*, a drama also backed by Japanese and Taiwanese investors.

But on 12 June 2004, Chang was forced to cancel her appearance in Hangzhou because of safety concerns. Outside the venue, a group of self-identified "patriots" held a banner that read "Pro-Taiwan Independence Green People Not Welcome," apparently reacting to the online circulation of a "green list" that supposedly identifies the political leaning of Taiwanese entertainers. In the next month and a half leading to Chang's scheduled solo concert in Beijing, tension loomed over the straits. Chang held a successful concert at Capital Stadium on 31 July 2004. But she had barely enough time to catch her breath before finding herself in the hot water of another patriotic test. On a radio show, Taiwan's Vice President Annette Lu urged Chang to weigh her career in China against the security of her fellow Taiwanese living in a "quasi-war state" (Wang and Chang 2004, p. 1). Chang told the media that politics should be left in the hands of "daren" [grown-ups, authorities][7] "I am just a singer doing what I am supposed to do. When I stand on the stage, I do my best to deliver a perfect performance. I don't have the capacity to join the world of the 'daren.' Let's leave the matter to 'daren' to handle since they know the best" (Yuan 2004, p. A3).

About a month after the public debate on Chang's dilemma quieted down in Taiwan, South Korean police were conducting its largest draft-dodging scandal investigation. The arrest of ten baseball players and two brokers led the police to identify athletes and entertainers who sought to get out of compulsory service. This included Song, who at the time was filming the music video of *Sad Love Story* in Australia. In a public statement to the Korean press and his fans, Song admitted having manipulated medical records to dodge conscription. He expressed regret for his misconduct and willingness to follow the government order. "I'd like to take this opportunity to be more mature," he wrote in an open statement. Song returned to Seoul to cooperate with the investigation after finishing shooting the music video. Support from his fan groups in Taiwan, China, Hong Kong, and Japan poured in to urge the Military Manpower Administration (MMA), the South Korean government, and related authorities to credit Song's contribution to the phenomenal "hallyu" in Asia. Following a very public physical checkup and an international send-off, Song began 24-month army service on 16 November 2004.

The above narratives weaves Chang's and Song's predicaments into a common "coming-of-age" story. Both stars have been subject to some kind of a patriotic test. The description juxtaposes the two entertainers whose unlike audiences and career paths became possible references for each other in the trans-Asian cultural traffic — a fertile soil for tapping into the materiality of what Kuan-hsing Chen (2001; 2005b) called a not-yet-postcolonial and not-yet-post-Cold-War Asia. Working primarily in the area of politics, Chen is committed to forming alliances with third world cultural critics and turning to alternative, non-western dominated frames of references to breathe new life into the practices of knowledge production. In "Asia as Method" (2005a), he further elaborates the potential gain in working toward a new Asian imagination, which makes it possible to own up to the historical legacies in the region from the colonial, cold-war, and imperial structures of power.[8]

In line with Chen's syncretic approach, the inter-referencing task of this chapter hopes to enlarge the critical discursive space on Asia by tackling the relations of the popular, political and public. I will comment on the critical intervention by academics (a kind of politicization of the popular), raise the possibility of popular cultural flows in inter-Asia as a space that accommodates publics, and end with a caution on the exclusion of the official-political by the popular-public.

Claiming to speak or write on "Asia," as suggested by critical historians (Ching 2000; Chun and Shamsul 2001; Sun 2000a; 2000b), has constituted a political practice. The movement of inter-Asia cultural studies has begun to tease out Asia's complex dynamics from various disciplinary locations.[9] This interventionist effort to complicate the meanings of Asia from intellectual circles is political, but its distance from the popular experience and discourses where politicized definitions of Asia could just as well emerge has not been sufficiently bridged.[10] A certain "public" has perpetually eluded the radar detection of academic discourses that speak in the name of the "popular." Criticizing leftist media critics in Taiwan for holding moralist standards on what is acceptable as the "public," Ning Ying-bin (2004) has pointed out that despite its exploitativeness, low-brow variety shows on commercial TV channels for publicity purposes are more accessible to the working class, the "deviant," and the truly marginalized people than public television programs. Though not quite so subversive, the at-large "public" in this research does imply various bodies (e.g., fans, academics, government) and styles (e.g., rational, affective) of interactions.

For those who have studied the cultural flows in Asia, the prospect of a pan-Asian identity is precarious and political. It demands a re-definition of terms by acknowledging experiences from different histories and positions. For instance, can trans-Asian cultural traffic, characterized by Morris (2004, p. 257) as a "new space of circulation that can tolerate, bear, and make use of relations of unlikeness, even while the liberating experiences of recognizing or constructing resemblances" be re-conceptualized as a public zone? My answer to it begins by accounting for, briefly, the personal — that is, my relationship, access, and sensitivity to the at-large public of Asia. Informed by interpretive, ethnographic, reflexive, and empirical strategies of inquiry, my pursuit of publics in Asia — which I can't and am unwilling to simplify to the likes of the "Chinese public" and the "Korean public" — led me to multiple issues of reconciliation. By reconciliation I mean working out spaces of recognition, not doing away the political with cultural. As Jing Wang (2001) suggests in her critique of the Chinese "popular," the popular can't be treated automatically in opposition to the state or to the high brow. The rise of creative culture industries and Korean popular culture indicate that government authorities are actively involved in producing popular culture. The issue comes down to our capacity to handle and translate their relationship in the non-fixed relations of the popular, public, and political.

Surviving Patriotism in the Post-national Age

The rise of Chang Hui-Mei is a classic Cinderella story in two senses. She lived out the promise of individual transcendence of the culture industry and she — a Puyuma descendant from Taitung — has made it to the top in a society dominated by Han-ethnic Chinese. The "A-mei phenomenon," coined after the sale of two million albums in 1996, was said to symbolize the advent of a new taste, the ascent of aboriginal culture, and the salvation of homesick urban audiences (Yang 1997; Lo 1998a; Lo 1998b; Wang 1998). No one ever doubted Chang's ability to sing, given her experience as a tested champion on a television audition and as a pub singer before her debut. She also proved to be a true live diva, capable of moving her audience with a powerful and versatile voice and unrestrained body language, whether it is in a cozy setting or a stadium show attended by tens of thousands of people. In 1999, Chang held sold-out concerts throughout Southeast Asia. Her concert in Beijing, the first solo pop concert ever held at the Workers Stadium with a seating capacity of 50,000 people, nearly paralyzed the nearby subway system. A veteran fan from Beijing, who walked two kilometers before she was able to hail a cab, recalled the intoxicated feeling: "I was sitting on the mezzanine, watching this tiny person perform on stage. But I was elated. My goodness, so many people were singing the same song with me" (Interview, 15 Oct 2005).

If politics is narrowly defined as the offensive game wheeled by the bigwigs, then this seems to be the story before Chang became politicized. The year 2000 was often perceived as the watershed year that ended the age of innocence following her performance of the ROC anthem at the inauguration ceremony of President Chen Shui-Bian and the subsequent mainland censorship. Rather than reducing the "political" problem to a tale of two nationalisms, the question inspired by Chang's predicament is this: In the experience of transnational cultural traffic in Asia, how does one negotiate with different modes of attachment that may not form in a necessary order one's sense of belonging? The response addresses the central thesis in Arjun Appadurai's grapple with the global staying power of patriotism, that is, to give recognition to social forms of alternative loyalty besides the kind prescribed by the nation-state (1993). Starting with a contextualization of Chang in the history of the "patriotic entertainer," I present in the following an account of the complex ways Chang's veteran fans in Taiwan and China negotiate with loyalty amid cross-strait tensions and competing political discourses. Their "being here" and "being there" for Chang over the past nine years is not just a simple display of loyalty, but a period in which they create opportunities for cross-border understanding.

Specter of Teresa

The politicization of Chang did not begin in 2000. It was embedded in an interpenetrated relationship between entertainers and politics under the Cold War framework. It was also linked to the legacies of one of the first trans-Asian pop stars and a model *aiguo yiren* [patriotic entertainer]: Teresa Teng. Born into a family of Kuomingtang (KMT) nationalist soldiers and debuting at a young age, Teng's sweet ballads brought solace to homesick mainlanders and the general population in Taiwan in the wake of the nation's secession from the United Nations in the 1970s. Teng's music became popular in China in the 1980s despite an official denouncement. Throughout her career, Teng performed for the purpose of relieving overseas Chinese residents like many patriotic entertainers, who were various kinds of performers (e.g., dance troupes, musicians, film actresses, Beijing opera singers) involved in entertaining the KMT troops on the front line, on ally ships, and in overseas Chinese communities following their retreat to Taiwan after 1945. For them, performing was tantamount to performing patriotism — a virtue many even valued over other gains like fame or wealth.[11] Teng was not only given a formal recognition for being a "patriotic entertainer" by the ROC Government of Information Office in 1981, but also remained politically active as seen in her support of the students movement in Tiananaman in 1989. After she died of acute asthma in Thailand in 1995, she was given a national burial in Taiwan which was broadcast live on television.

Although it has never been explicitly defined, the construction of patriotic entertainers in Taiwan has a transnational dimension delimited by the Taiwan-China relation in the Cold War structure. Teng and other "patriotic entertainers" only performed in the territories of "free China" and of its allies.

How does this history affect Chang and her Taiwanese fans, who grew up in a relatively democratized and depoliticized age where "patriotic entertainers" seemed to have become obsolete in the advent of merging Asian and Chinese-language markets under globalization?

As Chang's career began to cross over to China, the Taiwan press gave Chang and Teng similar rhetorical treatment particularly when their "mainland penetration" occurred in similar circumstances of cross-strait tension (Lee 2000a). In Chang's case, it was shortly after Lee Teng-Hui enunciated the two-state formula. A magazine reporter wrote: "Even at a low point in cross-strait relations a 'special harmony' existed. It showed the power of popular culture" (Shih 1999, p. 42). If anything, this familiar rhetoric of the triumph of popular culture over politics underscored the persistence — not irrelevance — of patriotism since, for people living in differing political realities, its definition can only complicate and pluralize. Nancy Guy's research (2002) on the reactions to Chang's singing of the ROC anthem reveal that for those who learned the song under the KMT regime, China's reaction only reinforced the image of an authoritarian state. As for the new DPP government, which desired to present the prospect of ethnic reconciliation in the context of Taiwan-centered indigenization *[bentuhua]*, keeping a song so tightly associated with KMT indoctrination was read by some as a compromise.

The "specter of Teresa" refers not to the ghost nation imagined under the KMT regime, or its presumed competitor, that is, the DPP's nation-building project. It is the lesson that the object of loyalty can no longer be thought of as so singularized and "safe." In 2004, President Chen Shui-Bian's attempt to "help" Chang by calling her a "patriotic entertainer" after what the Vice President had said received a news headline (Liu 2004), but it could not put a lid over the burning anxieties about prescript loyalty display like the *aitaiwan* [loving Taiwan] discourse or possible betrayal which plagues Taiwanese business professionals in China.[12] More significantly in the 2004 public discussion about Chang's predicament was the emergence of an aborigine voice that expressed a more chequered political subjectivity.

Can the virtual body of a celebrity escape the projection of political desire? The protest in Hangzhou revealed that patriotism mattered to segments of the public that may become *affected* — in the sense of transmission of intensities — by the circulation of popular symbols of stars whether or not they are fans. This demands a reconceptualization of publicness through the recognition of borders. Moreover, patriotism as a kind of structure of emotions is determined to intersect with the affective sensibility of fans particularly in Asia because the political and historical entanglements in this region have found unconstrained spaces of dialogues utterly wanting.[13] Drawing on the "new patriotism" discussion in a special 2003 issue of *Journal of Communication Inquiry*, patriotism is not automatically an irrational expression or a citizen virtue, as its definitions now include "multiple and changing political cultural loyalties not only in relation to the nation-state but also regarding intersections of global, local, national, regional, ethnic, and religious affiliations" (Gavrilos 2003, pp. 333–334). I now turn to the recasting of the structures of emotions in fandom in politically affecting terms.

From Mattering Map to Territorial Map

Drawing on my fieldwork with twelve veteran fans living mostly in Taipei and Beijing, I want to explicate the power of their affect generated from their experiences with Chang's music, encounters with each other, and responses to Chang's suffering. Seminal to this discussion is the definition of "affect" developed by Lawrence Grossberg in his work on fandom. He argues that fans of any kind should be understood in relation to a different sensibility distinguishable from the cultural critic's typical pursuit of "meanings" or "pleasure."

> Affect is closely tied to what we often describe as the feeling of life. You can understand another person's life: You can share the same meanings and pleasure, but you cannot know how it feels … Affect is what gives 'color,' 'tone' or 'texture' to our experiences. (1992, pp. 56, 57)

Grossberg's identification of the affective dimension is extremely important because he located a language that speaks to the realm of mattering — where things matter. Such "obvious" passion often takes a backseat to the behavioral description of the fans, which rarely gets to the bottom of "why" (e.g., why Elvis? Why Gucci bags?) What does it matter that it matters? Affect produces the so-called "mattering maps," which direct people's investments in the world and offers a place in the world for absorption (1992, p. 57).

This question must be dealt with in relation to the biographically situated researcher. I have come to see myself as a beneficiary of the affective investments by Chang's fans in Taiwan and China, but not so much in the straightforward sense that "I got information" from them. In the process of being let into an area of their mattering maps, real mileage was yielded and strait-crossing was made possible. My first trip to China, a research trip to meet Chang's fans in Beijing, was inspired by S1, a highly reflexive woman in her 30s from Taiwan who actively creates cultural and physical mileage by writing, traveling, and maintaining a website. Once in Beijing, my journey with the fans to see a *pinpan* [assorted] concert in Tianjin infolded me into their mattering maps, local and emotional. There was a fan who traveled from as far as Mongolia to see Chang perform that night. In 2002 and 2004, the Taipei-based S1 traveled to Shanghai and Beijing to see Chang's concerts and meet the fans who have been reading her website dedicated to Chang. Ever since Chang's debut, S1 has been actively visiting her tribes in Taitung during the off-peak seasons to understand the culture that has nurtured a proud claimant of aboriginal identity so disenfranchised in Taiwan's hegemonic Han culture.

The double points I am making are these: First, the fans have directed their affective energy from their mattering maps toward creating actual mileage and bonds. The distance covered is relative, but the recognition of the border and what makes the border-crossing possible are equally important. S8, a native of Beijing who brought his college schoolwork to study on the trip, said "if it wasn't for A-mei, I don't even know when I would get out of this town" (16 Oct 2005). The moments they spend waiting for Chang at the airport, talking about her (often finishing up each other's anecdotes) in between places, and seeing her perform form extraordinary narratives distinguishable from their routine everyday at home, school, or work. Second, my embodiment in this highly affective care allowed me to experience affect as the "encounter between the affected body and an affecting body" (Massumi, quoted in Shouse 2005). The "hotness" of this research experience is precisely how the fans' mattering map gets articulated to the researcher's mattering map. As Elspeth Probyn aptly put it: "When affect becomes hot, it becomes untouchable and untouched by that wonder and by a necessary gratitude to the ideas that allow us to think and write. Writing affect should inspire awe and awe inspire modesty" (2005, para. 14, 15).

The Irrational Forces of Politics

The political implication of affect has been suggested, such as in Van Zoonen's borrowing of "affective intelligence" — a quality mixing emotions and reasons — to explore political citizenship among the entertained constituencies in the West (2005). While she analyzes the convergence of the popular and the political (e.g., political celebrities, *West Wing*, *Big Brother*), the "popular" in her research already actively incorporates a political character. Yet in Chang's case, the popular cultural constituencies — from the star to the fans — did not want those two domains to mix, particularly when "politics" is monopolized by the state. Grossberg has suggested that the fan's relation to the culture need not be located on the terrain of commercial popular culture. The politicization of pop stars in Asia opens up the terrain promisingly, though probably not in the normative direction as suggested by Van Zoonen. In this section, I would like to sketch out some potential terrains that have been suggested in the responses of Chang's cross-strait fans.

The most obvious and also significant terrain is a passionate, tragic sensibility that Chang has been innocently and repeatedly maligned by the irrational forces of politics. S10, a doctor in her mid-20s working in Shandong, found the accusation of Chang's pro-Taiwan independence "non-sensible," especially when singing the ROC anthem could not have been her decision:

> I knew it. A-mei grew up in the mountains. How could she understand politics? She didn't mean anything by singing it. It got played into the hands of politicians. It's tragic. (Interview, 25 Oct 2005)

S6, a petite woman in her 30s from Beijing who was drawn to Chang's invigorating quality which made her "a contrast to the melodramatic soap world on television," simply asked: "How strong must the hearts of her fans get" (16 Oct 2005)? The chain of events that had been set off in 2000, which remained a difficult topic, has infused a darker hue into S6's world. When asked to compare, 2004 was more difficult to bear because "it's the feeling that you watch it unfold before your eyes and yet there's nothing you could do about it" (S6). The fans felt helpless watching her being protested against in Hanzhou and besieged back in Taiwan. The weeks following the cancellation of her concert were described as disorienting, despondent, and devastating.

This shared sentiment of tragicness is significant because it forms the affective reserves from which Chinese fans organize and expand their mattering maps. For instance, the prohibitive climate in 2000 prompted her fans to take a more pro-active stance toward building networks, which included the setup of a large fan organization in China. In the absence of promotional industry, the fans took on the promotional tasks themselves, staging sales events for Chang outside the biggest record shops in town and approaching shoppers with self-made gifts. S12, an enthusiastic young man recounted the experience:

> We just wanted her music to be heard … We played some material provided from Warner. But I actually felt Warner didn't have to provide us with anything. The fans were plenty resourceful. We could handle it. Of course, if we were talking about getting her on TV or something,

then we probably couldn't. But we will for sure build a reputation for A-mei. The vigor was very real. (15 Oct 2005)

Just an elementary school kid when he first heard Chang's song on the radio, S12 is now 21 and a computer science major in college. To give Chang a collective birthday gift, he once spent a week producing a song file by arranging a composition from Chang's repertoire, coordinating fans from different places to record the singing, and editing the segments into a mp3 file. Like many other Chinese fans I came in contact with, S12 felt close to Chang and was moved by her amazing threshold of tolerance and giving spirit.

The affective terrain of the fans grew into other forms and practices — in fact, it must by the nature of affective investment. Here I want to keep the discussion at this core and dynamic level for the purpose of elaborating the divergent cross-strait experiences. Specifically, while fans on both sides of the Taiwan Strait felt that Chang was catapulted into the throes of politics by irrational forces during the second half of his career, the emotional basis can be different. For one thing, Chang's performance at the 2000 presidential inauguration was a moment of pride, at least for the Han-ethnic Taiwanese. A fan in her late 20s who went swimming on the morning of the inauguration witnessed swimmers streaming out of the pool almost in unison just to watch on a rarely noticed television Chang perform (Interview, 23 Sep 2005). The pride came not from a natural respect for the ROC anthem, but from its being noticed *as if for the first time* by the general public. In this case, the political helped justify the fans' taste. But for S5, a 20-year-old student in eastern Taiwan who grew up between her Taroko tribe and the Hualien city, she did not experience the same "pride," or even the same "tragicness" even though she empathized with Chang's repeated and reluctant entanglement with politics. Much more outspoken about her political views than the twentysomething Taiwanese fans I met,[14] S5 situated Chang's plight in the history and media representation of aborigines in Taiwan rather than in the Taiwan-China tension. As S5 became engaged in active learning of the aboriginal culture and politics, Chang's meaning for her also changed from that of a role model to a mainstreamed, co-opted star relativized by the more "authentic" aboriginal entertainers.

The emotional responses presented here were generated in different research circumstances, generations, and the interviewees' historical awareness of their identity formation. Since the Taiwanese fans I met spanned four different generations, their political experiences are expectedly more heterogeneous than the Chinese fan group raised in post-socialist China. A fan told me in a "just-telling-it-like-it-is" manner: "Chang's fans are already divided between blue and green camps" (Interview, 12 Aug 2005). This is a reality that any Taiwanese fan involved in the heated online debate in 2004 could clearly sense. But even this political configuration is limited by a statist imperative. Despite its unifying pitch, the cross-strait notion of fans as publics must accommodate unshared sentiments about Chang's predicament as well as unaffected sentiments with each other.

Different Questions of Border-Crossing

I would like to offer an exemplar of the cross-strait relationship that illustrates experiences of affecting and affected feelings about the star and about each other. I return to S1, who was moved by the passion and hospitality of the Chinese fans. Their online (e.g., collective writing) and offline (e.g., concert going) interactions have come to create a vocabulary casting Chang as a queen figure in a warm, generous, love-giving and ever expanding cosmos. My purpose here is not so much to present an ideal or inevitable cross-strait relationship, as to acknowledge the historicized emotional structures behind the obvious strait-crossing.

S1 situates herself in a *bensheng* Taiwanese generation that experienced political liberalization but may still lack perspectives to completely swim out of KMT ideological teachings and de-stereotype the mainland Chinese. She has only become able to associate with the mainland Chinese after recognizing even more boundaries that relativize the statist agenda, beginning from the marginal position of aboriginal cultures. S1's job puts her in contact with two groups of teenagers with drastically different resources and value systems. On the one hand, she is surrounded by the most privileged ethnic-Han, urban, middle-class kids in Taipei; on the other hand, she also works with aboriginal, less-confident, much less resourceful children in the countryside. Chang's debut was a shocking statement to her:

> She debuted at a time when there was a lot of news about child prostitution in Jianshih. But she proudly announced that 'I am aborigine.' She's got to be the healthiest aborigine in history, completely comfortable with her identity and family. This attitude is so different from the culture I have come to know. What's going on? (12 Aug 2005)

Driven by a curiosity to understand Chang's ability to publicly claim her marginal identity, S1 began visiting Chang's tribe in Taitung regularly. Her purpose was more "ethnographic" than "star-chasing," as she avoided the congested festivals for tourists and documented her visits in the format of special reports posted on her website. Despite her repeated visits and gradual familiarization with the area, S1 still felt ambivalent about her tourist gaze. She warns other fans wishing to visit the tribe: "Save the trip if you are going for a chance to meet Chang Hui-mei!" S1 carries an attitude of productive yielding as she turns travel experiences into opportunities to de-naturalize the image of aborigines as being optimistic and big-hearted since it is actually the outcome of unequal power relations.

Since 1999, S1's in-depth writing and multi-media presentations of Chang's performance have made her website an inviting forum of exchange. This is also how her interactions with several veteran Chinese fans began. They exchanged and commented reflectively on each other's writing about Chang's music. S1 surprisingly felt an ease in communicating with a group of young people who were interested in discussing Chang's music and still possessed a knowledge of classical Chinese literature. Once a staff member in a large fan organization in Taiwan, S1 now keeps a distance from other fan groups mainly because of the failure to evolve into a more open-minded community. Besides, she is deeply affected by the Chinese fans' raw passion and urgency to introduce Chang's music to a broader audience. Thus she runs her website according to an inclusive principle that makes Chang's performances accessible without requiring registration or membership. She said:

> I don't want anything. I don't want money or nothing. I just want you [A-mei] to be good, to be known by everyone. I call this "doing reputation." If you want to get to know her, you can get to know her. You don't need to pay because she is good. Good stuff. I have always thought this should be the way it is (16 Sep 2005).

The practice of "doing reputation" in this case is analogous to the fan-initiated sales efforts mentioned by S12. According to her, fans acting as agents of dissemination are only fitting for a diva like Chang. Significantly, *muyi tianshia*, a classical Chinese expression referring to exemplary wives of ancient Chinese statesmen is evoked by S1 to refer to the magnanimous, noble demeanor of Chang following the political brouhaha. The precise expression as well as related descriptors (e.g., loving, tolerant) were also used by several of the Chinese fans I met. They were particularly using it to describe Chang's having survived the injuries with an unbelievable and rightful kindness.

Getting to know the Chinese fans allowed S1 to be critical of Taiwan's stereotypes of mainland Chinese and of the island politics. Having seen Chang perform in China also made her more sympathetic to the predicaments of Taiwanese business professionals and workers in China. She witnessed how hardworking they were in a not-necessarily-friendly environment. She said:

> ... when you look at the faces of Taiwanese business professionals, each and everyone has homesickness written on it. It's a pity that they are called *taibao* [Taiwan compatriot] there and "Chinese pigs" when they come back. (16 Sep 2005)

S1's ability to perceive Chang as a transnational worker whose work identity is not given enough recognition brings us back to the heart of the matter, that is, there are many borders that have yet to be foregrounded to effectively problematize patriotism. The overriding family trope in fandom breaks down here because while S1 cared for Chang like a family member, she saw Chang as a young woman working away from home, with the home's name being multiple and ambivalent. After visiting Orchid Island, she remarked: "why doesn't Orchid Island go independent?!"

Feeling Patriotism From a Distance

Just as Chang's patriotic dilemma would not make sense unless contextualized in the historical formation of "patriotic entertainers" in Taiwan under the Cold War structure and growing economic dependence on China, the patriotic implication of Song Seung-Heon's draft scandal is rooted in historical and emotional structures of South Korea's gendered citizenship. The economy and discourse of the Korean Wave complicate exclusive ideas of national loyalty for Song as a transnational celebrity, his fans participating in trans-Asian cultural traffic, and various culture industry agents with vested interests in domestic and regional markets. Using these contexts as my base to grasp from a distance[15] the gravity of draft-dodging in South Korea, I probe the meanings of overseas fans' mobilization during the crisis when a major draft-dodging investigation interrupted Song's starring part in the highly anticipated television drama production, *Sad Love Story*.[16] Significant as inter-referential springboards for Chang's fans is the similarly tragic, affective, and communicational experience through which Song's fans remake the meaning of the star amid an adverse atmosphere. Although the fans' actions were not directly confrontational to the geopolitical problematic inscribed in South Korean conscription, their mobilization leading up to the spectacular send-off outside the boot camp in Chunchon, Kangwon Province, should be considered a crucial feminized, transnational initiative calling into question a not-yet-post Cold-War Asia.

Conscription Anchored

From the start of the investigation Song had been quick to admit publicly the "mistake" he made while at his career break. While filming the music video for the drama in Australia, he faxed the Korean press a handwritten letter of apology which also explained his pressing commitment in remorseful anguish. When he returned to Seoul on September 20th, a thinner Song apologized in front of the press for "having evaded conscription as a South Korean man" (www.nocutnews.co.kr). The scandal involving Song and other celebrities[17] drew heavy public debate in the media and internet polling sites. One poll that drew the intense participation of Taiwanese fans was posted on *Joongang Ilbo* (Central Daily), which asked netizens to determine "what should happen to Song on the matter of military service?" from the following choices: "join immediately," "finish filming the drama before service," "substitute service," and "no service." There was much speculation among his fans that such public opinion indicators would influence Song's fate in the drama production.

Despite its airtight stipulation, conscription as an institution in South Korea rests on something more dynamic than Article 3.1 of the ROK Military Service Law. The institution survives through mutual persuasion, co-optation, and constant negotiation between government authorities and different publics. The morality of military service can be found in major media stories. It wasn't too long ago that two public figures implicated in draft-dodging scandals received punishing consequences. One case was the defeat of the Grand National Party presidential candidate Lee Hoi-Chang (also Yi Hoe-Chang), who was expected to have an easy win in the 1997 election until his two sons were found to have avoided military service by suspicious methods. The second case was Yoo Seung-Jun, a pop teen idol who angered the Korean public after he became an American citizen in 2002, which allowed him to obtain a service waiver. Earlier in his budding singing and dancing career, Yoo had announced that he would perform his military duty as a Korean citizen. This was a praiseworthy gesture for a 1.5 generation *yoen-uh-jok* (salmon) who had immigrated to the United States with his parents when he was only 14 years old. However, after acquiring American citizenship, Yoo went from a role model citizen to an "ugly American" whose English name — Steve Yoo — was sarcastically adopted by Korea's mainstream media (Lee 2003). His presence was considered such a corrupting force that the Ministry of Justice denied his entry into Korea several weeks later upon request from the Military Manpower Administration (MMA). These media stories of transgression suggest that the power like fame and public office, that comes with celebrities as public figures can be jeopardized — denied even — when they trip upon values central to the collective identities of a group. In this case, the seemingly universal demand for a healthy Korean man to perform the military service not only reflects on one's character, but also sustain the ideology of patriarchy.

Nevertheless, patriotism in South Korea should not be viewed as an unchanging national characteristic. Ideological teachings in South Korea from literature to war memorials have championed different heroic male figures in a history narrated as a patriarchal lineage in continuous crisis (Jager 2003). According to Insook Kwon, conscription anchors in 1990s political culture because it is still serviceable to anti-communism and nationalism, the twin-engines driving the narrative of self-sacrifice for one's nation. Thus, not only has there been an absence of resistance to conscription in South Korea's rich protest history, popular support for conscription has only intensified in the period following the pro-democracy movements which threw military dictators out of public office and the supposed end of the Cold War (Kwon 2001, p. 29). This is indicative in the newly amended (4 May 2005) Nationality Law which prohibits Korean males holding dual citizenship to give up their Korean citizenship until they have fulfilled their military service.

Perhaps more powerful in Kwon's feminist exploration of conscription is that the system has been the indispensable glue binding some of the most crucial notions of being authentically Korean, such as masculinity, femininity, motherhood, and fatherhood. Mothers become symbolically important during the men's conscription experiences, playing the nurturing role that grants them the historically justified patriotic motherhood. *The Youth Report*, a weekly variety show that puts conscripts and celebrities together during prime-time hours, also exploits the culturally powerful mother-son bond by dressing the mother-guest in traditional garb as she waits for her chance to meet her conscripted child on the show (Moon 2005b, p. 79). For women not in the mother's role, this entertaining show also unites selected couples to create the expectation of heterosexual romance. The show personalizes conscription and contributes to the moral structure of feeling along with other accessible storytelling formats like news, television dramas, and films.

The above historicized background to South Korean conscription aims to illuminate the indispensability of conscription as a legal, social, and ideological process. The gravity of draft-dodging in general must then confront the multiple subjectivities enabled by the military service and its discourses. It would also be necessary to observe how the associated patriotic morality gets reinvented — perhaps in the absence of critical opinion even from the progressive movements — in the infrastructure of South Korea's nationalist political culture.[18] Specific to Song's draft-dodging incident, however, is his embodiment of a different type of masculinity generated and celebrated by the Korean culture industry as evidence of Korea's own transnational cultural prowess. Albeit difficult, this new circumstance from popular culture seems to call for reasons to address South Korean conscription beyond the terms of domestic politics.

Conscription Meets the Constituencies in Hallyu

> I was really shocked to see his picture from the airport. It wasn't so much that he looked disconcerted. I have never seen Song Seung-Heon like that. He was always dashing, with makeup and hairstyling. But we all felt he looked like a prisoner in that photo taken at the airport. Not the typical dashing, spirited Song we are used to seeing. (A1, 8 Sep 2005)

A veteran fan from Taiwan who had seen Song in person on many other occasions conveyed her thoughts on pictures of Song returning from Australia to cooperate with the police investigation. A series of news photos had been posted on a major fan forum,[19] showing a very "un-star like" Song donning a white sweatshirt, blue jeans, and carrying his own bag making a statement to the press. In another picture published on the day of physical checkup, Song was shown wearing a blue medical gown and a metal name plate. He waited expressionlessly in a fluorescent-lit office with his hands folded on his abdomen, looking no different from two other actors — Chang Hyuk and Hae Jae-suk — in the same boat. Stripped of the rakish looks of his *Sad Love Story* character whose images had begun to circulate around the same time, Song appeared more and more "civilian" as it became clear that MMA would draft him almost immediately. He was well on his way to transforming into the idealized Foucauldian docile body — a soldier.

For the fans, what Song went through was an enormously difficult subject. It would not be an exaggeration to say that watching him go through public criticism and speculation "was like the end of the world."[20] Even after a year had passed, the incident was a emotional trigger for a veteran Taiwanese fan (A4) representing a large fan organization who declined my interview request. Nonetheless, corresponding with her cued me to the fans' feelings, particularly their self-aware vulnerability and low-key assertiveness to protect their star from any unfavorable judgment. For instance, A4 did not see any point discussing Korean conscription. "So what?" she asked me and cited the ineffectiveness of this line of criticism from Korea's most valued market — Japan. Even A1, who cordially opened up her rich involvement in transnational fan networking, emphasized that the fans were not trying to appeal to the South Korean authorities for any "special treatment" like a service exemption. That is why the "United Support Letter" issued by five fan organizations from Taiwan, China, and Hong Kong prior to Song's return to Korea adopted a non-confrontational and non-imploring tone to influence the resolution of the crisis. According to A1, respecting the decisions of the Korean government was also a measure to protect Song from sinking into deeper water.

The immediate question facing the overseas fans was indeed practical — that is, to drum up and lend support to Song. It seemed meaningless and groundless to critique the impact of South Korean conscription. The lack of apparent justification is understandable. Kwon's interviews with Korean women activists during the students movement and democratization movement in the 1980s also revealed a curious lack of motivation and agenda to challenge conscription altogether (2001). So if the most anti-establishment women in Korea found it difficult to formulate a debate around mandatory military service in their own country, what could Asian women outside Korea — who are doubtless the constituencies of the Korean Wave — do tempering with issues concerning the "boys" and a foreign government?[21] And what good does raising the agenda do now that Song's "heavenly body" is squarely disciplined by the Korean MMA?

I spell out these points of contention not to bypass or lay "tough" readings on the fans' experiences. Rather, I hope to pursue further articulation of the interpenetration between trans-Asian cultural traffic and regional politics. Song's status as a red-hot *hallyu* star predicated that his draft-dodging would be no simple domestic affair. In fact, the Steve Yoo incident had already illuminated the power of the transnational entertainment workings and the porousness of Korean national loyalty. As Hee-eun Lee (2003) pointed out, the Korean pop music industry is the "biggest habitat for salmons" like Yoo. The hybridized reality of Korean popular culture has not prevented the invention of the "other" category from within. Could a different mode of hybridity in *hallyu* — rendered in the realm of transnational fandom specifically — make a difference in the definition of Korean national loyalty? Following Shin Hyunjoon's suggestion to mine regarding the under-represented cultural practices in intra-Asian cultural traffic (2005), I will turn to examine the communicational practices engaged by Song's fans in Taiwan and China as a way to interject the "Chinese-Asian" experience in the Korean Wave.

To Whom It May Concern: Without Song, Korean Wave Is a Sad Love Story[22]

The dramatic gathering of hundreds of women fans from Korea, Japan, Taiwan, and Hong Kong to send Song off outside the Chunchon preparatory camp on the morning of 16 November 2004 was a telling testament to Song's transnationalized stardom built at the juncture of inter-Asian cultural traffic and market legitimation. It was the crystallization of fan mobilization and a media event with dramatic elements. According to a Taiwanese fan (A3) who provided her narrative account and 52 news photos from that day, Song was surrounded by a crowd while inching toward the camp entrance.[23] Close-up pictures from *Yonhap News* showed the mini dramas of Song looking down, frowning, biting his lower lips, and exhaling through his teeth during this supposedly short walk. A3 used "war-like" to describe the meeting between cameras (reporters) and guns (camp guards) at the moment Song entered the camp, since the reporters were trying to get Song to answer questions. Song eventually came out, still lowering his head frequently, exhaling through his teeth, and unsuccessfully containing rolling tears from spilling over.

This moment fraught with femininity and emotions casts a melodramatic aspect that seems to find resonance in many gendered Korean conscription stories. As a result it does not reveal the complexity of fan mobilization and the different strategies overseas fans have exercised to influence this sentimental outcome which unfortunately is devoid of critical possibilities. Instead of analyzing this staged event,[24] I would like to discuss the issuance of the "United Support Letter" by fans in China, Taiwan and Hong Kong and a letter-writing campaign from a large fan organization in China. There were many other mobilization efforts by overseas fans during this period, but these two are highlighted here to complement what was not as visible at the send-off scene — the Chinese-speaking fans (particularly those from China) — as well as to illuminate Chinese fans' nuanced and non-unison attempts to communicate with the non-exclusive audience of Korean government authorities.

Encouraged by news reports, public opinion climates, and personal communication from Korea, both efforts were organized during a worrisome period before anyone really knew who had the final say on Song's fate and when. From the cultural producers and capitalists (e.g., Song's management agency, broadcasting station, drama production agencies, overseas investors) to the equally image-conscious national governmental units (e.g., MMA, Tourism Bureau), multiple companies apparently had an inter-related ideological or economic stake in Song's participation in *Sad Love Story*. What did the overseas fans say to these Korean authorities and how did they present their arguments to the selected ears and eyes out there?

According to A1, who maintained communication with key fan organizers from other places during the crisis, the open letter was not intended to appeal to the Korean authorities. The letter begins by empathizing with Song's suffering from the overwhelming publicity. It then describes how encounters with Song's work in the Korean Wave had led the overseas fans to new experiences like traveling and taking an interest in Korean culture. Praising his professional ethics and giving nature, the letter states the fans' unwavering stance behind his courage to tell the truth and closes with a warm and firm stance to stand by him throughout the hardship. The letter takes a nuanced position without suggesting to anyone in any decision-making place what to do. Yet when the letter was reported in a Taiwanese news story, the headline pleaded explicitly to the Korean authorities, using the exact words to designate government authorities: "Please *daren*, don't conscript Song Seung-heon" (Wu 2004, p. C4). The difference in tone and meaning was clarified on the fan site but it was also pointed out that the reporter found a fan making the plea.

For the present purpose, which is to understand the moment at which the popular meets the political, what is intriguing is the smart third (with the first and second being, respectively, a direct imploration to the MMA and a demand for his staying on the drama) route carved out by the United Support Letter's self-aware purpose and strength as dissemination. I am referring to the central problematic of dissemination and communication in John Peters's *Speaking into the Air* (1999). Trekking historical, discursive, and philosophical terrains from Socrates' time to our technological utopia, Peters fleshes out the dialectical conundrum between human desire (including that of the communication theorists!) for genuine connection and the cold hard evidence of irreconciliation as small or as large as unrequited love, unanswered letters, and unheard voices.

> Dialogue ideology keeps us from seeing that expressive acts occurring over distances and without [an] immediate assurance of reply can be desperate and daring acts of dignity. That I cannot engage in dialogue with Plato or the Beatles does not demean the contact I have with them. (Peters 1999, p. 152)

If we judge by the outcome, the open letter by the fans in Hong Kong, China, and Taiwan seemed inconsequential.[25] It didn't even make a demand! But if we understand it as a disseminational practice that acknowledged the probable divide between adoring Chinese-Asian female fans and Korean officialdom — a relation that also implies the gender hierarchy in Korean society, then we are beginning to see the open letter not as a failure, but a revelation of politics, bodies, and language.[26]

In at least two ways, the open letter did more than "merely express" unconditional support for Song. It became politicized by the Taiwanese news report that hailed the addressee. The letter's outline also provided the model argument for a subsequent letter-writing campaign from China that addressed directly to the Korean authorities, and which had a specific request (to postpone Song's conscription until he finishes filming *Sad Love Story*), and enabled the materialization of nationalized, feminized, and pressing voices.

> To all of our members, to support more effectively our beloved Seung-heon, the management team would like to solicit open letters to relevant Korean governmental bodies that include the Ministry of Foreign Relations, the Ministry of Culture and Tourism, and the Military and Manpower Administration. Please leave messages here: Write down your love and support for Seung-heon! Write down your expectation for him to carry on the promotion of Korean culture to China! The management team shall print out everyone's messages and send them to the concerned governmental bodies by international express mail. Sisters, let's take action! Use our love to protect our Seung-Heon!

These words, posted on 23 September 2004 on a large mainland Chinese fan site, were part of a transnational mobilization effort that tried to steer the public opinion climate toward favoring the postponing of Song's conscription. In fact, two online polls in Korea showed over 50 percent of support for this resolution.[27] Already in the Korean press, there was a debate weighing the cost of Song's contribution as a *hallyu* star against the gain of his immediate draft. A group of pro-government UriParty lawmakers even submitted a petition to the MMA to demand the draft postponement (Park 2004).

Still, the fans were not in very much control, especially judging from their just-in-time realization of the Korean holiday delay on the likelihood of an official announcement. The 54[28] postings responding to the above solicitation from 23 to 27 September seemed at first like melodramatic messages that amounted to a mad "essay contest," which, in the Chinese context, has come to mean a game of pure performance devoid of substance.[29] To illustrate, X20 began her letter by expressing her "vehement impulse to shout and desire for release" which she had to put into writing to convince "your honorable nation" of the "significance of Mr. Song Seung-Heon to China's hundreds of millions of Chinese." But this performance — which probably mattered in the larger sense only as a performance because it was unlikely to be read by the media or by authorities carefully — cannot be dismissed as uniform and unsophisticated. In fact, in the unlikely prospect of scrutiny, these messages managed to produce rhetorical variations that knowingly deployed hyperbolic elaborations of Song's virtues (e.g., a real man for taking the fall for a more general social problem) and contribution (e.g., exceptional cultural ambassador).[30]

Furthermore, many letters adopted a diplomatic language (e.g., "your honorable country"; "no intention to interfere with other nation's domestic politics") to gear up for a criticism of the Korean government. Some fans admonished the South Korean government's misjudgment of Song's national loyalty. X29 disputed the conflation between draft-dodging and unpatriotism. X9 called on Korea's double standards in allowing "national" athletes shorter terms of service while overlooking the perennial private interest in sports. She wrote: "He [Song] brought a handsome income and worked hard to promote the Korean culture to the world. Isn't this patriotic conduct? Why must conscription be the only patriotic embodiment?" Following this logic, many fans advised the South Korean government to be kind to their people (X30). When this piece of advice was ignored, some fans flung down the gauntlet and signaled a suffering bilateral relationship that all had a beginning because of Song.

The fans revealed themselves to be ordinary fans, a poor student, a middle-class office worker, a 60-year-old lady, a mother, a rational star chaser, a motivated fan-webmaster, a trend-setter in China, an overseas fan, and one of the 4000 powerful Chinese fans of Song. Though the veracity of these fans' self-proclaimed identities should be taken with a grain of salt, they spoke as Chinese citizens and exercised this positionality to address to those running South Korea — a country which many said did not exist in their mental map until Song made it stand out from the "undifferentiated color mass" on the map (X7).

How do we interpret the imperial pitch exercised by Song's fans in China during this crucial time? By adopting an ambassadorial rhetoric, the fans found a way to engage with Korean nationalism in a bilateral relationship. It probably reveals more about the nationalist and gendered uses of *hallyu*. Keeheyung Lee's chapter in this volume critiques the framing of *hallyu* as a nationally-endorsed cultural phenomenon. The backing of local politicians, government agencies like the Ministry of Culture and Tourism, and academics has made *hallyu* serviceable to the Korean national image. It is just that within the hierarchy of masculinities in South Korea, militarized masculinity still takes precedence over other — softer, more economically inclined — notions of masculinity. The conflict occurs at both a transnational but gendered moment.

Caught *Shiris*[31] in Trans-Asian Straits

This chapter has juxtaposed the predicaments of two popular Asian stars — Chang Hui-Mei and Song Seung-Heon — whose transborder capacities from their respective positions in mandarin pop and *hallyu* became limited around 2004. As pop stars, they were agents of love and affect, singing love ballads and playing tender roles. But this time, they underwent an overwhelming test of patriotism from "the political and public at large" within and outside their fan base. Chang's and Song's dilemmas in this circumstance provided an opportunity for understanding patriotism as a political and popular force in trans-Asian popular culture. Surely, we can discuss patriotism independently of the stars. But when they intersect — and they do more often than is acknowledged — "love for a star" and "loyalty for a political-cultural affiliation" unleash and feed on similar reserves of emotions.

This chapter deals with Asian pop stars as popular, political and public sites. In the two juxtaposed cases, the celebrities clearly bridged the individual and public culture of the democratic age as suggested by P. David Marshall (1997). The fans were involved in the political realm, whether it was by communicating with government authorities or articulating their political identities. Though full of tension, the intersections between non-fan publics and the stars and fans as the embodiment of the popular were clear in both cases. This is at least a result of the stars themselves bearing important public experiences and morality. In Chang, we see the public of Taiwanese transborder workers in China facing the same dilemma as well as the publics who find power in her inclusive representability. In Song, we see the Korean national subjects that support the necessity of Korean conscription, perhaps still under the effect of militarized modernity (Moon 2005a). Some fans emerged as politicized bodies, speaking, as Song's Chinese fans did, as Chinese citizens. Other fans, as in the strategic coalition by fans in Taiwan, Hong Kong, and China, carved out a space neither purely occupied by fans nor by national subjects.

In the words of the stars, fans, and other publics, there were traces of emotional structures, thus traces of histories. A position this chapter has taken is that popular culture does not resolve political issues by being politics' naïve "other." Kuan-Hsing Chen's reading of *Dousan* and *Banana Paradise* passionately uncovers the need to give mutual recognition to the sorts of emotional structures different populations occupying the same social space inherit from different trajectories of histories (2002a; 2002b). A more recent Taiwanese film, *Love of May* (2004), not only deals with the issue of inter-generational, cross-strait reconciliation, but also suggests the bridging power of popular music — specifically, the music of the Taiwanese band May Day. These stories become resources in popular culture narratives for grasping divergent experiences, but they are not, in themselves, sufficient spaces for reconciliation. In the world where narratives of stars, of fans, and of different publics intersect, the emotional structures of different groups of people need even more spaces for interaction and inter-referencing. Perhaps the mode of entering the Asian space is not through the trope of fluidity and mobility, but by being caught at the border or by some kind of terrain. Then it becomes necessary and meaningful to seek out the configurations of the terrains under the currents.

12

When the Korean Wave Meets Resident Koreans in Japan: Intersections of the Transnational, the Postcolonial and the Multicultural

Koichi Iwabuchi

Introduction

In the last decade, East Asian media flows and connections have intensified. Media markets have rapidly expanded and transnational partnerships have been closely formed among media corporations which pursue marketing strategies and joint production ventures spanning several different markets. The circulation of popular culture is no longer limited to the national borders but finds a broader transnational acceptance in the region, leading to the formation of new links among people in East Asia, especially the youth. This trend has shown no sign of letting up. Asian markets have become even more synchronized, East Asian co-projects in film and music have become more common, and singers and actors from around the region are engaged in activities that transcend national borders.

In this development, Japanese media culture took the initiative in the 1990s. However, many other East Asian regions too are creating their own cultural forms of international appeal within the social and cultural contexts specific to their countries and media flows are becoming more and more multilateral. Most notably, in the early twenty-first century, Korean popular culture is sweeping over Asian markets. Korean TV series and pop music are now receiving an even warmer welcome in places like Taiwan, Hong Kong, and China than their Japanese equivalents.

Japan, too, is embracing the Korean Wave. While local channels such as Fukuoka TVQ had begun to broadcast Korean TV drama series as early as in 1996, it is especially since the late 1990s that Korean films and TV dramas have been well received in Japan. As far as TV dramas are concerned, in 2002, a national-network channel TV Asahi, for the first time broadcast *All about Eve* at prime time. The series was not successful in terms of rating, but it opened the door for Korean TV dramas' entry into the major media space in Japan. Finally, as the chapters of Mori and Hirata in this volume discuss in detail, *Winter Sonata* was phenomenally popular since 2003 and this clearly marked the landing of the Korean Wave in the Japanese market, which has been hitherto exclusive to other Asian TV dramas.

The purpose of this chapter is to examine the complexity of the impact of the Korean Wave in Japanese society and consider the possibility of transnational dialogues through popular cultural connections. First I will look at how the reception of other East Asian media cultures proves to be an opportune moment for Japanese audiences to critically review the state of their own lives, society and history. I will do this by comparing the reception of the Korean Wave, and *Winter Sonata* in particular, with the fervent reception of Hong Kong popular culture in the late 1990s. While the sense of nostalgia is a key feature to the both cases, the nostalgia perceived by consuming Korean TV dramas has more to do with personal sentiments and memories and this leads to more self-reflective post-text activities such as learning the Korean language, visiting Korea and even studying the history of Japanese colonialism.

However, there is another crucial difference between the reception of Hong Kong and Korean popular culture. It is the existence of postcolonial subjects within Japan. To understand the complexity of transnational media connections promoted by the Korean Wave, I will argue, it is also crucial to consider how the media flows from South Korea have influenced, both constructively and unconstructively, the social positioning and recognition of resident Koreans in Japan, most of whom are the descendants of expatriates under Japanese colonial rule. I will consider this by examining the representation of and audience responses to a popular Japanese TV drama series that for the first time deals with socio-historical issues about resident Koreans at prime time. It will be suggested that while the social recognition of resident Koreans has been much improved as the Korean Wave significantly betters the image of Korea, it tends to disregard the understanding of historically embedded experiences of resident Koreans. They are instead effortlessly associated with the culture and people of South Korea in a way in which postcolonial and multicultural issues are subsumed under inter-national relations. This consideration highlights the importance for the study of trans-Asian media and cultural flows to go beyond the nation-centered framework by examining how the transnational intersects with the postcolonial and the multicultural.

Nostalgia and Self-reflexivity

The Korean Wave is not the first instance where other Asian media texts have been well received in the Japanese market. Various kinds of films (mostly of Hong Kong) and stars such as Bruce Lee, Jackie Cheng and Dick Lee have been favorably received as they appealingly represent different kinds of cultural expressions and imaginations of being modern in Asia. Most recently, there was a Hong Kong boom in the late 1990s, which is still fresh in our memories.[1] A comparison of the reception of Hong Kong media culture in the late 1990s and that of the Korean Wave in the early twenty-first century elucidates both similarities and differences between them in intriguing ways.

First of all, the scope and intensity of media and cultural flows from South Korea is not comparable to those from other Asian regions and countries. In particular, the passionate reception of *Winter Sonata* reaches an unprecedented level. The Hong Kong boom was promoted by women's magazines and film and music industries, it did not attract much attention from most of the mainstream media, especially TV. Extra efforts were thus needed for audiences to watch videos and get information about the stars and they faced difficulties in sharing their interests in Hong Kong media culture with friends and colleagues. Accordingly, its audiences were relatively limited to devoted fan communities. Yet, precisely because of this, many fans were proud to have an "advanced" taste, which enabled them to differentiate themselves from mass consumers of the mainstream media culture in Japan.

It is crucial here to remember that Hong Kong TV dramas have never been shown in Japan but TV dramas as well as films are the main vehicles of the Korean Wave and thus terrestrial national channels, which are the most influential media in Japan, are main promoters of the boom. Notably, *Winter Sonata* was broadcast on NHK, a public TV channel, which has the most extensive penetration all over the country. In addition, various kinds of mass media such as newspaper and magazines regularly cover the story about the drama, actors and audience responses.

The Hong Kong boom and Korean Wave have something in common in that the well received media texts represent modern cultural scenes in urban settings. While sharing the experience of negotiating with American (and perhaps to a lesser extent Japanese) influences of production styles, Hong Kong and Korean media industries have developed their own styles of films, pop music and youth-oriented dramas that attain transnational appeal in terms of the representation of "here and now" in Asian urban contexts. They lucidly articulate the intertwined composition of global homogenization and heterogenization in a different way from those of Japanese media texts. For audiences, it can be argued, similar and different, close and distant, fantasizing and realistic, all of these intertwined perceptions subtly intersect so as to arouse a sense of cultural identification, relatedness and sympathy in the eyes of young people in East Asia under regional cultural dynamics (see Iwabuchi 2004 for the case of Japanese TV dramas).

It can be argued that one of the main reasons for the success of Korean TV dramas is their depiction of family matters and relationships, which enable them to appeal to a wider range of viewers than Japanese programs. Even for young viewers in East Asia, South Korean dramas are preferable to Japanese ones in terms of realism and their ability to relate to the characters and story lines. In my interviews with Taiwanese university students in 2001, I was told that Japanese series tended to focus solely on young people's loves and jobs, and this restricted the scope of their stories and thus audience identification. Korean dramas, on the other hand, while featuring young people's romances as a central theme, tend to portray the problems and bonds of parents and children, grandparents, and other relatives. This makes them look more similar to the actual lives of young people living in Taiwan. The restricted and closed relationships and daily lives of young people featured in the world of Japanese TV dramas, which Ito (2004) describes as a "microcosm," have attracted many followers in the Asian region. While Korean TV drama production might have been influenced by this kind of Japanese drama production (Lee 2004), Korean dramas have achieved a different kind of realism in portraying East Asian urban imaginaries.

However, this does not fully account for the favored reception of *Winter Sonata* in Japan. It is rather the sense of nostalgia that marks its adoring reception. This shows another similarity in the reception of Hong Kong and Korean media texts in that the main audiences are women in their 30s, 40s, 50s and 60s who tend to express their nostalgic feelings for the things that used to be in Japan in their reception of Hong Kong and Korean media texts. In the case of Hong Kong culture, it reminded Japanese audiences of the vigor of the society that has supposedly been lost in Japan. This sense of nostalgia was strongly contextualized in the situation in which Japan struggled with an economic slump after the so-called bubble economy while other Asian nations enjoyed high economic growth from the early 1990s. In this suffocating socio-economic atmosphere, Japanese audiences' consumption of Hong Kong media culture was sharply marked by a nostalgic longing for lost social vigor. This mode of reception shows a highly ambivalent posture in the appreciation of cultural neighbors. An awareness of "familiar" cultural differences through the consumption of Hong Kong popular culture arouses contrasting senses, a sense that Hong Kong's level of being modern still lags behind Japan, albeit slightly, and a sense of contemporaneity in living in the same temporality that promotes cultural dialogue on equal terms. On the one hand, Japanese audiences' emphasis on the temporal difference rather than spatial one occasionally displays their failure and refusal to see other Asians as modern equals who share exactly the same developmental temporality. This might attest to a historically constituted Japan's double claim for being similar but superior to "Asia". Orientalist thinking that attempts to understand Asia's present by equating it with Japan's past good times occasionally resurfaces in the nostalgic appreciation of Hong Kong culture (Iwabuchi 2002 ch.5).

On the other, however, it also shows their appreciation of a different mode of Asian modernity on more than equal terms with Japan in terms of the negotiation with the West and the sophistication of cultural hybridization. Hong Kong's present was appreciated as a promising vivacity of another Asian modernity that looked in stark contrast to Japan's present. By realizing that Hong Kong is no less developed and modernized than Japan and positively identifying themselves with its sophisticated media texts, Japanese female audiences themselves tried to regain vigor and energy (Iwabuchi 2002 ch.5). By watching media texts produced in other parts of Asia, Japanese audiences realize that they now inhabit the same developmental time zone as people in other Asian regions and that the peoples of Asia, while being washed by similar waves of modernization, urbanization, and globalization, have experienced these phenomena in similar yet different ways in their own particular contexts. This may prove to be an opportune moment for Japanese people to critically review the state of their own modernity. Belief in Japan's superiority over the rest of Asia — a condescending mode of thinking that, while accepting that the country belongs geographically and culturally to Asia, makes a distinction between Japan and Asia — remains firmly rooted in society, but such attitudes are being shaken as countries in Asia become more and more interconnected through popular cultural flows.

The same is true with the reception of *Winter Sonata* in Japan, as the comment of a news reporter from Korea made a point of: "Cultures of other Asian countries evoke, touch and revive the emotions and dreams that have been lost in one country. This is a wonderful gift of cultural diversity" (*Asahi Shinbun* 18 May 2004). Revived emotions furthermore induce self-reflexive attitudes in audiences and drive them to search for a better present. However, nostalgia projected onto the Korean TV drama, *Winter Sonata*, is slightly but significantly different. While both nostalgias are socio-historically structured and self-reflexive, in Hong Kong's case nostalgia is projected more onto a societal loss perceived as such by individuals, but in the case of *Winter Sonata*, it is projected less onto the social vigor Japan allegedly has lost than onto personal memories and sentiments in terms of emotions of love and interpersonal relationships. This causes a crucial difference in the perception of coevalness (see Fabian 1983). In contrast to highly a precarious way of interpreting the cultural difference of Hong Kong in a temporal framework, the reception of *Winter Sonata* and other Korean TV dramas in general seems to more often escape the pitfall.

Actually this perception is more often than not found in the media discourse about the phenomena which aims to dismiss Korean TV dramas as the belated equivalent of Japanese dramas in the 1960s and 70s and to mock dissatisfied middle-aged women audiences who find a savior in Korean TV dramas that actually reflect the behind-the-time standing of the society (see Li 2004). This is mostly evident in men's weekly magazines, while the depiction is more sympathetic to the experiences of audiences in the magazines whose target readers are women and whose articles are mostly written by women.

It can be argued that Japanese audiences of *Winter Sonata* still perceive a temporal gap, given that most audiences are elder women compared to their Korean counterparts. Those middle aged women are reminded of the pure passion for love and caring in human relationships which according to them, they used to have in their youth. However I found the audiences do not seem to associate the temporal gap to that between the two societies even if they compare *Winter Sonata* with Japanese dramas of the 1970s and 80s, precisely due to the fact that the longing for things that used to be is induced more at the level of personal memories and love sentiments rather than at the level of social loss. If, in the Hong Kong case, the sense of nostalgia is closely related to the discourse of vanishing (Ivy 1995) discourses about social loss in the course of modernization, in the Korean case it has more to do with the personal recovery of vanished sentiments. And this longing is also related to the vanishing of discourse, the failure of Japanese media industries to produce media narratives that inspire emotions in a positive and humane manner. Most obviously, it is a pure, single-minded loving affectionate and caring interpersonal relationship depicted in *Winter Sonata* that attracts Japanese audiences. Especially much-admired is the man's magnanimous tenderness that subtly combines embracing leadership and sincere respect for the partner that is attractively performed by Bae Yong Jun. These are something that cannot be found in Japanese TV dramas as one producer acknowledged that

Japanese TV producers would not be able to make such dramas since such pure love stories have been replaced by stories with more ironic twists (*Asahi Shinbun* 21 May 2004).

Interestingly the highly personalized longing provoked by the reception of the Korean drama has strong marks on the vivacity of post-text social praxis, which is crucially different from the Hong Kong case. Many audiences told me that they consciously tried to become more caring and gentle to others and respect family members after watching *Winter Sonata*. More significantly, compared to Hong Kong's case in which many audiences tended to consciously indulge in the act of consuming media images and did not pay much interest in directly connecting with the people and culture of Hong Kong, audiences of *Winter Sonata* are much more actively making contact with Korean culture, society and people. Fascination evoked in the media texts more directly and actively leads to interests in knowing and encountering "real" Korea. As detailed in Hirata's chapter, no small number of them join *Winter Sonata* tours to Korea to experience the drama scenes, experience local culture and people, and start learning the language. Furthermore, many audiences are learning the history of Japanese colonialism in Korea. The nostalgic longing evoked by *Winter Sonata* is less motivated by the will to identify with the modernizing energy of the society, but precisely because of this personal-oriented desire, it is more engaging and emancipatory. Personal is indeed political!

Inter-national Cultural Exchange and Beyond

The historical relationship is also an important factor in understanding the development of the Korean Wave in Japan and its difference from its Hong Kong counterpart. Particularly important here is the history of Japan's colonialism, which has long rendered the relationship between the two countries geographically and culturally close yet politically and emotionally distant. The recent upsurge of the Korean Wave in Japan, which is based on the contemporaneous appreciation of its cultural neighbour, can be seen as a positive kind of reaction to the postwar closure of bilateral cultural exchange. Japan did have a history of imperial invasion to Hong Kong too. No small number of people in Hong Kong still hold a strong anti-Japan sentiment, as is clearly shown by the demonstrations over the dispute about the possession of the senkaku islands. The point is, however, how the (post)colonial historical relationship is perceived and discussed in Japan. It is not a historical fact but the public perception of history and postcolonial presence that is at stake in the consideration of the way in which the history of Japanese colonialism inscribes the manner of the Japanese reception of other Asian cultures. Japan's colonial relationship with Hong Kong has never been a big public issue in Japan — let me reiterate that this is not to say it is insignificant — but the fact that South Korea is a former Japanese colony and no small number of people in South Korea have a strong antagonism against Japan has long been widely recognized in Japan.

The bilateral relationship between Japan and South Korea has significantly improved since the late 1990s. The Seoul Olympics in 1988 was perhaps the first instance that changed Japanese images of South Korea, from a backward, still undeveloped country to an urbanized modern country. The event attracted many tourists from Japan and activated grassroots exchange among the populaces. More significantly, two momentous events in the late 1990s greatly improved the cultural relationship between Japan and South Korea. One was the South Korean government's decision in late 1998 to abolish the long-term regulation policy of banning the import of Japanese culture. This announcement clearly signified a new epoch for the bilateral relationship and was particularly welcomed in Japan, since it seemed to mark the sign of historical reconciliation at least on the part of the ex-colonizer.

The Japanese government has been interested in the potential of media culture facilitating cultural dialogue, particularly in terms of its capacity to improve Japan's reputation and to make smooth Japan's historical reconciliation with other East and Southeast Asian countries. This idea of cultural diplomacy in Asia has been discussed and its policy has been implemented by the governmental circle at least since the 1970s when the so-called Fukuda doctrine was schemed, but it is mostly targeted toward Southeast Asia. North-East Asia, especially Korea and China, whose colonial relationship with Japan is more direct and harsh but has not been seriously faced by the Japanese government since 1945, did not then quite fit the scheme of cultural diplomacy. Therefore, the recent development of popular cultural exchange between Japan and South Korea is a great advancement of the application of cultural diplomacy to East Asia.

It is in this context that the concert of a Japanese duo, Chage & Aska in Seoul in 2000 attracted massive media coverage in Japan. The duo had been actively entering other Asian markets. They had staged concerts in Taipei, Singapore, Hong Kong, Beijing and Shanghai since 1994, but could not make it to South Korea due to the cultural regulation policy. Their inroads into East Asian markets might have been motivated by commercial reasons, but they are quite conscious of their role in overcoming Japanese imperial history (see e.g., *Views*, July 1996: 78). In August 2000, Chage & Aska finally held a concert in Seoul. The Japanese media enthusiastically covered it, reporting that this was a historic concert being the first performance by Japanese pop musicians in the Japanese language, which clearly marked the cultural thaw between Japan and South Korea. Chage & Aska themselves expressed the sense of accomplishment at the concert: 'Let us younger generations make a future together!' (*Asahi Shinbun*, 28 August 2000).

Yet what has become prominent is not just the entry of Japanese popular culture into South Korea but even to a greater degree, the advent of Korean popular culture into Japan. The two-way flow of popular culture has significantly contributed to the people mutually finding intimate human faces and the immediate attractiveness of cultural neighbours. It is also greatly enhanced by the other historic event, the co-hosting of the FIFA world cup soccer tournament. In 1996, to everyone's surprise, South Korea and Japan were assigned to co-host the FIFA world cup soccer in 2002. The two countries harshly competed with each other to win the bid and thus were not quite happy with the decision. However, the co-hosting process eventually resulted in having a tremendous impact on the betterment of the cultural relationship between the two nations at the official level as well as a grass-root level. It engendered many government-sponsored events, media collaborations such as the co-production of TV dramas and various kinds of people's cultural exchanges. When Korea proceeded to the semi-final, people from Japan and Korea, including resident Koreans, all gathered together to cheer Korea in Shin-Okubo, a renowned Korean town in Tokyo.

Supporting this trend, some surveys showed the drastic improvement of people's mutual perceptions and the positive view about the future relationship between Japan and Korea, with Japanese responses apparently being more positive. Likewise, many audiences of *Winter Sonata* expressed that the drama had totally changed their images of Korean society, culture and people, which were hitherto negative. By experiencing Korea through post-text activities, they come to further realize the close ties the two countries have and the fallacy of Orientalist images of Korea that have been dominantly held in Japanese society. According to a survey, about sixty percent of audiences came to have a better image of South Korea and forty percent of audiences are paying more attention to the media coverage of the Japan-Korea political and historical relationship (Hayashi 2004). Some warn that this development is just a transient boom and whether media consumption of *Winter Sonata* will lead to a substantial understanding of Korea is highly doubtful (e.g. Chon 2004, Son 2004). However, if we look closely into the audience reception as detailed in Mori's chapter, the change cannot be easily dismissed. In the post-text activities that characterize the *Winter Sonata* syndrome, some even start learning what Japanese colonialism did in the Korean peninsula and realise how it still casts a shadow on the current situation. It probably will not lead to drastic political change in the short term, but the imagination and practice in everyday life is the basis of societal constitution. Through such mundane change, audiences will become indeed active political agents.

Having said this, admittedly the caution is an important reminder against uncritical celebration on the role of popular culture in the enhancement of inter-national relationships. Too excessive an expectation in popular culture for the enhancement of inter-national relationships needs to be carefully examined. Being concerned mostly with the relationships between nations, it tends to conveniently use popular culture for the promotion of national interests. What is problematic here is that such discourses can only be put in the foreground by not attending to the complexity of transnational popular cultural flows that (re)produce not just dialogue but also unevenness (see Iwabuchi 2002, 2004). Most imperatively, such a view tends to subtly re-demarcate the national boundaries and disregard, and even suppress, the issues of existing differences, marginalization and inequality within each society in terms of gender, sexuality, ethnicity, race, class, age, region etc. It needs to be remembered that what is being promoted is the exchange and dialogue between cultures that are dominant and popular in each country. If we take cross-border dialogue engendered by media cultural flows seriously, we must go beyond the national framework and consider how the complicated transnational circulations of people, capital and media texts crisscross local multicultural and postcolonial issues. Then, if we are to take the Korean Wave in Japan seriously, the examination of how the Korean Wave has impacted on the inter-national relationship between Japan and South Korea is not enough. The examination of its impact, I would suggest, on the social positioning of resident Koreans in Japan who have long been discriminated against as second-rate citizens would be a significant touchstone in the consideration of the (im)possibility of mediated transnational cultural dialogue.

Korean Wave and the Recognition of Korean Residents

Resident Koreans are those who migrated to Japan during Japan's colonial rule and are their descents. At the time of the end of the war, roughly 2 million Koreans lived in Japan as Japanese nationals under colonial rule. More than 1.3 million people returned to Korea after the war, but about 60,000 Koreans remained in Japan due to the difficulty of starting a new life and finding a job in Korea. Most of those remaining in Japan were the earliest immigrants who had firmly established their families in Japan and lost a substantial connection with Korea. By the implementation of the San Francisco peace treaty in 1952, the Japanese government one-sidedly deprived Japanese nationality to those Koreans who had stayed in Japan and subjected them to the rigid control of Alien Registration Law. Koreans had then two options other than to remain stateless residents in Japan; either to return to Korea or naturalize to Japanese, but neither was persuasive to many, though some of them repatriated to North Korean after 1959, responding to Kim Il Sung's encouragement of repatriation. The start of the diplomatic relationship between Japan and South Korea in 1965 made it possible for Koreans in Japan to obtain permanent residency if they became South Korean nationals. Still those who supported and identified themselves with North Korea remained stateless, neither Japanese nor South Korean. In either case, as a non-Japanese, Koreans had to be registered as a foreigners living in Japan and used to carry a registration card, which included fingerprints until 1991 when their status as special permanent residents were fully acknowledged by the Japanese government.[2]

Some might wonder why many Koreans did not naturalize into Japanese despite the fact that they eventually lived in Japan for good. It is mostly due to the lingering structural discrimination against resident Koreans and the Japanese government's authoritarian immigration policy in order to keep the nation apparently "homogeneous". In the application of the procedure of naturalization, resident Koreans have to experience a long, inhumane examination about the qualifications of becoming "properly Japanese" and it eventually requires them to adopt a Japanese name. Due to the strong assimilation policy, to become a Japanese citizen, Koreans are required to forget and hide their descent. Thus, many choose not to become Japanese citizens and this posture has been an important part of their identity formation in the resistance against the repression of the Japanese government. "Residing in Japan" (*zainichi*) is "an alternative to becoming naturalized" and the construction of their identity is centered on the sense of belongingness to Korean nations (Tai: 2004: 356), while the number of Koreans who naturalize into Japanese has been increasing recently.

When we consider the impact of the Korean Wave in Japan, as suggested above, the presence of resident Koreans as (post)colonial subjects in Japan is decisively different from the Hong Kong case. The issue at stake here is whether and how the presence of problematic (post)colonial subjects has some bearing on the reception of popular culture from the country they have ethno-historical "roots and routes" and/or how the reception has had an impact on local multicultural and postcolonial issues.

Ashley Carruthers (2004), in his analysis of the Japanese consumption of Vietnam exotic, argues that while it is a subjectless multiculturalism that tries to pleasurably domesticate multicultural situations in highly a consumerist manner without seriously engaging with the presence of actual subjects, what marks the Japanese case is a striking tendency that exotic Vietnamese cultures are introduced, exhibited and promoted by Japanese people themselves. Here, the relative absence of Vietnamese residents in the Japanese public sphere as a significant other makes it much easier for people in Japan to consume Vietnamese culture as exotic:

> The fact that the Vietnamese are not significant national others is crucial to any understanding of the exceptional commodifiability of the Vietnamese exotic in Japan … Vietnameseness in Japan is not embodied in a threatening way. It can be safely conceptualised in the abstract, untroubled by the prospect of encountering the concrete "ethnic" subject and its strange cooking smells and noisy music. (Carruthers 2004: 416)

Perhaps this point is applicable to the reception of Hong Kong culture too. The relative absence of Hong Kong subjects in the public sphere renders the consumption of Hong Kong culture idealized and commodified.

Yet, as Carruthers points out, this is never the case with Korean culture. "The commodification of Koreanness is disrupted by a general distaste for the national otherness represented by diasporic or hybrid Korean identities" (2004: 416). Resident Koreans have long been forced to live as a second-rate citizens in Japan and suffered considerable discrimination and prejudice and many of them have been forced to live by passing as Japanese, hiding their ethnic backgrounds and adopting Japanese names in public. Koreanness is not something that can be comfortably consumed as a mass exotic commodity in the Japanese public imaginary unless its origin is suppressed or "Japanized" as is often the case with celebrities who willingly or unwillingly conceal their ethnic descents in public. Resident Koreans' cultural expressions have occasionally gained social recognition as shown by several writers winning prizes for their novels by but they are not for pleasurable mass consumption. "Impure" identity construction that is neither Japanese nor Korean in a full sense has been a serious issue for them. Their cultural expressions thus tend to deal with the agony and ambiguity about their own precarious lives in the social positioning as *zainichi* who are historically torn apart between the Japanese and Korean peninsula. And this in turn evokes something uneasy for Japan since its postcolonial subjectivity never allows it to cheerfully forget the history of colonialism.

In this context, the advent of the Korean Wave and the improvement of the images of Korea in general pose intriguing questions about its relations to the social positioning and recognition of resident Koreans. As Taylor (1994) argues, social recognition of difference is a significant aspect of the multicultural politics of the marginalized. Then, the question is how resident Koreans whose otherness cannot be easily contained by subjectless multiculturalism are recognized via the fetishization of Korean popular culture? Does the recognition work to empower or disempower resident Koreans? How are positive perceptions of South Korea through the Korean Wave related to the perception of resident Koreans in Japan? How is their untameable postcolonial subjectivity that resists easy cultural consumption repositioned within Japan through the positive consumption of Korean popular culture and the advance of bilateral cultural exchange?

Of course it depends. There are no straightforward answers to this nor can we generalize the diverse experiences of resident Koreans. It cannot be denied that the rise of the Korean Wave and the betterment of Korean images in Japan have significantly improved the imaged of resident Koreans, and this has empowered no small number of resident Koreans. Some, especially the younger generations, have gained the confidence to live as Koreans in Japanese society without naturalizing into Japanese. Others have become more willing to bridge the two countries by positively taking advantage of his/her impure existence through the activities that introduce various cultures such as film and popular music to each other. The presence and issues about resident Koreans have come to be more frequently dealt with and attract more attention in the public media space such as popular magazines and TV wide-shows. While *All under the Moon* (1993) is the first commercially successful film about resident Koreans in Japan (see Iwabuchi 2000), recent films such as *GO* (2000) and *Pacchigi* (2005) are even better received.

At the same time, the impact of the Korean Wave still tends to be constrained by the dominant attention paid to inter-national relationships, which overpowers the concern with resident Koreans. The sense of frustration is often expressed by resident Koreans themselves in that Japanese people might embrace the Korean Wave but the structure of social discrimination and indifference has not changed. For many resident Koreans, job opportunities are still limited and it is at times difficult to rent a room. The improvement of these situations has not interested the Japanese government that is solely interested in using the recent cultural exchange for the easing of the historically strained relationship between Japan and South Korea. In August 2004, the LDP (Liberal Democratic Party), the party in office, invited the director of *Winter Sonata* to a seminar on the bilateral relationship between Japan and South Korea and the then party secretary, Abe, also celebrated the development of mutual cultural exchange by referring to the popularity of the drama in his official visit to South Korea. Yet, he kept his silence to the Korean president's question about the issue of history textbooks and the granting of voting rights for local elections to resident Koreans in Japan. In the above-mentioned survey (Hayashi 2004), about a quarter of respondents said that they had become more interested in resident Koreans and their history, which is not negligible but yet much lower compared to their increasing interest in South Korea. Even worse, according to Asahi Shinbun (21 August 2004), to the question about the interests that are roused by the Korean Wave, only few mentioned historical issues or resident Koreans.

Furthermore, it should be noted that the improvement of the image of South Korea is simultaneously occurring with the demonizing of North Korea. Since the North Korean government officially acknowledged their involvement in the abduction of Japanese nationals, there has been a massive and antagonistic media bashing of North Korea. Racist attacks have also been made against resident Koreans who identified themselves with North Korea. North Korea-affiliated high school female students who wore Korean ethnic dress as school uniforms were assaulted in the city[3] and a self-claimed resident North Korean boxing champion's homepage had to close due to a flood of blackmail messages.

A clear divide between North and South Korea in the public perception among Japanese has an influence on the recognition and naming of resident Koreans according to their belonging either to South Korea or North Korea. The naming of resident Koreans — *zainichi chousenjin* (resident North Koreans or resident Koreans in general as *chousenjin* signifies ethnicity rather than national identification), *zainichi kankokujin* (resident South Koreans to differentiate it from resident Koreans who identify themselves with North Korea), *or zainichi kankoku-chousenjin* (resident North and South Koreans to include both kinds of political identifications) — is highly political, as it involves the issue of political identification with two Korean countries. In either case, however, remaining as Korean nationals is important for many since it signifies the resistance against the disgraceful naturalization into a Japanese national, as explained earlier. Recently, resident Korean communities have tried to be more open to the diversity within and to widen membership irrespective of his/her nationality or national identification. The name, *zainichi Korian*, which uses the English term "Korean", has been often used partly because of its apparent political neutrality, while it is often criticized for the very same reason. In addition, it has also the merit of making it possible to include those who have been naturalized into Japanese as the emphasis is put more on historically embedded "Koreanness" than on national identification or the kind of passport they have.

However, with the advent of the Korean Wave, the reference to resident South Koreans (*zainichi-kankokujin*) has become used more often than before in Japanese media. The new categorization of South Korean nationals living in Japan does not just accompany the suppression of resident Koreans who identify themselves with North Korea. No less importantly, this manner of naming signifies the ahistorical recognition of resident Koreans that is apt to understand their existence in association with the contemporary culture and society of the nation-state called South Korea which now produces attractive media cultures. For example, in a book titled, "I want to know that person's country, South Korea" (2004), there is a small section about resident South Koreans, which is included in the chapter of the history of South Korea. The author of this section is a resident Korean and she introduces the ambivalent identity of resident Koreans who do not clearly belong to either nation in a positive manner. However, such an approving account of ambivalent identity construction embraced in the lives of resident Koreans is diminished by the categorization of their experiences as those of the people of South Korea. In this instance, *zainichi-kankokujin* signifies less resident-South-Koreans than South-Korean-nationals-living-in-Japan in an ahistorical and nationalized framework. Crucial in this nationalized recognition of resident Koreans is the disregard of the collective historical memories and experiences that are shared irrespective of nationality and that have been passed down from generation to generation. In the last scene of the popular film, *GO*, the protagonist, a third generation resident Korean man shouts to his Japanese lover when she calls him resident South Korean, "you Japanese do not feel at ease unless you categorize and name us in any way. Do not confine me in such a narrow category". This line that strongly rejects the effortless categorization of resident Koreans takes on a more imperative meaning with the advent of the Korean Wave in Japan.

Tokyo Bayscape *and the representation of resident South Koreans in Japan*

While there are positive impacts of the Korean Wave on the social recognition and positioning of resident Koreans in Japan, there can be discerned a confusion in the understanding their existence through the prism of South Korea, which accompanies the segregation of shared historical experiences of resident Koreans. How the Korean Wave has constructively and unconstructively impacted on media representations and recognition of resident Koreans is elucidated in a TV drama series, *Tokyo Bayscape* (Fuji TV, Monday 9–10pm), which was broadcast from July to September 2004. The drama is about the romantic relationship between a third-generation resident South Korean woman and a Japanese man and their aspiration to overcome the obstacle of ethnic difference. The story begins with the scene in which the depressed heroine sends a message to a web site from a mobile phone, "please find the real me". This is the key word of the drama and motif that signifies her desire to be recognized and loved just as she is, as a woman who was born in Japan of Korean ancestry. The production of the drama was clearly motivated by the recent popularity of Korean TV dramas and films as the producer clearly acknowledged. The drama is epoch-making in that it is the first TV drama series in the prime time of a major commercial TV station that features a resident Korean as the protagonist. This testifies to another positive impact of the Korean Wave on media representations of resident Koreans whose existence has long tended to be disregarded in the mainstream media.

However, it is apparent that the drama effortlessly uses resident Koreans as spice to the story in terms of acting as a hindrance to the relationship. In the drama, the story revolves around the anguish of a third generation daughter whose economically successful second-generation father stubbornly insists on her marrying resident Koreans and opposes her wish to marry a Japanese man. He is much concerned with the historically constituted discrimination against resident Koreans in Japan. At the same time, he has a bitter memory of his dead wife's passionate but tragic relationship with a Japanese man before their marriage and how she never forgot her sense of longing for him. To him, the daughter appears to fatefully follow her mother's forbidden love relations with Japanese men. While parental opposition to children marrying Japanese nationals might to some extent reflect the real life experiences of resident Koreans, the drama depicts the issue with an exclusive focus on the personal distress of resident Koreans without giving due attention to the structured discrimination in Japanese society. Issues are reduced to the personal anguish of well-to-do Korean residents in Japan and social and historical issues are separated from the personal. Furthermore, the stubborn closed-ness of the resident Korean community is to blame for her agony, as symbolized by the protagonist's father who is represented as ethnocentric, obstinate and who thus cannot understand the developing relationship between Japan and Korea (Ogura 2004). It is as if resident Koreans were all responsible for drawing the sharp exclusive line between Japanese and resident Koreans.

In relation to this, the protagonist's distress is depicted as the sharp divide between the two nations, South Korea and Japan. Japan's relationship with South Korea and its people is again confounded with that of resident Koreans whose historically contextualized experiences and subjectivities are thus interpreted in terms of those of South Korean nationality. This is shown by the catchphrase of the drama, "the love that transcends the national boundaries between Japan and South Korea". The father of the heroine often states that there is a deep gulf between Japan and Korea that is sharply divided by the Sea of Japan. Even a Korean star who acts in *Winter Sonata* appears in the end of one episode to send a message to the audiences that people of both nations will be best friends by going beyond what happened in the past.

This is a striking confusion between Koreans and resident Koreans in Japan, as one viewer sharply criticised on the web-site:

> I think the issue of resident Koreans needs to be distinguished from the Korean Wave in Japan. Maybe they have the same nationality. Yet how is it plausible to deal with those Koreans who have been brought up in South Korea and those third generation resident Koreans who have been brought up in Japan on par? … It is very good in any case that the neighboring country South Korea is in the media limelight and the friendship between Japan and South Korea is being deepened. However, resident Koreans are someone living next to you, not in the neighboring country. They might be your neighbors, colleagues or friends, if you are not aware of this. No sea divides Japan and resident Koreans.[4]

Yet, looking into the official web site of the drama series,[5] most audiences' contributions seem to affirm the drama narrative of inter-national relationship between Japan and Korea: "Unexpectedly I am addicted to the drama, because it deals with the contemporary issues between Japan and South Korea we are currently embracing"; "This drama aims to bring Japan and South Korea closer, isn't it? If so, unless the drama has a happy ending, the relationship between the two nations will remain distant"; "I am deeply impressed with the drama that depicts the loves who struggle to overcome national boundaries". These messages suggest that many audiences expect the drama series to contribute to the improvement of the relationship between Japan and Korea, but at the expense of the understanding of the complexity of experiences and social positioning of resident Koreans, as it is reduced to those of South Korean nationals living in Japan.

While the desire for suppressing the fallacy of racial and cultural homogeneity in Japan appears in the form of a subject-less multiculturalism in the case of the consumption of Vietnamese culture, *Tokyo Bayscape* confers a kind of social recognition to resident Koreans that renders them easily consumable historical subjects through interpellating them as South Korean nationals. The positive image of South Korea that the Korean Wave promotes eventually works to newly marginalize and suppress postcolonial complexity and nuisances embodied in the historical subjectivity called "resident Koreans". This is an attempt to conveniently understand his/her precarious experience and identity formation, which resist clear categorization in any sense since they are constructed in the situation in which s/he is forced to live with the vague feeling of uneasiness and strain in Japanese society (So 2003). Social recognition is given only when historical nuisance is tamed by and for the majority. While showing new positive developments about the social recognition of resident Koreans in Japan, the representation of resident Koreans in the drama nevertheless displays a postcolonialism without history. The past is acknowledged as something that has gone and which no longer determines the present, an acknowledgement of the past not to remember but to leave behind.

The drama also displays the replacement of multiculturalism by multinationalism that attempts to understand the issue of multiculturalism in terms of nationality as a unit of analysis (see Iwabuchi 2005). The existence of resident Koreans in Japan is grasped from the view point of the inter-national relationship between Japan and South Korea, which disregards those whose experience and identity formation are torn between the two nations. The existence of South Korean nationals living in Japan rather than resident Koreans in Japan can be publicly recognized as they are more tolerable foreign nationals who are safely separated from the past, present and future of the Japanese imagined community. The factual mark of difference in terms of nationality and passport, the lack of the right to vote and the lingering difficulty of marrying Japanese nationals are dealt with in the drama, but not in a way in which the myth of Japanese homogeneity that has severely marginalized resident Koreans is fundamentally questioned. This is reminiscent of the Japanese government's recent encouragement for resident Koreans to acquire Japanese nationality. As Tai (2004) warns, even if the naturalization process becomes softer and resident Koreans can more easily "come out" by publicly using Korean names and/or acknowledging his/her ethnic roots, this does not ensure the acceptance of resident Koreans as full-citizens. Unless the lingering social discriminations and the racially and ethnically essentialist definition of "Japanese" are seriously overcome, "resident Koreans are encouraged to 'come out', but only in a contained way". The naturalization with Korean ethnic marks would result in their assimilation "only as a second-class Japanese" (369).

Critique for the Future

My critical analysis of the impact of the Korean Wave on the social positioning and recognition of resident Koreans in Japan should not be taken as totally rejecting positive changes. Critique is a necessary detour to further the potentiality of the emergent change and to actualize transnational dialogue through media consumption. Thus it is no less imperative to carefully attend to the sign of change as well. Pessimism of the intellect needs to be embraced by optimism of the intellect. One should not dismiss how the Korean Wave, especially the popularity of *Winter Sonata*, has made Japanese people understand Korea and resident Koreans much deeper than before. Let me end my arguments by looking at such promising signs in audiences' responses to *Tokyo Bayscape* on the web site.

Tokyo Bayscape was discussed on the fan sites of *Winter Sonata* too.[6] Apparently the fans were motivated to watch the drama by their interest in how its production was influenced by *Winter Sonata*, but there were also many comments on the issues of social discrimination against resident Koreans such as the historical dis/continuity, the adaptation of Japanese names and the categorization as "resident Koreans". One person who began the discussion was so overwhelmed by the intensity of discussion that followed that she concluded that she would like to keep on studying the history of the two countries and how it had had significant impacts on resident Koreans in Japan. While, as she states, the vivacity of the discussion itself is the impact of *Winter Sonata*, the production and consumption interaction of the two dramas, *Winter Sonata* and *Tokyo Bayscape* positively actually urge audiences to rethink the history of Japanese colonialism and resident Koreans in Japan.

In the official site of *Tokyo Bayscape* that is organized by Fuji TV, there are also some insightful comments about the relationship between *Winter Sonata* and the drama:

Watching the drama, I came to think more about the historical relationship of Japan and South Korea. I am a Japanese who is sick of the recent Korean boom … Its craze looks so superficial and I thought that there was no consideration about history … It is not *Winter Sonata* but *Tokyo Bayscape* that roused my interest in the history of Japan and South Korea.

I am also a third generation resident Korean and attending a Korean school. To tell the truth, I have some reservations about the recent Korean boom in Japan. I am frustrated with the craze of Japanese people who do not even know about our history … But *Tokyo Bayscape* changed my view. We should try to let such people know about ourselves!!

The positive suggestion of the latter comment, apparently from a young female resident Korean to educate Japanese people about history and resident Koreans should not be regarded as a one-way appeal from resident Koreans. Such an attitude would easily lead to the evasion of responsibility by the majority who are inclined to effortlessly ask the minority to teach them what to do. Her comment should be read as an appeal for both Japanese and resident Koreans to work together. She might have been encouraged by the fact that the Japanese mass media produced a drama that dealt with the anguish of young resident Koreans as well as by reading various comments on the web site that are critical of the current situation in Japan. In any case, her expression of hope embodies a possibility of cultivating a new kind of alliance through the consumption of media culture.

Similarly, many resident Koreans, who sympathetically identify themselves with the protagonists, express a sense of empowerment by watching the drama:

> I am myself a third generation resident Korean and had the same experience of the break-down of marriage with a Japanese man. So the drama does not look like another person's affair … I was also distressed about who I am, but could not tell of my anguish of living as a resident Korean in Japan to my Japanese friends. But I now feel healed by the drama.

> I am also a third generation resident Korean. I am really empowered by the drama that having two homelands is a nice thing. … Thanks a lot.

> I have never felt it wonderful to be born a resident Korean, but the drama encourages me to straightly face what I am. Thanks to all the production staff for giving me a touching story.

While these comments make us realize the significance of the drama that deals with the hitherto disregarded issue about resident Koreans, there are also critical comments against the drama in that it fails to attend to the complexity of the lives and existence of resident Koreans by confounding South Koreans and resident Koreans and lacking historical depth.

> I am ambivalent about the recent Korean boom. I am glad that many people have more interests in South Korea but they still continue to be uninformed of resident Koreans. The drama story is nice but it is still far from our reality, as it is depicted from a Japanese point of view.

> I had quite a mixed feeling when I first watched this drama … My grandfather was forcibly brought to Japan during the colonial rule. There

are many children and grand children of such people living in Japan. Young people would think that such old incidents are none of their business, but at least for the first generation resident Koreans it is not something of the past that is finished. The recent Korean Wave has improved the relationship between South Korea and Japan. To further mutual understanding, the history needs to be more firmly grasped.

I am sure that the drama has let many Japanese people know about resident Koreans whose existence has long been out of the front stage of Japanese society (but, let me remind you, not as foreign nationals who are living in Japan but as resident Koreans who are living traces of a tragic history). Still now, it is not easy for resident Koreans to rent an apartment. Fact is stranger than fiction. There are more intricate troubles and incidents in reality. I wish those who watch *Tokyo Bayscape* will become more interested in resident Koreans. And I wish more dramas will be produced that deal with the issue of resident Koreans.

The co-existence of divergent views on *Tokyo Bayscape* expressed by resident Koreans is a testimony of diverse social positions and experiences of resident Koreans who cannot be understood as a homogeneous ethnic group. However, either positive or negative, they are expressed by someone who has long been positioned as a second-rate citizen in Japanese society. We need to understand the complexity and the depth of the issues by seriously listening to the voices of resident Koreans who sympathetically find their anguish and hope in the drama, without effortlessly celebrating the empowering effect of the drama.

> None of my good friends knows about my ethnic roots. I always fear that they would dislike me when the fact is known. I was really moved by the scene where Mika (protagonist) confesses her ethnic background and nationality to her lover. I had the same experience once. I was so moved to shed my tears ... I really wish for a happy ending.

Needless to say, her tears do not simply testify to the positive impact of the Korean Wave or the moving narrative of the love story. It is a historical present of resident Koreans living with the lingering structure of social discrimination that give a special power to the drama narrative.

Answering to the wishes of many audiences, the drama has a happy ending. Yet, her wish for a happy ending is not of the same kind as that of Japanese audiences. Here lies the expectation for real life. No matter how much strongly resident Koreans are empowered by the drama and the Korean Wave in Japan, the crucial question still remains as to how to connect cultural empowerment with actual social transformation. The above-mentioned appeal of "let's work together" by a resident Korean needs to be more actively made from the people whose social positions are more privileged ones. For this purpose, a critical examination of how the transnational media flows intersect the postcolonial and the multicultural is imperative.

Notes

Introduction   East Asian TV Dramas

1. For further analysis of TV dramas in the PRC, see Sun (2002).
2. Comparative analyses of audience reception to Japanese trendy dramas in the rest of Asia can be found in K. Iwabuchi (2004).
3. I have attempted at best an outline in the conceptualization of this sphere in Chua (2004).
4. Interview with station public relations officer.

Chapter 1   The Growth of Korean Cultural Industries and the Korean Wave

1. I thank Richard Seow for this translation.
2. Won is the basic unit of currency in Korea, with US$1 roughly valued at 1,150 won in the early 2000s.
3. Yoon (2005), however, remarks that such unfair conventions have ameliorated in recent years.

Chapter 2   Renting East Asian Popular Culture for Local Television

1. I would like to thank Assistant Professor Lee Dong-Hoo of Incheon University, South Korea, Professor Koichi Iwabuchi of Waseda University, at Tokyo, and Professor Chua Beng-Huat, at the Asia Research Institute, National University of Singapore, for their invaluable assistance and insightful comments.

2. See speech by Mr David T. E. Lim, Acting Minister for Information, 'Communications and the arts', at the opening of the 'Asia television forum, Asia animation and Asia film market and conference 2002' on 3 December 2002. Website: http://www.mita.gov.sg/pressroom/press_021203b.html/.

3. See November 2005 issue of Television Asia, in the section entitled 'Rise and shine: Part 1' when Television Asia conducted a brief survey among satellite operators such as BBC World, Star, AXN Asia, CNBC Asia, MTV Asia, National Geographic, and more, of the continuing rosy economic growth in Asia-based media growth as 'multi-channel advertising sales are on the up and up'. Available at http://www.tvasia.com.sg/home?wid= 150&func= viewSubmission&sid=388/ [accessed 12 Dec 2005].

4. See http://e-broadcastnewsasia.blogspot.com/2006_02_01_e-broadcastnews asia_archive.html [accessed on 27 Apr 2006] where Singapore's MediaCorp Technologies, InfoComm Development Authority and China Film Digital intended to cooperate on building a digital content distribution network.

5. See Singapore's Free Trade Agreements at website http://www.fta.gov.sg/ as well as industry comments about the intensification of regional free trade agreements in East Asia at website: http://www.bilaterals.org/article.php3? id_ article=1035 [accessed 12 May 2005].

6. *Oriental Daily*, 2004. Available: http://orientaldaily.com.hk/photo/20041105/ ent/1105enew01b1.jpg/ [accessed 13 Nov 2005]. See also *Ta Kung Pao* and *The Sun* (2004) 'TVB's Limited Edition of "War and Beauty" DVD'. 5 November.

7. Bourdieu 1984. He refers to these people as those in jobs that involve presentation and representation (sales, marketing, advertising, public relations, fashion, decoration and so forth) and in all the institutions providing symbolic goods and services' (359).

8. For information on *Heaven's Coins* (1995), see www.sempai.org/~mwduncan/ heavens_coins.shtml/. The Korean remake is mentioned on several websites like http://asianfanatics.net/forum/lofiversion/index.php/t79406.html. The SBS homepage for *A Spring Day* is at http://tv.sbs.co.kr/bomnal/ [accessed 20 Jan 2006].

9. Debord (1967: 10) cited in Kellner (2003). According to Kellner, Guy Debord's *The Society of the Spectacle* (1967) was published in translation in a pirate edition by Black and Red (Detroit) in 1970, and has gone through multiple reprints.

10. See *Time Asia* magazine's review and interview with director Zhang on the movie in Richard Corliss (2002), 'In the mood for swordplay', 23 December, available: http://www.time.com/time/asia/magazine/article/0,13673, 501021223-400044,00.html/[accessed 17 Mar 2005]. Also see reviews in http:/ /www.kungfucinema.com/reviews/hero2002.htm/[accessed 20 Mar 2005].

11. See Hong Kong Film Archive newsletter for a seminar entitled 'Another night in Hong Kong: Hong Kong–Japan film exchange in the 1950s and

1960s'. Available: http://www.lcsd.gov.hk/CE/CulturalService/HKFA/
english/newsletter02/e-34-more-happenings.pdf/ [accessed 22 Jan 2006].

12. There is an inter-mingling of Chinese and Korean history in the storyline of *Musa* that lends a creative license to this transnational co-production. See http://www.imdb.com/title/tt0275083/ [accessed 5 May 2005].

Chapter 3   Mediating Nationalism and Modernity

1. Clausen, p. 13.
2. This is part of a research funded by Japan Foundation.
3. Hesmondhalgh, p. 179.
4. Ibid.
5. Donald and Keane, p. 8.
6. Zhao, p. 205.
7. Ibid, p. 186.
8. Ibid, p. 188.
9. Harrison, p. 167.
10. Some of the regulations include strict categorization of TV programmes any cooperation with foreign TV units have to be permitted by the State Ministry of Broadcasting Films and Television.
11. Donald and Keane, p. 9.
12. Wehrfritz and Hewitt, 'One Billion Couch Potatoes', *Newsweek International*, http://www.msnbc.msn,com/id/8018605/site/newsweek/.
13. See analyses of satellite TV in China, Harrison, p. 171, and Chan, p. 165.
14. The StarTV incident was the one when the authorities issued a ban in 1993 on reception of foreign satellite service, when Rupert Murdoch owned StarTV was beginning an aggressive profile in Chinese TV market. The ban also ensued a broader movement against westernization. Harrison, p. 173.
15. Harrison, p. 167.
16. Keane, p. 80.
17. Ibid, p. 83.
18. Ibid, p. 89.
19. There is a convenient reference of 'Hallyu' to avian flu that they both spread across China like pandemic.
20. Xinhua Net, http://www.xinhuanet.com, 7 Apr 2005.
21. The popularity of several K-pop idols (H.O.T. in 1998, and BoA).
22. *Jealousy* was followed by *What Is Love, Endless Love, The Men in the Bathing House Boss's Family,* all of which scored blockbuster success. *Jiang Nan Shi Bao,* http://www.xinhuanet.com, 10 Sep 2004.
23. Other popular dramas include *In Love with the Female Anchor, The Temptation of Eve, Glass Slippers.*
24. Analysis of the preference of Korean TV dramas for different provinces

shows that various factors are at force in affecting consumption of Korean TV dramas: geographical location, the habit of the channels they consume and the genre of dramas. The audience in Canton is largely influenced by Hong Kong TV stations, while Beijing audience seem to be used to watching Korean dramas from CCTV. Shanghainese audience, on the other hand, seem to be consumed with their own trendy channels (Zhang Jing Jing, 'Cool Thinking over Korean Wave', 2004).

25. According to the list of national Top 10 Korean dramas, *Watch Again* is the favourite of the audience in Beijing and Chengdu, *Hotelier* tops the list in Shanghai, *Stairway to Heaven* in Guangzhou, *Wedding and Conspiracy* in Wuhan (Zhang, 2004).

26. *Da He Bao (Big River Post),* 21 Nov 2005.

27. The peak ratings of *Dae Jang Geum* in Korea was 50%.

28. According to Ms Xiao, Programme Director of Hunan Satellite TV, it was during a corporate visit to Taiwan where the CEO of Hunan TV, Eoyang Chang Lin, discovered the huge popularity of *Dae Jang Geum*, then shown on TV8 in Taiwan, that he immediately made the offer to buy the drama's broadcasting rights from Taiwan.

29. *Xin Min Wan Bao,* 30 Jul 2005.

30. *Nan Fang Dou Shi Bao,* 8 Nov 2005.

31. *Sun Daily,* 2 Oct 2005.

32. *Nan Fang Dou Shi Bao* 〈南方都市报〉, 8 Nov 2005.

33. The discussion generated both on newspaper commentaries and online discussion websites are tremendous. Over 3000 websites can be found on one single search engine that discusses the drama.

34. Programmes such as 〈水着大长今〉 talks about the period of Korean history featured in *Dae Jang Geum*.

35. 〈职场〉 discusses office politics, 〈小宫女〉 analyses the hierarchies involved in the Korean palace, 〈播客秀〉 uses animated characters to explain about the drama. These dramas are shown before the viewing of Daejanggeum.

36. Please refer to the booklet 〈大长今〉 published by Hunan TV.

37. Keane, p. 83.

38. Ibid, p. 85.

39. A typical night's performance would include comedians telling jokes, magic, and performers singing old tunes as well as popular songs.

40. Extracted from interviews with Ms Xiao and Ms Liu of Hunan TV station.

41. *Yang Chung Evening News,* 29 Sep 2005.

42. It was reported that having lost the battle over *Dae Jang Geum*, CCTV quickly bought another blockbuster from Taiwan, *Mist in Imperial Capital* 〈京华烟云〉.

43. *Yang Cheng Evening,* 29 Sep 2005.

44. Interview with Ms Chan, Programme Director of the Shanghai TV Station, 18 Nov 2003.

45. *Nan Fang Dou Shi Bao,* 8 Nov 2005.
46. Leung, 2004, p. 65.
47. *Nan Fang Dou Shi Bao,* 8 Nov 2005.
48. Hong Kong Commercial News, 10 Jun 2005, C07.
49. There is a lot of discussion on seeking for information about Korean history around Chosun Dynasty, political structure around that period, Korean cuisines, and herbal medicine in Korea. See various websites.
50. *People's Daily,* 21 Oct 2005.
51. Zhang is producer of a few TV dramas that became household names: *My Life,* epic dramas such as *The Eloquent Ji Shao Lan* and *Kang Xi's Personal Tours.*
52. Sohu.com, 1 Oct 2005, 15:07.
53. Ibid.
54. Ibid, 1 Oct 2005, 21:02.
55. Ibid, 2 Oct 2005, 12:22.
56. *Yang Cheng Evening News,* 29 Sep 2005.
57. *Ming Pao,* 5 Oct 2005.
58. Coined in one response on Sohu.com, 1 Oct 2005.
59. CCTV International Website, 22 Nov 2005.
60. *Beijing Youth Post,* 16 Oct 2005.
61. *Qian Jiang Evening News,* 11 Oct 2005.
62. CCTV International Website, 22 Nov 2005.
63. *Da Di Bao,* 22 Nov 2005.
64. *Youth Post (Shanghai),* 16 Feb 2006.
65. *Financial Times,* 20 Feb 2006.

Chapter 4   Structure of Identification and Distancing in Watching East Asian Television Drama

1. The unevenness has become a source of complaint among media practitioners in the PRC who see the popularity of Korean pop culture as a 'cultural invasion' (*The Sunday Times* 16 October 2005).
2. For greater detail on the idea of 'dominant' meaning and the 'encoding-decoding' process, see Morley (2003).
3. For a survey of these canonical texts on reception in Europe and America, see Brooker and Jermyn (2002).
4. There are interesting politics of language in this multi-Chinese lingual community that have been discussed in terms of the general issue of Chinese identity (Chun 1996; Ang 2001).
5. Cross-national joint productions of films among the East Asian locations have been on the increase in the past decade. However, unlike television programmes, films tend not to be dubbed, thus increasingly their 'multi-

Asian-lingual' character, including multi-accented Mandarin(s) in Chinese language films.

6. TV programs, on the other hand, are often broadcast in 'dual sound', so that the audience can choose between dubbed local-language and the original language with local language subtitles.

7. Before dubbing can take place, a translation of the given script has to be undertaken; this is followed by the 'synchronization of the translated dialogue so that it matches the actors' mouth movements and the other images as closely as possible' (Martinez 2004: 4).

8. In addition to lip-synchrony, dubbing must also pay attention to 'kinetic synchrony' — synchrony with body movements on screen, and, 'isochrony', synchrony in timing of screen characters' utterances (Varela 2004: 41).

9. For its popularity in PRC, see Lisa Leung's chapter in this collection. In Singapore, the series was first screened on cable television. It was so popular that it was re-broadcast immediately after the series ended. It was subsequently screened a third time on a free-to-air channel.

10. Significantly, many in Singapore prefer the Cantonese to the Mandarin version because of 'greater authenticity' effect of colloquial expressions, rather than the relative 'stiffness' of the Mandarin version.

11. In recent years, Japanese TV stations have been broadcasting PRC produced *'wuxia' anime* series, dubbed in Japanese. These Japanese versions are then re-exported to Singapore, a component of Pop Culture China, rather than the original Mandarin version.

12. An interesting comparison is with the popularity of *Dae Jang Geum* among mainland Chinese audiences, which exceeds that of the locally produced large-scale period drama *Emperor of the Han Dynasty*; according to one commentator, the former series 'resonates with modern viewers' (*The Sunday Times* 16 October 2005), implying the latter does not because it is presumably too historical.

13. See the chapter by Yukie Hirata in this volume.

14. For a very quick summary of the different theories of audience reception, see Eldridge, Kitzinger and Williams (1997: 125–133).

15. For an excellent discussion of the complex history of modern Japan with the rest of Asia see Sun Ke (2000).

16. See Iwabuchi's chapter in this volume.

17. As Thomas observes, there are also Vietnamese who see consumerism driven capitalist modernization as 'cultural contamination' and destruction of wholesome local cultural practices. Ambivalence towards capitalist consumerism is pervasive in all developing societies, not limited to Vietnamese (Chua 2000: 12–16).

18. Ko's emphasis on youth audiences possibly arose from a generational gap in the reception of Japanese TV dramas in Taiwan. Older Taiwanese, particularly the intellectuals, harking back to the history of the Japanese colonization of Taiwan, are wary of yet another 'invasion' of Japanese imperialism.

19. The researcher adds her commentary which reinforces the sense of 'we are all human' (Leung 2004: 94–95).
20. On the idea of social repertoires, see Taylor (2004).
21. 'The version of R's Chinese subtitling of *Pride* was extremely popular in the Hong Kong newsgroup through its online circulation by means of BitTorrent. As I learned from R, the marketing of another version of *Pride* produced by a Taiwanese-based leading pirated-Japanese-VCD company seems to be threatened, because R's version has already been so widely circulated among Chinese fans through the Internet' (Hu 2003: 178).
22. Hu is quoting Streeter (2003: 649).
23. The ideas of the newspaper as 'imagined geography' and 'occasional community of consumers' are elaborated in another essay (Chua 2006).

Chapter 5   Re-Imagining a Cosmopolitan 'Asian Us'

1. This chapter is based on a research project funded by a Strategic Research Grant (2004–05) awarded to Angel Lin by the City University of Hong Kong. The authors are also indebted to Professor Chua Beng-huat for his many useful critical comments on an earlier version of this chapter.
2. Hong Kong Statistic Department, 2002.
3. Department of Statistics, Singapore, 2002.
4. Hong Kong Statistic Department, 2002.
5. Department of Statistics, Singapore, 2002.
6. Department of Statistics, Singapore, 2002.
7. Department of Statistics, Singapore, 2002.
8. Department of Statistics, Singapore, 2002.
9. Economics and Social Commission for Asia and the Pacific (1999) *Gender Dimensions of Population and Development in South-East Asia*. New York: United Nations.

Chapter 6   *Winter Sonata* and Cultural Practices of Active Fans in Japan

1. The essay is based on part of a Japanese publication of my own in the book: *Nisshiki Hanryu*, where nine scholars contributed essays on trans-Asian popular culture, in particular, the Korean wave. See Mori (ed.) (2004), *Nisshiki Hanryu:* Winter Sonata *and the current situation of popular culture in Japan and Korea* (Japanese-style Korean Wave), Tokyo: Serica Shobo. By the term *'nisshiki hanryu'*, I propose the existence of the process of hybridization between trans-Asian countries, by focusing on consumer activity.
2. *Zainichi* are those who have North and South Korean nationality and who

live in Japan. Most of them moved (or were forced to move) to Japan in the colonial period and stay after the war. The number of *Zainichi* was 2,100,000 at the end of the war and is now about 600,000 because some went back to Korea while others were naturalized in Japan.

3. For detailed discussions on the 2002 World Cup by Japanese and Korean cultural studies scholars, see the themed issue of *Inter-Asia Cultural Studies*, 'Beyond FIFA's World Cup: Shared event, different experiences', (2004)5(1).

4. The basic data comes from NHK's website, http://www.nhk.or.jp/.

5. *Yomiuri Shimbun*, 27 July 2004.

6. Here I would deliberately call even 70 year-old-women middle-aged, because they looked much younger than I had expected and I am hesitant to call them 'old ladies'.

7. *AERA*, 16 August, 2004.

8. For example, see Matt, H. (2002), *Fan Cultures*, London: Routledge; and Lews, L.A. (ed.) (1992), *Adoring Audience: Fan culture and popular media*, Routledge: London.

9. Otsuka, E. (1989), *Monogatari Shohiron* (The theory of consuming narratives), Tokyo: Shinyosha.

10. The 38th Parallel North is a national boundary through the middle of Demilitarized Zone between South and North Korea made in 1953. This is often seen as a symbol of national division in Korea.

Chapter 7   Touring 'Dramatic Korea'

1. This article is based on and revised by Yukie Hirata on her 2004 chapter, "Manazasu monotoshiteno Nihon Josei Kan(kou)kyaku-Fuyuno Sonata Rokechimeguri ni Miru Transunashonaru na Tekusuto Dokkai", in Yoshitaka Mouri (ed.), *Nissiki Hanryu-Fuyuno Sonata to Nikkan Taisyubunka no Genzai (Japanese style Korean Wave: Winter Sonata and the current situation of popular culture in Japan and Korea)*, Tokyo: Serica Syobo.

2. According to a research by NHK, above 90% of people who participated in the research knew the Korean drama, *Winter Sonata* by September 2004 (Mitsuya, 2004).

3. Thirty women participants of the *Winter Sonata* tour and women who planned to visit Korea were interviewed from May to August 2004. (The women were in their 20s to 70s.) And fieldwork that included participation in local tours and individual tours was conducted several times. In addition to that, I interviewed 15 women (including 5 women who were interviewed in 2004) in 2005.

4. *Kisaeng* originally means traditional female entertainer in Korea. But now, it means women who work as prostitutes.

5. It was also linked to the "critical gaze for modern Japan and subsequent efforts to change themselves", suggested by Iwabuchi (2001).
6. The Japan Institute for Labor Policy and Training, www.jil.go.jp/press/rodo_sha/030306.html/.
7. Lee, 2003.
8. There are many Korean dramas, such as *The Stairway to Heaven, The Beautiful Days*, that embed sub-themes of secrecy of parentage and family relationships, with love relationships as the main theme.
9. Ironically, the 'family-centered thinking' based on Confucian concepts of the Japanese women over 40 is a frequent target of Korean feminists.
10. *SAPIO*, 18 August 2004, Shogakukan.

Chapter 10 Rap(p)ing Korean Wave

1. This is the concert version, in the original lyrics, it is "F*** your mother's c***, f*** your mother's c***, F*** Clon, F*** H.O.T." Clon and H.O.T. are two popular Korean bands in Taiwan.
2. This term is used by Shan Li (1998). She characterized the contemporary music scene in Taiwan as "the dominance of individuality and the dwindling of pop music." The term "alternative mainstream" also echoes many music critics' sentiments on Taiwan's lack of authentic rock music or on Wu Bai's selling out of rock for commercial success. This view is expressed in Chang Chao-wei's "Rethinking Rock Music" published in Milan Kun E-paper, June, 2000.
3. Rather than specifically debating about scatology as the essence of Taiwanese culture, this Tai-ke debate takes this as its premise. This shared understanding can be partially traced to the previous public debate on the LP (testicle) event. Many critics see scatology, especially the use of male sexual organs in the public sphere, as an expression of grassroots/local culture — something that needs to be acknowledged and redeemed, not debased. See Wei (2004) and Yang and Fan (2004).
4. Here I offer an example of a female fan's confession of her encounter with Bae. "I am so lucky, really lucky! As a fan of Yong-yang [Bae's nickname], I have finally realized my dream to have close bodily contact with him, chat with him, and shake hands with him, and most significantly, exchange eye contact with him!!!!! … [The moment I see him], my heart pumps from *putung putung* to *bang bang bang* … even my brain tells me to calm down, but I can't control my feelings. My brain becomes completely blank … until I see his familiar warm smile on TV … . He smiles at me, just like Joon-sang in *Winter Sonata* …" ("Blog Guide for Yong-yang Guest Room").
5. Heidegger defines standing reserve as : "Everything is ordered to stand by, to be immediately at hand, indeed to stand there just so that it may be on call for a further ordering" (1997: 17).

6. This interview was conducted in the summer of 2004. It was part of the Inter-Asia research project on the consumption of Korean dramas in Taiwan sponsored by the Korean Women's Institute of Development.. This interviewee is a 35 year-old housewife whose main job is to take care of her mother-in-law and her children.

Chapter 11 Existing in the Age of Innocence

1. This research was made possible with a collaborative funding from NHK under the project title: "Publicness of TV Broadcasting in East Asia" from April 2005–March 2006. An earlier draft was presented at the workshop, "East Asian Pop Culture: Transnational Japanese and Korean TV Dramas," organized by Asia Research Institute, National University of Singapore, on December 8–9 2005. I would like to thank Rong-Yu (Alice) Chi, Kai-Lang (Philip) Roh, Jing-He (Michael) Chuang, and Jing-Hui Feng for their research assistance during different stages of the project. I thank the fans of Chang Hui-mei in China and in Taiwan for their hospitality and time for communication. I also thank the Taiwanese fans of Song Seung-heon for their sharing of experiences. A note about the title: Though the paper I delivered at the workshop in Singapore was meant to be "Exiting the Age of Innocence," a typo on my part resulted in an inadvertent title, "Existing [in] the Age of Innocence." The workshop participants brought to my attention that "existing" makes more sense than "exiting" particularly when the paper challenges the "innocence" of "popular culture" and the "offensiveness" of "national politics." I thank the workshop participants for this pivotal insight. Without the opportunity to attend the workshop and the intellectual stimulation from the participants, I simply could not carry out the inter-referential ambition in this chapter. For that I especially thank Chua Beng-huat, Kuan-hsing Chen, Iwabuchi Kōichi and Shin Hyun-joon. I am solely responsible for any argument flaws, inaccuracies, and other problems in this work.

2. This is a question of perspectives. It is unpopular for those who feel stars should be left alone by politicians. But even those who see this ideal division — like Chang's fans — expressed ambivalence. In reality, many entertainers have used political opportunities (e.g., election) to boost their careers or launch new political careers.

3. In 2002, she led a protest on behalf of the Tao residents on Lan Yu (Orchid Island), an island 49 miles off Taiwan's eastern shore that has become a permanent storage site of nuclear waste from the mainland (Taiwan). Interestingly, one of the first things she did when she became a legislator was to sing the ROC anthem in front of the Presidential Office Building on New Year's day. Later on, she became critical of the Taiwanese aborigines'

compulsion to sing the ROC anthem (Tong 2005; Wang 2002; Lu 2002). Another famous entertainer-turned-legislator is Ko Jun-hisung, a veteran actor well known for playing patriotic roles in films like *823 Battle* (1986).

4. See, for instance, Chen Tsung-yi's magazine story (2004a; 2004b) about the gutsy Western stars who stood up against the human rights problem in China. The story is followed by his reporting of Chang Hui-mei's inability to call herself a Taiwanese while being interviewed on PRC's CCTV interview. But even the few examples that get recalled converge with Taiwan's larger political, that is, anti-communist and pro-American stance. John Wayne's anti-Native American stance was never mentioned by the Taiwanese as a problem.

5. Rock 'n' roll, alternative, and hip-hop music all have been acknowledged for their potential to challenge the political status quo. In contrast, popular music frequently receives "sell-out" dirty looks from more politicized musical performances. Shortly after Chang's Beijing concert in 2004, Taiwanese music critic Ho Tung-hong (2005) praised in an editorial American singer Michelle Shocked for standing up against a big promotional budget and Bush's politics. In the same piece Ho pointed out that Chang has never intervened in public affairs of the aborigines. While I agree with his position that Chang's performance in China cannot escape a political connotation, the criticism displays an attitude that denounces popular music for not being political enough (or at all).

6. I believe this is more of a rhetorical than real expectation to begin with.

7. *Daren* could mean grown-ups or adults. But it also refers to public officials or people holding important government positions in ancient China, including making a plea.

8. Drawing on Japanese historian Mizoguchi Yuzo's proposition of "China as a method," Chen suggests that Asia as method is a contemporary response to the inadequacy of nation-states. This "inter-Asia" project is linked up via heterogeneous movements and does not aim to prove Asia as different or unique from the West. It problematizes the northeast domination on the discourse of Asia and encourages diverse historical interpretations of the different linkages toward the making of new subjectivity (Chen 2005a, pp. 200–201).

9. See, for instance, Iwabuchi (2003; 2004), Chua (2004), and Erni and Chua (2005).

10. An example I have in mind is the distance between Japanophiles in Taiwan and the critical dialogues between Taiwan and Japan's leftist critics.

11. Even after she retired from public performances, she would still entertain the troops.

12. "Loving Taiwan" was originally invented as an election language aimed to mobilize the pan-green constituencies in Taiwan. The charge against Chang also needs to be situated in the so-called Hsu Wen-Long effect. Hsu, a rich

industrialist known for his outward support of Taiwanese independence, released an open letter in March 2004 in which he renounced the pro-Taiwan independence position as well as issued approval of China's Anti-Secession Law. The change of position of this long-time DPP benefactor (even a character in Kobayashi Yoshinori's political manga, *Taiwan Ron*) shocked the pan-green leadership and revealed the political predicaments of *taishang* [Taiwanese business professionals] in China. An editorial in *Business Weekly* linked Chang to Hsu with the headline: "Don't Worry A-mei, but please take care, Hsu Wen-Long" (Ho 2004, p. 18).

13. For example, even though Mizoguchi Yuzo, a Japanese historian of Chinese intellectual history, would like to respond to the question of Japanese wartime responsibility to the Chinese, it was simply impossible because there has been no discussion on historical memory in China "at any level" (Chen 2002b, p. 242).

14. In fact, she felt it strange that I would be so cautious about getting political opinions from the fans. She asked "why sensitive? I don't care about that. We've got the freedom of speech. I am not afraid of being taken away, by the police."

15. I speak as a woman whose high school experience in the US in the early 1990s acquainted me with many male parachute kids who left Taiwan before they turned 16. For some of them, avoiding military was at least part of the deal — if not the goal — for studying abroad. Also as a re-patriated Taiwanese in the early 2000s, I find it difficult to overlook the de-militarizing tendency in military service and the re-militarizing desire in the national defense budget. Currently the length of military service for Taiwanese men is one year and four months. I thank Shin Hyun-joon and Jungbong Choi for sharing experiences and views on Korean military and masculinity.

16. His part was eventually replaced by Yeon Jung Hoon.

17. Other implicated celebrities included actor Jang Hyuk, Han Jae-sok, and more than fifty former and acting baseball players (*The Korea Times* 5 Sep 2004; 6 Sep 2004).

18. The Military Manpower Administration (MMA) of South Korea does seem to have more work to do to maintain the hegemony of militarized masculinity. Since March 2005, it updated its communication platform and started to facilitate online applications for conscripts abroad (Jung 2005). It has also been answering questions in English from abroad concerning qualifications, rights, and procedures through its user-friendly English website since 2004. Still, the patriotic bond in conscription can be fragile. Before the revised dual citizenship law went into effect on 1 June 2005, immigration offices were swarmed by applications renouncing their Korean nationality (Kim 2005; Seo 2005).

19. To protect the identities of the fans, the name and URL of the fan website which I drew from substantially for researching this chapter will not be

used. I collected postings of discussions during the critical two-month period from 16 September to 16 October 2004.

20. From A2's posting on 21 Sep 2004.

21. There was evidence that Song's Korean fans were in close contact with fans in Taiwan, Hong Kong, and Japan. They called for help to vote on internet polls, encouraged them to write to Song's management company GM Entertainment, broadcasting station MBC, and MMA. Messages expressing gratitude in Korean were also translated into Chinese.

22. In addition to observing a Taiwanese fan site (see note 19), I also collected past postings from a large Chinese fan site. The quote was posted on 23 September 2004 by fan X14 as part of a letter addressed to the Korean authorities. Accessed on 28 Oct 2005.

23. From the Taiwanese fan forum under the posting: "Goodbye and Take Care, Seung-heon ... The Seeing-Off Day (16th) 16," posted on Nov 2004. Accessed 5 Sep 2005.

24. The event was staged in the sense that not only were reporters informed and played a part in this sentimental media event, some audience members from Japan were also invited by a television station to observe the send-off. Interestingly, there did not seem to be a fan group in the send-off troupe representing PRC fans, which likely indicated the presence of certain economic or other cultural barriers.

25. A1 did find it to be a success, for the publicity went beyond the circle of the fans.

26. Peters writes: "Too often, 'communication' misleads us from the task of building worlds together. It invites us into a world of unions without politics, understandings without language, and souls without bodies, only to make politics, language, and bodies reappear as obstacles rather than blessings" (1999, pp. 30–31).

27. Available on www.chosun.com (22 Sep 2004). I thank Kai-Lang Roh for assistance on the Korean-Chinese translation.

28. Of the 54 postings, 30 were addressed by different individuals to the Korean government authorities stated in the solicitation. The rest were supplementary comments, reactions to the call, and encouragement.

29. Right from the start, a fan with a science background called for help from the more literary-inclined "sisters." Some of the high-flying language by the fan included describing *Autumn Fairytale*'s effect on the Chinese cultural market as an "atomic bomb" (X20).

30. A fan quickly remarked in between letters that "To fight for all possibility, I have done all I could to praise the Koreans. Sigh ... I don't know what else to say ... Bless you!" (X18).

31. *Shiri,* South Korea's blockbuster film in 1999, refers to a species of fish that lives in the waters between North and South Korea.

Chapter 12 When the Korean Wave Meets Resident Koreans in Japan

1. For a detailed analysis of the Hong Kong boom in Japan in the 1990s, please see chapter 5 of Iwabuchi (2002).
2. See for the details, Sonia Ryang (2000) and Tai (2004).
3. The uniforms are modeled after the traditional Korean costumes and the female students' Korean origins are easily recognizable by the uniform.
4. http://www.myprofile.ne.jp/blog/archive/acquire-mind/25/.
5. http://wwwc.fujitv.co.jp/wankei/index2.html/.
6. http://www.innolife.net/bbs2/list.php?bbs=bbs1&pg=25/.

References

Introduction   East Asian TV Dramas

Allen, Robert C. (ed., 1995), *to be continued ... Soap operas around the world.* London: Routledge.

Chua Beng Huat (2004), 'Conceptualizing an East Asian popular culture', *Inter-Asia Cultural Studies* 5: 200–221.

Iwabuchi, Koichi (2004), *Feeling Asian Modernities: Transnational consumption of Japanese TV dramas.* Hong Kong: Hong Kong University Press.

Kim, Hyun-mee (2002), 'The inflow of Japanese culture and the historical construction of "fandom" in South Korea'. Paper presented at the International Conference in the Age of Informatization: East Asia into the 21st century. Institute of East and West Studies, Yonsei University, Seoul, Korea, 16 November.

Lee, Ming-tsung (2004), 'Travelling with Japanese TV drama: Cross-cultural orientation and flowing identification of contemporary Taiwanese youth', in K. Iwabuchi (ed.), *Feeling Asian Modernities.* Hong Kong: Hong Kong University Press, pp. 129–154.

Lu, Sheldon (2001), 'Soap opera: The transnational politics of visuality, sexuality and masculinity', in *China, Transnational Visuality, Global Postmodernism.* Stanford: Stanford University Press, pp. 213–238.

Rofel, Lisa (1995) 'The melodrama of national identity in post-Tiananmen China', in Allen (ed.), *to be continued ... Soap operas around the world.* London: Routledge, pp. 301–320.

Sun, Wanning (2002), 'Arriving at the global city: Television dramas and spatial imagination', in *Leaving China: Media, migration and transnational imagination.* Lanham, MD, US: Rowan and Littlefield Publishers, pp. 67–90.

Chapter 1 The Growth of Korean Cultural Industries and the Korean Wave

Broadcast Worldwide. 2005. http://2005.bcww.net/about2005_w.asp (accessed 26 November 2005).

Choe, Hun. 2005. Mexico is a bridgehead of Central and South American markets (Mexico-neun Jungnammi sijang gyodubo). *Joong-Ang Ilbo,* 12 September, p. 6.

Choe, Yong-shik. 2001. Asia dreaming of Korea's pop singers and actors. *Korea Herald,* 31 August.

Chon, Gina. 2001. Golden Summer. *Asiaweek,* 26 October, 46–49.

Cinema Service. 2006. http://www.cinemaservice.com/ (accessed 23 February 2006).

CJ Entertainment. 2006. http://www.cjent.co.kr/ (accessed 23 February 2006).

Gu, Hiryeong. 2004. Drama bodyguards: Change the lead role's fate (Deurama chinwidae juingong unmyeong-do bakkwo). *Joong-Ang Ilbo,* 16 July, p. 22.

Heo, Jin. 2002. The "Hanryu" phenomenon and the acceptability of Korean TV dramas in China. *Korean Journal of Broadcasting 16*(1): 496–529 (in Korean).

Hong, Junhao. 1998. *The Internationalization of Television in China.* Westport, US: Praeger.

Hwang, Sang Cheol. 2001. Venture capital, brisk film investment (Bencheo jabon, younghwa tuja hwalgi). *Hankyoreh,* 3 January, p. 24.

Im, Beom. 2000. Lee Gangbok, CEO of CJ Entertainment. *Hankyoreh,* 8 December, p. 33.

Joong-Ang Ilbo. 2005. Soft power soft Korea 4. 6 January, p. 5 (in Korean).

Kang, Woo-suk. 2002. Looking back on the Korean cinema in 2002 (Dorabon 2002nyeon hanguk younghwa-gye). *Chosun Ilbo,* 23 December, p. 63.

Kim, Dong Ho. 2005. *A History of Korean Film Policy.* Seoul: Nanam.

Kim, Haksu. 2003. *Pioneers of the Korean cinema industry.* Seoul: Inmul-gwa Sasang-sa.

Kim, Hyeon Gi. 2004. The fever of *Winter Sonata* not cooling down (Sikji anneun Gyeo-ul Yeonga yeolgi nollawoyo). *Joong-Ang Ilbo,* 28 July, p. 24.

Kim, Mi-hui. 2000. A year of money and accolades for Korean films. *Korea Herald,* 30 December.

Kim, Mi-hui. 2002. Korean netizens invest in local pix. *Variety,* 1 January, p. 35.

Kim, Mee-hyun. 2005. Analysis of the Present State of Korean Film Exports and Related Trends. Paper presented at the 3rd USSH-KAREC International Symposium, Ho Chi Minh City, Vietnam, 26–27 September.

Kim, Min Gyeong. 2004. Korean cinema in full bloom after Samsung Entertainment Group's death (Samsung Sa-eopdan Jugeo Hanguk younghwa kkot piwotne). *Weekly Dong-A,* 6 May, pp. 72–74.

Kim, Seunghyeon and Jinman Han. 2001. *Korean Society and Television Drama.* Seoul: Hanul (in Korean).

Kim, Tae-jong. 2006. Aside from film quota cut, industry faces challenges. *Korea Times,* http://times.hankooki.com/ (accessed 8 February 2006).

Kim, Young-han. 2001. The broadcasting audience movement in Korea. *Media Culture and Society 23*(1): 91–107.

Ko, Jae Yeol. 2004. The recent performance code is "luxury" (Yojeum heunghaeng kodeu-neun "leoksyeori"). *The Sisa Press,* 30 September, pp. 112–113.

Ko, Jae Yeol. 2005a. The future of Korean Wave: We want to know it (Hallyu-eui mirae Guegeot-i algo sipda). *The Sisa Press,* 6 January, pp. 72–76.

Ko, Jae Yeol. 2005b. Those who were deserted make splendid resurrection (Beorim badeun geudeul hwaryeohan buhwal). *The Sisa Press,* 20 September, pp. 92–94.

Ko, Jae Yeol. 2005c. The enemy inside is more problematic than the 'Anti-Korean Wave' (Naebu-eui jeog-i hyeom-hallyu-boda deo museopda). *The Sisa Press,* 8 November, pp. 88–91.

Kookmin Ilbo. 1994. Youngsang soft san-eop-eul jabara (Seize the media content industry). 12 December, p. 9.

Korea Culture and Tourism Policy Institute. 2005. Thinking of the Korean Wave (Hallyu-reul saenggak-handa). *Culture/Gaze 1*(1): 29–56.

Korea Times. 2004. 'Winter Sonata' actor gets warm welcome in Japan. 5 Apr. http://times.hankooki.com/ (accessed 8 April 2004).

Korean Broadcasting Commission. 2006. http://www.kbc.go.kr/ (accessed 22 February 2006).

Korean Film Council. 2006. http://www.kofic.or.kr/ (accessed 22 February 2006).

Korean Overseas Information Service. 2004. Korea Wave crashes on Asian shores. http://www.korea.net (accessed 26 August 2004).

Lee, Myung-ho. 2004. Yon-sama syndrome and the power of housewives (Yonsama sindeurom-gwa ajumma-eui him). *The Sisa Press,* 23 December, p. 97.

Lee, Samuel. 2003. Seoul Survivor. *Straits Times,* 8 April.

Lee, Sangbok. 2005. Television drama still going strong, although ratings ↓ ("Deurama gangse yeojeon, sicheongryul-eun ↓"). *Joong-Ang Ilbo,* 5 October, p. E15.

Li, Xueying. 2005. S. Korea rides high on soft power. *The Straits Times,* 30 November, pp. 1–2.

Lotte Cinema. 2006. http://www.lottecinema.co.kr/ (accessed 23 February 2006).

Ministry of Culture and Tourism. 2001. *Culture Content: The Next-Generation Growth Industry.* Press release, August 16 and August 24.

Ministry of Culture and Tourism. 2005. http://www.mct.go.kr/ (accessed 27 November 2005).

Park, Chung-a. 2005. The power of Korean dramas. *The Korea Times.* 27 October, http://times.hankooki.com/ (accessed 28 October 2005).

Shim, Doobo. 2002. South Korean Media Industry in the 1990s and the Economic Crisis, *Prometheus 20*(4): 337–350.

Shim, Doobo. 2006. Hybridity and the rise of Korean popular culture in Asia. *Media, Culture and Society* 28(1): 25–44. http://dx.doi.org/10.1177/0163443706059278/.

Showbox. 2006. http://www.showbox.co.kr/showbox/history.asp/ (accessed 23 February 2006).

Sisa Press. 2005. Actress Yang Mi-kyoung is a civilian diplomat (Yang Mi-kyoung ssi-neun mingan oegyogwan). *The Sisa Press*, 8 November, p. 91.

Waterman, David and Everett Rogers. 1994. The economics of television program production and trade in Far East Asia. *Journal of Communication* 44(3): 89–111.

Weekly Chosun. 1995. Chaebol and media business. 19 January, p. 76 (in Korean).

Won, Yong-jin. 1998. *Diagnosis of Korean Press Democratization*. Seoul: Communication Books (in Korean).

Yi, Jiyoung. 2004. Conventional materials are made into social issues sophisticatedly (Tongsok-jeok sojae-reul seryeon-doege sahoe isyuhwa). *Joong-Ang Ilbo*. 15 October, p. 23.

Yi, Man-je. 2004. Television networks richer, independent productions poorer. *Kookmin Ilbo*. 2 November.

Yoon, Tae-jin. 2005. Production structure of the popular culture. *Studies of Broadcasting Culture 17*(2) (in Korean).

Yun Seok-jin. 2004. Cry and laugh following "Candyrella" ("Kaendirella" ttara ulgo utneunda). *The Sisa Press*. 30 September, p. 114.

Chapter 2   Renting East Asian Popular Culture for Local Television

Agarwal, S. (2006) 'Lure of mobile TV', editorial, in *Television Asia* [online]. Available: http://www.tvasia.com.sg/home?wid=150&func=view Submission&sid=417/ [accessed 28 Apr 2006].

Asianfanatics Forum (2005) '*War and Beauty* vs *Jewel in Palace* aka *Da Jeung Gum*', Available: http://asianfanatics.net/forum/lofiversion/index.php/t106038.html/ [accessed 17 Nov 2005].

Bachtiar, A. (2002) 'Indonesia tolerance for ethnic Chinese soars', *The Asahi Shimbun Asia Network* [online]. 1 November. Available: http://www.asahi.com/english/ asianet/column/eng_021101.html/ [accessed 12 Apr 2005].

Bourdieu, P. (1984/1979) *Distinction*. Cambridge, MA: Harvard University Press.

Chadha, K. and Kavoori, A. (2000) 'Media imperialism revisited: Some findings from the Asian case', *Media, Culture & Society*, vol.22, pp. 415–432.

Channel NewsAsia.com (2005) 'MediaCorp Studios licenses "Project Superstar" to Malaysia's 8TV', by Johnson Choo. 14 November. Available: http://www.channelnewsasia.com/stories/singaporelocalnews/view/178558/1/.html/ [accessed 2 Dec 2005].

Chua, Beng Huat. (1998) 'World cities: Globalisation and the spread of consumerism: a view from Singapore', *Urban Studies*, no.35, pp. 981–1000.

Chua Beng Huat (2000) 'Consuming Asians: Ideas and issues', in Chua, B.-H. (ed.), *Consumption in Asia: Lifestyles and identities*, Routledge: London, pp. 1–34.

Chua Beng Huat (2004) 'Conceptualizing an East Asian popular culture', *Inter-Asia Cultural Studies* [online], vol.5, no.2, pp. 200–221. Available: SwetsWise Journals database [accessed 20 Jan 2005].

Electronic Engineering Times (2005) [online] 'Mobile entertainment industry to drive wireless data usage in Asia', 25 October. Available: http://www.eetasia.com/ART_ 8800379931_499488_b654ec99_no.HTM/ [accessed 25 Apr 2006].

Flew, Terry (2002a) 'Creative industries', in *New Media: An introduction*, Melbourne, Australia: Oxford University Press, pp. 114–138.

——— (2002b) 'E-education and cyber-learning', in *New Media: An introduction*, Melbourne, Australia: Oxford University Press, pp. 162–182.

Fung, A. (2004) 'Copying, cloning and copying: Hong Kong in the global television format business', in Moran, A. and Keane, M. (eds.), *Television across Asia: Television industries, programme formats and globalization*, London: RoutledgeCurzon, pp. 74–87.

Giammarco, T. and Paquet, D. (2006) 'Upcoming films', Koreanfilm.Org. Available: http://www.koreanfilm.org/new.html/ [accessed 28 Jan 2006].

Groves, D. and Rothrock, V. (2005) *Variety.com* [online], available: http://www.variety.com/index.asp?layout=miptv2005&content= jump&jump= features&articleID=VR1117920479/ [accessed 22 October 2005].

Hara, Y. (2004) 'Import and export of Japanese television programs', *JAMCO International Symposium* [online], Feburary–March. Available: http://www.jamco.or.jp/english/index.html/ [accessed 20 May 2005].

Harvey, D. (1990) *The Condition of Postmodernity: An enquiry into the origins of cultural change*, Cambridge, MA: Blackwell.

Herskovitz, J. (2000) 'Some of the best-known TV formats are from Japan.' *Variety* [online]. 12 August. Available: http://www.findarticles.com/cf_vrty/ m1312/4_ 379/62981188.html/ [accessed 22 Jan 2002].

Hesmondhalgh, D. (2002) *The Cultural Industries*, London: Sage.

Hong Kong Film Archive (2006) 'Another Night in Hong Kong: Hong Kong–Japan Film Exchange in the 1950s and 1960s'. Seminar newsletter. Available: http://www.lcsd.gov.hk/CE/CulturalService/HKFA/english/newsletter02/ e-34-more-happenings.pdf/ [accessed 22 Jan 2006].

Iwabuchi, K. (2001) 'Becoming "culturally proximate": The a/scent of Japanese idol dramas in Taiwan', in Moeran, B. (ed.) *Asian Media Productions*, Surrey: Curzon Press.

Kitley, P. (2004) 'Closing the creativity gap — Renting intellectual capital in the name of local content: Indonesia in the global television format business', in Moran, A. and Keane, M. (eds.) (2004) *Television across Asia: Television industries, programme formats and globalization*, London: RoutledgeCurzon, pp. 138–156.

Langdale, J. V. (1997) 'East Asian broadcasting industries: Global, regional, and national perspectives', *Economic Geography* [online], July, vol.73 no.3, pp. 305–321. Available: ABI/Inform Global online search [accessed 21 May 2005].

Lee, D-H. (2004) 'Cultural strategies of remakes: The case of *Yojolady*', paper presented at the '13th JAMCO Online International Symposium', February–March. Available: http://www.jamco.or.jp/2004_symposium/en/lee/index.html/ [accessed 12 July 2005].

Lee, D-H. (2005) 'Transnational imagination: Co-produced dramas and national identity', unpublished manuscript.

Liu, Y-L. and Chen, Y-H. (2004) 'Cloning, adaptation, import and originality: Taiwan in the global television format business', in Moran, A. and Keane, M. (eds.) *Television across Asia: Television industries, programme formats and globalization*, London: RoutledgeCurzon.

Ma, E. K-W. (1999) *Culture, Politics, and Television in Hong Kong*, London and New York: Routledge.

MDA News Releases (2004) 'Rouge — Asia's first regional TV drama series for youth premieres on MTV in nine countries'. 6 October. Available: http://www.mda.gov.sg/wms.www/thenewsdesk.aspx?sid=581/ [accessed 23 Oct 2005].

Moran, A. (1998) *Copycat Television: Globalisation, program formats and cultural identity*, Luton, UK: University of Luton Press.

——— (2004) 'New television, new formats', in Adair, D. and Moran, A. (eds.) *At the TV Format Coalface: Mark Overett and David Franken in Conversation*, No.2, Working Papers in Communications, Griffith University, Brisbane, pp. 1–17.

Moran, A. and Keane, M. (eds.) (2004) *Television across Asia: Television industries, programme formats and globalization*, London: RoutledgeCurzon.

Ng, W-M. (2002) 'The impact of Japanese comics and animation in Asia', *Journal of Japanese Trade & Industry* (JJTI)/*Financial Times Global News Wire* [online], 1 July. Available: LexisNexis.com news search [accessed 2 July 2002].

Osaki, T. (2002) 'Mad about Manga', *Asia Image — Animation Special: Country Focus*, November, Issue No. 102, pp. 14–16.

Russell, M. (2005) 'Sector report: Korea', published in Hollywood Reporter.com. 24 May. Available: http://www.hollywoodreporter.com/thr/international/feature_display.jsp?vnu_ content_id=1000930566/ [accessed 22 January 2006].

Sinclair, J. (1998) 'Culture as a "market force": Corporate strategies in Asian skies', in Srinivas R. M., Shields, P., Agrawal, B.C. (eds.), *International Satellite Broadcasting in South Asia: Political, Economic and Cultural Implications*, Lanham, MD: University Press of America, pp. 207–225.

Sony Pictures (2005) [online] 'The Amazing Race format makes a pit stop in Asia Pacific — BVITV-AP announces "The Amazing Race" format deal with AXN Asia, set to wow over 76 million households', press releases. Available: http://www.sonypictures.com/corp/press_releases/2005/10_05/101405_amazingrace.html/ [Accessed 14 Nov 2005].

Tanner, J. C. (2004) 'Pay-TV pirates of the Asia Pacific', *Television Asia* [online]. December. Available: http://www.telecomasia.net/telecomasia/article/articleDetailjsp?id=136907/ [accessed 18 May 2005].

The Manila Times (2005) 'GMA 7 premieres Korea's record-breaking soap', 3 November. Available: http://news.yehey.com/news3.asp%3Fc%3D5%26i%3D132934/ [accessed 14 November 2005].

The Star Online (2006) 'A shining star', by Li Ee Kee. 17 February. Available: http://star-ecentral.com/news/story.asp?file=/2006/2/17/music/13366529&sec=music/ [accessed 20 Feb 2006].

TheUrbanWire.com (2005) [online] 'The 16th Edition', by Jingson Xu. 11 August. Available: http://www.theurbanwire.com/stories/index.php?option=content&task=view&id=383/ [accessed 15 November 2005].

TV Asia (2005) Available: http://www.tvasia.com.sg/home?wid=150&func=viewSubmission&sid=388/ [accessed 12 Nov 2005].

TVB Annual Report (2004) [online] 'Management Discussion and Analysis'. Available: http://www.tvb.com/affairs/faq/anreport/2004/eng/F106.pdf/ [accessed 10 November 2005]

Wang, G. (1993) 'Satellite television and the future of broadcast television in the Asia Pacific', *Media Asia*, vol.20, no.3, pp. 140–148.

Wang, G., Servaes, J. and Goonasekera, A. (eds.) (2000) *The New Communications Landscape Demystifying Media Globalization,* Routledge: London and New York.

YesAsia.com (2005) Available: http://global.yesasia.com/en/Search/SearchResult.aspx/ [accessed 12 Nov 2005].

Chapter 3   Mediating Nationalism and Modernity

Appadurai, Arjun (1996), *Modernity at Large: Cultural Dimensions of Globalization,* Minneapolis: University of Minnesota Press.

Chan Joseph Man (2002), 'Administrative boundaries and media marketization: A comparative analysis of the newspaper, TV, and Internet markets in China,' in Chin Chuan Lee (ed.), *Chinese Media, Global Contexts,* London: RoutledgeCurzon Press, pp. 159–176.

Clausen, Lisbeth (2003), *Global News Production,* Copenhagen: Copenhagen Business School.

Fung, Anthony and Eric Ma (2002), '"Satellite Modernity": Four modes of televisual imagination in the disjunctive socio-mediascape of Guangzhou,' in Stephanie Hemelryk Donald, Michael Keane and Yin Hong (eds.), *Media in China: Consumption, Content and Crisis,* London: Routledge. **PAGE NO.??**

Harrison, Mark (2002), 'Satellite and cable platforms: Development and content,' in Hemelryk Donald, Keane and Hong (eds.), *Media in China: Consumption, Content and Crisis,* London: Routledge, pp. 167–178.

Hemelryk Donald, Stephanie and Michael Keane (2002), 'Media in China: New convergences, new approaches,' in Hemelryk Donald, Keane and Hong (eds.), *Media in China: Consumption, Content and Crisis,* London: Routledge, pp. 3–18.

Hesmondhalgh, David (2004), *The Cultural Industries,* London: MacMillan.

Keane, Michael (2002), 'Send in the clones: Television formats and content creation in the People's Republic of China', in Hemelryk Donald, Keane and Hong (eds.), *Media in China: Consumption, Content and Crisis,* London: Routledge, pp. 80–91.

Lee Chin Chuan (2003), 'The global and the national of the Chinese media: discourses, market, technology and ideology', in *Chinese Media, Global Contexts,* London: Routledge, pp. 1–31.

Leung Yuk Ming Lisa (2004), '"Ganbaru" and its transcultural audience: Imaginary and reality in Japanese TV doramas,' in Koichi Iwabuchi (ed.), *Feeling Asian Modernities: Transnational Consumption of Japanese TV dramas.* Hong Kong: Hong Kong University Press. pp. 89–106.

Zhao Yue Zhi (2003), 'State and ownership in Chinese media,' in Pradip N. Thomas and Zaharom Nain (eds.), *Who Owns the Media? Global Trends and Local Resistances,* New York : Zed Books, pp. 196–210.

Various newspapers

Mainland China
Xin Min Wan Bao
People's Daily
Yang Cheng Evening News
Beijing Youth Post
Qian Jiang Evening News
CCTV International Website
Da Di Bao
Da He Bao
Nan Fang Dou Shi Bao
Youth Post (Shanghai)

Hong Kong
Ming Pao
Sun Daily
Hong Kong Commercial News

Overseas

Financial Times

Chapter 4   Structure of Identification and Distancing in Watching
East Asian Television Drama

Agost, Rosa (2004). 'Translation in bilingual contexts: Different norms in dubbing translation', in Pilar Orero (ed.), *Topics in Audiovisual Translation*. Amsterdam/ Philadelphia: John Benjamin Publishing Company, pp. 63–83.

Ang, Ien (2001). *On Not Speaking Chinese*. London: Routledge.

Brooker, Will and Deborah Jermyn (eds.) (2002). *The Audience Studies Reader*. London: Routledge.

Chua Beng Huat (2000). 'Pop Culture China', *Singapore Journal of Tropical Geography* 22(2): 113–121.

Chua Beng Huat (2000). *Consumption in Asia: Lifestyles and Identities*. London/ New York: Routledge.

Chua Beng Huat (2006). 'Gossips about stars: Newspapers and Pop Culture China', in Wanning Sun (ed.), *Media and the Chinese Diaspora: Community, Communication and Commerce*. London: RoutledgeCurzon, pp. 75–90.

Chun, Allen (1996). 'Fuck Chineseness: On the ambiguity of ethnicity as culture and identity', *Boundary 2*, 23: 111–138.

Eldridge, John, Jenny Kitzinger and Kevin Williams (1997). *The Mass Media and Power in Britain*. New York: Oxford University Press.

Hartley, John (1996). *Popular Reality: Journalism, Modernity and Popular Culture*. London and Sydney: Arnold.

Hu, Kelly (2003). 'The power of circulation: Digital technologies and the online Chinese fans of Japanese TV drama', *Inter-Asia Cultural Studies* 6: 171–186.

Ko, Yufen (2004). 'The desired form: Japanese idol dramas in Taiwan', in Koichi Iwabuchi (ed.), *Feeling Asian Modernities: Transnational Consumption of Japanese TV Dramas*. Hong Kong: Hong Kong University Press, pp. 107–128.

Leung, Lisa Yuk-ming (2004). '*Ganbaru* and is transcultural audience: Imaginary and reality of Japanese TV dramas in Hong Kong', in Iwabuchi (ed.), *Feeling Asian Modernities*. Hong Kong: Hong Kong University Press, pp. 89–106.

MacLachlan, Elizabeth and Geok-lian Chua (2004). 'Defining Asian femininity: Chinese viewers of Japanese TV dramas in Singapore', in Iwabuchi (ed.), *Feeling Asian Modernities*. Hong Kong: Hong Kong University Press, pp. 155–176.

Martinez, Xénia (2004). 'Film dubbing, its process and translation', in Pilar Orero (ed.), *Topics in Audiovisual Translation*. Amsterdam/Philadelphia: John Benjamins Publishing Company, pp. 3–8.

Morley, David (2003). 'The nationwide audience', in Brooker and Jermyn (eds.) *The Audience Studies Reader*. London: Routledge, pp. 95–104.

Shim Doboo (2002). 'South Korean media industry in the 1990s and the economic crisis' *Prometheus* 20: 337–350.

Sun Ke (2000). 'How does Asia Mean?' *Inter-Asia Cultural Studies* 1: 13–48 and 331–341.

Taylor, Charles (2004). *Modern Social Imaginaries*. Durham, NC: Duke University Press.

Thomas, Mandy (2004). 'East Asian cultural traces in post-socialist Vietnam', in Koichi Iwabuchi, Stephen Muecke and Mandy Thomas (eds.), *Rogue Flows: Trans-Asian Cultural Traffic*. Hong Kong: Hong Kong University Press, pp. 177–196.

Tsai, Eva (2005). 'Kaneshiro Takeshi: Transnational stardom and the media and culture industries in Asia's global postcolonial age', *Modern Chinese Literature and Culture* 17: 100–132.

Varela, Frederic Chaume (2004). 'Synchronization in dubbing', in Pilar Orero (ed.), *Topics in Audiovisual Translation*. Amsterdam/Philadelphia: The John Benjamins Publishing Company, pp. 35–52.

Chapter 5   Re-Imagining a Cosmopolitan 'Asian Us'

Ahearn, L. M. (2001) Language and Agency. *Annual Review of Anthropology*, 30: 109–137.

Aksoy, A. and Robins, K. (1992) 'Hollywood for the 21st Century: Global Competition for Critical Mass in Image Markets'. *Cambridge Journal of Economics*, 16.

Ang, I. (1985) *Watching Dallas: Soap Opera and the Melodrama Imagination*. London and New York: Methuen.

Ang, I. (2004) The Cultural Intimacy of TV Drama, in K. Iwabuchi (ed.), *Feeling Asian Modernities: Transnational Consumption of Japanese TV Dramas*. Hong Kong: Hong Kong University Press.

Baym, N. K. (2000) *Tune in, Log on: Soaps, Fandom, and On-line Community*. Thousand Oaks, London and New Delhi: Sage Publications.

Besley, C. (1994) *Desire: Love Stories in Western Culture*. Oxford and Cambridge: Blackwell Publishers.

Brown, M. E. (1994). *Soap Opera and Women's Talk: The Pleasure of Resistance*. London: Sage.

Bourdieu, P. (2001/1998) *Masculine Domination*. Stanford: Stanford University Press.

Chua, B. H. (2004). 'Conceptualizing an East Asian popular culture'. *Inter-Asia Culture Studies*, 5(2): 200–221.

Dyer, R. (1986) *Heavenly Bodies: Film Star and Society*. London: Macmillan.

Felski, R. (1995) *The Gender of Modernity*. Cambridge: Harvard University Press.

Felski, R. (2000) *Doing Time: Feminist Theory and Postmodern Culture*. New York and London: New York University Press.

Fiske, J. (1989) *Understanding Popular Culture*. Boston: Unwin Hyman.

Guat, T. L. (1996) 'Singapore', in G. C. L. Mak (ed.), *Women, Education and Development in Asia*. New York and London: Garland Publishing.

Harvey, D. (1990) *The Condition of Postmodernity*. London: Blackwell.

Hayashi, K. (2005) 'Assessing the Popularity of "Winter Sonata": How do Women's Emotions Affect the Public Sphere in Japan?' Paper presented at the International Conference on Culture Industry and Cultural Capital, Hallym University, South Korea, 28 February 2005, Korea.

Hinderman, S. (1992) 'I'll Be Here With You: Fans, Fantasy and the Figure of Elvis', in L. Lewis (ed.), *The Adoring Audience: Fan Culture and Popular Media*. London: Routledge.

Iwabuchi, K. (ed.) (2004) *Feeling Asian Modernities: Transnational Consumption of Japanese TV Dramas*. Hong Kong: Hong Kong University Press.

Iwabuchi, K. (2004) Introduction: Cultural Globalization and Asian Media Connections, in K. Iwabuchi (ed.), *Feeling Asian Modernities: Transnational Consumption of Japanese TV Dramas*. Hong Kong: Hong Kong University Press.

Ko, Y. F. (2004) 'The Desired Form: Japanese Idol Dramas in Taiwan', in K. Iwabuchi (ed.), *Feeling Asian Modernities: Transnational Consumption of Japanese TV Dramas*. Hong Kong: Hong Kong University Press.

Langlois, A. J. (2001) *The Politics of Justice and Human Rights: Southeast Asia and Universalist Theory*. Cambridge: Cambridge University Press.

Leon, C. T. and Ho, S. C. (1994) 'Hong Kong: The Third Identity of Modern Chinese Women: Women Managers in Hong Kong', in N. J. Adler and D. N. Izraeli (eds.), *Competitive Frontiers: Women Managers in a Global Economy*. Blackwell.

Lee, D. H. (2004). 'Cultural Contact with Japanese TV Dramas: Modes of Reception and Narrative Transparency', in K. Iwabuchi (ed.), *Feeling Asian Modernities: Transnational Consumption of Japanese TV Dramas*. Hong Kong: Hong Kong University Press.

Lee, Kuan Yew (1984) 'Make Time for Your Children'. *Straits Times*, February.

Lee, M. and Cho, C. H. (1995). 'Women Watching Together: An Ethnographic Study of Korean Soap Opera Fans in the United States', in G.. Dines and J. M. Humez (eds.), *Gender, Race and Class in Media*. Thousand Oaks: Sage.

Leung, L. Y. M (2004) 'Ganbaru and Its Transcultural Audience: Imaginary and Reality of Japanese TV Dramas in Hong Kong', in K. Iwabuchi (ed.), *Feeling Asian Modernities: Transnational Consumption of Japanese TV Dramas*. Hong Kong: Hong Kong University Press.

Lin, A. (2002). 'Modernity and the Self: Explorations of the (Non-)Self-determining Subject in South Korean TV Dramas'. *M/C: A Journal of Media and Culture*, 5(5), http://www.media-culture.org.au/mc/0210/Lin.html/.

Lin, A., Kwan, B. and Cheung, M. (2004). 'Korean Media Flows and Koreans' Unique Contribution to Asian Modernities'. Paper presented at the Korean Workshop at the Faculty of Humanities and Social Sciences, City University of Hong Kong, 27 August 2004, Hong Kong.

Lin, A. and Kwan, B. (2005) 'The Dilemmas of Modern Working Women in Hong Kong: Women's Use of Korean TV Dramas'. *Asian Communication Research*, 2 (2): 23–42.

Lin, A. and Tong, A. (2007) 'Crossing Boundaries: Male Consumption of Korean Dramas and Negotiation of Gender Relations in Modern Day Hong Kong'. *Journal of Gender Studies* (in press).

Lin, A. and Tong, A. (2005) 'Modernity and the Self: TV Dramas and the Formation of New Women Identities in Hong Kong, Singapore and Japan'. Research report, Department of English and Communication, City University of Hong Kong, Hong Kong.

Maclachlan, E. and Chua, G. L. (2004) 'Defining Asian Femininity: Chinese Viewers of Japanese TV Dramas in Singapore', in K. Iwabuchi (ed.), *Feeling Asian Modernities: Transnational Consumption of Japanese TV Dramas*. Hong Kong: Hong Kong University Press.

Mamoru, I. (2004) 'The Representation of Femininity in Japanese TV dramas of the 1990s', in K. Iwabuchi (ed.), *Feeling Asian Modernities: Transnational Consumption of Japanese TV Dramas*. Hong Kong: Hong Kong University Press.

Marshall, B. L. (1994) *Engendering Modernity: Feminism, Social Theory, and Social Change*. Boston : Northeastern University Press.

Marshall, B. L. (2000) *Configuring Gender: Explorations in Theory and Politics*. Peterborough, Ontario: Broadview Press.

Poovey, Mary (2002) 'The Liberal Civil Subject and the Social in Eighteenth-century British Moral Philosophy'. *Public Culture*, 14(1): 125-145.

PuruShotam, N. (1998) 'Between Compliance and Resistance: Women and the Middle-class Way of Life in Singapore', in K. Sen and M. Stivens (eds.), *Gender and Power in Affluent Asia*. London and New York: Routledge.

Robertson, R. (1995) 'Globalization as Hybridization', in M. Featherstone, S. Lash and R. Roberston (eds.), *Global Modernities*. London: Sage.

Saw, S. H. (1999) *The Population of Singapore*. Singapore: Institute of Southeast Asian Studies.

Shim, D. (2004) 'Hybridity and the Rise of the Korean Media in Asia'. Unpublished paper.

Toru, O. (2004) 'Producing (Post-)Trendy Japanese TV Dramas', in K. Iwabuchi (ed.), *Feeling Asian Modernities: Transnational Consumption of Japanese TV Dramas*. Translated by Nasu Madori. Hong Kong: Hong Kong University Press.

Wee, C. J. W. L. (2002) 'From Universal to Local Culture: The State, Ethnic Identity, and Capitalism in Singapore', in C. J. W. L. Wee (ed.), *Local*

Cultures and the 'New Asia': The State, Culture and Capitalism in Southeast Asia. Singapore: Institute of Southeast Asian Studies.

Wee, C. J. W. L. (2003) *Culture, Empire, and the Question of being Modern.* Lanham, Md.: Lexington Books.

Wee, C. J. W. L. (2004) 'Staging the Asian Modern: Cultural Fragments, the Singaporean Eunuch, and the Asian Lear'. *Critical Inquiry,* 30.

Wilen, T. and Wilen, P. (1997) *Asia: For Women on Business.* Berkeley, California: Stone Bridge Press.

Wu, C. L., and Tseng, H. Y. (2002). *Popular Korean Dramas and Cultural Identities of the Audience in Taiwan.* Research report, Centre for Communication Research, National Chia Tung Unversity, Taiwan.

Chapter 7   Touring 'Dramatic Korea'

Ariyama, Teruo (2002). *Kaigairyokou no Tanjou* (The Dawn of the Overseas Travel). Tokyo: Yoshikawakoubunkan.

Baudrillard, Jean (1998). *The Consumer Society: Myth and Structures.* London: Sage.

Bobo, Jacqueline (1988). "The Color Purple: Black Women as Cultural Readers", E. Pribram (ed.), *Female Spectators.* London: Verso.

Felski, Rita (1995). *The Gender of Modernity.* Massachusetts: Harvard University Press.

Ghose, Indira (1998). *Women Travellers in Colonial India: The Power of the Female Gaze.* New York: Oxford University Press.

Hirata, Yukie (2003). *Ilbon 20, 30dae Yoson dul wi Hanguk Kanguan wi Guanhan Yongu* (Research on Japanese Women Tourists to Korea in Their 20s and 30s). M.A. thesis, Yonsei University.

Iwabuchi, Koichi (2001). *Transnational Japan: Ajia wo Tsunagu Popular Bunka* (Recentering Globalization: Popular Culture and Japanese Transnationalism). Tokyo: Iwanamishoten.

Jong, Daegyun (1995). *Kankoku no Imeiji* (The Images of Korea). Tokyo: Chukoshinsyo.

Leed, Eric (1991). *The Mind of the Traveler: From Gilgamesh to Global Tourism.* New York: Basic Books.

Lee, Dong-Hoo (2003). "*Nihon no Terebidorama tono Bunkateki Sessyoku: Juyou no Youshiki to Katari no Toumeisei*" (Cultural Contact with Japanese TV Dramas: Modes of Reception and Narrative Transparency), in Iwabuchi, Koichi (ed.), *Gurobaru Purisumu: <Asian Dorimu> toshiteno Nihon no Terebi Dorama* (Global Prism: Japanese TV Dramas as "Asian Dream"), Tokyo: Heibonsya, pp. 254–285.

Macky, Vella (2003). *Gurobaluka to jendahyousyou* (Globalization and Representation of Gender). Tokyo: Ochanomizushobo.

Mies, Maria (1986). *Patriarchy and Accumulation on a World Scale.* London: Zed Books.

Mitsuya, Keiko (2004). "*Yoronchousa kara Mita Fuyusona Gensyou* (Winter Sonata Phenomenon from the Standpoint of Opinion Polls: Surveys on Winter Sonata)". *Housoukenkyu to Chousa* (The NHK Monthly Report on Broadcasting Research and Survey), No. 54(12), pp. 12–25.

Mulvey, Laura (1975). "Visual Pleasure and Narrative Cinema", *Screen*, 16(3), pp. 6–18.

Park, Jung-gyu (2003). "*Television Drama 'Winter Sonata' wa diaspora jok Jonchaesung* (Television Drama 'Winter Sonata' and diasporic identity)". *Hanguk Munhwa Inryuhak* (Korean Cultural Anthropology), 36(1), pp. 219–245.

Rojek, Chris (1985). *Capitalism and Leisure Theory.* London: Routledge.

Rosald, Renato (1989). "Imperialist nostalgia". *Representation* 26.

Sekikawa, Natsuo (1987). *Tokyo Kara Kita Nagune* (Traveler from Tokyo). Tokyo: Chikumashobo.

Urry, John (1990). *The Tourist Gaze: Leisure and Travel in Contemporary Societies.* London: Sage.

Wang, Ning (2000). *Tourism and Modernity: A Sociological Analysis.* Pergamon Press.

Yatabe, Yuko (2003). *Fuyunosonata Kouyuroku: Net de Hanasaku Idobatakaigi* (The Records of the Website for Fans of Winter Sonata). Tokyo: Tokimeki Publishing (Kadokawa Shoten).

Chapter 8   Popular Cultural Capital and Cultural Identity

Bourdieu, Pierre (1997). *Outline of a Theory of Practice.* Cambridge University Press.

Bury, Rhiannon (2005). *Cyberspaces of Their Own: Female Fandoms Online.* New York: Peter Lang.

Choi, Sook Hee (2005). "Korea: Coping with Low Fertility rate". KET Issue Report 2005, 19 Nov., 13–20.

Chua, Beng Huat (2004). "Conceptualizing an East Asian Popular Culture". *Inter-Asia Cultural Studies*, 5(2).

Darling-Wolf, Fabienne (2004). "SMAP, Sex and Masculinity: Constructing the Perfect Female Fantasy in Japanese Popular Music". *Popular Music and Society*, 27(3), 357–370.

Fiske, John (1992). "The Cultural Economy of Fandom", in Lisa A. Lewis (ed.), *The Adoring Audience: Fan Culture and Popular Media.* London and New York: Routledge.

Iwabuchi, Koichi. (2002). *Recentering Globalization: Popular Culture and Japanese Transnationalism.* Duke University Press.

Iwabuchi Koichi (eds.)(2004). *Feeling Asian Modernities: Transnational Consumption of Japanese TV Dramas.* Hong Kong University Press.

Hu, Kelly (2005). "The Power of Circulation: Digital Technologies and the Online Chinese Fans of Japanese TV Drama". *Inter-Asia Cultural Studies*, 6(2).

Kim, Hyun Mee (2003). "J-Pop Consumption and the Formation of 'Fandom'", *Korean Cultural Anthropology*, 36(1) [in Korean].

Kim, Young-Chan, and Lee, Kee-Hyeong (2003). "'Ne Mutdaero Haera': An Ethnographic Study on Mania Fans' Cultural Practices", *Program/Text* 9 [in Korean].

Leung, Lisa Yuk Ming (2001). "Romancing the Everyday: Hong Kong Women Watching Japanese Dorama", *Japanese Studies*, 22(1).

Lee, Dong-Hoo (2004). "A Local Mode of Programme Adaptation", in Albert Moran and Michael Keane (eds.), *Television Across Asia*. London: RouteledgeCurzon.

Lin, Angel and Kwan, Becky (2005). "The Dilemmas of Modern Working Women in Hong Kong; Women's Use of Korean TV Dramas". *Asian Communication Research* 9, 23–42.

Mazzarella, Saron (ed.)(2005). *Girl Wide Web*. New York: Peter Lang.

Muggleton, David and Weinzier, Rupert (eds.)(2003). *The Post-Subcultures Reader*. New York: Berg.

Thomas, Mandy (2002). "Re-orientation: East Asian Popular Cultures in Contemporary Vietnam". *Asian Studies Review*, 26(2), 189–204.

Yoon, Kyong-Won and Na, Mi-Su (2005). "Cultural Regionalization and Subcultural Practice: The Appropriation of Japanese Pop Culture in Korea Youth Culture", *Korean Journal of Journalism and Communication Studies*, 49(1), 5–28 [in Korean].

Chapter 9   Mapping Out the Cultural Politics of "the Korean Wave" in Contemporary South Korea

Acland, C. (2003). *Screen Traffic: Movies, Multiplexes, and Global Culture*. Durham: Duke University Press.

Appadurai, A. (1996). *Modernity at Large: Cultural Dimensions of Globalization*. Minneapolis: University of Minnesota Press.

Barker, C. (1997). *Global Television: An Introduction*. London: Blackwell.

Bennett, A. and Kahn-Harris, K. (ed.)(2004). *After Subculture: Critical Studies in Contemporary Youth Culture*. New York: Palgrave.

Cho, H. (2002). *Hanryu and Popular Cultures in Asia*. Seoul: Ttohanauimunhwa.

Hall, S. and du Gay, P. (ed.)(1996). *Questions of Cultural Identity*. London: Sage.

Hartley, J. (2005). *Creative Industries*. Oxford: Blackwell Publishing.

Hirata, Y. (2005). *The Consumption of Korea in Japan: Hanryu, Women, and Drama*. Seoul: Chaeksaesang.

Hwang, S. (2005). "On Hanryu Fever in Japan." *Creation and Critique* 127, pp. 369– 374.

Iwabuchi, K. (ed.)(2004a). *Feeling Asian Modernities.* Hong Kong: Hong Kong University Press.

Iwabuchi, K. (2004b). "When Hanryu meets Korean Japanese." *Program/Text* 11, pp. 87–120.

Iwabuchi, K. (2002). *Recentering Globalization: Popular Culture and Japanese Transnationalism.* Durham: Duke University Press.

Jang, S. (ed.)(2004). *Why China Receive Hanryu.* Seoul: Hakkojae.

Jenkins, H. (2004). "Pop Cosmopolitanism: Mapping cultural flows in an age of media convergence," in Marcelo Suarez-Orozco et al. (ed.), *Globalization.* New York: The Ross Institute.

Kang, N. (2000). *Neoliberalism and Culture.* Seoul: Cultural Science.

Kim, H. (2003). "The Consumption of Japanese Popular Culture and the Fandom. Korean Journal of Cultural Anthropology," 36(1), pp. 149–186.

Kim, S. and Yang, E. (2005). "The Politics of Identity and Cultural Flows in East Asia." Korean Association of Journalism and Communication Studies Convention. 20 May.

King, A. (ed.)(1991). *Culture, Globalization, and the World-System.* Binghamton: SUNY Press.

Lee, D. (2005). "Is There an Asian Cultural Studies?" International Seminar on Asian Popular Culture, Seoul, South Korea, 22 Feb.

Lee, D. (2004). "Limits of Transnational Imagination." *Korean Journal of Broadcasting,* 18(4), pp. 358–397.

Lee, K. (2004). Hanryu and Television Drama. *Program/Text* 11, pp. 41–64.

Lee, K. (2005). "The Emergence of Transnational Popular Culture and the Cultural Politics of 'the Korean wave.'" *Media and Society* 13(2), pp. 189–213.

Lin, Angel et al. (2004). "The Dilemma of Modern Female Office Workers in Post- Confucian Asia: Women's Reception of South Korean TV Dramas." *Program/Text* 11, pp. 121–139.

Marcus, G. (1998). *Ethnography Thick and Thin.* NJ: Princeton University Press.

McChesney, R. (2004). *The Problem of the Media.* New York: Monthly Review Press.

McChesney, R. and Nichols, J. (2002). *Our Media, Not Theirs.* New York: An Open Media Book.

Miller, T. and Yudice, G. (2002). *Cultural Policy.* London: Sage.

Muggleton, D. and Weinzier, R. (ed.) (2003). *The Post-Subcultures Reader.* Oxford: Berg.

Murphy, P. and Kraidy M. (ed.)(2003). Global Media Studies: Ethnographic Perspectives. New York: Routledge.

Oren, T. and Petro, P. (ed.)(2004). *Global Currents.* NJ: Rutgers University Press.

Paik, W. (2005). "The Condition of Formation and Possibility for Cultural Regionalism in Asia." Asian Culture Symposium, Kwangju, South Korea, 24 Feb.

Pieterse, J. N. (2004). *Globalization and Culture: Global Melange*. Lanham: Rowman & Littlefield.

Shim, D. (2004). Hanryu as International Communication Phenomenon and Hybridity. *Program/Text* 11, pp. 65–86.

Shin, H. (2005). "Cultural Politics of K-Pop: Out of Gayo Nationalism into Pop Asianism." International Seminar on Asian Popular Culture, Seoul, South Korea, 22 Feb.

Yoo, S. et al. (2005). *The Secret of Hanryu DNA*. Seoul: Sangkakuinamu.

Yoo, S. and Lee, K. (2001). "A Comparative Study on the Cultural Similarity of the Television Dramas in East-Asian Countries." *Korean Journal of Journalism and Communication Studies*, 45(3), pp. 230–267.

Chapter 10   Rap(p)ing Korean Wave

"About the Story of CommonWealth." *CommonWealth Magazine*. 14 Nov 2005. http://www.cw.com.tw/about/philosophy03.jsp/.

Ahmed, Sara. "Communities that Feel: Intensity, Difference, and Attachment." *Conference Proceedings for Affective Encounters: Rethinking Embodiment in Feminist Media Studies*. Ed. Anu Koivunen and Susanna Paasonen. E-book at: http://www.utu.fi/hum/mediatutkimus/affective/proceedings.pdf/. University of Turku, 2001, pp. 10–24.

Berlant, Lauren. "The Female Complaint." *Social Text* 19/20(1988): 237–257.

"Blog Guide for Yong-yang [Bae Yong-jun] Guest Room." *ET Mall*. 28 Nov 2005. http://etmall.com.tw/XML/Content/room/p3_3.html/ (accessed on 28 Nov 2005)

Chang, Chao-wei. "Rethinking 'Rock Music.'" Milan Kun E-paper. June 2000. http://enews.url.com.tw//archiveRead.asp?scheid=9612/ (accessed on 24 Feb 2006).

Cho, Haeojoang. "Constructing and Destructing 'Koreaness' in the 1990 South Korea." Trans. Chia-hsuan Lin. *Taiwan: A Radical Quarterly in Social Studies*, 30(1999): 65–102.

Chu, Shao-wen. "Introduction to Classics: 'The World Is Flat: A Brief History of the Twentieth Century.'" *CommonWealth* (1 Aug 2005): 142–148.

"Come and Take a Picture with the Water Cup that Bae Just Drank From." *China Times*, 20 Aug 2005: D3.

"Crossing the Ocean to Pursue Bae Yong-jun, Fans Offer Loads of Gifts." *Liberty Times*, 20 Aug 2005.

Debord, Guy. *The Society of the Spectacle*. Trans. Donald Nicholson-Smith. NY: Zonebooks, 1994.

"Declaration for a Beautiful Vision of Taiwan in 2020, Zhiben." 14 Nov 2005. http://www.cw.com.tw/about/philosophy03.jsp/.

Deem, Melissa. "From Bobbit to SCUM: E-memberment, Scatological Rhetorics, and Feminist Strategies in Contemporary United States." *Public Culture,* 20(1996): 511–538.

Di, Ying, Shelly Li, and Shi-fen Lyu. "Understanding Li Ying-ai's Charm of Ordinariness." *Rising Korea.* Taipei: Commonwealth Publications, 2005, pp. 67–84.

"Fans Thrilled Out of Control to Have Handsome Bae's Hugs." *Liberty Times,* 22 Aug 2005: D4.

Foucault, Michel. "The Order of Discourse." *Untying The text: A Post-Structuralist Reader.* Ed. Robert Young. Boston: Routledge and Kegan Paul, 1981, pp. 48–78.

"God! Handsome Bae's small pouting mouth." *Liberty Times,* 20 Aug 2005, D2 [caption].

Grace, Helen. "Business, Pleasure, Narrative: The folktale in our times." *Nation, Culture, Text: Australian Cultural and Media Studies.* Ed. Graeme Turner. New York: Routledge, 1993, pp. 199–210.

"Handsome Bae reveals his secret code!" *Liberty Times,* 22 Aug 2005: D2 [caption].

"Hard to Say Good-bye to Handsome Bae, the Airport Is Wild and Chaotic." *Liberty Times,* 22 Aug 2005: D2.

Heidegger, Matin. "The Question Concerning Technology." *The Question Concerning Technology, and Other Essays.* New York: Harper & Row, 1977.

"His gesture for drinking water is super-elegant!" *Liberty Times,* 22 Aug 2005: D2 [caption].

Hsiau, A-chin. "The Development of Cultural Nationalism in Taiwan Since the 1980s: An analysis of Taiwan's 'national' literature." *Taiwan Sociology Studies,* 3(1999): 1–51.

Hsiau, A-chin. *Contemporary Taiwanese Cultural Nationalism.* New York: Routledge, 2000.

Kipnis, Laura. "(Female) Desire and (Female) Disgust: Reading Hustler." *Cultural Studies.* Eds. Grossberg, Nelson, and Treichler. New York: Routledge, 1992. 373–391.

Li, Shan. "The Dwindling of Pop Music and the Dominance of Individuality: Contemporary Taiwanese Popular Music in the New Times." *Sinorama* 23.4 (1998). http://www.sinorama.com.te/c/1998/199804/704134c1.html/ (accessed on 24 Feb 2006).

Li, Shelly. "Let Fans Around the Globe Be Korean Fans." *Rising Korea.* Taipei: Commonwealth Publications, 2005, pp. 133–143.

Li, Shelly. "There Is No Future for the People." *CommonWealth,* (1 Jan 2005): 72–76.

Li, Shelly and Pei-yu Sun. "Touching Modern People's Heart with Traditional Values." *Rising Korea.* Taipei: Commonwealth Publications, 2005, pp. 189–200.

Li, Xiu-ying. "If Koreans Can Do it, Why Can't We: New Korean Force Use Movies to Win Economy." *Digital Times,* 81(2004): 116–117.

Lin, Chi-po. "From Margin to Mainstream: New Taiwanese Songs Fight Back." *Taiwan Panorama*, 2002. http://www.sinorama.com.tw/ch/print_issue. php3?id=200259105026c.txt&ma=past/ (accessed 25 Jan 2006).

Lin, Qi-bo. "Handsome Actors and Pretty Actresses: Taiwan Drowned in the Korean Wave." *Sinorama*, 26.7 (2001): 98–101.

Liu, Yu-xi. "Taiker Brand, [Facing East Asia], Blooms in Warm Spring?" *China Times*, 22 Aug 2005.

"Look, without wearing socks, Bae is still very cute." *Liberty Times*, 20 Aug 2005: D2 [caption].

"Look at him eating, it's/he's delicious." *Liberty Times*, 22 Aug 2005: D2 [caption].

Lu, Chi-fang. "How does Our Job disappear?" *Cheers*, Nov 2005. http://marketing.chinatimes.com/ItemDetailPage/MainContent/05MediaContent.asp?MMMediaType=CheersMG&MMContentNoID=22732/ (accessed 10 Nov 2005).

Morris, Meaghan. *The Pirate's Fiancee: Feminism, Reading, Postmodernism*. New York: Verso, 1988.

Mulvey, Laura. 1992. "Visual Pleasure and Narrative Cinema," in *The Sexual Subject: A Screen Reader in Sexuality*. London and New York: Routledge, 1992, 22–34.

"People Wall Crumbling Down with the Arrival of Handsome Bae: 66-year-old Grandma Tripped in the Crowds at the Bottom of Human Pyramid But Still Insisted on Chasing after Bae" *China Times*, 20 Aug 2005: D1.

Song, Dong. "Globalization: The Invasion of the Third Wave of Tsunami." *CommonWealth*, 328 (Aug 2005): 106–114.

Stabile, Carol. "Nike, Social Responsibility, and the Hidden Abode of Production." *Critical Studies in Media Communication*, 17.2 (2000): 186–204.

Stallybrass, Peter and Allon White. *The Politics and Poetics of Transgression*. Ithaca: Cornell University Press, 1986.

"Oh, Oh, the shoelace is loose! Wish I could tie it for him." *Liberty Times*, 22 Aug 2005: D2 [caption].

Ong, Aihwa. "Re-Engineering the Chinese Soul in Shanghai." *Neoliberalism as Exception: Mutations in Citizenship and Sovereignty*. Durham: Duke University Press. 2006, 219–240.

"Tai-ke and Korean Wave." Editorial. *China Times*, 23 Aug 2005.

"Tai-ke Pissed at Korean Wave, Singling out Bae Yong-jun as the Target of Foul Language." *China Times*, 20 Aug 2005: D6.

"Tai-ke rocker Chang Chen-yu Swears at Bae Yong-jun." *Liberty Times*, 20 Aug 2005: D6.

"The Blissfull Smile Blog." *ET Mall*. 28 Nov 2005. http://etmall.com.tw/XML/Content/room/p2.html?&WT.mc_id=_noPH/.

Wang, Chun-rui. "The Invasion of Korean Wave Creates a New Historical High for Economic Deficit." *United Evening News*, 19 Oct 2004.

Wang, Li-Jung. "Economic Discourse in Cultural Policy: From Elite Culture to

Cultural Economy." *Router: A Journal of Cultural Studies* 1 (2005): 169–196.

Warner, Michael. "The Mass Public and the Mass Subject." *Habermas and the Public Sphere.* Ed. Craig Calhoun. Cambridge: Massachusetts Institute of Technology Press, 1992. 377–401.

Warner, Michael. "Publics and Counterpublics." *Public Culture* 14.1(2002): 49–90.

Wei, Hsing Lin. "Grassroots Culture: The Origin of Taiwan's Life Resource." *China Times,* 5 Oct 2004.

"Wow! Wow! Wow! Handsome Bae exposes his small belly" *Liberty Times,* 20 Aug 2005: D2 [caption].

Wu Bai. "Do Not Let Tai-ke Become Another Excuse for Our Degeneration." *China Times,* 17 Aug 2005. Recorded by Huang Jun-jie.

Wu Bai. "Tai-ke Performance, How to Be Taiker, How to Rock." 20 Nov 2005. http://www.eslitebooks.com/cgi-bin/eslite.dll/search/article/all_article_reader.jsp?/.

Wu, Wang-yu. "Editorial: The Rise or Disappearance of Your Job?" *Cheers,* Nov 2005. http://marketing.chinatimes.com/ItemDetailPage/MainContent/05MediaContent.asp?MMMediaType=CheersMG&MMContentNoID=22660/ (accessed 10 Nov 2005).

Wu, Yi-jing. "Globalization: The Need to Step Out Courageously." *CommonWealth,* (March 2001): 48.

Wu, Ying-chun. 2001a. "Emptification? Globalization?" *CommonWealth,* (1 Feb 2001): 52–64.

Wu, Ying-chun. 2001b. "Two-Way Operation: Global and Local." *Commonwealth,* (5 June 2001): 54–65.

Yang, Chang-Zhen. "From Negro to Local Tai-ke." *China Times,* 21 Aug 2005.

Yang, Fang-chih and Fan, Yun. "The Language Hierarchy of LP and Ruan-pa." *China Times,* 7 Oct 2004.

Yang, Wen-Chia. "Reflections on the Reversal of the Meanings of 'Tai-ke.'" *Liberty Times,* 20 Aug 2005.

Yin, Yun-peng. "Preface: Because of Qing, We Can Step Forward." *Rising Korea.* Taipei: Commonwealth Publications, 2005, pp. 10–14.

Yudice, George. *The Expediency of Culture: Uses of Culture in the Global Era.* Durham: Duke University Press, 2003.

Chapter 11 Existing in the Age of Innocence

Appadurai, Arjun. "Patriotism and Its Futures." *Public Culture* 5.3 (1993): 411–429.

Chen, Kuan-Hsing. "America in East Asia: The Club 51 Syndrome," *New Left Review* (12 November–December 2001): 73–87.

———. "Why is 'Great Reconciliation' Im/possible? De-Cold War/Decolonization, or Modernity and Its Tears." (Part I) *Inter-Asia Cultural Studies* 3.1 (2002a): 77–99.

———. "Why is 'Great Reconciliation' Im/possible? De-Cold War/Decolonization, or Modernity and Its Tears." (Part II) *Inter-Asia Cultural Studies* 3.2 (2002b): 235– 251.

———. "Asia as Method." *Taiwan: A Radical Quarterly in Social Studies* 57 (2005a): 139– 218.

———. "Yazhou Duli de Wenti" [The Question of Asia's Independence] *Dushu* (Jul 2005b): 38-46. Reprinted on *Cultural Studies Monthly,* http:// hermes.hrc.ntu.edu.tw/csa/ journal/48/journal_park370.html/ (accessed 1 Aug 2005).

Chen Tsung Yi. "A-Mei Shijian Chongji Taiwan Yishi" [The impact of the A-Mei incident on Taiwanese consciousness]. *New Taiwan News Weekly* (14– 20 Aug 2004a): 14–16.

———. "Oumei Jushing Hanwei Ziji Zhuzhang" [Euro-American super stars defend their stances]. *New Taiwan News Weekly* (14–20 Aug 2004b): 17–18.

Ching, Leo. "Globalizing the Regional, Regionalizing the Global: Mass Culture and Asianism in the Age of Late Capital." *Public Culture* 12.1 (2000): 233–257.

Chou Yi-Chien. "From the Stars to the Fan: the Formation of Gender Subjects in Fandom in Popular Music." *Mass Communication* 56 (1997): 105–133.

Chua, Beng Huat. 2004. "Conceptualizing an East Asian Popular Culture." *Inter-Asia Cultural Studies* 5.2 (2004): 200–221.

Chun, Allen and A. B. Shamsul. "Other 'routes': the Critical Challenge for Asian Academic." *Inter-Asia Cultural Studies* 2.2 (2001): 167–176.

Darling-Wolf, Fabienne. "Virtually Multicultural: Trans-Asian Identity and Gender in an International Fan Community of Japanese Star." *New Media and Society* 6.4 (2004): 507–528.

DeAngelis, Michale. *Gay Fandom and Crossover Stardom.* Durham and London: Duke University Press, 2001.

Dyer, Richard. *Stars.* London: BFI Publishing, 1979.

———. *Heavenly Bodies: Film Stars and Society.* New York: St. Martin's Press, 1986.

Erni, John Nguyet and Siew Keng Chua, ed. *Asian Media Studies: Politics of Subjectivities.* Malden, MA: Blackwell, 2005.

Fung, Anthony and Michael Curtin. "The Anomalies of Being Faye (Wong): Gender Politics in Chinese Popular Music." *International Journal of Cultural Studies* 5.3 (2002): 263–290.

Gallagher, Mark. "Masculinity in Translation: Jackie Chan's Transcultural Star Text." *Velvet Light Trap* 39 (1997): 23–41.

Gavrilos, Dina. "Editor's Introduction: Communicating the 'New Patriotism'": What does it mean to be a citizen in a global context?" *Journal of Communication Inquiry* 27. 4 (2003): 333–336.

Grossberg, Lawrence. "Is There a Fan in the House? The Affective Sensibility of Fandom." *The Adoring Audience: Fan Culture and Popular Media.* Ed. Lisa A. Lewis. London and New York: Routledge, pp. 50–65.

Guy, Nancy. "'Republic of China National Anthem' on Taiwan: One Anthem, One Performance, Multiple Realities." *Ethnomusicology* 46.1 (2002): 96–119.

Ho Chang-Peng. "A-mei Fanghsing, Hsu Wen-Long Ching Paochong" [Don't Worry A-mei, but Please Take Care Hsu Wen-Long]. *Business Weekly* (21 Jun 2004): 18.

Ho Tung-Hong. "Liushing Yinyue de Zhengcheng yu Xuwei" [The Sincerity and Hypocricy of Popular Music]. *China Daily,* 2 Aug 2004.

Ip Iam Chong. "Why Does Lee Young-ae Support Korean Farmers?" *Ming Pao,* 20 February 2006. Reprinted on Coolloud, http://www.coolloud.org.tw/news/ database/Interface/Detailstander.asp?ID=110115/.

Iwabuchi, Koichi. *Recentering Globalization: Popular Culture and Japanese Transnationalism.* Durham and London: Duke University Press, 2003.

Iwabuchi, Koichi, ed. *Feeling Asian Modernities: Transnational Consumption of Japanese TV Dramas.* Hong Kong: Hong Kong University Press, 2004.

Jager, Sheila Miyoshi. *Narratives of Nation Building in Korea: A Genealogy of Patriotism.* New York: M.E. Sharpe, 2003.

Jung, Sung-Ki. "Conscripts Abroad Can Apply for Enrollment Online." *The Korea Times,* 31 March 2005. Hankooki.com/ (accessed 12 Sep 2005).

Kim, Rahn. "Young Men Abandoning Nationality over New Law." *The Korea Times,* 11 May 2005. Hankooki.com/ (accessed 12 Sep 2005).

Kwon, Insook. "A Feminist Exploration of Military Conscription: The Gendering of the Connections between Nationalism, Militarism and Citizenship in South Korea." *International Feminist Journal of Politics* 3.1 (2001): 26–54.

Lee Chi-Min. "Shinbun ni miru 'Yon-sama' Shintō Gensō" [Looking at the penetration of "yon-sama" phenomenon in the news]. In *Nisshiki Kanryu: Fuyu no Sonata to Nikan Taishu Bunka no Genzai.* Ed. Yoshitaka Mouri. Tokyo: Serika Shobo, 2004, pp. 83–111.

Lee, Coral. "From Little Teng to A-Mei: Marking Time in Music." *Sinorama* (Feb 2000a): 34–44.

Lee Dong-wook. "Let's Forgive Yoo Seung-joon." *The Korea Times,* 4 Jun 2003. Hankooki.com. Accessed on 12 Sep 2005.

Lee, Hee-Eun. "Home Is Where You Serve: Globalization and Nationalism in Korean Popular Music." Paper Presented at the International Communication Association Convention, San Diego, CA, 23–27 May 2003.

Liu Pao-Yi. "Bianzan A-mei: Aiguo Yiren" [A-Bian Praises A-Mei: Patriotic Entertainer]. *United Daily* (7 Aug 2004): A3.

Lo Yi-Hsiou. "Discovering the New Home of Urbanites" [Fashian Duhuiren de Shinyuanhsiang]. *Global View Magazine* [Yuan Jian] 138 (1998a): 85.

———. "Reading the A*mei Phenomenon" [Jiedu A*mei Hsianhsiang]. *Global View Magazine* [Yuan Jian] 140 (5 Feb 1998b): 118–122.

Lowenthal, Leo. "Triumph of Mass Idols." In *Literature, Popular Culture and Society*. Palo Alto: Pacific Books, 1968, pp. 109–140.

Lu Guo-Chen. "Who Told Her to Be 'Entertainer' Jin Su-mei?" *The Journalist* 792 (9 May–15 May 2002): 58–60.

Marshall, David. *Celebrity and Power: Fame in Contemporary Culture*. Minneapolis: University of Minnesota Press, 1997.

Martin, Fran. "The Perfect Lie: Sandee Chan and Lesbian Representability in Mandarin Pop Music." *Inter-Asia Cultural Studies* 4.2 (2003): 264–279.

Moon, Seungsook. *Militarized Modernity and Gendered Citizenship in South Korea*. Durham and London: Duke University Press, 2005a.

——. "Trouble with Conscription, Entertaining Soldiers: Popular Culture and the Politics of Militarized Masculinity in South Korea." *Men and Masculinities* 8. 1 (2005b): 64–92.

Morris, Meaghan. "Participating from a Distance." *Rogue Flows: Trans-Asian Cultural Traffic*. Ed. Koichi Iwabuchi, Stephen Muecke and Mandy Thomas. Hong Kong: Hong Kong University Press, 2004, pp. 249–261.

Na, Jeong-ju. "Pro-baseball Players Held for Draft Dodging." *The Korea Times,* 5 September 2004. Hankooki.com/ (accessed 12 Sep 2005).

Nakamura, Lisa. "Race in the Construct and the Construction of Race: The Consensual Hallucination of Multiculturalism in the Fictions of Cyberspace." *Race, Ethnicity, and Identity on the Internet*. New York and London: Routledge, 2002, pp. 61–85.

Ning Ying-Bing. "Gongguan Dianshi yu Gongguan Dianshi" [Public Television and Publicity Teleivsion]. In *Body Politics and Media Criticism*. Ed. Ning Ying-Bing. Zhongli: Central University Sex Studies, 2004, pp. 213–226.

Peters, John. *Speaking into the Air: A History of the Idea of Communication*. Chicago and London: The Chicago University Press, 1999.

Probyn, Elspeth. "A-ffect: Let Her RIP." *M/C Journal* 8.6 (2005): 18 pars. http://journal.media-culture.org.au/0512/03-probyn.php/ (accessed 1 March 2006).

Raine, Michael. "Ishihara Yujiro: Youth, Celebrity, and the Male Body in Late 1950s Japan." In *Word and Image in Japanese Cinema*. Ed. Dennis Washburn and Carole Cavanaugh. Cambridge: Cambridge University Press, 2001, pp. 202– 225.

Schickel, Richard. *Intimate Strangers: The Culture of Celebrity in America*. Chicago: Ivan R. Dee, 1985/2000.

Seo, Dong-Shin. "Lawmaker Fuels Controversy over Dual Citizenship Law." *The Korea Times,* 20 May 2005. Hankooki.com/ (accessed 12 Sep 2005).

Shih Chun. "The Chang Hui-Mei Phenomenon: Cultural Exchange Transcends Cross-Strait Politics." *Exchange* 47 (Oct 1999): 38–42.

Shin, Hyunjoon. "Cultural Politics of K-Pop: Out of 'Gayo' Nationalism into Pop Asianism." Paper presented at the International Seminar on Asian Popular Culture, Seoul, South Korea, 22 Feb 2005.

Shouse, Eric. "Feeling, Emotion, Affect." *M/C Journal* 8.6 (2005): 15 pars. http: //journal.media-culture.org.au/0512/03-shouse.php/ (accessed 26 Dec 2005).

Stacey, Jackie. *Star Gazing: Hollywood Cinema and Female Spectatorship.* London: New York: Routledge, 1994.

Sun, Ge. "How Does Asia Mean?" (Part 1). *Inter-Asia Cultural Studies* 1.1 (2002a): 13– 47.

——. "How Does Asia Mean?" (Part 2). *Inter-Asia Cultural Studies* 1.2 (2002b): 319–341.

Tong Ching-feng. "She Took Back Taiwan's Right to Historical Interpretation." *Yazhou Zhoukan* (16 Oct 2005): 36–37.

Tsai, Eva. "Kaneshiro Takeshi: Transnational Stardom and the Media and Culture Industries in Asia's Global/Postcolonial Age." *Modern Chinese Literature and Culture* 17.1 (2005): 100–132.

Wang Chi-Jun. "Kao Jin Su-mei as a Legislator Only Earns 20000 a Month." *Business Weekly* (22 Apr 2002): 48–51.

Wang Hsiao-Wen and Yun-Pin Chang. "A-Mei Blasted for Not Taking a Stand." *Taipei Times* (7 Aug 2004): 1.

Wang, Jing. "Guest Editor's Introduction." *Positions* 9.1 (2001): 1–27.

Wang Shou-Hua. "Radiating: A*mei Fires up Taipei" [Mei-li Fangsong: Chang Hui- Mei Renshou Taibei]. *Business Weekly* [Shangyie Zhoukai] (19 Jan 1998): 90–92.

Wu Chi-Zong. "Chiuchiu Daren Bierang Song Cheung-Hsian Dangbing" [Please Authorities, Don't Conscript Song Seung-Heon]. *Mingsheng Pao* (20 Sep 2004): C4.

Yang Yi-Feng. "Solving the Puzzle of Chang Hui-Mei's Fame" [Chang Hui-Mei de Chengming zhi Mi]. *The Journalist* [Shin Shinwen] 530 (1997): 115–118.

Yuan Hsi-Pei. "A-mei Wunai: Zhiyao Heping Daren de Shih Daren Jiejue" [A-mei just wants peace; let grown-ups resolve grown-up matters]. *United Daily* (7 Aug 2004): A3.

Chapter 12 When the Korean Wave Meets Resident Koreans in Japan

Carruthers, Ashley (2004). 'Cute logics of multicultural and the consumption of the Vietnamese exotic in Japan', *Positions* 12 (2): 401–429.

Fabian, Johannes (1983). *Time and the Other: How anthropology makes its object,* New York: Columbia University Press.

Hayashi, Kaori (2004). "Dorama Fuyu no Sonata no Seijiteki naru mono" (Political aspects of *Winter Sonata*), *Journal of Information Studies, Interfaculty Initiative in Information Studies,* The University of Tokyo, No. 69: 56–81.

Ito, Mamoru (2004). "The Representation of Femininity in Japanese Television Drama of the 1990s", in K. Iwabuchi (ed.), *Feeling Asian Modernities:*

Transnational consumption of Japanese TV drama, Hong Kong: Hong Kong University Press.

Ivy, Marilyn, (1995). *Discourses of the Vanishing,* Chicago: Chicago University Press.

Iwabuchi, Koichi (2000). "Political correctness, postcoloniality and the self-representation of 'Koreanness' in Japan", in S. Ryang (ed.), *Koreans in Japan: Critical voices from the margin,* London: Routledge: 55–73.

—— (2002). *Recentering Globalization: Popular Culture and Japanese Transnationalism,* Durham: Duke University Press.

—— (2004) (ed.). *Feeling Asian Modernities: Transnational consumption of Japanese TV drama,* Hong Kong: Hong Kong University Press.

—— (2005). "Multinationalizing the multicultural: The commodification of 'ordinary foreign residents' in a Japanese TV talk show", *Japanese Studies,* 25 (2): 103–118.

Lee, Dong-Hoo (2004). "Cultural Contact with Japanese TV Dramas: Modes of Reception and Narrative Transparency", in K. Iwabuchi (ed.), *Feeling Asian Modernities: Transnational consumption of Japanese TV drama,* Hong Kong: University of Hong Kong Press.

Li, Chimin (2004) " Shinbun ni miru Yon-sama shintou genshou" (Examining Yon-sama phenonema through Japanese newspaper), in Mori Yoshitaka (ed.), *Nisshiki Kantyu* (Japanese style, Korean Wave), Tokyo: Serika Shobo.

Ogura Chikako (2004). "The spice of love story: from disorder to obstacle", *Weekly Asahi,* 13–20 August.

Ryang, Sonia. (ed.) (2000). *Koreans in Japan: Critical voices from the margin,* London: Routledge.

Tai Eika (2004). "'Korean Japanese': A new identity option for resident Koreans in Japan", *Critical Asian Studies,* 36:3: 355–382.

Taylor, Charles (1994). "The Politics of Recognition", in C. Taylor and A. Gutmann (eds), *Multiculturalism and Examining the Politics of Recognition,* Princeton: Princeton University Press, 1992.

Index